SEXUALITY

Recent Titles in
Contributions in Psychology

SEXUALITY

New Perspectives

Edited by **Zira DeFries, Richard C. Friedman, and Ruth Corn**

Contributions in Psychology, Number 6

Greenwood Press
Westport, Connecticut • London, England

Library of Congress Cataloging in Publication Data

Main entry under title:

Sexuality, new perspectives.

(Contributions in psychology, ISSN 0736-2714 ; no. 6)
Includes bibliographies and index.
1. Sex—Addresses, essays, lectures. 2. Women—Sexual
behavior—Addresses, essays, lectures. 3. Sex role—
Addresses, essays, lectures. 4. Sexual ethics—
Addresses, essays, lectures. 5. Sexual disorders—
Addresses, essays, lectures. I. DeFries, Zira.
II. Friedman, Richard C., 1941-   . III. Corn, Ruth.
[DNLM: 1. Sex Behavior. 2. Sex Disorders. Wl CO778NHH
no. 6 / HQ 21 S5195]
HQ21.S477   1985   306.7   84-28991

ISBN 0-313-24207-0 (lib. bdg.)

Library of Congress Catalog Card Number: 84-28991
ISBN: 0-313-24207-0
ISSN: 0736-2714

First published in 1985

Greenwood Press
A division of Congressional Information Service, Inc.
88 Post Road West
Westport, Connecticut 06881

Printed in the United States of America

10 9 8 7 6 5 4 3 2 1

Contents

Preface

This volume is a collection of articles by clinicians and nonclinical academicians on diverse aspects of sexual behavior. Its goal is to direct attention toward important areas rather than to provide the all-inclusive coverage of a textbook. In its emphasis on variety, the volume is similar to a symposium or conference at which professionals with different specialized perspectives discuss topics under a common umbrella. This feature of *Sexuality: New Perspectives* highlights a quality of the behavioral sciences that is both stimulating and troublesome. Scholars from different disciplines often discuss behavior in such different ways that any general agreement about potentially controversial issues is surprising. The interdisciplinary nature of the field of human sexuality warrants emphasis. One has only to contrast the backgrounds of Sigmund Freud (a psychiatrist), Alfred Kinsey (an entomologist), and William Masters (a gynecologist) to realize that when behavioral scientists discuss sex they ofen do so from knowledge perspectives that differ widely.

The editors of this volume are clinicians. The selection of chapters was particularly influenced by the experience of one of us (Richard C. Friedman) in the preparation of the most recent edition of the *Diagnostic and Statistical Manual of Psychiatry* (*DSM*-III) and another (Zira DeFries) with the academic communities of Barnard College and Columbia University.

The *DSM*-III attempted to summarize the state of psychiatry in 1980. The selection on psychosexual disorders was particularly challenging because the approach was so radically different from that of the previous edition, *DSM*-II. As we worked on revising the *Diagnostic Manual*, it became clear that the problems with which the psychosexual disorders group struggled, although obviously different in content from those of other groups (e.g., affective disorders, schizophrenia), were astonishingly similar. The similarities stemmed from key features of the state of the clinical behavioral sciences in 1980, which remain just as true today. First, *facts* about huge areas of behavior were hard to come by. In their absence, clinical authorities with discomforting frequency grounded their judgments in ideology that was usually called theory. Subspecialization need not inevitably lead to fragmentation, but the lack of common ground and of generally agreed-on facts, the paucity of accepted methods of procedure, and the absence of generally agreed-on models of the mind imposed considerable strain on the attempt to achieve an integrated view. Although the situation has improved since 1980, when *DSM*-III was published, one has only to overhear a discussion between psychoanalysts and anthropologists or between clinicians and researchers on the topic of homosexuality to realize how much bridge-building remains to be done.

While one of us was working on *DSM*-III, another (Zira DeFries) was actively involved with academic and clinical issues as director of Mental Health Service at Barnard College. Her ongoing dialogue with nonclinical academicians convinced her that richness of presentation is enhanced by including material that is both directly clinical and more traditionally "academic" or basic.

The experience of all three editors supported the view that women's issues continue to be of substantial relevance. We are concerned that the literature in which models of male behavior are used as the norm for both genders still have great impact in this field. It should not be assumed that male-oriented models of sexual behavior apply to both genders. There are more articles on female psychology in this volume than on any other single subject. We selected topics that are either of particular relevance to public health or that provide a new perspective on models of the mind.

The editors of this volume are committed to interdisciplinary dialogue as a requisite for progress in the clinical behavioral sciences. There are many ways of fostering interdisciplinary interest. We have chosen here to present discussions by individuals from divergent backgrounds, and we hope that the sacrifice of homogeneity is compensated for by the intellectual stimulation produced. Consider, for example, Chapter 12, "Menstrual Cycle Symptoms from a Developmental Perspective" by Sharon Golub. Behavior and the menstrual cycle, an area often omitted from books on sexuality, is a field that could hardly be more multidisciplinary in interest and in collaboration. Scientific study of behavior and the menstrual cycle was spurred on by research in the 1930s between a medical psychoanalyst and a gynecologist. Subsequent literature has been of interest to descriptive, dynamic, and forensic psychiatrists; clinical, social, and developmental psychologists; nurses; social workers; general physicians; gynecologists; endocrinologists; pharmacologists; psychobiologists; neurologists; anthropologists; and sociologists—and this list is not all-inclusive. Chapter 12 was written not by a psychoanalyst or a gynecologist or a clinician but by an academician-researcher, because we felt this would enhance a scholarly critical posture toward the material. In this particular topic the mind-set of investigators has resulted in a large amount of literature that emphasizes negative associations between behavior and the menstrual cycle. Negative attitudes and values present throughout the general culture tend to be reinforced by scientific and clinical work because the attention of professional behaviorists is directed at areas dictated by the general cultural context. A recurrent theme not only in Chapter 12 but also throughout this volume is that cultural context may influence the way clinicians and researchers view human sexuality.

In addition to women's issues, we selected broad areas for inclusion in this volume on the basis of what we judged to be relevance to modern and rapidly changing concepts about human sexuality. In the field of sexual psychopathology, for example, concepts about gender identity, sexual orientation, and the relation between sexual behavior and the "borderline syndromes" are all in a state of rapid evolution. Chapter 10, on AIDS (acquired immune deficiency syndrome), and Chapter 13, on sleep physiology, resulted from our desire to focus on the impact medical and physiological data have on current thought about sexuality. We were particularly concerned that the subject of sexuality and ethics be discussed in this volume, and by a philosopher who specializes in ethics as a general field.

We are aware of the practical problems imposed by space limitations in the areas of sex differences and sexual development. For example, we would have preferred to have chapters on rapists as well as on rape victims and to provide an inclusive life-cycle approach. Bowing to practical constraints, we elected not to present parallel articles on male and female sexual behavior and to limit the developmental perspective mostly to adolescence and to the later phase of the life cycle.

This volume has been exciting to produce. The editors have profited from and enjoyed their contacts with the individual authors, who in turn have consistently welcomed critical feedback. Each contributor has helped make editing this book a gratifying experience which we hope will prove equally gratifying to our readers. Each made his or her unique contribution to a genuinely collegial atmosphere. Our thanks go to Ms. Pat Cobb and Ms. Camille Castro, who were so helpful in providing the secretarial assistance needed for completion of the manuscript. Thanks are also due to Barnard College for providing a Spivak grant which helped in the initial undertaking of this volume.

Zira DeFries, M.D.
Richard C. Friedman, M.D.
Ruth Corn, M.S.W.

Contributors

Jeffrey Blustein, Ph.D., Professor of Philosophy, Mercy College, Dobbs Ferry, New York

Susan Coates, Ph.D., Assistant Professor of Medical Psychology, Roosevelt Hospital, Columbia University, New York, New York

Ralph Colp, Jr., M.D., Senior Attending Psychiatrist, St. Luke's Hospital, New York, New York

Zira DeFries, M.D., Assistant Professor of Clinical Psychiatry, College of Physicians & Surgeons, Columbia University, Director of Mental Health Services, Barnard College, New York, New York

Shelley R. Doctors, Ph.D., Assistant Clinical Professor of Pediatrics, Albert Einstein College of Medicine, New York, New York

Teofilo Gautier, M.D., Professor of Pediatrics, Universidad de Santo Domingo, Robert Reed Cabrol Hospital, Dominican Republic

Sharon Golub, Ph.D., Associate Professor of Psychology, College of New Rochelle, New Rochelle, New York

Julianne Imperato-McGinley, Associate Professor of Medicine, Cornell University Medical College, New York, New York

Jeffrey Laurence, M.D., Associate Professor, Division of Hematology-Oncology, Cornell University Medical College, Guest Investigator, Department of Immunology, The Rockefeller University, New York, New York

Stanley A. Leavy, M.D., Clinical Professor of Psychiatry, Yale University School of Medicine, Training and Supervising Psychoanalyst, Western New England Institute for Psychoanalysis, New Haven, Connecticut

Ahmed Mobarak, M.D., Assistant Professor of Psychiatry, Cornell University Medical College, New York, New York

Harriette Mogul, M.D., Assistant Clinical Professor of Pediatrics, College of Physicians and Surgeons, Columbia University, Director of Health Service, Barnard College, New York, New York

Carol C. Nadelson, M.D., Professor of Psychiatry, Tufts University School of Medicine, Boston, Massachusetts

Malkah T. Notman, M.D., Professor of Psychiatry, Tufts University School of Medicine, Boston, Massachusetts

Ethel Spector Person, M.D., Clinical Professor of Psychiatry, College of Physicians and Surgeons, Columbia University, Director of Training and Supervising Analyst, Columbia University Center for Psychoanalytic Training and Research, New York, New York

Ralph E. Peterson, M.D., Deputy Director of Veterans Administration, Washington, D.C.

Charles A. Shamoian, M.D., Associate Professor of Clinical Psychiatry, Cornell University Medical College, New York, New York

Michael H. Stone, M.D., Professor of Clinical Psychiatry, Columbia Presbyterian Medical Center, New York, New York

Erasmo Sturla, M.D., Practice of Endocrinology, New York, New York

Marvin Wasserman, M.D., Assistant Clinical Professor of Psychiatry, Cornell University Medical College, New York, New York

PART ONE

FEMALE SEXUAL ISSUES: SELECTED TOPICS

CAROL C. NADELSON and
MALKAH T. NOTMAN

Behavioral-Psychological Aspects of Pregnancy and Abortion

PREGNANCY

It has been only two decades since pregnancy was considered a disease of nine-months' duration. We now understand pregnancy as a normative function with special characteristics that make it similar to other "developmental crises" of the life cycle, such as puberty (1). When a woman becomes pregnant, particularly for the first time, she is confronted with new challenges. These may precipitate the emergence of earlier identifications and unresolved issues, but at the same time there is an opportunity for further growth and maturation. Even a woman who chooses not to continue a pregnancy can experience it as a positive indication of her normal physical functioning as a woman.

Pregnancy is a complex physical, social, and psychological process that has different meanings for each person, although there are some universal components. Inevitably one must come to terms with multiple changes in relationships and roles. While pregnancy has been called a fulfillment and a creative act (2), it may also be a stressful time. Bibring and Valenstein (3) emphasize that pregnancy involves both physical and psychological changes that are immutable and alter the basic reality of one's life; once one has had a child one cannot turn back from having become a parent. In this chapter we will first address the pregnancy that leads to birth and parenthood, then look at miscarriage.

When a woman recognizes that she is pregnant, especially for the first time, regardless of whether the pregnancy was desired, she often experiences fear and ambivalence. The beginning is simple, but the implications are lifelong and the changes are permanent and progressive. Anxieties about future roles and responsibilities, including relationships and career, often arise. Concerns about her adequacy as a mother, changes in relationships with her own parents and the baby's father, and conflicts about other life goals are prominent.

An important aspect of pregnancy involves the revival of feelings about the woman's own mother and the opportunity to resolve the woman's relationship with her mother. Mother and daughter must both come to terms with changing roles, identities, and relationships. Past conflicts may cause feelings of guilt, anger, ambivalence, and remorse (1, 3–5). Competitive feelings may emerge, and it is necessary to deal with the loss of one's own status as a child while at the same time looking forward to the new role as an equal to one's own mother. Shereshefsky and Yarrow (6), in their study of the psychological aspects of a first pregnancy, found women who recalled their own mothers as warm, empathic, close, and happy in their role as mothers were more self-confident and less anxious about their pregnancy and their child. Melges (7), in his retrospective study of women with postpartum difficulties, found that women who consciously rejected their mothers as models were often upset at finding themselves acting like their mothers in their postpartum period, thus indicating some identification with the "disturbed" or "bad" mother. Even women who have relatively comfortable relationships with their mothers but wish to raise children differently can find themselves using techniques or behaviors their mothers used which they consciously rejected. Nilsson and Almgren (8), from prospective data, reported that women who identified positively with their mothers did better in the early postpartum period. In cases where there was conflict in the relationship with the mother, however, they reported that a good relationship with the baby's father was especially important for a positive outcome. Becoming aware of these identifications during the pregnancy or afterward can help make changes possible.

For the prospective grandparents the experience may be rewarding and joyful, a new beginning, or a chance to repair damaged relationships. It may also mean a confrontation with aging and mortality and evoke anxiety about loss of youth, sexuality, and power.

In examining the experiences of pregnancy, the father-to-be is often neglected. While pregnancy confirms his virility and may reinforce his masculine identity, he may feel threatened if he sees the child as a potential competitor (9). In a desire to redo his own past, he may overidentify with the child, perceiving the child as a narcissistic extension of himself. He may also see the child as a burden or an inhibitor of his freedom. Finally, the father-to-be may see parenthood as a new chance. All these feelings can occur at the same time.

Pregnancy has multiple meanings for both parents together as well as for each of them individually. Each parent must develop a concept of self as a parent, not as a child, and each must deal with some ambivalence about this new role and its implications, for example, further separation and individuation from his or her own parents and the loss of the gratifications as well as the limitations of childhood. For each couple, the child's sex or position in the family also has meaning, and all family members respond in some way to these factors.

Motivations for Pregnancy

Motivations for pregnancy are complex and multiple, and they differ from motivations for childrearing and the gratifications that come from relationships with children. To some extent, ambivalence about pregnancy and parenthood is universal, although most people do expect to have children. One important aspect of the desire to become a parent is the wish to foster the growth of the next generation and to achieve a kind of immortality through that generation. While one often hears about "good" and "bad" reasons for becoming a parent, few reasons can objectively be judged better than others.

Desires for love as well as concerns about the ability to love and to be loved are important motivating factors. Women often express the fantasy that having a baby guarantees them love and an important and close relationship with someone else. This is particularly true of a teenager who may feel lonely and unloved and seek a child in order to be a child herself and to feel loved. For example, a woman may want a child because she wants a mother (10) and because in mothering the child she hopes to master an early life experience of deprivation.

A pregnancy may also be used in an attempt to resolve a loss or to answer questions about the reality or endurance of a particular relationship (10). It may also serve to affirm gender identity and sexual adequacy, especially in adolescents and young adults (11, 12). However, while a pregnancy provides physical confirmation of one's sexuality and gender, the psychological or developmental aspects of becoming an adult may not be resolved. Particularly for the adolescent, pregnancy may be an attempt to facilitate separation from parents or to resolve long-standing conflicts in family relationships (11, 13).

Freud (14) hypothesized that bearing a child was the fulfillment of or a substitute for the wish to have a penis and that this was a central source of the motivation for having a baby. Deutsch (4) added that when pregnancy occurs the drive toward aggressiveness and masculinity in the healthy woman is given up for a more passive role until she actually becomes a mother, when maternal activity is considered appropriate. This is consistent with the earlier classical view that aggressive drives are associated with masculinity and that healthier women are more passive. Women fulfill a developmentally central goal in life by having a child. Few today can entirely accept these views (15, 16). However, one aspect of the motivation for pregnancy for some women is the resolution of Oedipal issues; having a child is both a way of resolving the competition with one's mother and a way of identifying with her.

In adolescent pregnancy, lack of information and understanding about sex and sexuality, or the inability to conceptualize and plan, both of which are developmental characteristics of adolescence, may be factors in bringing about a pregnancy. For an adolescent, becoming pregnant may also be supported by peer pressure, romantic fantasies, or denial that pregnancy can result from sexual intercourse. Teenagers who do not use contraceptives often believe "it won't happen to me," which may be a way of saying "I'm not really a woman" or "I'm special." Guilt about sexuality may result in an unwanted pregnancy, where the punishment—getting pregnant—is built into the experience.

Similar issues exist for the adolescent boy, who may see himself as more of a man if he is responsible for a pregnancy. Impregnating a girl may be an expression of his attempt to resolve gender identity issues or to settle competitive feelings. Although he is not as directly affected by a pregnancy and the girl is usually blamed, many teenage fathers today do feel involved and responsible, and they may feel hurt and displaced if they are excluded from the decision-making process. Others are frightened and run away, although this response is not as universal as sometimes assumed.

Physiological Changes and Psychological Concomitants of Pregnancy

Shereshefsky and Yarrow's (6) study confirms our understanding that greater external stress and difficulties unrelated to pregnancy increase problems in adapting during the pregnancy and the early postpartum period. Although this has been the subject of debate, some researchers have concluded that "childbirth is not just a life event but a specific stress and (can be) a true causal factor in the genesis of . . . psychosis" (17). Women with previous emotional problems, as well as those with life stress, are more likely to have difficulty with pregnancy or the postpartum period. Very early in pregnancy, reactions that occur result both from emotional responses to the implications of pregnancy and from physiological changes. Some symptoms, such as fatigue, nausea, and vomiting, are almost universal. Studies suggest that nausea and vomiting in early pregnancy are more common in Western cultures and vary from group to group (18, 19). Some reports indicate that nausea and vomiting are relatively unknown in many primitive cultures (20). When these symptoms are severe, they have sometimes been attributed to ambivalence about the pregnancy, but there is no clear evidence on this, or about specific etiologic factors. Some researchers focus on psychological factors (e.g., ambivalence about the pregnancy), others emphasize endocrine and other physiological determinants (21). However, one recent study concluded, "There is little evidence to support the notion that vomiting represents either a conscious or an unconscious rejection of the pregnancy" (22).

The early nausea, vomiting, and fatigue are often accompanied by a sense of disappointment because these symptoms interfere with the expected sense of excitement and well-being. Many women believe that they will be immune to such responses because of their genuine desire for the pregnancy, so the presence of these symptoms may represent failure to them. With the second trimester, these symptoms usually abate and a sense of well-being increases.

In the first trimester, emotional lability and anxiety are frequent and depression is not uncommon. Studies show that a certain amount of anxiety and distress in pregnancy is usual, as are other effects, such as insomnia, drowsiness by day, insecurity and dependency, loneliness, and mood swings (23, 24). While these feelings occur during most pregnancies and are considered normal, they also have been reported more often when feelings of guilt or ambivalence are prominent. One study concluded, "Anxiety appears to be the single most discriminating measure for presaging complications of pregnancy" (25).

Until quickening occurs, the fetus may be perceived as a foreign object that produces unpleasant feelings. Today such obstetric techniques as ultrasound give evidence of the reality of the baby before quickening. This can be shared with the father, involving him earlier in the pregnancy. Quickening makes it possible to begin to perceive the fetus as a real person and enables the woman to begin the task of differentiating herself from the fetus and begin bonding with it. This complex process requires establishing a new relationship with the baby as a separate person and a permanent change of identity for the woman, who must now begin to see herself as a mother (10). Quickening can be elating, but it can also precipitate anxiety, since the baby as a reality to come cannot now be denied.

The availability of amniocentesis as a prenatal diagnostic technique has changed the experience of pregnancy for many women. This procedure is most often performed for women over 35, for those who already have children with genetic abnormalities, or for those with a family history of specific disorders or risk factors, including translocation carriers, those with x-linked recessive diseases (e.g., hemophilia or Duchenne's muscular dystrophy), or those with a risk for trisomy-21 children (Down's syndrome). Amniocentesis for such other reasons as revealing the sex of the baby has been the subject of complex ethical discussion.

Although an estimated 95 to 98 percent of women undergoing amniocentesis or other procedures for prenatal diagnosis have favorable genetic results (26) (e.g., there is no detectable genetic abnormality), those who learn of an abnormality must make a decision about abortion. The psychological reassurance provided by favorable test results is substantial for most, and their adaptation to the pregnancy can be significantly altered (26). In a study by Silvestre and Frescoe (27) of 62 women and 25 of their male partners, it became clear that the experience of pregnancy is vastly different when prenatal diagnostic testing is expected. In fact, several of the respondents in their study waited to know the results before notifying anyone of the pregnancy. It is interesting to note that knowing the sex of the child is met with mixed feelings. Some did not want to be told, in order to protect themselves against a possible loss of the child and to prevent further "medicalization." For others, knowledge of the baby's sex facilitated preparation (27).

The new technique of chorionic villi biopsy promises substantial changes in the field of prenatal diagnosis, since it enables first-trimester diagnosis. However, perfection of the technique may increase the number of those desiring it and again raise complex ethical issues (28).

The second trimester of pregnancy brings a greater sense of well-being, decreased anxiety, and increased energy, but late in the second trimester some women begin to report increased feelings of dependency, passivity, and a desire to be alone. This is added to by the growing burden of the size of the fetus.

These feelings peak in the third trimester and may not disappear until sometime in the postpartum period (1). They may occur in part for physiological reasons, but they also have psychological concomitants involving the relationship of the mother to an unseen baby and the development of new identifications.

Regressive fantasies may also occur as part of the experience of pregnancy. Oral concerns and fantasies are prominent and have some cultural importance. Sometimes childhood fantasies of oral impregnation are temporarily revived. The idea that eating certain foods produces specific characteristics or abnormalities in the baby, for example, eating strawberries produces nevi (a Middle Eastern belief) or eating sharp foods will make the baby strong (a Polish belief), supports the belief in the power and control of the mother. The influence of prenatal nutrition is certainly important, and ingestion of particular substances has recently been further connected with fetal well-being in ways that have become more clearly recognized (e.g., in the fetal alcohol syndrome). Thus, complex environmental and genetic factors interact.

The feelings and fears experienced during pregnancy are frequently intense and varied. Women often express concern about their ambivalence in areas they had previously thought were conflict-free, such as their future roles and responsibilities, the effect of the pregnancy on a marriage, or the development and direction of career plans. There is also anxiety about sexual relations and physical attractiveness during the pregnancy and following delivery (1, 10). Women speak of embarrassment and guilt related to the exhibition of their sexuality, which is definitively demonstrated by the pregnancy. Many kinds of sexual and even homosexual fantasies also can occur. Sexual problems, including sexual dysfunction and extramarital affairs, particularly on the part of husbands, often begin during a pregnancy. Today, with pregnancy occurring later for many women, some of these fears emerge even prior to pregnancy and serve to increase ambivalence about whether to have a baby.

Some special issues revolve around sexual activity during pregnancy. The increased production of hormones which occurs during pregnancy leads to an increase in sex drive for some women and a decrease in others (29). Increased pelvic vascular engorgement also leads to increased sexual arousability for some. In general, however, pregnancy has often been associated with gradually decreasing frequency of sexual intercourse (30). In one study of 19 white middle-class primiparas, 14 were found to have from mild to marked decrease in coital frequency and sexual desire in the first trimester. Frequency and desire increased in the second trimester, although it was still lower than pre-pregnancy levels. By the eighth month of pregnancy, 15 subjects had ceased sexual activity altogether (31). Another study of women who delivered at birthing centers in Jerusalem during a two-year period reported that 90 percent of the women had intercourse during the seventh month of pregnancy, 66 percent had intercourse during the eighth month of pregnancy, and only 39 percent reported intercourse during the ninth month of pregnancy (32). Other studies show that although pregnant women feel an increased need to be touched and held, sexual activity tends to fluctuate and most couples report diminution in desire and in frequency of sexual intercourse (33).

The question of whether sexual activity can have a harmful effect on the fetus has received considerable attention. One study of 155 women reported that more than 20 percent had prevented orgasm during the last two months of their pregnancies because they or their doctor feared that orgasm would hurt the baby or for other reasons (34). The data indicated that of those who reported orgasm less than 24 hours before the onset of labor, none had prematurely ruptured membranes. This study reported no association between intercourse and orgasm, and prematurity or birth weight. Another study of 100 women who were sexually active during pregnancy concluded, "It does seem prudent to recommend orgasmic abstinence during certain pregnancies such as in gravidas with ripe cervix after 31 weeks of pregnancy and for those with poor reproductive history" (35).

A study of 413 women reported that "orgasm within one week of delivery is reported more commonly with increased maternal age and more years of formal education" (36). However, there was no association between recent intercourse and orgasm, and pregnancy complications (third-trimester bleeding, premature rupture of membranes, premature rupture of membranes with intrapartum infection, postpartum uterine infection, and neonatal sepsis). The consensus is that in normal pregnancy there is no valid medical reason to abstain from sexual activity prior to the rupture of the membranes (33).

As a pregnancy nears term, anxiety and fears often increase (1, 10). One study reported that a wide range of life experiences were associated with fear of childbirth, including negative experiences during childhood and early life, especially involving sexuality and anxiety-proneness (37). The pain and process of labor and possible difficulties with delivery are causes for worry. The sex and health of the infant and possibilities of death or injury to mother or child can preoccupy a woman during an often sleepless and restless period in the last trimester (1, 10). The support available from the relationship between the partners is especially important at this time. Shereshefsky and Yarrow (6) found that relationships generally improved as adaptation to the new roles as parents occurred, except where there was substantial marital discord.

A study of 55 women to assess depression and anxiety levels at various points during pregnancy and in the immediate postpartum period found overall increasing levels of depression and anxiety as the pregnancy progressed and high correlations of ratings of emotional state during pregnancy and during the postpartum period (38). The authors concluded that it is useful to assess emotional symptoms during pregnancy in order to predict which women are most at risk for developing postpartum problems.

During the course of pregnancy, expectant fathers also experience increased anxiety and other conflicts, including competitive feelings with the baby, or guilt. A substantial number of physical symptoms similar to those of pregnancy occur in men. Shereshefsky and Yarrow (6) report that the figure is 65 percent. Signs and symptoms include fears of damage to the woman or child, envy of the pregnancy, and even an increase in accidents and drinking. Some of these are related to the man's feeling of being excluded. The couvade ritual and many of the symptoms serve to enable the father to identify with his partner. This may be especially important when men do not have other supports for integration of their new role. The recent tendency for fathers to be more involved in the pregnancy has helped them feel less excluded and less competitive.

If there is ambivalence about the pregnancy or the relationship, acting out may occur. Men who are stressed by the pregnancy or by their impending fatherhood, however, have been reported to begin wife-battering during a pregnancy and may experience decreased sexual interest in their partners. These issues, fears of damage to themselves or their partners, or the reemergence of early oral or Oedipal conflicts, may lead to extramarital affairs. Pregnancy may stir up feelings and memories of their mothers' pregnancies and their relationships with siblings.

Even among men with few manifest emotional disturbances, "pregnancy-related stresses may arouse irritability, neglect of their wives, belittling or other forms of aggression" (39). Some other reasons for these reactions to pregnancy and fatherhood include increased financial responsibilities; the triggering of concerns about and feelings of latent homosexuality by reduced sexual activity during pregnancy; arousal of unresolved childhood anger toward parents or siblings; and frustration of dependency demands by the partner's attention to the pregnancy or baby (39). Studies of male patients with prior bipolar disorders show that pregnancy can precipitate episodes of affective illness (40). One study concluded, "Childbirth and pregnancy present the necessity for reviewing self-identity, which may be difficult and painful for the bipolar patient to achieve. Impending parenthood provokes a recrudescence of previous childhood ties, including feelings toward parents, particularly around issues of separation and loss" (40).

Labor and Delivery

There are a number of alternatives available today for the conduct of labor and delivery, in contrast to a generation ago, when there was almost uniform use of heavy sedation or anesthesia and the woman was inevitably in a supine position in a bed. There are suites for labor where the father and in some cases the other children can be present, and birthing rooms with homelike surroundings. The woman can sometimes choose to use a special chair or bed where she can assume a squatting position or any other more comfortable position. The LeBoyer method of delivery in dim light with the newborn baby immersed in warm water aims to minimize the trauma for the baby in the transitions of birth (41). In addition, there are complex techniques for monitoring the process of labor and the progress of the fetus. Nevertheless, the human experience, with considerable uncertainty, anxiety, drama, and excitement, still exists.

Anxiety may be reinforced by the way the labor and delivery are handled, and it may interfere with these processes. Often this anxiety is related to feelings about giving up a sense of unity with the unborn child. The sex of the baby, the sibling order, and the special meanings of that particular baby to the parents also affect feelings surrounding the birth.

The effects of heavy medication and the consequent failure of the mother to experience the delivery consciously and fully may interfere with early mothering. Women who have been anesthetized or heavily medicated are apt to report feeling out of touch with reality, disbelief that they have borne a child, and uncertainty that the child presented to them is actually their child (42). However, this does not preclude development of attachment and adequate mothering where other circumstances are not problematic. Considerable unhelpful anxiety can be generated if some aspect of the labor and delivery process does not go according to plan or expectations.

"Natural childbirth" instruction, aimed at conscious participation of the mother and father and thus reduction of fear and tension, can lead not only to pain reduction (43) but also to enhancement of the experience of birth and the development of the early relationship between the mother and child. It has been hypothesized that childbirth preparation classes reduce the need for pain medication because they give the woman something else to focus on, thereby reducing her perception of pain and her anxiety during the birth (25). However, there are multiple reasons for difficulty in childbirth, which may be physiologicallyand/ or psychologically determined. One study (44) reported that congruence between the doctor's and patient's points of view regarding labor and delivery led to shorter labors. It is important for those involved in care during labor to be flexible and to avoid making uniform rules or having unrealistic expectations regarding the rate of progress or the degree of discomfort, thereby conveying the idea that the mother has failed if she has not adhered to a particular plan, such as using no medication. In one study, 83 percent of the women who had received childbirth training by the orthodox Lamaze method requested epidural anesthesia against their instructor's advice (45). Another study concluded that natural childbirth should not be uniformly recommended because some couples are not suited for it (46).

For both parents, the effect of watching and participating in the delivery varies with the preparation, the anxiety level, and the underlying feelings stimulated by the events. Shereshefsky and Yarrow (6) found that feelings ranged from fear of anatomical assault and concerns about body intactness to a sense of completion and discovery. When either natural childbirth or heavy sedation is presented as the "best" way without full appreciation of individual needs and abilities, a woman whose delivery has been difficult may feel inadequate and/or guilty about not being a good enough woman or mother and may experience greater anxiety (47). It is not possible to draw direct conclusions about effects on later adaptation from a single experience. Likewise, analgesics or anesthetics may not only increase the risks for both mother and infant but also impair the mother's sense of mastery (48). A hospital environment originally designed to promote safety by permitting quick intervention when needed may enhance the need for medication because unfamiliar surroundings exaggerate the fear-tension-pain cycle (49–51). An avoidance of *all* intrusions, however, would prevent using the interventions that *are* needed to increase safety to mother and child (50).

The author of a review of the controversy surrounding home vs. hospital delivery (52) argues that some of the data used to support either home delivery or hospital delivery are difficult to interpret. United States data which indicate that prenatal mortality in home confinements is four times higher than in hospital confinements might lead to a conclusion that births at home are four times more dangerous. If, however, we consider that only 1 percent of all births in this study took place at home, and that many of these births were not planned to occur at home, then the perinatal mortality in this group was higher than that for completely unattended births in a random sample of the pregnant population in the Third World. One must wonder about the unreported facilities and supports in the unattended Third World group and question the comparability of the groups. We are left with only one conclusion. This group of home confinements in the United States appears to refer to a small and highly pathological group. In a well-controlled study in a small town in the Netherlands (52), the perinatal mortality for hospital deliveries was 12 times higher than that for planned home confinements (all deliveries planned and starting at home but ending in the hospital because of an emergency were considered home confinements). In the Netherlands there is no correlation between perinatal mortality and later hospitalization.

In 1981 the American College of Obstetrics and Gynecology indicated that there is a 10 to 25 percent chance that a pregnancy will end with a Cesarean section (52); in 1970 there was only a 5 percent chance. In the same town in the Netherlands referred to above, the percentage was 2 percent in 1970 and 1 percent in 1981. Kloosterman (52) points out that since the population in the Netherlands study was biologically similar on both occasions, there must be other variables operating, including environmental and social factors.

It is interesting to note that in the United States, where childbirth education classes have not been systematically encouraged or supported by regular medical channels as they have been in other countries, there are both more instruments and more drugs used during deliveries than among a similar population in the Netherlands, where there is more active support for childbirth education (25). Early-1970 figures for U.S. deliveries reported that over 90 percent were hospital deliveries, with episiotomies in 100 percent, the use of analgesics in 85 to 95 percent, the use of forceps in 33 percent, and Cesarean sections in 9 to 12 percent (25). This may be different in the 1980s. The United States has a relatively high infant mortality rate (21.8 per 1,000 births), even though most births are medically attended and take place in hospitals (25). When considering these data, however, it is important to note that we are not dealing with reports on comparable populations with regard to age, socioeconomic status, and so forth. These data, as well as those concerning home vs. hospital deliveries, make it apparent that further well-controlled studies of comparable populations in comparable circumstances must be done before definite conclusions can be reached. The variables are complex and are affected by historically specific factors, and it is difficult to interpret data when no more information about the medical or psychological state of the population is given.

Pain in Labor

The issue of whether pain is intrinsic to childbirth is usually answered by attempts to extrapolate from primitive societies. However, cultures also vary with regard to how pain is experienced or dealt with (52), and there are wide sociocultural as well as individual differences (53–55). In fact, a recent article (56) suggests that "there is probably considerably more pathology associated with obstetrically unattended childbearing and childbirth in developing countries than has been realized so far." While it does appear that anxiety and fear play a large role in the experience of what may be perceived as pain, anxiety and pain may be consequences of changes in body and self-image and accompany fears of pregnancy, loss of control, and fears about adequacy and damage. Bradley (57) has observed that women may be made more vulnerable to obstetric pain because of a particular form of socialization that discourages them from being sufficiently insistent on their own comfort or makes them feel ashamed of bodily exposure or functions.

Crandon (58, 59) has suggested that high levels of anxiety during pregnancy might be a predisposing cause of increased incidence of maternal and perinatal mortality and morbidity. Others (60), however, have disputed these findings. Lederman et al. (61, 62) conclude that there is a relationship between a number of variables: anxiety, epinephrine blood levels, and progress in labor. Maternal stress may represent a preventable cause of fetal distress, especially in the case of a compromised fetus who is unable to tolerate even a minimum decrease in uterine blood flow, and prevention of maternal stress during labor may contribute to maintenance of a normal uterine-placental blood flow. Another study (25) found evidence of an increased perinatal mortality rate among animals who were anxious or disturbed during labor and delivery. While it is difficult to extrapolate from this information, the data clearly point to the need for more complex studies of the interrelationships between anxiety, other stress, pain, and physiological factors in the outcome of pregnancy.

It is clear that there is some pain in childbirth. The variations in pain and the relationship of that pain to anxiety and preparation can be understood by comparing the experience of suturing a three-centimeter chin laceration on an 18–year-old football player and repairing the same size wound on a confused and frightened 4–year-old (63). Similarly, genuine pain in the chest muscles when running the final stretch of a winning race is associated with pride and mastery rather than with humiliation and dependency.

Since anxiety and the discomfort of labor may be intensified by stress and resulting fear, it may conversely be relieved to some extent by measures designed to remove the component of fear. The experience of pain does appear to be diminished by familiarizing the pregnant woman with the process of childbearing and by fostering self-confidence and active mastery. Recent work on endorphins makes it possible to conjecture that we will be able to "learn" to release and utilize intrinsic rather than extrinsic substances for pain relief (64). This may, in fact, be an aspect of the mechanism that accounts for the success of prepared childbirth.

Psychoprophylactic preparation, however, is often accompanied by the expectation of natural childbirth. Preparation is helpful, but unmedicated childbirth may not be suitable for every woman, and often men and women feel pressured to proceed regardless of the demands of the real obstetrical situation or their interest or ability to participate. Ballou (65) reported on two husbands who decompensated in the postpartum period. She attributed this to pressure for them to be in the delivery room. Women who feel pushed into natural childbirth may also experience adverse consequences. Anxiety may be increased or a sense of failure may be engendered, even if obstetrical intervention is necessary because of high risk or complications. Learning the techniques without insisting they be used may be enormously helpful, but it is important to be able to define indications, contraindications, and special problems better and to relate these to long-term outcome. In addition, as Seiden (48) points out, prepared-childbirth techniques tend to reach predominantly middle-class married couples. Thus, those who may have the greatest need may have the fewest resources. Women whose sense of mastery might be most vulnerable are likely to be poorer, adolescent, and unmarried mothers.

The Cesarean Birth

One of the most neglected aspects of the labor and delivery process is the woman's response to the need for a Cesarean birth. When the Cesarean is unexpected, anxiety may be overwhelming: in addition to the danger of any surgical procedure, there is apt to be a feeling of "failure" on the part of the woman, a suspicion that it might not really have been necessary.

When an operative delivery occurs, the birth of the baby can be treated as a side effect of an abdominal operation. Lipson and Tilden (66) add that, in addition to individual coping skills and ego strengths, important factors in adaptation were the circumstances of and the woman's actual experience in relation to the Cesarean birth, her prior plans as to natural childbirth, her relationship with her doctor, the amount of time she had to prepare for the surgery, the reason for the surgery, the duration of her labor, the presence of her husband during the surgery and recovery period, her contact with the infant, and any medical complications. The authors noted that in the immediate postoperative phase the patients in their study manifested "shocked numbness" with affective flatness. In the first few postpartum days feelings of disappointment and a flood of emotions emerged, for example, relief, guilt, anger, disappointment, or envy of others. Several women reported feelings of detachment and lack of enthusiasm for their infants. "The blues" began, but they were not easy to distinguish from responses to the surgical procedure. After discharge from the hospital, difficulty was heightened by the demands of the newborn infant and the process of recovery from surgery. Women reported feeling a need to be taken care of, and many reported disappointment in their mothering skills, which were hampered by the postoperative recovery period. Breast-feeding may be more difficult because of fatigue and incisional pain. The Cesarean birth was blamed for some difficulties that would ordinarily exist in the postpartum period for non–Cesarean births, so it was difficult to differentiate responses. These included nightmares and feelings of failure, as well as self-image problems. Between two months postpartum and the end of the first year, a combination of repression and denial of some negative aspects of the experience occurred, with the surfacing of unexpected feelings and memories for many of the women. Finally, a resolution appeared to occur with acceptance of the experience. In general, the more positively the woman perceives the experience to have been, the more "normal" the resolution process is (66). This is analogous to the resolution of a grief or traumatic experience.

Stewart (46) describes the clinical histories of five women and four men who sought psychiatric treatment after the "failure" of natural childbirth. They experienced a variety of symptoms and were described as highly organized people who needed to be in control and who responded to psychiatric intervention in ways that "one might expect for symptoms precipitated by acute stress."

Fetal Monitoring

The recent technological advances that make fetal monitoring during labor possible do not come without psychological as well as fiscal cost. It has been suggested that mother-infant bonding can be impaired, and data indicating that the progress of labor is affected by cultural and psychosocial factors, including support systems and beliefs about pregnancy and delivery, suggest other risks (49, 67, 68). For example, Rosengren (67) found that women who regarded pregnancy as an illness had longer labors than women who did not. In the absence of high risk to the fetus, therefore, the use of monitoring might be ill-advised for some because it might reinforce the medical model and illness concept of labor and delivery. While the effect of anxiety produced by the presence of the fetal-monitoring machine itself must be considered, the reassurance that monitoring provides to some women may far outweigh this negative aspect (69, 70). In a study of fetal monitoring, most women preferred to be able to see the front of the monitor. Those women who could see the front of the monitor during labor, whose husbands were present during labor, and who had attended prenatal classes felt a greater degree of reassurance.

Puerperium

There is substantial evidence that the psychological implications of the physical separation of mother and baby immediately after delivery, as was the norm in the recent past, can impair early mother-child bonding (71). We do not know the extent to which such separation affects later development in a lasting way or whether inadequate bonding occurs when it does because human mothers and infants lack dependable "instinctual" bonding repertoires. And we do not know how much social learning and current obstetric and pediatric practice interfere with otherwise adequate bonding potential. It is important to consider the way obstetric and early pediatric care is delivered in relation to this important early development as well as the support of the mother and child and other family members. There is evidence from studies of lower primates that even their "instinctive" nurturant behavior is heavily dependent on the mother's prior life experience and learning (72).

Because drugs used in labor can interfere with the attention and alertness of both mother and baby, they may affect activity in those areas of the brain involved in early mother-child interaction. These drug effects appear to last longer in the infant than in the mother and have been shown to alter brain activity in the human infant. Therefore, when drugs are used during labor it is more likely that the baby's initial response to the mother will be interfered with (50). Moreover, medication-induced depression of the infant's sucking, especially when combined with mother-child separation during the early hours of life, can delay the development of adequate sucking until after engorgement of the breasts has occurred. Thus the infant may fail initially to receive colostrum, and lactation can be delayed or even prevented (50).

Maternal response is also highly dependent on the infant's response to its mother. There is some evidence suggesting that a critical period occurs during the first postpartum hours (42). Since eye contact with the infant may be a critical releaser of the mother's emotional response, there is reason to question any practice that sedates infant or mother immediately postpartum or that separates them or interferes with eye contact during this time (42).

This area is still under study. One recent paper (73) suggests that medically abnormal pregnancies, difficult labors and deliveries, neonatal separation, and other separations in the first six months of life all place a child at risk for maltreatment. In emphasizing the importance of early parent-child interaction, Lynch (74) found that 66 percent of abused children had been separated from their parents 48 hours or more in the first week of life, while only 3 percent of the same children's nonabused siblings had been separated from their parents. Another study (75) reported that parents who did not visit their infant in an intensive care unit were likely to mistreat the child later. Still another study (76) has noted that disruption in parent-infant bonding predicts greater risk for maltreatment. When the mother has had an active role and has been an active participant in the process of childbirth, and when there are fewer drugs and medical complications as well as fewer Cesarean births and induced labors, there is reduction in the risk of child maltreatment (77, 78). One must put these findings into context, however, since we also know that many separations do occur and that where substitute care is adequate, adverse effects are not documented. The emphasis on separation also does not take into account the adequacy and quality of the relationship with the caretaker.

Mothering has traditionally been regarded as based primarily on instinctual responses, but studies show that this is not the case. For example, Erikson (79) has pointed out that social experience is important in achieving satisfactory motherhood. His thesis is that in order to be a good mother a woman must (a) have had the experience of being mothered, which provides a model for her new experience, (b) have a conception of mothering that is shared with a husband or others in her environment, and (c) have a world image linking past, present, and future.

Harlow et al. (72) demonstrated that even monkeys reared in isolation do not react as "natural" monkey mothers, but show rage at their infants and fail to take care of them. The behavior of human infants, particularly visual fixation and smiling, intensifies maternal feelings. Attachment is not an immediate phenomenon, but it grows with the mutual interaction of mother and infant during the first months. In studies of mothering patterns in other cultures, Whiting (80) finds a consistent cross-cultural belief that children need to be taught how to respond to and care for infants.

The evidence seems to indicate that some mothering behavior may be learned by mothers in much the same way as fathers seem to learn it. Feedback and interaction are critical in the experience of motherhood and fatherhood, but we have yet to fully understand the problems that occur when interruptions or pathological processes interfere with the early experiences of parenthood.

The Later Postpartum Period

In our society, the prevalence of small, isolated nuclear families has changed pregnancy from an experience with family involvement, concern, and attention to one that might be quite isolated, where a woman may be alone and feel unsupported (80). When delivery occurs in a foreign environment, the early postpartum feelings of dependency, which are normal, and the frequently occurring transitory depression may be accentuated by the isolation and unfamiliar surroundings. Changes in many hospital policies today, however, make it possible for husbands to be more involved in the labor and delivery.

In the early postpartum period one of the mother's most important concerns may be breast-feeding. Anxiety may be accentuated if a woman feels that her performance in this area will determine her adequacy as a mother or as a woman. Support or criticism from family or from her own mother, social pressures either to continue breast-feeding or to give it up, and the presence or absence of people to support and to learn from may affect a woman's decision and her experience with breast-feeding.

In the postpartum period there may be depressive feelings related to the loss of the pregnant state and the sense of oneness experienced with the infant during pregnancy. The state of ego depletion is manifested by a feeling of inability to tolerate any additional burdens or stresses, however minor they may seem.

A number of responses to the early postpartum period can be seen as part of the adaptational process (1). The "three-day blues," or mild depressive symptoms and emotional lability, begin within a few days and have been reported to occur in almost 80 percent of women. These generally last a few days. Some degree of depression is cross-cultural, and studies have reported the presence of postpartum depression in Tanzania, the West Indies, and the United Kingdom, with incidences and symptom patterns similar to those found in the United States (81). A number of studies document this clinically familiar pattern. One prospective study (82) of 42 postpartum women of varying parity, social class, and age revealed that the major symptoms consist of worry, anxiety, tension, and depression. Another study reports that "women drink more, sleep less, lose weight, and often have mild oedema" during the postpartum period (81). The woman who is experiencing postpartum depression may weep without apparent reason, feel that she is "falling apart," and sense that she is unable to cope with any more than the most immediate details of living and caring for her child. Minor inconveniences may be viewed as major trauma. New and intense feelings experienced by the mother include worry about whether she is able to meet the tasks and responsibilities of motherhood, which can seem monumental. The etiology of these postpartum depressive symptoms is unclear, but genetic, endocrine, and psychological factors appear to be important.

The process of adaptation is gradual and this depression or "blues" period may go on for several weeks. The sleep-wake cycle of the infant, its feeding patterns, how successful the mother feels she is in caring for the baby, and the strain of having to care for a fussy infant can play a large part in the progression of responses in the postpartum period. Sleep deprivation can be a major factor in the etiology of emotional distress in new parents. There may also be a longer-lasting depression that has its onset anywhere within a few weeks postpartum and may take several weeks to resolve.

While women with severe ego deficits prior to pregnancy are more likely to develop severe postpartum problems, one must distinguish between a postpartum psychiatric disorder precipitated by childbirth and a disorder that occurs then but is not directly linked to childbirth. Studies indicate that there is a greater incidence of psychotic disorders after childbirth than at any other time in life (17), but patients who evidence postpartum mania are "less likely to have recurrent episodes of illness outside the postpartum period" (83).

Severe emotional disorders or postpartum psychoses precipitated by pregnancy occur at approximately the rate of one to two per 1,000 live births (40). They are more often associated with obstetrical abnormalities such as toxemia, malpresentations, hydramnios (excessive amniotic fluid), and placental defects. There does not seem to be a specific relationship between prepartum emotional disorder and postpartum psychosis; in fact, it is unusual to find them both occurring in the same pregnancy. Symptoms of postpartum psychosis usually appear between the first and fourth postpartum weeks. One-third of the women who experience puerperal psychosis develop similar difficulties in subsequent pregnancies (17, 83). Other important etiological factors in postpartum psychosis are the possibility of organic (biochemical, endocrinological) causes (81, 82) as well as psychological causes, including unresolved conflicts about pregnancy, childrearing, and the relationship with the child's father (17, 39, 40). Although there is some increasing evidence to support genetic factors, a definitive formulation as to etiology has not been reached.

Reliable predictions as to which women will develop severe postpartum reactions are difficult to make (17). One study found that "previous history of neurotic depression, mood changes during pregnancy, and previous postnatal depression" were all associated with more severe symptoms in the first postpartum week (84). Another study (40) reported that women with previous bipolar affective disorders were more at risk for postpartum psychosis and concluded that "bipolar illness tends to run in families [and] is thought to have a strong, genetic component." This study also reviewed the cases of 40 male bipolar patients. The findings were that 21 had "episodes of primary affective disorder occurring during the perinatal course of the spouse, or within one year postpartum."

For milder disorders, no one etiology has been found. The fact that adoptive mothers, fathers, and grandparents experience postpartum symptoms points to the importance of psychosocial factors. Patients with postpartum psychosis can present initially with delirium, restlessness, mood lability, and confusion; depression usually occurs later. Those caring for such patients must be alert to potential self-destructive acts or the danger of a mother's hurting the infant. While postpartum psychosis represents one end of the spectrum, women with ego deficits or other life traumas are more likely to experience difficulty at some point during a pregnancy or in the postpartum period.

Certain elements in a woman's history can alert caretakers to her greater vulnerability to severe postpartum reaction and make it possible to anticipate her reactions and to resolve conflicts:

1. A history of psychiatric treatment or hospitalization
2. A history of difficulties at other critical maturational stages, such as puberty
3. A history of early maternal deprivation or loss
4. Conflicts involving separation from parents
5. Conflicts about sexual identity
6. Severe conflicts about the role of mother and concerns about adequacy as a mother or her ability to care for a child
7. Marital or other family difficulties
8. Past difficulties with pregnancy, delivery, or postpartum depression
9. Major individual or family problems, including recent losses (death)
10. Familial or congenital diseases

11. Previous birth of a defective child and/or the possibility of defective birth with this pregnancy
12. Extreme youth
13. Previous poor relationships with physicians

Some concerns of the pregnant woman which can alert caretakers include diverse symptoms that may be highly subjective. Experience with pregnant women makes it possible to know when to take these concerns seriously:

1. Excessive worry or fear of damage to oneself, the child, the marriage, or one's parents
2. Fantasies, thoughts, or preoccupations with being "out of control"
3. Intense separation anxiety
4. Loss of emotional responsiveness
5. Unusual or extreme mood swings
6. Denial of the pregnancy or failure to plan realistically for the baby
7. Excessive uncertainty or indecisiveness
8. Overconcern with body changes, such as stretch marks, feeling fat, or worry about "showing," especially very negative feelings about such changes

Miscarriage or Spontaneous Abortion

Many women have miscarriages and do not know they have been pregnant. Others have one or more spontaneous abortions as well as successful pregnancies. A small number of women have been unable to carry any pregnancy to term.

A woman is defined as a "habitual aborter" if she has had three or more spontaneous abortions or miscarriages. "By the time a woman has had three successive miscarriages a recurrent factor is suspected" (85). After three miscarriages a woman's chances of carrying a fetus to term are only 16 in 100; after four miscarriages her chances of carrying a fetus to term are less than 6 in 100. It is estimated that habitual abortions result in the loss of 50,000 fetal lives each year in the United States (85). Spontaneous abortions occur in an estimated 15 percent of all pregnancies (86).

Studies of the effects of spontaneous abortions on women have concluded that "even though a woman may not be unhappy about the termination of pregnancy, the experience . . . may be emotionally upsetting for her" (86). Women describe feelings of sadness, anxiety, depression, and hostility following spontaneous abortion (86). One study (87) reported several unique factors that contribute to delayed or pathological grief reactions on the part of the woman who has experienced a miscarriage: people often do not know that the woman is pregnant since the pregnancy may have been in the earliest stage; the woman may feel embarrassed to say that she lost a baby; the woman may not have resolved the ambivalence that is typical of the early, narcissistic stages of pregnancy; the woman rarely sees the lost fetus, and there is no funeral or other ritual to help with the loss. There is also often no support from caretakers, friends, and family to acknowledge that the loss is significant (87). The sense of helplessness that often occurs adds to a sense of guilt, which has been found to be "a nearly universal feeling" following a miscarriage (87).

The importance of emotional factors has been stressed in studies of habitual aborters because in many of these cases "no abortogenic pathology" can be demonstrated (85). When habitual aborters were compared with women who had no history of abortion, several psychological factors were found to be more common among those with abortion histories. However, an unwanted pregnancy is usually not aborted, even by someone very distressed, so the psychogenic etiology is difficult to demonstrate.

Newer techniques, such as temporary surgical treatment of a cervix that dilates prematurely, have provided help for some. For those who cannot carry a pregnancy to term, the disappointment can be intense, with cycles of anticipation and depression. These responses are similar to those aroused by other fertility problems, with the added element of a recurrent crisis.

In conclusion, a pregnancy represents a complex biological, psychological, and social experience with many ramifications and developmental implications. A first pregnancy provides a unique bridge from one role to another in a time-limited framework with some elements that are highly personal and others that are universal.

ABORTION

Recent controversy about ethical issues involved in abortion and questions about access to abortion have provoked new arguments and renewed claims that abortion should be considered a psychologically damaging procedure (88) in addition to having other detrimental consequences. In the past, physicians and other health professionals opposed abortion because it seemed to violate the Hippocratic oath and because it was not a safe medical procedure, especially compared with the risks of childbirth. Before 1960, professionals believed that guilt and shame resulting from abortion would lead to serious depression and disturbance in relationships (89).

As medical techniques improved and resulted in a revision of mortality rates, so that childbirth carried a greater risk than abortion, medical risk was no longer a possible argument (90). Currently, for an early pregnancy, *under* 16 weeks, the risk of death from abortion ranges between one per 25,000 abortions and one per 400,000. The estimated mortality to be expected in childbirth is one case in every 10,000 births, the same as the abortion risk for a pregnancy *over* 16 weeks. The risk of maternal death from illegal abortion is estimated to be one per 3,000.

Prior to 1973, in most states, abortions were permitted for "therapeutic" reasons: to preserve the life and/or health of the mother. Most states differed on grounds and indications, and hospitals as well as physicians accepted different criteria. For example, in one hospital a woman would have to attempt suicide in order for the pregnancy to be considered a danger to her life, but in another hospital a statement of suicidal intent would be sufficient. Few abortions were performed for purely medical reasons, because over the past several decades the technical ability to preserve life throughout pregnancy had improved to the extent that disorders that would threaten life during pregnancy were rare. Thus, the vast majority of therapeutic abortions were performed for psychiatric reasons, although guidelines and criteria were poorly defined (91).

The myth of inevitable or frequent psychological damge following abortion persisted, despite Ekblad's 1955 study (92) of 479 women who had legal abortions in Sweden for psychiatric reasons. Of the 1 percent of women who demonstrated emotional consequences following abortion, all had a history of emotional disorders. Ekblad found little evidence that abortion had serious effects on the mental health of women. Furthermore, he stated, "The problem of abortion for psychiatric reasons is far more often the question of judging the effect of the addition of another child to a household or mother or both, under stress, than predicting the likelihood of madness or suicide" (92).

This report did not evoke much interest until 1963, when Kummer (93) surveyed 32 psychiatrists who frequently saw women after an abortion. Some 75 percent of the psychiatrists stated that they had never seen severe emotional aftereffects, and 25 percent stated that such aftereffects occurred only rarely. Other studies began to challenge the views that had been so pervasive and to develop methodologies for more systematic investigation. In fact, Peck and Marcus (94) found that some women who had already been diagnosed as psychologically ill benefited from the procedure. Symptoms of depression and anxiety precipitated by the pregnancy were relieved, and new symptoms were mild and self-limited. Another study (95) reported that women who were psychologically healthy, as well as those who were not, responded to abortion with transient symptoms but were generally improved following the abortion. Furthermore, this study reported an increased risk of neurotic or depressive illness if an unwanted pregnancy was not terminated.

In 1969 the Group for the Advancement of Psychiatry reviewed the moral, ethical, psychological, and medical issues involved in abortion and supported the view that the decision to terminate a pregnancy should rest primarily with the pregnant woman (96). They noted the lack of serious postabortion complications and recommended that the physician explore the motivation for the decision with the woman and be able to recommend or provide counseling.

This position was echoed by other groups (97, 98). One report (99) noted that psychiatrists were unable to predict which women would suffer from emotional disturbances if therapeutic abortion was denied, and recommended that the woman and her family, not the psychiatrists, make the decision. Another report stated that "there are no unequivocal psychiatric indications for therapeutic abortion" (100). Studies from Great Britain (101) following the changes in their law making abortion more easily available refocused the issue on the stress of bearing an unwanted child. They reported that psychological symptoms following this type of birth were likely to occur in the overburdened multipara and the single woman without support. Women who had a pregnancy terminated, however, had little overt psychiatric disturbance. The attitude that has greatest clinical acceptance today holds that an abortion can be stressful for an individual but that assessment of the psychological effects must be related to the significance of the pregnancy and the abortion for the individual, with regard as well for the values and beliefs of her culture.

The Unwanted Child

Although earlier studies (102, 104) made it clear that psychiatric risks of abortion must also be considered along with preventive gains, little attention was paid to this recommendation. In 1954 Caplan (102) had reported that special problems were apt to develop between mother and child when an unsuccessful attempt at abortion had been made during the pregnancy. Hook (103) studied 213 children born to women who had been refused therapeutic abortion and found that, compared with controls, unwanted children were both physically and mentally impaired.

In a classic study by Forssman and Thuwe (104), 120 Swedish children born after a therapeutic abortion was refused were followed for 21 years. These children were matched with controls of the same sex born in the same hospital or district on the same day. The results indicated that the unwanted children fared worse in almost every way, even when illegitimacy was considered. They had a higher incidence of psychiatric disorders, delinquency, criminal behavior, and alcoholism. They were more often recipients of public assistance and were exempted from military service for medical or psychiatric reasons, and they had less schooling than the control group. The study concluded that the very fact that a woman even applies for a legal abortion means that her prospective child will have greater difficulty surmounting social and mental handicaps than his or her peers. The authors recommended that these factors be seriously considered when recommendations for ''therapeutic'' abortion are made. Subsequent studies of child abuse and neglect repeat these warnings about the fate of unwanted children (105, 106).

The Effect of Legalization of Abortion

As the climate of opinion about abortion began to change and some states liberalized their laws, investigations began to focus on counseling and crisis intervention in the decision-making process. Senay (107) emphasized counseling, particularly when a woman seemed to be pressured toward an abortion decision by her family or friends. Marder (108) reported observing negative attitudes on the part of hospital personnel toward women who opted for abortion; and that inadequate counseling contributed directly to the incidence of postabortion guilt, remorse, and depression.

Others (109–112) reported that for most women abortion was indeed therapeutic when they had made a decision that this was the best course for them. One study (113) found that "tired mothers," who might also request sterilization, were particularly benefited by abortion. These women reported that they found new meaning in life when they were no longer in the position of having obligatory pregnancies.

Another study (114) pointed out that when the law required severe prior psychiatric illness for abortion to be allowed, one would find a group least likely to respond favorably to abortion as a therapeutic procedure since they were more likely to be a group of emotionally disturbed women. Of the 207 women followed after abortions (average age 18), the reasons for seeking abortion included depressive feelings (most frequently), guilt, anxiety, fears (of hurting parents, of having and raising a child, social stigma, rejection, malformed fetus, and losing a job). Some 74 percent of this group had experienced contraceptive failure. Naiveté was prominent in many (e.g., the belief that one can't become pregnant the first time). These women reported that 98 percent of them felt that their general health was the same or better after the abortion, and 94 percent felt that their emotional health was the same or better. Most of the symptoms reported (depression, anxiety, and guilt) decreased with time. The authors found few patients who required psychiatric treatment. In fact, a history of previous psychiatric symptoms or illness was not a predictor of those who would have a negative emotional response to abortion. Another report (115) emphasized that healthier, more knowledgeable women were able to get therapeutic abortions more readily than those who were disturbed, because the latter had difficulty negotiating the process.

One study (110) that did measure anxiety, depression, anger, guilt, and shame in the preabortion and postabortion period found that the pattern of response was similar to that of other instances of crisis reaction and resolution. In the 24–hour postabortion observation period, relief and feelings of well-being predominated. Over the six-month period the absence of grief, sadness, or depression suggested that abortion was not experienced as a major loss by most women. The women in this group who were most vulnerable to conflict following abortion were those with:

1. A previous history of mental illness or serious emotional conflict
2. Immature interpersonal relationships or an unstable, conflicted relationship with men
3. A negative relationship with their mothers
4. Strong ambivalence or uncertainty and helplessness with regard to abortion
5. A religious or cultural background where there were negative attitudes toward abortion

In addition, single women, especially those who had not borne children, were more susceptible to conflict following abortion.

The authors cautioned that these factors are not to be interpreted as contraindications to abortion. They pointed out that at their six-month follow-up evaluation women in the vulnerable groups believed that their decision to have an abortion was the correct one. They concluded that the opportunity to play an active role in resolving the crisis of an unwanted pregnancy and to choose or reject abortion promoted successful adjustment and maturation. Thus, rather than making a decision for or against abortion on tenuous grounds, a variety of crisis-intervention and therapeutic techniques may be employed preventively to provide benefits for the women seeking an abortion. The apparently contradictory findings concerning the effects of psychiatric history on predicting postabortion problems can be explained by the differences in criteria and categories of mental illness in each group. In any case, a history of emotional disturbance does not always imply that there will be postabortion symptoms.

In another report, Freeman (116) considered the implications of abortion for women from another perspective. The women she studied did not perceive themselves to be active and instrumental in their own lives and thus chose abortion out of "necessity." After the abortion, however, these women felt that the experience resulted in a "different awareness about themselves," especially since for many it was their first experience with a major individual decision where the consequences were important and affected others as well as themselves. The author also confirmed reports that contraceptive use increases after an abortion (117, 120).

Although in 1973 the U.S. Supreme Court eliminated the "reason" for abortion and the need for psychiatrists to "approve" a "therapeutic" abortion, the belief that abortion was psychologically damaging persisted. While the evidence runs counter to this view, it is also clear that abortion cannot be seen as a minor procedure without significance to the individual. The decision for abortion is an important one, requiring careful consideration, which may be facilitated with counseling. For many women this may extend into the postabortion period. When counseling is provided in an atmosphere where a woman's decision is respected and her right to make that decision is not interfered with, fewer adverse reactions are to be expected.

REFERENCES

1. Bibring, G. Some considerations of the psychological processes in pregnancy. Psychoanalytic Study of the Child, 14:113–121, 1959.
2. Benedek, T. The psychobiology of pregnancy. In: Anthony, J., and Benedek, T., eds., Parenthood: Its Psychology and Psychopathology. Boston: Little, Brown, 1976.
3. Bibring, G., and Valenstein, A. Psychological aspects of pregnancy. Clinical Ob. Gyn., 19(2):357–371, 1976.
4. Deutsch, H. The Psychology of Women: A Psychoanalytic Perspective, Vol. II, Motherhood. New York: Grune and Stratton, 1945.

5. Bibring, G.; Dwyer, T.; Huntington, D., et al. A study of the earliest mother-child relationship. Psychoanalytic Study of the Child, 16:9–72, 1961.
6. Shereshefsky, P., and Yarrow, L. Psychological Aspects of a First Pregnancy and Early Postnatal Adaptation. Monograph, National Institute of Child Health and Human Development. New York: Raven Press, 1973.
7. Melges, F. Postpartum psychiatric syndromes. Psychosomatic Medicine, 30:95–108, 1968.
8. Nilsson, A., and Almgren, P. Para-natal emotional adjustment: a prospective investigation of 165 women, part II: the influence of background factors, psychiatric history, parental relations, and personality characteristics. Acta Psychiat. Scand. Supp., 63–141, 1970.
9. Gurwitt, A. Aspects of prospective fatherhood. Psychoanalytic Study of the Child, 31:237–271, 1976.
10. Nadelson, C. Normal and special aspects of pregnancy. Obs. Gyn., 41(4):611–620, 1973.
11. Schaffer, C., and Pine, F. Pregnancy, abortion, and the developmental tasks of adolescence. J. Child Psychiatry, 14:511–536, 1975.
12. Nadelson, C.; Notman, M.; and Gillon, J. Adolescent sexuality and pregnancy. In: Notman, M., and Nadelson, C., eds., The Woman Patient: Medical and Psychological Interfaces, Vol. I. New York: Plenum Press, 1978.
13. Nadelson, C. The pregnant teenager: problems of choice in a developmental framework. Psychiatric Opinion, 12(2):6–12, February 1975.
14. Freud, S. Some psychical consequences of the anatomical differences between the sexes. In: Strachey, J. ed., Standard Edition, Vol. XIX. London: Hogarth Press, 1961 (orig. 1925).
15. Nadelson, C. The woman's movement and changing sex roles. In: Noshpitz, J., ed., Basic Handbook of Child Psychiatry, Vol. IV. New York: Basic Books, 1979.
16. Notman, M., and Nadelson, C. Changing views of femininity and childbearing. Hillside Journal of Clinical Psychiatry, 3(2):187–202, 1981.
17. Editorial. Puerperal Psychosis. The Lancet, 2:908–909, 1981.
18. Kroger, W. Psychosomatic aspects of nausea and vomiting. In: Kroger, W., ed., Psychosomatic Obstetrics, Gynecology, and Endocrinology. Springfield, Ill.: Charles C. Thomas, 1962.
19. Fairweather, D. Nausea and vomiting in pregnancy. Am. J. Obs. Gyn., 102(1):135–175, 1968.
20. Taylor, H. Nausea and vomiting of pregnancy: hyperemesis gravidarum. In: Kroger, W., ed., Psychosomatic Obstetrics, Gynecology, and Endocrinology. Springfield, Ill.: Charles C. Thomas, 1962.
21. Lennane, K., and Lennane, R. Alleged psychogenic disorders in women: a possible manifestation of sexual prejudice. N. Engl. J. Med., 288(6):288–292, 1973.
22. Zechnich, R., and Hammer, T. Brief psychotherapy for hyperemesis gravidarum. American Family Physician, 26(5):179–181, November 1982.
23. Grimm, E. Psychological and social factors in pregnancy delivery and outcome. In: Richardson, S., and Guttmacher, A., eds., Childbearing: Its Social and Psychological Aspects. Baltimore: Williams and Williams, 1967.
24. Robin, A. The psychological changes of normal parturition. Psychiatr. Q., 36:129, 1962.

25. Chalmers, B. Psychological aspects of pregnancy: some thoughts for the eighties. Soc. Sci. Med., 16:323–331, 1982.
26. Milonsky, A. The Prenatal Diagnosis of Hereditary Disorders. Springfield, Ill.: Charles C. Thomas, 1973.
27. Sylvestre, D., and Frescoe, N. Reactions to prenatal diagnosis. Am. J. Orthopsych., 50(4):610–617, 1980.
28. Kolata, G. First trimester prenatal diagnosis. Science, 221:1031–1032, 1983.
29. Chernick, A., and Chernick, B. Commentary. ICEA Review, 6(1):6–7, April 1972.
30. Morris, N. The frequency of sexual intercourse during pregnancy. Arch. Sex. Behav., 4:501–507, 1975.
31. Falicov, C. Sexual adjustment during first pregnancy and postpartum. Am. J. Obs. Gyn., 117:991, 1973.
32. Mills, J.; Harlap, S.; and Harley, E. Should coitus in late pregnancy be discouraged? The Lancet, 1:136–138, 1981.
33. Alouf, F., and Barglow, P. Sexual counseling for the pregnant and postpartum patient. Obs. Gyn., 2(96):1–13, 1978.
34. Perkins, R. Sexual behavior and response in relation to complications of pregnancy. Am. J. Obs. Gyn., 134:498–505, 1979.
35. Goodlin, R.; Keller, D.; and Raffin, M. Orgasm during late pregnancy: possible deleterious effects. Obs. Gyn., 38:916–920, 1971.
36. Zlatnick, P., and Burmeister, L. Reported sexual behavior in late pregnancy: selected associations. J. Reprod. Med., 27(10):627–632, October 1982.
37. Areskog, B.; Uddenberg, N.; and Kjessler, B. Background factors in pregnant women with and without fear of childbirth. J. Psychosom. Obs. Gyn., 2(2):102–108, 1983.
38. Ballinger, C. Emotional disturbance during pregnancy and following delivery. J. Psychosom. Res., 26(6):629–634, 1982.
39. Ketai, R., and Brandwin, M. Childbirth-related psychosis and familial symbiotic conflict. Am. J. Psychiatry, 136(2):190–193, February 1979.
40. Davenport, Y., and Adland, M. Postpartum psychoses in female and male bipolar manic-depressive patients. Am. J. Orthopsych., 52(2):288–297, April 1982.
41. LeBoyer, F. Birth Without Violence. New York: Knopf, 1975.
42. Robson, K., and Moss, H. Patterns and determinants of maternal attachment. Pediatrics, 77:976–985, 1970.
43. Enkin, M.; Smith, S.; Dermer, S.; et al. An adequately controlled study of the effectiveness of PPM training. In: Norris, M., ed., Psychosomatic Medicine in Obstetrics and Gynecology: Proceedings. Basil, Switz.: Karger, 1972.
44. Rosengren, W. Social sources of pregnancy as illness or normality. Soc. For., 29:260, 1961.
45. Melzack, R.; Taenzer, P.; Feldman, P.; et al. Labour is still painful after prepared childbirth training. Can. Med. Assoc. J., 125:357–363, 1981.
46. Stewart, D. Psychiatric symptoms following attempted natural childbirth. Can. Med. Assoc. J., 127:713–716, October 15, 1982.
47. Doering, S., and Entwisle, D. Preparation during pregnancy and ability to cope with abortion and delivery. Am. J. Orthopsych., 45:825–837, 1975.
48. Seiden, A. The sense of mastery in the childbirth experience. In Notman, M., and Nadelson, C., eds., The Woman Patient: Medical and Psychological Interfaces, Vol. I. New York: Plenum Press, 1978.

49. Niswander, K., and Gordon, M. The Collaborative Perinatal Study: The Women and Their Pregnancies, 1st edition, National Institute of Neurological Diseases and Stroke. Philadelphia: W. B. Saunders, April 1972.
50. Phillips, O. Preferable methods of pain relief in labor, delivery, and late pregnancy complications. In: Reid, D., and Christian, C., eds., Controversy in Obstetrics and Gynecology II. Philadelphia: W. B. Saunders, 1974.
51. Quilligan, E. Introduction. In: Aladjem, S., ed., Risks in the Practice of Modern Obstetrics. St. Louis: C. V. Mosby, 1972.
52. Kloosterman, G. The universal aspects of childbirth: human birth as a sociopsychosomatic paradigm. J. Psychosom. Obs. Gyn., 1(1):35–41, 1982.
53. Szasz, T. The communication of distress between child and parent. British. J. of Medical Psychology, 32:161–170, 1959.
54. Sontag, S. Illness as Metaphor. New York: Farrar, Straus, and Giroux, 1978.
55. Lipsett, D. The painful woman: complaints, symptoms, and illnesses. In: Notman, M., and Nadelson, C., eds., The Woman Patient: Medical and Psychological Interfaces, Vol. III. New York: Plenum Press, 1982.
56. Sich, D. Modern obstetrics and confrontation with the traditional birthing system— an example from Korea. J. Psychosom. Obs. Gyn., 1(2):61–71, 1982.
57. Bradley, R. Husband-Coached Childbirth. New York: Harper and Row, 1965.
58. Crandon, A. Maternal anxiety and neonatal wellbeing. J. Psychosom. Res., 23:113–115, 1979.
59. Crandon, A. Maternal anxiety and obstetric complications. J. Psychosom. Res., 23:109–111, 1979.
60. Beck, N.; Siegel, L.; Davidson, N., et al. The prediction of pregnancy outcome: maternal preparation, anxiety, and attitudinal sets. J. Psychosom. Res., 24:343–351, 1980.
61. Lederman, R.; Lederman, E.; Work, B., et al. The relationship of maternal anxiety plasma catecholamines and plasma cortisol to progress in labor. Am. J. Obs. Gyn., 132:495–500, 1978.
62. Lederman, R.; Lederman, E.; Work, B., et al. Relationship of psychological factors in pregnancy to progress in labor. Nurs. Res., 28(2):94–97, 1979.
63. Shaffer, I. Naturally it hurts—but not that much. Med. World News, 10(40):17–18, 1969.
64. Snyder, A. The opiate receptor and morphine-like peptides in the brain. Am. J. Psychiatry, 135(6):645–652, 1978.
65. Ballou, J. The Psychology of Pregnancy. Lexington, Mass.: Lexington Books, 1978.
66. Lipson, J., and Tilden, V. Psychological integration of the Caesarian birth experience. Am. J. Orthopsych., 50(4):598–609, 1980.
67. Rosengren, W. Some social psychological aspects of delivery room difficulties. J. Nerv. Ment. Dis., 135:515–521, 1961.
68. Parlee, M. Social factors in the psychology of menstruation, birth, and menopause. Primary Care, 3(3):477–490, 1976.
69. Youngs, D., and Erhart, A., eds. Psychosomatic Obstetrics and Gynecology. New York: Appleton-Century-Crofts, 1980.
70. Jackson, J.; Vaugn, M.; Black, P., et al. Psychological aspects of fetal monitoring: maternal reaction to the position of the monitor and staff behavior. J. Psychosom. Obs. Gyn., 2(2):97–103, 1983.

71. Brazelton, T., and Keefer, C. The early mother-child relationship. In: Nadelson, C., and Notman, M., eds., The Woman Patient, Vol. II. New York: Plenum Press, 1982.
72. Harlow, H.; Harlow, M.; and Hansen, E. The natural affectional system in rhesus monkeys. In: Rheingold, H., ed., Maternal Behavior in Mammals. New York: John Wiley and Sons, 1966.
73. Garabino, J. Changing hospital childbirth practices: a developmental perspective on prevention of child maltreatment. Am. J. Orthopsych., 50(4):588–597, 1980.
74. Lynch, M. Ill health and child abuse. The Lancet, 2:317–319, 1977.
75. Kennell, J.; Voos, P.; and Klaus, M. Parent-infant bonding. In: Helfer, L., and Kempe, C., eds., Child Abuse and Neglect: The Family and the Community. Cambridge, Mass.: Ballinger, 1976.
76. Grey, J. Prediction and prevention of child abuse and neglect. J. Child Abuse and Neglect, 1:45–58, 1977.
77. Elkins, V. The Rights of the Pregnant Parent. New York: Two Continents, 1976.
78. Hughey, M.; McElin, T.; and Young, T. Maternal and fetal outcomes of Lamaze-prepared patients. Obs. Gyn., 51:643–647, 1978.
79. Erikson, E. Childhood and Society. New York: W. W. Norton, 1950.
80. Whiting, B. Folk Wisdom and Childrearing. Presentation, American Association for the Advancement of Science, 1971.
81. Stein, G.; March, A.; and Morton, J. Mental symptoms, weight changes, and electrolyte excretion in the first post-partum week. J. Psychosom. Res., 25(5):395–408, 1981.
82. George, A., and Wilson, K. Monoamine oxidase activity and the puerperal blues syndrome. J. Psychosom. Res., 25(5):409–413, 1981.
83. Kadrmas, A.; Winokur, G.; and Crowe, R. Postpartum mania. Brit. J. Psychiatry, 135:551–554, 1979.
84. Stein, G. The pattern of mental change and body weight change in the first post-partum week. J. Psychosom. Res., 24(3/4):165–171, 1980.
85. Grimm, E. Psychological investigation of habitual abortion. Psychosom. Med., 24(4):369–378, 1962.
86. Seibel, M., and Graves, W. The psychological implications of spontaneous abortion. J. Reprod. Med., 25(4):161–165, October 1980.
87. Stack, J. Spontaneous abortion and grieving. American Family Physician, 21(5):99–102, 1980.
88. Pasnau, R. O. Psychiatric complications of therapeutic abortion. Obs. Gyn., 40(2):252–256, 1972.
89. Deutsch, H. The Psychology of Women, Vol. II. New York: Grune and Stratton, 1945.
90. Tietze, C. Somatic consequences of abortion. Paper presented at the National Institute of Child Health and Human Development and National Institutes of Mental Health Workshop on Abortion, Bethesda, Md., December 15–16, 1969.
91. Nadelson, C. Psychological issues in therapeutic abortion. JAMWA, 27(1):12–15, 1972.
92. Ekblad, N. Induced abortion on psychiatric grounds. Acta Psychiat. Scand., Supplement 99, 1955.
93. Kummer, J. Post-abortion psychiatric illness—a myth? Am. J. Psychiatry, 119:980–983, 1963.

94. Peck, A., and Marcus, H. Psychiatric sequelae of therapeutic interruption of pregnancy. J. Nerv. Ment. Dis., 143:417–425, 1966.

95. Simon, N.; Senturia, A.; and Rothman, D. Psychiatric illness following therapeutic abortion. Am. J. Psychiatry, 124:59–65, 1967.

96. Group for the Advancement of Psychiatry. The Right to Abortion: A Psychiatric View. GAP 7 (no. 75):196–227, 1969.

97. American Psychiatric Association Position Statement on Abortion. Am. J. Psychiatry, 126:1554, 1970.

98. American Psychoanalytic Association Position Statement on Abortion, San Francisco, Calif., 1970.

99. Whittington, H. Evaluation of therapeutic abortion as an element of preventive psychiatry. Am. J. Psychiatry, 126:1224–1229, 1970.

100. Sloane, R. The unwanted pregnancy. N. Engl. J. Med., 22:1206–1213, 1969.

101. Pare, C., and Raven, H. Follow-up of patients referred for termination of pregnancy. The Lancet, 1:635–638, 1970.

102. Caplan, G. The disturbance of the mother-child relationship by unsuccessful attempts at abortion. Mental Hygiene, 38:67–80, 1954.

103. Hook, K. Refused abortion: a follow-up of 249 women whose applications were refused by the National Board of Health in Sweden. Acta Psychiat. Scand., Supplement 168, Vol. 39, 1963.

104. Forssman, H., and Thuwe, I. One hundred and twenty children born after application for therapeutic abortion refused: their mental health, social adjustment, and educational level up to the age of 21. Acta Psychiat. Scand., 42:71–88, 1966.

105. Resnick, P. Child murder by parents: a psychiatric review of filicide. Am. J. Psychiatry, 126(3):325–334, 1969.

106. Kempe, C. Approaches to prevention of child abuse: a health visitor's concept. Am. J. Dis. Child, 130:941, 1976.

107. Senay, E. Therapeutic abortion. Arch. Gen. Psychiatry, 23:408–415, 1970.

108. Marder, L. Psychiatric experience with a liberalized therapeutic abortion law. Am. J. Psychiatry, 126:1230–1236, 1970.

109. Ford, C.; Castelnuono-Tedesca, P.; Long, I. Is abortion a therapeutic procedure in psychiatry? JAMA, 218:1173–1178, 1971.

110. Payne, E.; Kravitz, A.; Notman, M., et al. Outcome following therapeutic abortion. Arch. Gen. Psychiatry, 33:725–733, 1976.

111. Osofsky, J., and Osofsky, H. The psychological reaction of patients to legalized abortion. Am. J. Orthopsych., 42(1):48–60, 1972.

112. Osofsky, H., and Osofsky, J. The Abortion Experience: Psychological and Medical Impact. New York: Harper and Row, 1973.

113. Ford, C.; Atkinson, R.; and Bugonier, J. Therapeutic abortion: who needs a psychiatrist? Obs. Gyn., 38:206–213, 1971.

114. Partridge, J.; Spiegel, T.; Rouse, B., et al. Therapeutic abortion: a study of psychiatric applicants at North Carolina Memorial Hospital. North Carolina Med. J. 32:132–136, 1971.

115. Morris, T. Abortion: psychiatric implications. Progress in Gynecology, 5:249–256, 1970.

116. Freeman, E. Influence of personality attributes on abortion experiences. Am. J. Orthopsych., 47(3):503–513, 1977.

117. Dauher, H.; Zalar, M.; and Goldstein, P. Abortion counseling and behavioral change. Family Planning Perspective, 4(2):23–27, 1972.
118. Margolis, A.; Rindfuss, R.; Cochland, P., et al. Contraception after abortion. Family Planning Perspective, 6:55–60, 1974.
119. Smith, E. A follow-up study of women who request abortion. Am. J. Orthopsych., 43(4):574–585, 1973.
120. Tietze, C. Contraceptive practice in the context of a non-restrictive abortion law. Family Planning Perspective, 7(3):197–202, 1975.

CAROL C. NADELSON and
MALKAH T. NOTMAN

Rape

In 1981 almost 82,000 rapes were reported, and 76 percent of these were rapes by force (1). Estimates vary widely regarding the percentage of reported rapes compared with the number of actual incidents. One survey of over 900 adult women reported that 44 percent of them had experienced a rape or an attempted rape (2). This study concluded that there is a 46 percent probability that a woman will be a victim of a rape or an attempted rape in her lifetime. Other researchers report that one in every ten women will experience a sexual assault at some time in her life (3).

The most frequent rape victim is an adolescent female (4, 5, 2). A study of 117 rapes reported that 50 percent were females between the ages of 15 and 24 and that 32 percent of these were between the ages of 15 and 19 (4). Male and homosexual rape is reported less frequently, and the actual incidence is not known. It has been suggested that the stigma associated with male rape deters many victims from reporting (6).

The 1980 FBI (Federal Bureau of Investigation) figures on rape reporting estimate that between 40 and 50 percent of all rapes are never reported. Because knowledge of the assailant is a factor in reporting, and victims who know their assailants are less likely to report, there is an underrepresentation of all cases that appear for prosecution (7). A 1980 study reported that 35 percent of over 600 female rape victims knew their assailants (5), and another study concluded that the number of victims who know their assailants is probably higher than 50 percent (7).

Other factors affect reporting. "Victims who knew their attackers were more likely to delay contacting police for an hour or longer" (8), and there is a higher incidence of reporting among white women than among minorities. Victims are more likely to report the assault to a husband or boyfriend first; he thus has an impact on influencing her to report officially (9). Many women will not report a rape if they perceive that social support is lacking. They are more likely to report if they believe that their sense of self-esteem and well-being will be restored by so doing (9).

The legal issues involved in rape cases are complex. Before a prosecutor files a rape complaint there must usually be medical evidence of penetration, lack of victim consent, and threat or use of force (7). In many states, mandatory sentences for rapists are so harsh that lesser charges are frequently substituted (7). It is most likely that a rapist will be booked and convicted if the victim does not agree to the initial contact with the rapist (e.g., does not accept a date with him), if the offender is a stranger to the victim, if the offender uses a weapon, and if the victim is injured (7). "In many states rape remains the only violent crime for which corroboration is required. . . . One of the consequences of the corroboration requirement is that the victim is the one who stands trial" (10).

According to FBI figures, 48 percent of reported cases of rape in 1980 resulted in arrest. Although this figure seems high, it must be remembered that between 40 and 50 percent of all rapes are never reported. Thus the actual number of rape arrests and convictions is much lower. In a study of 115 rape victims admitted to the emergency ward during a one-year period, only nine of these cases led to conviction for rape or abuse of a child (11).

Socioeconomic factors lend support to the view that "rape is a crime of opportunity" (12). Rape is largely an intraracial event and is "ecologically bound," occurring as it does predominantly between members of the same race, economic class, and geographic neighborhood (13). Rape is most likely to occur in areas with higher unemployment rates and lower median incomes and in areas where there are higher numbers of unemployed youths between the ages of 14 and 21 (7).

In addition to the emotional effects of rape, described below in more detail, many victims also suffer nongenital physical injury. A study of over 600 rape victims reported that 25 percent had sustained extragenital injuries (5). Another study of 117 rape cases revealed that 38 percent of these had suffered nongenital abrasions and contusions (4). Other studies of postrape victims (4, 14) report evidence of venereal disease as a consequence of the rape. In one study, there was evidence of gonorrhea in 12 percent of victims (4); between 3 and 4 percent of another group of rape victims developed gonorrhea, and there was evidence of syphilis in 0.1 percent (14). The authors feel that these percentages are high enough to warrant treating all rape victims prophylactically (with penicillin or spectinomycin) to guard against the possibility of venereal disease (4, 14).

The profound impact of the stress of rape is best understood when rape is seen as a violent crime against a person and not as a specifically sexual encounter. Rape is a personal violation accompanied by a loss of autonomy and control. The experience of rape can be viewed as a crisis situation in which a traumatic external event breaks the balance between the individual's adaptive capacity and the environment. As such it is similar to other traumatic situations described in the literature on stress, including community disasters (15), war (16–19), and surgical procedures (20). Its unexpected nature and the variability of the victim's coping resources are critical factors in how the victim responds to this life-threatening catastrophe.

Initial reactions to rape range from calm to confusion, anxiety, and extreme emotion. Victims may also demonstrate restricted attention span and automatic or stereotyped behavior. Symonds (21) emphasizes the disordered perception, thinking, and judgment that may occur, and the helplessness and regression, which he terms "frozen fright."

Sutherland and Scherl (22) have reported on one form of acute reaction that is characterized by shock, disbelief, emotional disorganization, and disruption of normal patterns of behavior and function. A posttraumatic stress disorder syndrome has been observed in rape victims (23). This sudden, unexpected, and life-threatening experience leaves the victim unable to develop adequate defenses. It involves intentional cruelty or inhumanity, makes the victim feel trapped and unable to fight back, and often involves physical injury (23). The victim may be unable to talk about what has happened and may have difficulty telling family or friends or reporting to the hospital or police. Guilt may be prominent, with fears that poor judgment may have precipitated the rape. A 1969 study by the National Commission on the Causes and Prevention of Violence reported that only 4.4 percent of rapes were victim-precipitated (24), but guilt and self-blame are still high among victims. One study reported that 74 percent of victims blamed themselves behaviorally (e.g., "I should not have walked down that street alone") and 19 percent blamed themselves characterologically (e.g., "I'm too naive")(24).

During the early postrape phase concrete concerns, such as whether the victim should tell her family what happened, demand attention. The implications of telling or not telling family may determine future relationships with them. The victim is often concerned about publicity, about the likelihood of pregnancy or venereal disease, about her responsibility to report the crime or her reactions to doing so, about being able to identify the rapist, and about the impact of possibly seeing the rapist again or being the victim of revenge if she does report and prosecute.

Burgess and Holmstrom (25) define a specific rape trauma syndrome in two stages: an immediate or acute response in which the victim's life-style is disrupted by the rape, and a long-term process in which the victim reorganizes herself. There are two types of acute response (26–28): "the expressed style," in which the victim is emotional and visibly upset, and the "controlled style," in which the victim may appear to be calm to the casual observer. Guilt and self-blame are prevalent in this initial phase. The primary acute reaction is related to the fear of physical injury, mutilation, and death. Mood swings are common, as are feelings of humiliation, guilt, shame, self-blame, and fear of another assault by the assailant. A reorganizational stage has elements in common with other stress responses, although it varies for each individual.

In the first stage, there is often surprisingly little clinical evidence of anger in rape victims, compared with the outrage stimulated in others who hear about the rape. Feelings of anger and a desire for revenge often appear somewhat later. A primary defense may be an attempt to avoid thinking about the rape, although this is difficult. The wish to undo the event may appear in fantasies of how an individual might have handled the situation differently.

A wide variety of physical and psychological reactions may occur during this period. These depend, in part, on the location and the extent of the injuries sustained. Specific symptoms such as sleep disturbances, nightmares, and appetite disturbances are common. In one study, 35 percent of the victims reported loss of interest in normal activities, 20 percent reported decreased concentration, sleep disturbances, and appetite disturbances, and 11.8 percent reported loss of energy (3). The individual may also find herself reviewing her responses and, judging whether they are adaptive or maladaptive, may often question her own reactions. A positive or negative view of her ability to cope may affect the course of resolution of the trauma and her future capacity to respond to stress. Self-esteem may be enhanced or damaged during this phase.

Group support enables most disaster victims to feel less isolated and helpless. In fact, support may be one of the most crucial determinants of outcome. Obviously a victim who is alone, such as the rape victim, can only hope for support later. She is often disappointed by the failure of her usual support group, including family, friends, and the community, to validate her experience. In fact, their responses may be quite the opposite from what she expects or requires.

The acute stage may last from a few days to weeks. It is followed by a reorganizational process with manifestations depending on the victim's personality style, available support system, and the treatment she encounters from others. Changes in life-style are prominent, with impaired levels of function at work, home, and school. Indeed, work seems to be an area that is particularly vulnerable to the victim postrape. One study reported that victims continued to have difficulty with work up to eight months after the rape (29). Another study of 27 rape victims reported that almost half had lost or quit their jobs within one year postrape (30). Other life-style changes include living arrangements. Some women may move to another residence, while others are fearful of leaving their homes at all or give up autonomy by returning to their families.

Sleep disturbances often continue, with vivid dreams and nightmares. Early, dreams with reenactments of the actual rape are frequent. These later progress to a point where mastery of the rape may begin taking place and the victim may apprehend the rapist or assailant of her dream. Phobias which seem specifically determined by the nature of the rape experience may appear, with fears of crowds or of being at home or outside, depending on the location of the assault.

Sexual problems are common, with a decline of interest as well as withdrawal from a partner. Prior sexual experience does not seem to be a factor in postrape sexual problems. This reinforces the view that "the trauma of rape involves considerably more than the sexual act" (31). In one study of 92 adult victims and 23 preadult victims, 66 percent reported decreased sexual activity postrape, 38 percent gave up sex for at least six months after the rape and 41 percent reported difficulty experiencing orgasm or any sexual feeling postrape (31). In this study, victims were interviewed immediately postrape; at three, six, and nine months postrape; and again from four to six years later (31). Another study of 83 victims interviewed one year postrape reported that most still experienced some sexual dysfunction, especially fear of sex or difficulty with arousal or desire (32).

Specific situations increase the complexity of the reaction to rape. The victim who is raped by a friend or relative, an event more frequent with children and adolescents, often has a greater psychological burden than would be true if the assailant were a stranger. She must also deal with issues of trust and sometimes with the added burden of secrecy, which prevents seeking help. The existence of psychological problems and/or maladaptive coping patterns prior to the rape increases the likelihood of maladaptive coping patterns following the rape. Serious medical or psychiatric problems either prior to or as a result of the rape are likely to affect the outcome. Victims with psychological problems such as anxiety or depression prerape are more likely to recover slowly from postrape depression (33).

A period of outward adjustment beginning within several days to weeks after the rape, with an apparent temporary resolution of the immediate anxiety-provoking issues, has been described in some victims (22, 27, 28). The victim often returns to her usual life patterns and attempts to behave as if all is well, reassuring both herself and those close to her. Denial of difficulty and suppression of feelings are prominent during this period. The impact of what has happened is often not faced at this stage. Although it may be mild, depression frequently occurs. One study reported that 75 percent of the victims studied experienced mild to severe levels of depression immediately postrape (33). One year later, 26 percent of this group were still depressed as a result of the rape. Another study reported that 24 percent of the victims seemed to have symptoms consistent with a major depressive disorder (3). In general, it is believed that the more supportive the social network is perceived to be by the victim, the less depressed she is likely to become postrape (3).

Later, other responses or symptoms may develop. The victim often needs to talk about what has happened in order to integrate the event with her self-image and to resolve her feelings about the rapist. The earlier attitude of tolerance and understanding of the rapist may be replaced by anger toward him. She may also wonder if she colluded in some unknown way with the rapist. At this time, the realization that the self-reassuring mechanisms which had previously fostered a sense of invulnerability were not effective may result in a decrease of self-esteem. The victim then blames herself for her lack of perception or attention to the danger.

When an individual continues to question herself and the ability of the group or society to be protective, a traumatic neurosis may be developing (34, 35). This is defensively protective against further exposure to trauma, but it is psychologically costly, especially since it may result in a loss of self-esteem and ability to take risks or to be innovative in other situations. Symptoms may change the individual's life-style and functioning; for example, she may develop an inability to go out alone, which may be an aftermath of rape. Most of the work which has been done on rape has been organized around a crisis model of conceptualizing the experience. This model suggests that the rape victim enters a stable state by the end of a year and appears to recover her previous level of functioning. More recent studies have cast doubt on the reality of this view. McCahill, Meyer, and Fischman (36) followed up 213 victims and found that at the end of one year at least one-third of the victims still had symptoms, including changes in eating habits and sleeping patterns, increased fear of being out on the street alone, increased negative feelings toward unknown men, decreased social activities, and worsened sexual relations with their partners.

Burgess and Holmstrom (37), four years after their original study, reinterviewed 81 women and found that, by the victims' self-assessment, the majority of the sample (74 percent) felt "recovered" at the time of the interview, four to six years following their rapes. However, half these recovered women felt that it "took years," and only one-third of the total sample reported feeling "recovered" within a period of months.

Nadelson et al. (38) reinterviewed 41 rape victims 15 to 30 months postrape. Terror, fears, and suspiciousness remained the outstanding persistent feelings. More than half the victims continued to feel that their freedom to venture out was restricted. Half reported sexual difficulties, and almost half the victims stated that they continued to be depressed despite lack of evidence for previous history of mental illness. Another study reported that probably one-third of rape cases do not resolve the rape crisis (10). This lack of resolution leads to long-term consequences for the victim, including mistrust and avoidance of men, sexual dysfunctions, phobias and chronic anxiety, and depression and self-esteem problems (10). Of 179 victims studied from three to five years postrape, 83.7 percent reported sleeping problems, 79 percent reported continued depressed feelings, 63 percent had eating problems, and 32 percent reported persistent sexual dissatisfaction (39).

Other studies have reported some positive outcome, including feelings of greater self-reliance, inner strength, thoughtfulness, and seriousness, which may serve to counteract the invasive fears. These qualities should be noted by counselors because of their therapeutic implications.

Unfortunately, there is not much data available on the effects of rape on the significant others in the victim's life. It has been established, however, that myths about rape often lead to inappropriate reactions on the part of family members, such as anger toward the victim (10). Often spouses or boyfriends focus on their own discomfort, such as fear, self-blame, and rage, and are less able to respond to the needs of the victim (3). One study reported that four of the five married victims in a group of 27 were divorced within 18 months of the rape (30). While there is no proof that the rape was a precipitant, the data do suggest a connection.

Underreporting of the rape and difficulty of maintaining contact with victims who do report has led to a general lack of data available for study. Among a group of 25 women who were treated for rape from February 1978 to May 1979, some 68 percent terminated follow-up in less than three months (40). Twenty-two of these women broke off contact within one year, three continued after one year, four had their phones disconnected, and one moved and could not be located (40).

LIFE-STAGE CONSIDERATIONS

In addition to the responses already noted, there are reactions that relate to specific life stages. Since the single young woman between the ages of 17 and 24 is the most frequently reported rape victim, an understanding of the special issues of this age-group is critical. The young woman is usually inexperienced, and her relations with men have frequently been limited to family and friends, so that she has little sophistication and may easily become involved in an unwelcome sexual encounter. In this age-group, rape victims frequently have a prior acquaintance with the rapist. This may be the reason for her refusal to identify the rapist or prosecute. She may reproach herself because she could have been more active in preventing the rape, and she experiences shame and guilt, regardless of the circumstances. These feelings, coupled with the victim's sense of vulnerability, may color her future relationships with men. This is especially true for the very young woman, who may have had her first sexual experience in this context. The result can be a confusion of sexuality and violence.

The rape experience for a young woman may revive concerns about separation and independence. She may feel inadequate to care for herself. Parents, friends, and relatives often respond by offering to take care of her again in an attempt to be supportive and reassuring, but in doing this they may foster regression and prevent mastery of the stress. A balance of support and permitting independence is optimal.

Another problem for the younger rape victim is her perception of and tolerance for the gynecological examination that is part of the care she receives if she goes to a hospital. Because she may have suffered physical trauma, is susceptible to venereal disease, and may become pregnant, examination is indicated. It may be perceived as another rape, especially by an inexperienced or severely traumatized woman. Thus, while she may be concerned about the intactness of her body, she will have difficulty with necessary procedures if they stimulate memories or seem to reproduce in any way the original rape experience.

THE AFTERMATH OF RAPE

In the immediate aftermath of the rape, issues of personal safety and control emerge as primary concerns. The victim's immediate needs are for a sense of physical safety as well as for assistance in assuming some control over her life.

The presence of an empathic and supportive counselor, clinician, and/or friend will enhance her sense of safety.

She should be encouraged to talk with reassurance and validation of her responses. Whether this occurs in the police station, the physician's office, or the hospital emergency room, the issues are the same. In order to be effective, the counselor must have information about medical and legal procedures available so that the victim can be informed. Decisions about procedure, including reporting to the hospital or law enforcement agencies, must be made. While the counselor may have opinions about what the victim ought to do with regard to reporting, it is the victim who must make the decision.

Burgess and Holmstrom (26) propose a short-term issue-oriented counseling approach to the rape victim, with the goal of restoring the victim to her previous level of function as quickly as possible. Since the crisis disrupts the victim's life-style in four areas (physical, emotional, social, and sexual), all these issues must be addressed. Hilberman (41) summarizes appropriate areas for initial counseling intervention:

The assault: The circumstances; her relationship to the assailant; details of the event including physical and verbal threats; details of behavior; amount and kind of resistance; the use of alcohol or drugs by either victim or assailant; the victim's emotional and sexual reactions. Knowledge in these areas will help the counselor ascertain which issues to address. For example, the focus may be on the rape as a first sexual encounter, or intense guilt for not putting up a fiercer struggle. Brussel (42) notes that "the victim who is beaten into senselessness may suffer far less emotional trauma than the woman who submits to rape when her life is threatened." The victim's coping strategy before and during the assault will become an issue after the assault (28).

Medical concerns: The quality of her treatment and interactions with medical and nursing personnel; extent and type of physical injury; the possibilities of pregnancy and venereal disease; the pelvic examination which is a frequent focus for the victim's anger and may be experienced as another rape. Victims also are fearful that their bodies are irrevocably damaged.

Legal issues: Does she plan to report; if she has reported, how was she treated; what kinds of questions was she asked; was she encouraged or dissuaded from considering pressing charges against the assailant; does she plan to cooperate with the police investigation or appear in court. This is often an issue of high priority for the victim, who must make this decision at a most difficult time. The victim's rationale for not wishing to prosecute may be quite realistic, or it may reflect her fears that she did indeed precipitate the rape. The counselor's role is to help the victim clarify these issues for herself and to support the victim's decision, whatever it may be.

Social support system: Who are the important people in the victim's life; whom does she plan to tell about the rape; what responses does she anticipate. How has the rape affected or changed her relationships with significant others? An evaluation of the personal support available will determine in part the extent to which continued counseling becomes necessary; the availability of a strong social support network will diminish the need for ongoing counseling intervention. In contrast to most personal crises where the counselor or therapist reinforces the importance of sharing the crisis with those who are significant in the person's life, no firm guidelines exist about communicating the event of the rape because of the real possibility that the revelation may disrupt the relationship. For example, a husband may perceive the rape as a deception by his wife, and the parents of an adolescent may project their own sense of guilt and become angry with the victim. At times, the counselor may have an important role in family counseling. Family and friends must be sensitized to the meaning of the rape so that they are able to support the victim. If the victim chooses not to tell close friends or family members, guilt or distancing may occur, for which the victim will need counseling assistance.

Physical safety: If the victim lives alone, or was raped at home, she is likely to be fearful of returning home. The assailant (who most often has not been apprehended) may have threatened to return, and the victim may be fearful of this even when a threat has not been made. A temporary resolution may involve identifying a friend with whom the victim can stay as well as available options for the future if necessary.

Those working with a rape victim can prepare her for the range of reactions likely to occur so that she becomes sensitized to her own feelings and has some awareness that the inevitable disruptions are normal. Mild sedation for sleep may be indicated as well. Knowledge that the victim is supported throughout this period provides additional reassurance that she will not be left in isolation.

The last decade has witnessed the spontaneous appearance of growing numbers of community-based rape crisis centers as part of a nationwide antirape movement (43–46). These centers may supplement medical care resources and are largely staffed by volunteers. Men are not usually accepted as volunteers in rape crisis programs, but in some programs men work with the significant men in the victim's life and provide services to male friends and relatives of rape victims. In many instances, men can also do effective rape counseling.

Direct services to victims attempt to meet the victim's needs for emotional support, information, and advocacy. Information about medical treatment and criminal justice procedures is provided. Counseling services are usually limited to immediate temporary support and short-term follow-up through the use of peer counselors.

The goal of the initial counseling is the return of autonomous functioning and control, and prolonged involvement is usually discouraged. Individual counseling is generally the rule, with group models reportedly less successful. Victim advocacy services include intervention and support with medical and law enforcement personnel. Continuing contact by phone and in person throughout the prosecutory phase is often provided.

Institutional or hospital-based rape crisis programs are not a substitute for community rape crisis centers, but they are an alternative. Community groups

may tend to attract younger and/or feminist women, while more traditional and/
or older women, or women with injuries or medical needs, will use institutional
services. Community programs also provide a wide spectrum of services not
easily accomplished by the professional, whether it is finding a safe place to
sleep when the victim is fearful of returning home after the rape, or a companion
to guide her through the criminal justice procedure.

While a great deal has changed in the way that rape is viewed and approached,
myths about victim complicity persist, and failure to understand the differences
between a sexual fantasy that may involve rape and the violent and degrading
reality of the experience continue to cause confusion. If we are to provide the
kinds of understanding and care that are imperative, rape must be viewed as an
assault both on the body and on the psyche of the victim.

REFERENCES

 1. Federal Bureau of Investigation. Uniform Crime Report, 1982 Preliminary Annual
    Release, U.S. Department of Justice, Washington, D.C., November 1982.
 2. Russell, D. and Howell, N. The prevalence of rape in the United States revisited.
    Signs, 8(4):688–695, Summer 1983.
 3. Frank, E., and Stewart, B. The treatment of depressed rape victims: an approach to
    stress-induced symptomatology. In: Clayton, P., and Barrett, J., eds., Treatment
    of Depression: Old Controversies and New Approaches. New York: Raven Press,
    1983.
 4. Everett, R., and Jimerson, G. The rape victim: a review of 117 consecutive cases.
    Obstet. Gynecol., 50(1):88–90, July 1977.
 5. Solola, A.; Scott, C.; Severs, H., et al. Rape: management in a non-institutional
    setting. Obstet. Gynecol., 61(3):373–378, March 1983.
 6. Groth, A., and Burgess, A. Male rape: offenders and victims. Am. J. Psychiatry,
    137(7):806–810, July 1980.
 7. Rapkin, J. The epidemiology of forcible rape. Am. J. Orthopsych., 49(4):634–647,
    October 1979.
 8. Wright, R., and West, D. Rape—a comparison of group offenses and lone assaults.
    Med. Sci. Law, 21(1):25–30, 1981.
 9. Feldman-Summers, S., and Ashworth, C. Factors related to intentions to report a
    rape. J. Soc. Issues, 37(4):53–69, 1981.
10. Shrier, D. Rape—myths, misconceptions, facts, and interventions. J. Med. Soc.
    N.J., 78(10):668–672, September 1981.
11. Holmstrom, L., and Burgess, A. Sexual behavior of assailants during reported rapes.
    Arch. Sex. Behav., 9(5):427–439, 1980.
12. Brownmiller, S. Against Our Will. New York: Simon and Schuster, 1975.
13. Amir, M. Patterns of Forcible Rape. Chicago: University of Chicago Press, 1971.
14. Wertheimer, A. Examination of the rape victim. Postgrad. Med., 71(3):173–180,
    March 1982.
15. Tyhurst, J. Individual reactions to community disaster: the habitual history of psy-
    chiatric phenomena. Am. J. Psychiatry, 107:764–769, 1951.

16. Glover, E. Notes on the psychological effects of war conditions on the civilian population, part 1: the Munich crisis. Int. J. Psychoanal., 22:132–146, 1941.

17. Glover, E. Notes on the psychological effects of war conditions on the civilian population, part III: the blitz. Int. J. Psychoanal., 23:17–37, 1942.

18. Schmideberg, M. Some observations on individual reactions to air raids. Int. J. Psychoanal., 23:146–176, 1942.

19. Rado, S. Pathodynamics and treatment of traumatic war neurosis (traumatophobia). Psychosom. Med., 4:362–369, 1942.

20. Deutsch, H. Some psychoanalytic observations in surgery. Psychosom. Med., 4:105–115, 1942.

21. Symonds, M. The psychological patterns of response of victims to rape. Paper presented at Seminar on Rape, John Jay College of Criminal Justice and American Academy for Professional Law Enforcement, New York, April 10, 1975.

22. Sutherland, S., and Scherl, D. Patterns of response among victims of rape. Am. J. Orthopsych., 40(3):503–511, April 1970.

23. Martin, C.; Warfield, M.; and Braen, G. Physician's management of the psychological aspects of rape. JAMA, 249(4):501–503, January 1983.

24. Janoff-Bulman, R. Characterological versus behavioral self-blame: inquiries into depression and rape, J. Pers. Soc. Psychol., 37(10):1798–1809, 1979.

25. Burgess, A., and Holmstrom, L. Rape trauma syndrome. Am. J. Psychiatry, 131(9):981–986, 1974.

26. Burgess, A., and Holmstrom, L. The rape victim in the emergency ward. Am. J. Nurs., 73(10):1740–1745, October 1973.

27. Burgess, A., and Holmstrom, L. Rape: Victims of Crisis. Bowie, Md.: Robert J. Brady Co., 1974.

28. Burgess, A., and Holmstrom, L. Coping behavior of the rape victim. Paper presented at Special Session on Rape, APA, Anaheim, Calif., 1975.

29. Resick, P.; Calhoun, K.; Atkeson, B., et al. Social adjustment in victims of sexual assault. J. Consult. Clin. Psychol., 49(5):705–712, 1981.

30. Ellis, E.; Atkeson, B.; and Calhoun, K. An assessment of long-term reaction to rape. J. Abnorm. Psychol., 90(3):263–266, 1981.

31. Burgess, A., and Holmstrom, L. Rape: sexual disruption and recovery. Am. J. Orthopsych., 49(4):648–657, October 1979.

32. Becker, J.; Skinner, L.; Abel, G., et al. Incidence and types of sexual dysfunctions in rape and incest victims. J. Sex. Marital Ther., 8(1):65–74, Spring 1982.

33. Atkeson, B., and Calhoun, K. Victims of rape: repeated assessment of depressive symptoms. J. Consult. Clin. Psychol., 50(1):96–102, 1982.

34. Kardiner, A., and Spiegel, H. War Stress and Neurotic Illness. New York: P. B. Hocher, 1941.

35. Kardiner, A. The Traumatic Neuroses of War. Medical Monograph II–III. New York: P. B. Hocher, 1941.

36. McCahill, T.; Meyer, L.; and Fischman, A. The Aftermath of Rape. Lexington, Mass.: Lexington Books, 1979.

37. Burgess, A., and Holmstrom, L. Recovery from rape and prior life stress. Res. Nurs. and Health, 1(4):165–174, 1978.

38. Nadelson, C.; Notman, M.; Zackson, H., et al. A follow-up study of rape victims. Am. J. Psychiatry, 139(10):1266–1270, October 1982.

39. Norris, J., and Feldman-Summers, S. Factors related to the psychological impacts of rape on the victim. J. Abnorm. Psychol., 90(6):562–567, 1981.
40. Binder, R. Difficulties in follow-up of rape victims. Am. J. Psychother., 35(4):534–541, October 1981.
41. Hilberman, E. The Rape Victim. Project of the Committee on Women of the American Psychiatric Association. Baltimore: Garamond/Pridemark Press, 1976.
42. Brussel, J. Comment following Menachim Amir, "Forcible Rape." Sexual Behavior, 1(8), 1971.
43. Center for Women Policy Studies. Rape and Its Victims: A Report for Citizens, Health Facilities, and Criminal Justice Agencies. The Police Response: A Handbook. Washington, D.C.: Law Enforcement Assistance Administration, 1975.
44. Schmidt, P. Rape crisis centers. Ms. Magazine, 14–18, September 1973.
45. Wasserman, M. Rape: breaking the silence. The Progressive, 19–23, November 1973.
46. National Center for the Prevention and Control of Rape. National Directory: Rape Prevention and Treatment Resources. Rockville, Md.: U.S. Department of Health and Human Services, NIMH, 1981.

Premarital Pregnancy and Childbirth in Adolescence: A Psychological Overview

We live at a time in which the American ideal regarding conception and childbirth involves a context defined by the simultaneous occurrence of mature sexuality, marriage, and economic adulthood (1). Further, mental health professionals include the attainment of mature object relations as an aspect of the ideal circumstances for the experience of conception and childbirth, and perhaps this is implicit in the commonly accepted understanding of the phrase "mature sexuality." From this point of view, adolescent out-of-wedlock pregnancy and mothering represents an extensive departure from the social, cultural, and psychological norms of the United States at this time. When an out-of-wedlock pregnancy occurs, it raises dual questions. There is first the question of how such a deviation could occur and then the question of what the effects of such a deviation might be.

This chapter will review the evidence available with an eye to delineating the factors that precede the occurrence of adolescent conception and childbirth outside marriage. It includes an examination of patterns of sexual activity and contraceptive behavior in adolescents and involves a look at the psychological features of adolescence, whether normative or pathological, which might contribute to the failure to attain the societal ideal. The effects of conception and childbirth will be reviewed, from both an immediate and long-range point of view. Short-term effects are seen as those stemming directly from personal knowledge of an unplanned out-of-wedlock pregnancy, including both the need to decide about such issues as abortion, delivery, and adoption, and the ways in which the conception is experienced and integrated into the ongoing development of the adolescent. Those who choose to abort will be considered sepa-

This chapter is based on work partially supported by the Robert Wood Johnson Foundation, Grant #4858.

rately from those who choose to bring their pregnancies to term. For each, the emphasis will be on developing an understanding of what meaning the adolescent attaches to the event and how this may contribute to behavioral decisions. The effects of abortion and childbirth on the developmental process will be considered, and known outcomes will be reviewed. No attempt will be made to report on the considerable difficulties attendant on adolescent mothering, nor will the related literature on the children of adolescent mothers be reviewed.

While it is obvious that each unplanned teenage conception or birth involves both a male and a female, the relevant literature is largely on adolescent girls. The fullest understanding of the phenomena will require insight into the possibly different paths by which boys and girls arrive at their respective responsibilities for conception and pregnancy. Before taking the literature bias as evidence of sexist orientation, it must be remembered that researchers are practical and opportunistic and that girls who become pregnant are far more likely to "get caught" in research by dint of participation in health-care services than are their male counterparts. This chapter is thus virtually exclusively composed of findings about adolescent females.

SEXUAL ACTIVITY IN ADOLESCENCE

An estimated 12 million to 13 million teenagers and preteens in the United States are sexually active (2). This statement refers to the number of adolescents believed to be engaging in sexual intercourse. More generally, adolescents are widely understood to be actively thinking and fantasizing about the various forms of sexual activity that precede sexual intercourse, since adolescence is a time of progressively attaining experience in the sequence of social-sexual acts which culminates in sexual intercourse. The order of social-sexual relations in Western culture begins with kissing, then kissing with open mouth and tongue (deep kissing), stimulation of a woman's breasts over clothes then under clothes, stimulation of the female genitals by the male, then stimulation of the male genitals by the female, then male and female genitals in opposition (next to one another), and thereafter sexual intercourse (3). Adolescents tend to move through this sequence in a stepwise fashion. The general increase in the prevalence of teenage sexuality means not only that large numbers of adolescents engage in sexual intercourse but also that there has been a general lowering of the age at which young people begin to kiss and "pet," that each form of social-sexual behavior tends to be attained at earlier ages than was true for previous generations, and that therefore the current generation is younger at first coitus than previous generations (4–6).

Given the repeated assertion that ever-younger adolescents are sexually active and experiencing intercourse, it would be desirable to have epidemiologicalstudies for the younger ages like those available for the older 15– to 19–year-old group (7). While Sorenson (9) did this in 1972 (and reported incidences of intercourse of 44 percent for boys and 30 percent for girls in the 13– to 15–

year-old group), parental objections resulted in a large sample loss in his population. As a result, his data have been criticized as biased toward overestimating sexual experience. In repeated studies of predominantly white boys and girls from upper-working-class to middle-class families in Michigan, Vener and Stewart (5, 8) demonstrated significant increases in reported intercourse for 14– and 15–year-old boys and girls. Their data (from the late 1960s and the early 1970s) report rates of intercourse for 14–year-olds as high as 7.1 percent for girls and 18 percent for boys, which while similar to rates reported by Sorenson (9) are higher than those reported for very young teenagers by Zelnick, Kim, and Kantner (6).

Rates of sexual intercourse can be reported with greater confidence in the older teenage group. In the 1970s the lowering of the age of first intercourse was marked. In 1971 only 1 in 12 U.S. females had had intercourse by the age of 16, and by age 19 the figure had been close to one-half. In 1976, as many as 1 in 5 U.S. females had had intercourse by the age of 16 and two-thirds had by age 19. Almost all that experience is outside marriage (6). Furthermore, this appears to be a trend that is progressive, since overall prevalence figures collected in 1979 show an increase from those reported in 1976 (7). It should be noted that the trends for black and white teenagers appear to be different. While the probability of having sexual intercourse remained greater for blacks than for whites at every age-group in 1976 (as it was in 1971), the probability of having sexual intercourse increased for whites at every age-group while at the same time it decreased at every age-group for blacks. The median age at first coitus for whites decreased by 0.5 year between 1971 and 1976, while for blacks it increased 0.6 year (6). Data for 1979 show no changes in prevalence for blacks, while prevalence percentages continue to rise for whites. Thus, although blacks in 1979 were 1.4 times as likely as whites to have had premarital intercourse, the racial difference in the prevalence of premarital intercourse among young women appears to be narrowing (7).

Demographic information available (7) describes those women who do become sexually active, but it must be remembered that demographics do not explain why some become sexually active. Age is by far the most potent single category, though family stability (including the presence of the natural father in the home) and religiosity are large factors for both races. A most striking racial difference involves the importance of socioeconomic status (SES). While the lower the SES the higher the prevalence of sexual activity overall for both races, the relationship is far weaker for whites than for blacks. For whites, the highest prevalence of intercourse is not found in the lowest SES group, whereas the decline in prevalence of sexual activity with increasing SES is much steeper for blacks than for whites. Even with such large factors as these, most of the variance remains unexplained (7). The possibility must be borne in mind that the paths to becoming sexually active are various rather than singular. Factors that are highly relevant to some girls' becoming sexually active at age 13 may be different from those that affect some others at age 16 and different still from factors affecting the same girls or others at age 18. Statistical models are hampered by cross-sectional differences (e.g., the population of 15–year-olds is heterogeneous in significant ways other than their sexual activities), and there are longitudinal differences (e.g., the 15–year-old will herself be different at 17 years of age). In simple terms, all sexually active 17–year-olds may not have traveled the same route. The data of Vener et al. (5), for example, appears to suggest that those initiating sexual intercourse at age 13 or 14 tend to have different partners more frequently and earlier than sexually experienced unmarried women in general. Thus any cross-sectional study will group newly active and more experienced 17–year-old girls together, and while both are currently active and the same age, their psychological makeup may be significantly different.

Most teenagers who engage in sexual intercourse tend to do so at their own home or at the home of their partner. There is evidence that the likelihood of a sexually experienced unmarried woman having several partners has increased, compared with previous eras, when out-of-wedlock sexual activity tended more to be confined to just one partner. However, the frequency of intercourse in adolescence remains lower than in later life. Half of those who never married but who are sexually experienced had no intercourse during the month prior to being surveyed, and fewer than three in ten had intercourse as many as three times in the month (10). A search of the literature revealed no studies that bear on the motivations for intercourse in adolescent females. Adults usually assume that adolescents are motivated by sexual desires, but none of the published papers on adolescent pregnancy mentions sexual feeling as a motivation for intercourse, though several report girls' being motivated by related affectional needs—touching, holding, and closeness (11).

PATTERNS OF CONTRACEPTIVE USE AMONG TEENAGERS

Since passage of the Family Planning Services and Population Research Act of 1970, federal funds supporting provision of family planning services have increased by more than 100 percent (12). There has also been a significant liberalization of laws and policies affecting teenagers' access to contraceptive services (13), although recent years have seen a challenge to this trend. These two factors may well be responsible for the large and rapid increase in enrollment of teenagers in clinics that provide family planning services—a shift from 453,000 in 1971 to 1.1 million in 1975 (2). The increasing availability of contraceptive information and devices appears to be related to the notable improvement in the numbers of unmarried teenage women who practice contraception which occurred at the same time (10). While there is good reason to believe that access to birth control is positively related to regular and successful use of birth control by teenagers (14, 15), factors other than widespread availability must come into play, because in the same period there has actually been a small rise in the proportion of teenagers who never use contraception (10).

Zelnick and Kantner (10, 16) surveyed women aged 15–19 in 1971 and 1976 and reported an increase in the percentage of teenagers always using contraception, an increase in the regularity of such use, and an increase in the use of the most effective medical methods of contraception. Overall, 38.7 percent of 13– to 19–year-olds reported using contraception in their first coital experience when surveyed in 1976. The general trend is both for the percentage to increase with increasing age at first coitus and for contraceptive use to increase over time with increasing coital experience. Thus 15– to 17–year-olds are far more likely than under-15–year-olds to use contraception at first intercourse, and 18– and 19–year-olds are even more likely to be so prepared. At the same time, increasing coital experience increases the likelihood of eventual contraceptive use.

Zelnick and Kantner (16) developed a scheme for analyzing contraceptive use which delineates four categories among sexually active teenagers: (a) those who used contraception at first intercourse and thereafter continued such use, (b) those who used contraception at first intercourse but sometime thereafter lapsed, (c) those who did not use contraception at first intercourse but sometime thereafter began use, and (d) those who did not use contraception at first intercourse and who never began such use.

The method of contraception chosen appears to be an important variable in understanding patterns of contraceptive use. Medical methods (the pill, intra-uterine device, or diaphragm) are utilized by one-quarter of those who use contraception at first intercourse, one-fifth of whites and nearly one-half of blacks. The difference is likely to be related to the increased availability of family planning clinic services proportionally more for blacks than for whites. While only one adolescent in ten is prepared with a medical method at first coitus, the attainment of such protection is strongly associated with consistent use of contraception, as 87 percent of those who began with such a method continued to use it, while only 64 percent of those who began with a nonmedical method continued to employ it regularly. However, there appears to be a delay in obtaining medical methods of contraception. One-third of those beginning with a nonmedical method later change to a medical method, while almost half the young women who did not use any method at first intercourse later began with a medical method. The delay in obtaining contraception is obviously critical. Racial differences do not appear to be significant in this regard (unprotected whites tend to seek contraception slightly sooner than unprotected blacks), but age differences are. The younger the age at first intercourse (among those not initially protected), the longer the delay in attaining contraceptive protection. Among those under age 15 at first intercourse who are initially not protected, there is a delay of 0.9 years for those eventually utilizing a nonmedical method, and a delay of 1.8 years for those eventually beginning with a medical method.

For those who do use contraception, therefore, initial protection with a medical method is most likely to result in consistent and reliable protection, while no protection or other forms appear to be steps along the path to eventually acquiring some reliable contraception. Nonetheless, 31 percent of sexually active teenagers

overall (27.7 percent of whites and 42.9 percent of blacks) never use any form
of birth control, and 45 percent of sexually active teenagers overall report using
no contraceptive protection in their last intercourse experience. Given the widespread availability of such devices, one wonders why they are not utilized.

UNDERSTANDING THE FAILURE TO USE
CONTRACEPTION EFFECTIVELY

Zelnick and Kantner (17) examined reasons given by sexually active teenagers
for not using contraception. A group of 15– to 19–year-olds who had intercourse
only once reported not using contraception because they thought they could not
become pregnant (64.6 percent) or, if they did think they could become pregnant,
because they did not expect to have intercourse (30.9 percent). Only one-third
of those who thought they could not become pregnant believed this to be true
on the basis of the time of the month they were having intercourse. The other
two-thirds believed that they were too young to become pregnant, that they had
intercourse too infrequently to become pregnant, or that they for some other
nonspecific reason could not or would not become pregnant. Among those 15–
to 19–year-olds who are more sexually experienced (having coitus more than
once) and still are not using contraception, the number who believe they could
not become pregnant is smaller (51 percent) but still substantial, considering
that over half these young women believe they could not become pregnant
because they are too young or are having intercourse too infrequently or for
some other nonspecific reason. Among this more experienced group, 20.3 percent
did not expect to have intercourse. Only a very small percentage of these teenagers (4.9 percent) believe contraceptive use to be wrong or dangerous, and a
similarly small percentage (3.1 percent) do not know about contraception or
where to get it. The broad picture is thus congruent with what is known about
teenage sexual activity—the unexpected, often infrequent character of the activity
can mitigate against the planning necessary to utilize contraception. In addition
to the suggestion of a degree of impulsivity which may be implied by the inability
to anticipate that which an adult might anticipate based on similar experience,
there are particular ideas that, while incorrect, are indigenous to adolescence
and that need to be examined to understand contraceptive-related behavior in
adolescence.

Although there are contraceptive programs specifically for teenagers, the overall continuation rate in those programs is not high (18). The setting itself and
the manner in which services are offered may make a considerable difference.
Free, personalized, confidential services that include education and provide for
close follow-up are far more successful than services that do not offer a consistent
staff and that pay less attention to individual concerns (19). Nonetheless, the
youngest teens (13–15) are most apt to be lost to follow-up in such programs,
which suggests again that developmental variables operate in the acquisition of
contraceptive behavior.

To examine the psychological and developmental competencies that must be present for effective contraceptive use, Urberg (20) has developed a theoretical framework based on a problem-solving model. The current discussion will emphasize the first step noted in her model, "problem recognition," since teens not using contraception because they believe they cannot become pregnant or because they do not anticipate intercourse (51% + 20.3% = 71.3% of sexually active 15- to 19–year-olds who do not use contraception [17]) can be seen as failing to correctly recognize the problem of remaining nonpregnant while sexually active.

Problem recognition logically begins with the assumption of sufficient intelligence as well as access to and mastery of accurate information on reproductive physiology and contraception. Adolescents are not alone in reporting erroneous beliefs, such as "conception cannot occur without orgasm." Gabrielson et al. (21) reported a high positive correlation between general sex and birth control knowledge and the ability to avoid pregnancy though sexually active. However, the functional capacity to utilize knowledge to think about probabilistic relationships requires a form of thinking which develops largely during adolescence. This form of thinking is necessary in order to think about the hypothetical, to reason abstractly, and to extend such thinking into the future. Formal operational thinking, as this was called in Piaget's developmental theory of cognition (22, 23), has been identified as a factor in effective contraceptive utilization (24, 25). The hallmark of formal operational thinking is the anticipation of future situations and the transposition of such hypothetical situations into present reality so that all logically possible solutions can be considered and solutions can be implemented before an actual situation materializes. Oskamp et al. (26) have reported research specifically linking the cognitive ability to plan into the future and effective contraceptive utilization.

For any problem to be recognized as personal and immediate rather than general or externalized, aspects of the self which predispose toward having the problem must be correctly and consciously identified. To recognize oneself as at risk for an unintended pregnancy, one must accept oneself as a sexually active person. A variety of authors have identified acceptance of one's own sexuality as an important variable in contraceptive use (27, 28), and one such study found this factor to be the most important correlate of contraceptive use examined, more important than sex education or knowledge about sex per se (29). The social-psychiatric view (30) emphasizes the difficulty of attaining sexual self-acceptance when large, vocal segments of society disapprove of premarital sex in particular and more generally subtly propagate the attitude that sex is "bad." Admitting forethought (e.g., anticipating pregnancy risk by using contraception) is therefore worse with regard to societal mores than being surprised and caught off guard (e.g., not using contraception). Prepared intercourse is especially difficult for young women because sexual activity remains more prohibited for them than for boys in this society, and young women may therefore fear being thought sexually experienced by their boyfriends.

An additional aspect of problem recognition is the capacity to experience oneself as vulnerable to external circumstances (Urberg [20] considers this a motivational aspect of problem-solving). If the self is not experienced as potentially vulnerable, problems in the world have no self-reference. Elkind (31) has advanced the view that adolescence is characterized by a cognitive egocentrism which has as its core a feeling of invulnerability. He has called the stories adolescents tell among themselves about their lives "personal fables" and describes a wide variety of instances in which adolescents seem to see the world as discontinuous with the self. From this vantage point, events such as auto accidents and pregnancy can be recognized but are seen as things that happen to other people. There is no recognition that they might happen to oneself as well. Not only do the majority of adolescents who do not use contraception believe they "can't" become pregnant, but most pregnant adolescents report feeling that pregnancy would not happen to them (32, 29). Some teenagers, even after having been pregnant, tenaciously hold to the belief that it could not happen to them, though it can and sometimes does happen again (33). Statements made by adolescents such as "I thought I was too young" or "I never thought it could happen to me" are manifestations of a developmental incapacity to experience vulnerability which can virtually block effective problem recognition.

During the adolescent years, both boys and girls are powerfully involved in the development of appropriately masculine or feminine identities. For both, this may involve adopting the sex-typed behaviors identified by the culture as well as passing through the "stages" that appear to mark the acquisition of mature male or female identities. "Machismo" no longer narrowly connotes the striving for masculine identity in Hispanic males but is more widely considered to mean the male wish to feel securely virile and potent. In some cultural subgroups this is best demonstrated by impregnating a woman (30). If a boy is struggling to attain a feeling of virility, contraceptive use by the girl may be experienced as a threat to him. However, motivations for impregnation remain speculative though widely held ideas. It may be safer to say that adolescent males generally view success in sex as a measure of manhood (34).

For girls, attaining a mature feminine identity may involve a period in adolescence of narcissistic dramatization of relationships and a concurrent romanticizing of sexuality. Deutsch (35) has described the intensely narcissistic love relationships that frequently occur in adolescence and has coined the word "pseudology" to describe the unreal quality that marks the teenage girl's crushes and fantasy relationships—her early experience of sexuality. The often noted tendency of adolescent girls to value the spontaneous aspects of sexual intercourse may then represent more than the episodic nature of their sexual encounters or a denial of forbidden sexual impulses. The ubiquitous romanticizing of sexuality can be seen as directly related to the adolescent girl's view that contraceptive preparedness would "cheapen the whole thing" (36). Thus, normal aspects of personality development may transiently render the adolescent female unlikely to recognize a practical problem; if she conceptualizes sexual intercourse as a spontaneous, romantic occurrence, she may indeed disdain behaviors that are antithetical to her ideas.

As Urberg (20) has pointed out, after the perception of a problem some motivation must exist to do something to avoid the problem. The assumption is that adolescents, if given the choice, would prefer to avoid pregnancy. Most authors agree that fewer than 10 to 15 percent of sexually active teenagers would find a pregnancy desirable or even acceptable (37, 38, 11), but there are some who question the assumption of minimal intentionality (39–41, 28). While these authors are inferring premeditation of pregnancy from post facto statements made by pregnant girls, such wishes may be present in a population of girls who are likely to "drop out" on the basis of failure, poverty, or passivity. The only group apt to be actually motivated to become pregnant are older teenagers who hope to coax a long-term boyfriend into marriage, though premarital pregnancy is increasingly unsuccessful in that regard (42). In any case, the motivation to care about the consequences of unprotected intercourse cannot be universally expected. Those who may have considered the possible benefits of pregnancy will be treated more fully in a later section.

Finally, any problem-solving model must culminate with the implementation of decisions. Adolescents often report that they intended to do something about contraception but that somehow they did not follow through (17). There is encouraging evidence that participating in modeling, role-playing, and rehearsal exercises in which decisions about dating, sexuality, and birth control are practiced can enhance problem-solving abilities and actually results in significant increases in mature behavior (43).

THE INCIDENCE OF PREMARITAL CONCEPTIONS

There is a remarkable degree of confusion in the literature as to the incidence of premarital conceptions in adolescence. While there is obvious interest in knowing the actual scope of the problem, no single group maintains such statistics. Because they must be gleaned by adding the number of live births (recorded by the National Center for Health Statistics of the Department of Health and Human Services) to the number of therapeutic abortions and spontaneous abortions (recorded by the Centers for Disease Control of the Department of Health and Human Services), confusion results when authors discuss rates of pregnancy and rely only on statistics about birth rates (44). In addition, authors often neglect to distinguish premarital pregnancies from those occurring within marriage (45). It has been pointed out, for example, that in 1974 some 42 percent of childbearing teenagers were married 18– and 19–year-olds (1). To complicate matters further, figures for those aged 15–19 are separate from the under-15–year-old group.

The best data available suggests that in 1976 about 800,000 premarital conceptions occurred in adolescents. Zelnick and Kantner (46) indicate that in 1976 a little more than 1 million 15– to-19–year-olds experienced a pregnancy. About

77 percent, or 780,000, of those pregnancies occurred outside marriage. If we consider that there are records of 13,000 deliveries in 1977 to those under age 15 (47), and if we assume that the ratio of live births to abortions in this age-group is roughly similar to that in the 15– to 19–year-old group (48, 49), then there may have been 6,500 abortions and therefore about 20,000 conceptions, assumed by age to be outside marriage in the under-15 age-group in 1977. The estimate of 800,000 yearly out-of-wedlock conceptions is made by adding 780,000 and 20,000.

Two points are worth noting. First, while the absolute number of younger adolescents who are conceiving outside marriage is small relative to the number of middle and older adolescents so conceiving, the likelihood of conception at the younger ages is increasing (6). This is supported by the finding that it is the 10– to 14–year-old group which is the only age-group for which birth rates are rising nationwide. Further, this group also has the highest abortion rate of all age-groups (50). Increasing birth and abortion rates mean increasing conception rates. Second, it is clear that while contraception is already a powerful delimiter of conception (the current conception rate in the 15– to 19–year-olds would almost double if these teens were not using contraception), the current conception rate for unmarried adolescents might be almost halved if all those who did not want a baby were practicing contraception consistently (16). Since, as we have seen, ever younger teens are becoming sexually active, and since the youngest groups are the poorest contraceptors, it becomes clear that a significant trend in conception is a function of trends in patterns of sexual activity and contraception; younger adolescents for whom developmental issues interdigitate with sexual precocity are increasingly at risk for early conceptions outside marriage.

THE IMPACT OF THE DISCOVERY OF CONCEPTION IN ADOLESCENCE

The most common reaction of the unmarried adolescent to the discovery that conception has taken place is denial, disbelief, and despair. Few girls are described as happy (51, 52). Indeed, the frequent report of unusual delay among pregnant adolescent girls in obtaining medical consultation is often a reflection of their extreme upset at the discovery of the pregnancy. Stress at this time is so great that some girls later report having thought of suicide (53). Anecdotal material indicates that the young woman becomes preoccupied with fears and fantasies of the responses of significant others. She sometimes hopes that her boyfriend will rescue her and marry her, while often fearing his rejection or painfully recognizing that she herself is unready or unwilling to marry. Fear of parental anger and rejection is common and often foreshadows the actual parental response. Copeland (54) has placed the event of an unplanned pregnancy in the context of the developmental tasks of adolescence. Given that adolescence is quintessentially a time of "disengagement from infantile dependencies" (55), a time of developing a sense of self with personal values and work which is differentiated from the family, as well as a time of stabilizing relationships and shifting loyalties from the family to the peer group, the discovery of conception can be seen as an event that challenges the main thrust of adolescent psychological development. The newly pregnant adolescent girl becomes dependent on others, in fantasy and fact, for a successful resolution (56). Her sense of herself is suddenly and radically revamped both psychically and physically. While normal adolescent growth proceeds from girlhood to womanhood, the pregnant adolescent girl must consider motherhood an intervening rather than a subsequent stage (57). Indeed, it is common for the entire family to experience a crisis when an unmarried adolescent announces her pregnancy (58). Several studies demonstrate that pregnant adolescents have suffered insult to or interference with their identity development (59, 60), though in the absence of prospective, longitudinal studies one cannot tell whether such a factor resulted from the pregnancy or contributed to a susceptibility to becoming pregnant.

In this context of denial, disbelief, despair, fear, and anxiety an unmarried teenager must decide (perhaps with the aid of family, friends, and community supports) what to do about the fact of her conception. The possibilities to consider are abortion or carrying the baby to term (whether this includes keeping the child by herself, marrying the boyfriend and creating a new family in which to raise the child, or giving the child up for adoption). In the sections to follow, the literature on those who abort and those who carry their pregnancy to term will be examined to elucidate the ways each group appears to differ from the other and to determine what is known about how each group experiences the pregnancy and how each group is affected by the experience both in the short run and over the longer term.

THOSE WHO CHOOSE TO ABORT

Unmarried adolescent abortion patients are not conspicuously different in social or psychological characteristics from their nonpregnant, sexually active counterparts (61). Any special configuration of features that may have been advanced as characterizing adolescents seeking abortion turns out to be spurious when they are matched with nonpregnant girls whose sexual experience is comparable. This is supported by studies using a wide range of samples and a variety of methods (62–65). Indeed, when pregnant and nonpregnant adolescents (matched for level of sexual activity) are compared, the only differences that emerge relate to a greater degree of caution regarding sexual activity on the part of those not pregnant. They tend to have been older at first intercourse, to be more consistent in their use of contraception, and to come from families in which the parents hold less permissive attitudes toward premarital sex (66). Thus it seems that adolescents seeking abortion are differentiated from those who are sexually active but not pregnant only by having been less careful about avoiding pregnancy.

When unmarried teenagers seeking abortion are compared with unmarried teenagers who choose to carry their deliveries to term, however, significant differences emerge (67, 68). Those who choose abortion are likely to come from small, intact families that enjoy a relatively higher socioeconomic status than the families of girls who choose to carry to term. The abortion patients (unlike those who choose delivery) tend to be functioning educationally on a par with their peers and may, in addition, demonstrate competence and independence by holding part-time employment. They may have a role model in the form of a sister in the family who herself has had an abortion (69, 63, 64). Racial and religious factors also apply. Whites obtain abortions at rates nine times that of blacks (46), and, as expected, proportionally fewer Catholics seek abortion (70).

Girls who choose to abort tend not to involve their boyfriends or their fathers in their decision. Differences within the group as to whether and how the mother is involved have been shown to correlate with the psychological experience of abortion (51).

Most published studies of adolescents who choose an abortion seek to measure the severity, frequency, or duration of upset. However, the developmental point of view assumes that the event (e.g., the need for an abortion) will be experienced in terms of and become active in the developmental tasks and issues of the age. Particularly because we see that adolescents who seek abortion are essentially similar to sexually active nonpregnant girls, much of what is published about the feelings of these girls can be seen as a window into the psychological makeup of adolescence, revealing both the developmental issues that become activated by the event of pregnancy and the ways that individual differences in levels of ego development interdigitate with the event of the pregnancy to produce various characteristic patterns of response to the event (51, 36).

During adolescence, the increasing growth and differentiation of the sense of self parallels and contributes to a further individuation from the family. Normal developments such as these always involve some progressive dissolution of old dependencies, whether one considers the reworking of the internal parental imago or the acutal state of independence in relation to the real parent-in-the-world. Conflicts around dependence and independence experienced on various levels are virtual hallmarks of adolescence. Pregnancy, at any age, has been recognized as producing in normal women a regression in the service of the ego (Winnicott's "primary maternal preoccupation" [71]), a regression that brings with it "the revival and simultaneous emergence of unsettled conflicts from earlier developmental phases" (72).

Schaffer and Pine (51) reported that for the adolescents they studied pregnancy and abortion "brought to the fore the conflict between being mothered (with the arousal of passive longings for the pregenital mother-of-infancy) and being a mother (to one's infant, to oneself, to others, with new identifications and the opportunity to make amends for the past, to attempt to begin life over)." The pregnancy and abortion appeared to be experienced as an opportunity to resolve this conflict. Resolutions both of a more regressive nature and of a more progressive nature were seen in the group. Those who either had an ongoing infantile relationship with the mother or moved in that direction during the time of crisis involved the mother in the abortion. They allowed the mother to make decisions and so externalized the conflict and reworked it in the real mother-child relationship, establishing or reestablishing passive-dependent and ambivalent ties. Those who were identified less with their own prospective infant and more with the "good mother" of infancy did not involve their mothers but mothered themselves and used the experience in a progressive way to establish feelings of mastery of their bodies and of the world. Midway positions and solutions were seen too. Both solutions can be seen as "acting out," the experience of pregnancy and abortion serving as a vehicle for the expression of internal conflict. Pregnancy and abortion appeared to produce a virtual dependence-independence conflict in exacerbation. The reemergence of more primitive conflicts at the time of the normal reworking of these same conflicts at higher levels may be an especially intense stressor. It does appear from Schaffer and Pine's report (51) that a range of more and less adequate solutions is possible.

Hatcher (36) also presents data that can be used to consider the experience of pregnancy as a function of the developmental stage. Her study advances the view that to make meaning of the experience pregnancy partakes of the affects and representations of self and others which are current at the stage. However, she confuses the adolescent's experience of pregnancy with factors that cause or motivate the pregnancy. Unfortunately, while her discrimination of three distinct stages of adolescence has much theoretical appeal, the reclassification of the subjects (aged 15–26) into early, mid, and late adolescence assumes that all people will move through all stages, given enough time. This obscures the possibility of looking at the variety of more and less mature experiences of the crisis. It is possible that the various experiences described in each of these developmental studies speak to the ways that level of ego development interdigitates with ongoing developmental issues exacerbated by pregnancy. Those who are more mature tend more to utilize pregnancy as a source of mastery and growth, while others experience a regressive pull, which interferes with progressive development.

For the most part, few severe psychiatric complications have been noted following induced abortion. The small number of serious problems that do occur are probably related to preexisting psychopathology (73). For the most part, teenagers are relieved to have an unwanted pregnancy terminated (34). Indeed, once the procedure is over, regardless of the way it had been anticipated, many teenagers want so much to forget about it that studies of adolescent aborters commonly note that as many as 50 percent of an initially studied group are lost to follow-up shortly after the procedure (73, 51, 36).

While relatively more teenagers than older women suffer transient feelings of anxiety, depression, sadness, guilt, or regret following abortion (74), such feelings vary significantly with the level of support available to them (75) and the type of procedure (76). Teenagers tend to think about abortion in absolutist terms that reflect their age (77). That is, there is a distinctly adolescent tendency to describe abortion as "murder" or to view an unplanned pregnancy as a just consequence of engaging in sexual activity. While such views are more likely to be held by younger teenagers than by older teenagers and as such probably reflect the lack of development of relative thinking which may come with greater maturity, such thinking is likely to be both a source of psychological conflict after an abortion and a cause of delay in seeking abortion. Adolescents have twice as many abortions performed after 16 weeks of pregnancy as do older women (78). Such abortions performed by the saline induction method cause the teenager to experience the expulsion of a fetus and often to see it. Thus the thinking and feelings characteristic of the age both delay the decision (sometimes causing a need for a much more noxious procedure) and may be the source of some of the transient psychological conflict experienced.

Medically, abortion is viewed as a generally safe procedure for adolescents. There appear to be fewer short-term complications and a lower mortality rate in adolescents than in older women. Overall, the risk of dying from pregnancy continuation is at least five times higher than that from pregnancy termination. This very low risk would be lower still if the fears of adolescents could be effectively addressed, since delays in requesting abortions and delays in reporting postabortion symptoms are factors in a large proportion of cases in which difficulties arise (79).

Adolescents are frequently appropriately concerned about whether induced abortion will threaten later desired pregnancies. Studies of late complications have produced conflicting results and make the subject of long-term sequelae an unresolved issue (80). For adolescents, the critical medical factor appears to be the caliber of dilatation required, both because the young adolescent with a smaller, tighter cervix is at greater risk for cervical trauma and because wider dilatation can be necessary when adolescents present at the later gestational age (81). However, the commonly utilized suction curettage procedure is apparently not associated with significant risk of adverse outcome in subsequent pregnancies.

Late psychological effects have not been shown to evolve from the experience of abortion per se. The only report in the literature which suggests that a suicide attempt may occur around the time a fetus would have come to term (82) is a report of two adolescents who appeared at very high risk for suicide attempts prior to the elective abortion. One had three major vehicular accidents, a previously undisclosed suicide attempt, and a history of drug and alcohol abuse, while the other had once been in a psychiatric hospital, had made a suicide attempt, and had five relatives who had committed suicide. The interpretation suggested by Gabrielson et al. (83) with regard to later suicide attempts in those who had borne children as teenagers is applicable: "The suicide attempt is not a direct result of pregnancy, but . . . both the pregnancy and the suicide attempt stem from a common process." The impulsive girls presented by Tishler (82) appear to have expressed their impulsivity in a variety of ways, including pregnancy and suicide attempts, but this does not demonstrate a causative link.

CHILDBIRTH OUTSIDE MARRIAGE

While the media sometimes make it seem as if there is an epidemic of adolescent pregnancies, suggesting thereby that larger numbers of births are occurring to teenage girls than ever before, this is not the case. We have seen a striking increase in adolescent sexual activity and out-of-wedlock conceptions, but both the increase in the use of birth control and the increase in abortions have tended to decrease the rate of childbearing in adolescence (44). What has occurred is more an epidemic of baby-keeping (1). The nature of the visible problem has changed in that younger adolescents are having babies, more births to adolescents are illegitimate, and vastly larger numbers of these babies are being kept by their mothers than ever before. While the birth rate for 15– to 19–year-olds dropped 9 percent between 1968 and 1973, the birth rate for 10– to 14–year-olds simultaneously increased 30 percent (84). During the same period of time (1966–1975), the illegitimacy rate has been rising for teenagers although it has been falling for all other groups of women. In 1975, some 51 percent of births to those ages 15–17 were illegitimate, as were 30 percent of births to those ages 18 and 19 (85). Finally, ever fewer babies are being relinquished by adolescents for adoption (2.6 percent of out-of-wedlock births in 1976, compared with 7.6 in 1971) (46). The best current estimate is that in 1976 approximately 573,000 births occurred to teenagers of all ages in the United States, 60 percent of which were conceived out of wedlock (44). The uproar in the popular press is related to the visible presence of close to 350,000 new babies yearly who require care from their unwed teenage mothers.

THOSE WHO CHOOSE TO CARRY THE PREGNANCY TO TERM

Unwed teenagers who choose to bring their pregnancies to term are far more likely to have come from larger, single-parent, lower-socioeconomic-level families than the teenagers who choose abortion. The term patients also tend to earn worse grades and to have more academic difficulties, and these problems predate both the pregnancy and any dropping out that follows (64, 69, 70). The demographic bulge in unwed adolescent pregnancy occurs in the 16– to 17–year-old age-group; among these women, pregnancy is most likely to result in childbirth.

Racial factors also apply, but they require interpretation because the picture is complex. Blacks have higher illegitimacy rates than whites, utilize abortion services less, and therefore are disproportionately represented among unwed adolescents who carry their babies to term (86, 87). This is consistent with the knowledge that black women overall have more children than white women and begin having their children at younger ages (88). This varies with socioeconomic status, as the higher the socioeconomic status of the black woman, the fewer children she tends to have, a finding that also holds true for adolescent blacks. While this tends to be true overall for whites as well, however, social class appears to have a stronger effect on the sexually related behavior of blacks (88). Black illegitimacy is decreasing, while white illegitimacy is increasing (61). Further, more and younger blacks have been utilizing abortion (89). It would therefore appear that while blacks remain disproportionately represented among teenagers who bear children, this is a result of disproportionate numbers of blacks being represented in the poorer classes in the United States. A social-class problem should not be mistaken for a racial problem. Indeed, at present the moderating effect of social striving seems stronger in the black culture than in the white culture.

Adolescents who choose to carry their babies to term are said to have a poorer self-image and a more compromised sense of competence and control than others their age (33, 36). For these girls, relationships to boyfriends have been described as longer, closer, and "more important" than for the girls who choose to abort. Further, the same girls are also more likely to be influenced by their mothers. There may well be a relation between the diminution of the sense of self and the continued dependence on an important other which is uninterrupted by any indication of a period of relative independence.

The effects of the decision to carry the pregnancy to term will be reviewed medically, educationally, socially, and psychologically before looking at the outcome for the society at large.

HEALTH CONSEQUENCES OF ADOLESCENT CHILDBIRTH

Reports published in the 1950s showed a higher incidence of a variety of medical complications among adolescents when compared with older child-bearing women, and when medical risk factors were stratified by age, it became apparent that most at risk are those 16 years old and younger (90). However, age may be only one of a number of other correlates, such as prenatal care. McAnarney (48, 49) demonstrated that when prenatal care was controlled teen-agers could achieve obstetric outcomes comparable to older women and that this could be achieved regardless of race or social class. The best current evidence suggests that it is only the very young teenager (under 15) who, as a function of physiological and anatomical immaturity, is at risk for toxemia, cephalopelvic disproportion, and abruptio placentae (91). For others, good outcomes are quite possible and largely related to utilizing and complying with good prenatal care.

THE QUESTION OF ADOPTION

Since a teenager carrying a pregnancy to term would eliminate the risk of any of the consequences of childbirth still to be discussed if she were to choose to give her child up for adoption, it is logical that we turn to adoption. The wide-spread availability and utilization of legal abortion has had a tremendous impact on adoption. Before the era of legalized abortion, 90 percent of children born to teenagers were given up for adoption. In the 1950s and 1960s, "maternity homes'' served as residences for middle- and upper-class girls during their pregnancies and as sources of babies for adoption agencies. Because this population of girls has had access to a far less life-disrupting resolution to pregnancy, these homes have all but disappeared. The small numbers of girls who now choose to give their babies up for adoption now usually do so after residing at home during the pregnancy. It is interesting to speculate about whether this factor has contributed to the decrease in numbers of children available for adoption. Living at home may provide the gradual, progressive acceptance of the situation which was not available before, when pregnant girls were ostracized and sent away before they "showed."

One study looked at girls residing in a "maternity home" (92). The decision to keep or adopt was related both to the girl's level of functioning and to the degree of male involvement she experienced. Those girls who had higher levels of personality functioning and less involvement with their boyfriends chose to give up their child for adoption, while those who functioned at lower levels psychologically and were more involved with their boyfriends chose to keep the baby. Although adolescents who choose adoption may avoid the consequences experienced by their counterparts who choose to keep their babies, it has been shown that after having placed their babies for adoption, mothers frequently suffer feelings of grief, guilt, and shame which continue to haunt them for some time (53).

EDUCATIONAL CONSEQUENCES OF ADOLESCENT CHILDBIRTH

Pregnancy is the most common reason for girls' failing to complete high school; 50–67 percent of female dropouts are pregnant (52). Moreover, follow-up after 11 years indicates that teenage mothers remain significantly less well educated than their counterparts who did not become pregnant during adolescence. This long-term finding is corroborated by Hardy et al. (93), who reported on more than 700 women who had children before they were 18. Follow-up 12 years later indicated that only 35 percent of them had ever completed high school. In general, the younger the woman when she bears her first child, the fewer years of schooling she completes. The strong relationship between age at first childbirth and years of school completed holds even when race and socioeconomic level is held constant (94, 95). While we have seen that girls who choose to carry to term tend to be adolescents who were doing more poorly in school than their nonpregnant or aborting counterparts before conception, their educational fate immediately following delivery has been identified as a key factor in determining whether subsequent premarital adolescent conception will occur. Early on, Barglow et al. (33) recognized that a second pregnancy was predicted not by any constellation of personality features, as had been anticipated, but by the failure to return to school and the presence of poor grades. This has subsequently been replicated by Furstenberg (52) and Trussell and Menken (96).

Whether this indicates that some adolescent females continue in a childbearing pattern in place of or in preference to other expected adolescent activities, or whether lower grades indicate lower innate levels of cognitive functioning, which both hampers effective contraceptive utilization and prevents participation in other meaningful life roles, remain unresolved questions at present.

SOCIAL, VOCATIONAL, AND ECONOMIC CONSEQUENCES OF ADOLESCENT CHILDBIRTH

There is typically a great deal of familial and social pressure for the pregnant teenager to marry, and about half the young women in this situation do so (42). However, those who remain single tend to do better subsequently, both educationally and vocationally, than those who marry (52, 97). The separation and divorce rate for adolescent marriages induced by conception is quite high. The likelihood of a marriage breaking up is three times as high for girls bearing first children between the ages of 14 and 17 as it is for those bearing children at age 20 or over (98).

Adolescent mothers have more children than do other women over the course of their childbearing years, and they report having more children than they intended to have (95, 96). The interval between the first birth and subsequent births is shorter for those bearing first children under the age of 18 than it is for older women. In the Johns Hopkins study (93), 40 percent of the teenagers delivering before age 18 had subsequent deliveries within one year, while this was true for only 22 percent of the older women. The finding that adolescents who bear children early are likely to have more subsequent children, more unwanted children, and more closely spaced children compared with older women holds up even when racial, educational, and religious differences are controlled.

Largely because of lower educational attainment, teenage mothers obtain less-rewarding and less-remunerative work over much of their working lives. Many of them are on welfare (95, 52). Bacon (99) established that there is a strong positive correlation between the age of the mother at first childbirth and income. An individual delivering at age 15 is two times as likely to reside at or below the poverty line as an individual delivering at age 19, and three times as likely to live at the poverty level as an individual who defers childbirth to age 22 or beyond. Furthermore, as a result of early childbearing, many adolescent mothers do not join the work force. A recent survey in New York City (2) indicated that 91 percent of women having their first babies between the ages of 15 and 17 had neither full-time nor part-time employment 19 months after delivery. Some 72 percent of these mothers were on welfare. The total numbers of women who are or were teenage mothers and require welfare support is extremely high. Moore (100) reported that almost half of all federal expenses for Aid to Families with Dependent Children (AFDC) in 1975, some $4.65 billion, were absorbed by households in which the woman gave birth to her first child during her adolescent years. Moore found that this relationship was independent of the other social correlates of teenage childbearing that are associated with poverty (race and educational level). This means not only that welfare dependency was related to teenage pregnancy because of common associated features but also, with those common associated features held constant, that childbearing during the teen years significantly increased the risk of long-term welfare dependency.

THE PSYCHOLOGICAL EXPERIENCE OF OUT-OF-WEDLOCK CHILDBIRTH

The decision to carry an out-of-wedlock pregnancy to term, to "have a baby," need not presume a prior wish for a baby. The decision reached by any one girl may result from the meaning she attributes to the event, and this will perforce follow from the interaction of her level of ego development and the psychological issues that are current for her. The opportunity is ripe for the pregnancy to partake of and to express the psychological conflicts she is experiencing. What function can it serve to choose to accept teenage motherhood?

One theme that emerges from the literature is that of "default." Furstenberg (52) speaks of girls who "drift" into teenage childbearing. For some hapless, hopeless girls, the pregnancy may be accepted as an opportunity for an identity and a role. These are the girls who seem to initially say they "didn't care" if they became pregnant (101) and for whom the pregnancy is experienced as a potential source of self-esteem (102). These young women seem to be aware of a pervasive, chronic emptiness in their lives and within themselves. They experience the pregnancy as an opportunity to fill the void and to create a new, adult role and life for themselves by having a baby (103). Lindemann and Scott (28) have advanced the view that this may be a viable alternative for low-income adolescents. A more psychological explanation would require tying the common conditions of poverty to the experience of "emptiness." While the bleakness of the culture of poverty may serve for some as the intervening link, it does not address the question of inner emptiness in adolescence.

A second though not necessarily independent theme in the literature on teens who choose childbirth is the singularly tenacious quality of symbiosis in the maternal line which is found repeatedly in families of girls who become teenage mothers (1). The difficulty many girls experience in achieving a flexible lessening of dependency on the mother may be related to the single-parent status of many of the households. Barglow et al. (33) noted the difficulties caused by the absence of a father to help a girl in the separation from her mother. Apprey (104) has written about the function of the father in aiding a girl's separation from her mother (and thereby contributing to the structuralization of her personality). Many of the "reasons" typically set forth as "motivations" for pregnancy—such as competing with mother, punishing mother, pleasing mother by giving her a child, escaping from mother, provoking mother's continued care and concern—can be understood in terms of the possible vicissitudes of unresolved separation-individuation problems acted out in adolescence. A baby may become the vehicle for effecting a spurious form of individuation, only to become heir to the same problem. The girl who speaks about her unborn child saying "I want something of my own," "I want someone to love," or "I want someone to love me" is demonstrating that the baby is not experienced as separate from her, not considered to be a potential person in its own right.

If, then, an adolescent is struggling to find an identity, perhaps in the face of a bleak environment that offers little or in the context of limited skills and limited prospects, and/or if this pressing search for identity and independence reflects a thwarted stymied thrust toward individuation from a "symbiotically" experienced mother, an infant may have special personal appeal. If amid this frustrating search for an independent identity a pregnancy occurs, stirring up the unresolved tensions between an unrequited need to be mothered and the wish to mother, those who experience few prospects for successful conflict resolution may find in the opportunity to bear a child an apparent solution to both the present dilemma and the underlying dilemma.

For older women in general, the experience of childbirth carries with it a far higher incidence of subsequent psychological disturbance than does the experience of abortion. While there is no apparent risk during pregnancy, the first three months postpartum carry a significant risk of psychosis (105). However, it appears that the psychological sequelae of teenage childbearing are not strongly associated with the biological event. Sequelae that have been described (high incidences of suicide [83]) appear to result from processes common to the childbearing and the later psychological event, such as impulsivity, a tendency to act out solutions, and/or the absence of higher-order channels for the resolution of conflict.

DISCUSSION AND CONCLUSIONS

Parents and educators try to protect teenagers from dire consequences by teaching, preaching, reminding, and pleading "If you must drink, don't drive." Educational programs, scare tactics, love, money, time, and effort notwithstanding, death and injury to adolescents from the combination of alcohol and vehicles is rampant. However, when a tragic motor vehicle accident occurs despite ample "warnings," barring flagrant pathology, no one suggests that the teenager wanted to have an accident. Instead, the general agreement is that the tragedy took place largely because of normally occurring features of adolescent development gone awry.

So it is with adolescent conception outside marriage. Aside from the very few who may wish to become pregnant, for the most part adolescent pregnancy results because more adolescents are having sex at earlier ages and because the attendant developmental issues mitigate against the most adequate contraceptive protection. The often incomplete state of the development of formal operational thinking—the hesitancy involved in accepting full sexuality (especially for females), the defenses erected against the experience of vulnerability, and the need, especially for females, to romanticize sexuality—are all influences against pregnancy prevention. Rather than considering motivations for pregnancy, it appears more helpful to consider the psychological experience of the discovery of out-of-wedlock pregnancy, for it is here that psychological features influence outcomes.

Pregnancies occur against the background of the developmental issues in flux. The disengagement from infantile dependencies, the development of the sense of self, the stabilization of relationships, and the shifting of loyalties from the family to the peer group are characteristics of adolescent development in our culture. Adolescents vary considerably in the level of maturity (level of ego development) that they bring to bear on these issues, as can be observed in the various styles which different adolescents exhibit as they experience, approach, and resolve the problems of their world. Pregnancy is a social and psychological crisis in adolescence which is given meaning by the status of the adolescent's progress in effecting developmental transitions and by the general maturity level of the personality. Pregnancy is not merely a biological event with singular, universal meaning and impact. It is a special case of what Schafer (106) meant when he stated, "Psychosexuality means mental sexuality—that is, a sexuality of meanings and personal relationships that have developed and been organized around real and imagined experiences and situations in a social 'world.' " Pregnancy is a potential vehicle for the experience and expression of multiple psychological and developmental issues.

The bifurcation that ensues as the paths followed by those who abort and those who choose to carry to term is not as absolute as it might appear. It must be remembered that some who may have wanted a baby are forced by families to consent to abortion, and some who may have really wished to abort their pregnancies delay too long and experience childbirth either by complete default or in preference to a saline induction abortion. Nevertheless, as a group, those who choose abortion seem healthier. Indeed, except for a lesser degree of caution with regard to birth control, they are indistinguishable from their nonpregnant, sexually active counterparts. The conception represents a developmental stressor, but lasting consequences are nil. Those who choose childbirth, on the other hand, appear to recognize fewer prospects within themselves and in the world which promise successful development. The choice of childbirth as a resolution to frustrated identity development greatly heightens their chances of social, vocational, and economic problems of significant magnitude. To the extent that they appear psychologically vulnerable before childbirth, the additional life stress that typically follows out-of-wedlock adolescent childbirth would appear to place this group at risk for poor overall mental health. Though the increased risk of later suicide has been demonstrated, the long-term mental health outcome for this group remains an important task for future research.

REFERENCES

1. Fisher, S., and Scharf, K. Teenage pregnancy: an anthropological, sociological, and psychological overview. Adolescent Psychiatry, 8:393–403, 1980.

2. Alan Guttmacher Institute. 11 Million Teenagers. New York: Planned Parenthood Federation of America, 1976.

3. Schofield, M. The Sexual Behavior of Young People. Boston: Little, Brown, 1965.

4. Luria, A., and Rose, M. Psychology of Human Sexuality. New York: John Wiley and Sons, 1979.

5. Vener, A.; Stewart, C.; and Hager, D. The sexual behavior of adolescents in Middle America: generational and American-British comparisons. J. Marriage Fam., 34:696–705, 1972.

6. Zelnick, M.; Kim, Y.; and Kantner, J. Probabilities of intercourse and conception among U.S. teenage women, 1971 and 1976. Fam. Plan. Perspect., 11:177–183, 1979.

7. Zelnick, M. Sexual activity among adolescents. Birth Defects, Original Article Series, 17:19–34, 1981.

8. Vener, A., and Stewart, C. Adolescent sexual behavior in Middle America revisited: 1970–1973. J. Marriage Fam., 36:728–735, 1974.

9. Sorenson, R. Adolescent Sexuality in Contemporary America. New York: World, 1972.

10. Zelnick, M., and Kantner, J. Sexual and contraceptive experience of young, unmarried women in the United States, 1976 and 1971. Fam. Plan. Perspect., 9:55–71, 1977.

11. Klein, L. Antecedents of teenage pregnancy. Clin. Obstet. Gynecol., 21:1151–1159, 1978.

12. Alan Guttmacher Institute Data and Analyses for 1976 Revision of DHEW Five-Year Plan for Family Planning Services. New York, 1976.

13. Paul, E.; Pilpel, H.; and Wechsler, N. Pregnancy, teenagers, and the law. Fam. Plan. Perspect., 8:16, Table 1, 1976.

14. Francome, C. Unwanted pregnancies amongst teenagers. J. Biosoc. Sci., 15:139–143, 1983.

15. Shaffer, D.; Pettigrew, A.; Wolkins, S.; and Zajicek, E. Psychiatric aspects of pregnancy in school girls. Psychological Medicine, 8:118–138, 1978.

16. Zelnick, M., and Kantner, J. Contraceptive patterns and premarital pregnancy among women aged 15–19 in 1976. Fam. Plan. Perspect., 10:135–142, 1978.

17. Zelnick, M., and Kantner, J. Reasons for nonuse of contraception by sexually active women aged 15–19. Fam. Plan. Perspect., 11:289–296, 1979.

18. Namerow, P., and Philliber, S. The effectiveness of contraceptive programs for teenagers. J. of Adolescent Health Care, 2:189–198, 1982.

19. Edwards, L.; Steinman, M.; Arnold, K.; and Hakanson, E. Adolescent contraceptive use: experience in 1,762 teenagers. Am. J. Obstet. Gynecol., 137:583–587, 1980.

20. Urberg, K. A theoretical framework for studying adolescent contraceptive use. Adolescence, 17:527–540, 1982.

21. Gabrielson, I.; Goldsmith, S.; Potts, L.; Matthews, V.; and Gabrielson, M. Adolescent attitudes toward abortion: effects on contraceptive practice. Pub. Health, 6:730, 1971.

22. Flavell, J. The Developmental Psychology of Jean Piaget. Princeton, N.J.: Van Nostrand, 1963.

23. Flavell, J. Cognitive Development. Englewood Cliffs, N.J.: Prentice-Hall, 1977.

24. Cobliner, W.; Schulman, H.; and Romney, S. The termination of adolescent out-

of-wedlock pregnancies and the prospects for their primary prevention. Am. J. Obstet. Gynecol., 115:432–444, 1973.

25. Cobliner, W. Pregnancy in the single adolescent girl: the role of cognitive functions. J. of Youth and Adolescence, 3:17–29, 1974.

26. Oskamp, S.; Mindick, B.; Berger, D.; and Motla, E. Predicting success versus failure in contraceptive planning. Paper presented at the 82nd Annual Convention of the American Psychological Association, New Orleans, 1974.

27. Cvetkovich, G.; Grote, B.; Bjorseth, A.; and Sarkissian, J. On the psychology of adolescents' use of contraceptives. Journal of Sex Research, 11:256–270, 1975.

28. Lindemann, C., and Scott, W. Wanted and unwanted pregnancy in early adolescence: evidence from a clinic population. J. of Early Adolescence, 1:185–193, 1981.

29. Goldsmith, S.; Gabrielson, M.; Gabrielson, I.; Matthews, J.; and Potts, L. Teenagers, sex, and contraception. Fam. Plan. Perspect., 4:32–38, 1972.

30. Tighe, P. The social psychiatry view of female adolescent contraception. In: Zackler, J., and Brandstadt, W., eds., The Teenage Pregnant Girl. Springfield, Ill.: Charles C. Thomas, 1975.

31. Elkind, D. Egocentrism in adolescence. Child Development, 38:1025–1034, 1967.

32. Luker, K. Taking Chances: Abortion and the Decision Not to Contracept. Berkeley: University of California Press, 1975.

33. Barglow, P.; Bornstein, M.; Exum, D.; and Wright, M. Some psychiatric aspects of illegitimate pregnancy in early adolescence. Am. J. Orthopsychiat., 38:672–688, 1968.

34. Earls, F., and Siegel, B. Precocious fathers. Am. J. Orthopsychiat., 50:469–480, 1980.

35. Deutsch, H. The Psychology of Women, Vols. I and II. New York: Grune and Stratton, 1944.

36. Hatcher, S. The adolescent experience of pregnancy and abortion: a developmental analysis. J. of Youth and Adolescence, 2:53–102, 1973.

37. Zelnick, M., and Kantner, J. In: Westoff, I. G., and Parke, R., eds., Demographic and Social Consequences of Population Growth. Washington, D.C.: U.S. Government Printing Office, 1972.

38. Tyler, L., and Josimovich, J. Contraception in teenagers. Clinc. Obstet. Gynecol., 20:651–663, 1977.

39. Ryan, G., and Sweeney, P. Attitudes of adolescents toward pregnancy and contraception. Am. J. Obstet. Gynecol., 137:358–366, 1980.

40. Cohen, J. Intentional teenage pregnancies. J. Sch. Health, 53:210–211, 1983.

41. Ulvedal, S., and Feeg, V. Profile: pregnant teens who choose childbirth. J. Sch. Health, 53:229–233, 1983.

42. Phipps-Yonas, S. Teenage pregnancy and motherhood: a review of the literature. Am. J. Orthopsychiat., 50:403–431, 1980.

43. Schinke, S.; Blythe, B.; and Gilchrist, L. Cognitive behavioral prevention of adolescent pregnancy. J. of Counselling Psychology, 28:451–454, 1981.

44. Blum, R., and Goldhagen, J. Teenage pregnancy in perspective. Clinical Pediatrics, 5:335–340, 1981.

45. Magrab, P., and Danielson-Murphy, J. Adolescent pregnancy: a review. J. of Clin. Child Psych., 8:121–125, 1979.

46. Zelnick, M., and Kantner, J. First pregnancies to women aged 15–19, 1976 and 1971. Fam. Plan. Perspect., 10:11–20, 1978.
47. Fielding, J. Adolescent pregnancy revisited. N. Engl. J. Med., 229–893, 1978.
48. McAnarney, E. Obstetric, neonatal, and psychosocial outcome of pregnant adolescents. Pediatrics, 61:199, 1978.
49. McAnarney, E. Adolescent pregnancy—a national priority. Amer. J. Dis. of Child., 132:125, 1978.
50. Kreipe, R.; Roghmann, K.; and McAnarney, E. Early adolescent childbearing: a changing morbidity? J. of Adolescent Health Care, 2:127–131, 1981.
51. Schaffer, C., and Pine, F. Pregnancy, abortion, and the developmental tasks of adolescence. J. Amer. Acad. Child Psychiat., 11:511–536, 1972.
52. Furstenberg, F. Unplanned Parenthood: The Social Consequences of Teenage Childbearing. New York: Macmillan, 1976.
53. Osofsky, J., and Osofsky, H. Teenage pregnancy: psychosocial considerations. Clin. Obstet. Gynecol., 21:1161–1173, 1978.
54. Copeland, A. The impact of pregnancy on adolescent psychosocial development. Adolescent Psychiatry, 9:244–253, 1981.
55. Blos, P. When and how does adolescence end? Adolescent Psychiatry, 5:5–17, 1977.
56. Lewis, C. A comparison of minors' and adults' pregnancy decisions. Am. J. Orthopsychiat., 50:446–453, 1980.
57. Schneider, S. Helping adolescents deal with pregnancy: a psychiatric approach. Adolescence, 66:285–292, 1982.
58. Bryan-Logan, B., and Dancy, B. Unwed pregnant adolescents. Nurs. Clinics North Am., 9:57, 1974.
59. Patten, M. Self-concept and self-esteem: factors in adolescent pregnancy. Adolescence, 64:765–778, 1981.
60. Protinsky, H.; Sporakowski, M.; and Atkins, P. Identity formation: pregnant and non-pregnant adolescents. Adolescence, 65:73–80, 1982.
61. Olson, L. Social and psychological correlates of pregnancy resolution among women: a review. Am. J. Orthopsychiat., 50:432–445, 1980.
62. Boyce, J., and Benoit, C. Adolescent pregnancy. N.Y. State J. Med., 75:872–874, 1975.
63. Cvejic, H. Follow-up of 50 adolescent girls 2 years after abortion. Canad. Med. Assoc. J., 116:44–46, 1977.
64. Evans, J.; Selstad, G.; and Welcher, W. Teenagers: fertility control behavior and attitudes before and after abortion, childbearing, or negative pregnancy test. Fam. Plan. Perspect., 8:192–200, 1976.
65. Perez-Reyes, M., and Falk, R. Follow-up after therapeutic abortion in early adolescence. Arch. Gen. Psychiat., 28:120–126, 1973.
66. DeAmicis, L.; Klorman, R.; Hess, D.; and McAnarney, E. A comparison of unwed pregnant teenagers and nulligravid sexually active adolescents seeking contraception. Adolescence, 16:11–20, 1981.
67. Bracken, M.; Klerman, L.; and Bracken, M. Abortion, adoption, and motherhood: an empirical study of decision making during pregnancy. Am. J. Obstet. Gynecol., 130:251–262, 1978.
68. Fischman, S. Delivery or adoption in inner-city adolescents. Am. J. Orthopsychiat., 47:121–133, 1977.

69. Freeman, E. Abortion: subjective attitudes and feelings. Fam. Plan. Perspect., 10:150–155, 1978.
70. Kramer, M. Legal abortions among New York City residents: an analysis according to socioeconomic and demographic characteristics. Fam. Plan. Perspect., 7:128–137, 1975.
71. Winnicott, D. Primary maternal preoccupation. In: Collected Papers, Through Pediatrics to Psychoanalysis. London: Tavistock, 1958.
72. Bibring, G. Psychological processes in pregnancy. In: Psychoanalytic Study of the Child, Vol. XIV. New York: International Universities Press, 1959.
73. Barglow, P., and Weinstein, S. Therapeutic abortion during adolescence: psychiatric observations. J. of Youth and Adolescence, 2:331–342, 1973.
74. Bracken, M.; Hackamovitch, M.; and Grossman, G. The decision to abort and psychological sequelae. J. Nerv. Ment. Dis., 158:154–162, 1974.
75. Moseley, D.; Follingstad, D.; Harley, H.; and Heckel, R. Psychological factors that predict reaction to abortion. J. of Clinc. Psych., 37:276–279, 1981.
76. Rooks, J., and Cates, W. Emotional impact of D & E versus instillation. Fam. Plan. Perspect., 9:276–278, 1977.
77. McCormick, E. Attitudes Toward Abortion. Lexington, Mass.: Lexington Books, 1975.
78. Cates, W., and Tietze, C. Standardized mortality rates associated with legal abortion: United States, 1972–1975. Fam. Plan. Perspect., 10:109–112, 1978.
79. Cates, W. Adolescent abortions in the United States. J. of Adolescent Health Care, 1:18–25, 1980.
80. Cates, W. Late effects of induced abortion: hypothesis or knowledge. J. Reprod. Med., 22:207–212, 1979.
81. Russell, J. Sexual activity and its consequences in the teenager. Clin. Obstet. Gynecol., 1:683–698, 1974.
82. Tishler, C. Adolescent suicide attempts following elective abortion: a special case of anniversary reaction. Pediatrics, 68:670–671, 1981.
83. Gabrielson, I.; Klerman, L.; Currie, J.; Tyler, N.; and Jekel, J. Suicide attempts in a population pregnant as teenagers. Am. J. Pub. Health, 60:2289–2301, 1970.
84. Jekel, J. Primary or secondary prevention of adolescent pregnancy? J. Sch. Health, 47:457, 1977.
85. U.S. Department of Health, Education, and Welfare, National Center for Health Statistics. Teenage childbearing: United States 1966–75. Monthly Vital Statistics Report, Natality Statistics, HRA 77–1120, 26, no. 5, Washington, D.C., 1977.
86. Dignan, M., and Anspaugh, D. Permissiveness and premarital sexual activity: behavioral correlates of attitudinal differences. Adolescence, 13:703–711, 1978.
87. Centers for Disease Control. Abortion Surveillance: Annual Summary. Atlanta, 1977.
88. Washington, A. A cultural and historical perspective on pregnancy-related activity among U.S. teenagers. Journal of Black Psychology, 9:1–28, 1982.
89. Ezzard, N.; Cates, W.; Kramer, D.; and Tietze, C. Race-specific patterns of abortion use by American teenagers. Am. J. Pub. Health, 72:809–814, 1982.
90. Tyrer, L. Complications of teenage pregnancy. Clin. Obstet. Gynecol., 21:1135, 1978.
91. Dott, A., and Fort, A. Medical and social factors affecting teenage pregnancy. Am. J. Obstet. Gynecol., 125:532, 1976.

92. Leynes, C. Keep or adopt: a study of factors influencing pregnant adolescents' plans for their babies. Child Psychiat. and Human Devel., 11:105–112, 1980.

93. Hardy, J.; Welcher, D.; Stanley, J.; and Dallas, J. Long-range outcome of adolescent pregnancy. Clin. Obstet. Gynecol., 21:1215, 1978.

94. Moore, K., and Waite, L. Early childbearing and educational attainment. Fam. Plan. Perspect., 9:220–225, 1977.

95. Card, J., and Wise, L. Teenage mothers and teenage fathers: the impact of early childbearing on the parents' personal and professional lives. Fam. Plan. Perspect., 10:199–205, 1978.

96. Trussell, J., and Menken, J. Early childbearing and subsequent fertility. Fam. Plan. Perspect., 10:209, 1978.

97. Klerman, L., and Jekel, J. School-Age Mothers: Problems, Programs, and Policy. Hamden, Conn.: Linnet, 1973.

98. McCarthy, J., and Menken, J. Marriage, remarriage, marital disruption, and age at first birth. Fam. Plan. Perspect., 11:21–30, 1979.

99. Bacon, L. Early motherhood, accelerated role transition and social pathology. Soc. Forces, 52:333–341, March 1974.

100. Moore, K. Teenage childbirth and welfare dependency. Fam. Plan. Perspect., 10:233, 1978.

101. Presser, H. Early motherhood: ignorance or bliss? Fam. Plan. Perspect., 6:8–14, 1974.

102. Kane, F., and Lachenbruch, P. Adolescent pregnancy: a study of aborters and non-aborters. Am. J. Orthopsychiat., 43:796–803, 1973.

103. Falk, R.; Gispert, M.; and Baucom, D. Personality factors related to black teenage pregnancy and abortion. Psychology of Women Q., 5:737–746, 1981.

104. Apprey, M. "I hate light blacks: they are sneaky": a pregnant adolescent's protest at father's anonymity. J. of Psychoanalytic Anthropology, 4:393–412, 1981.

105. Pugh, T.; Jerath, B.; Schmidt, W.; and Reed, R. Rates of mental disease related to childbearing. N. Engl. J. Med., 268:1224, 1963.

106. Schafer, R. Problems in Freud's psychology of women. In: Blum, H., ed., Female Psychology: Contemporary Psychoanalytic Views. New York: International Universities Press, 1977.

Female Sexual Identity: The Impact of the Adolescent Experience

It is generally believed that men suffer more from gender-identity problems and that women suffer more from sexual problems. While it is true that men experience more gender-identity problems, the extent and nature of sexual problems in women are not well documented. The latter (frigidity and anorgasmia) are most frequently believed to result from cultural inhibitions. The corollary belief is that such problems, particularly among young women, have now vanished because of the beneficial and sweeping influence of "sexual liberation."

Yet these popular beliefs are wrong. In discussing consciousness-raising groups during the 1960s, noted novelist and feminist Alix Kates Shulman says, "I was surprised to hear so many women who had come of age in the sixties talk resentfully about their sexual experience, for I had believed the media version of the great sexual revolution among the young. But far from having felt freed by the so-called sexual revolution of the sixties, those young, dedicated women— many of whom had been politicized in the New Left—actually felt victimized by it" (1: p.23). Her observation remains true of young women today.

Orgasmic sex continues to be difficult to achieve for adolescent and young adult women in heterosexual relationships because of sexual and social differences between the sexes that blight heterosexual encounters and because of persisting social conventions that act to inhibit female sexuality. The resulting sexual problems should be attributed not to female hyposexuality or to disordered individual development but to the failure of both sexes to translate the findings of sex researchers into new behaviors that might promote more sexual pleasure in women. Some psychological barrier still exists that precludes the utilization of objective information. It appears that the sexual revolution has promoted sexual activity without addressing those differences between women and men that create problems in realizing sexual pleasure for women, with obvious consequences for sexual self-esteem and sexual identity.

If one assumes that the achievement of orgasmic sexual pleasure is requisite for consolidation of a well-integrated sexual identity, the opposite also obtains—problems in achieving orgasmic sex result in a problematic sexual identity. (This is true of either a heterosexual or a homosexual identity, though the focus in this chapter is on heterosexual identity.) As an example of the necessity of confirming sexual identity by actual sexual experience, consider the frequent fears expressed by college men who have not yet had heterosexual intercourse that they may be homosexual—this despite the absence of any homosexual behavior or fantasies on their part (2). Similarly, lack of experience or sexual problems on the part of young women impedes consolidation of their mature sexual identities.

Insofar as sexual problems derive from common contextual causes (e.g., as a result of socialization) and not from intrapsychic conflicts, the corresponding problems in sexual identity may be considered normative, not neurotic. Most often such problems are normative, not the result of disordered psychosexual development. They frequently surface in the adolescent induction into sex—an experience that is different for females and males. The impact of the adolescent experience continues to exert a profound effect on the subsequent course of sexuality.

I propose here to define sexual identity, describe the path of its normal consolidation in late adolescence, elaborate on the normative problems that interfere with sexual gratification in many young women during adolescence and young adulthood and thereby interfere with the consolidation of sexual identity, and outline the conflictual problems.

SEXUAL IDENTITY AND GENDER IDENTITY

Although it has experiential roots going back to infancy and early childhood, sexual identity becomes patterned only during the Oedipal phase and fully established following puberty, when fantasy and desire can be melded into physical sexuality. However, establishment of sexual identity does not occur automatically on a predetermined timetable and may not be fully consolidated until much later, if ever. The ultimate consolidation of sexual identity rests on the attainment of an actualized sexual life, characterized both by the assumption of a sociosexual role and the achievement of sexual gratification.

Sexual identity is difficult to define precisely, first, because identity itself is such a poorly defined concept. Moreover, the fact that in sex one is both the desiring subject and someone else's desired object makes the definition of sexual identity necessarily complicated and elusive. Whereas both subject and object self-identifications play a role in sexual identity, one or the other facet is often exaggerated, to the impoverishment of the other—the male more often overidentifying as subject, the female as object. In either instance, extreme self-typing as subject or object leads to a marred or incomplete sexual identity. Finally, although sexual identity refers to one's self-definition as a sexual being, it is not a unitary construct. Its two major components are sexual role and "sex print."

Sexual role is most accurately thought of as a sociosexual role assumed by the individual to indicate that she or he is following sexual expectations within a societal or cultural context. Sexual role, as culturally defined, is not insignificant. It may take priority over subjective desire when the two are not congruent.

The "sex print" (3) refers to the experience of desire, sexual arousal, and discharge as well as to the behaviors and fantasies that stimulate them. An individual's sexual horizons are progressively narrowed from infancy and childhood (the stage of polymorphous perverse sexuality) to adulthood, at which time sexuality has most often crystallized out into a definite pattern, the "sex print." The sex print is the mature individual's erotic signature. It conveys more than just preference for a particular sexual object and a particular sexual activity; it also reflects the individualized script that elicits erotic desire. It often includes an individual's strong preference for specific erotic techniques. From the subjective point of view, the sex print is experienced as sexual "preference."

Yet gender identity seems to be more fundamental to personality development than sexual identity. It begins to develop intertwined with the development of a self-identity and is integral to any well-articulated concept of self. Gender identity, the feminine-masculine polarity, reflects a psychological self-image and can loosely be defined as an individual's self-evaluation of psychological femaleness or maleness—the belief that "I am feminine" or "I am masculine" as measured against societal standards of feminine or masculine behavior. It refers to those culturally determined and institutionalized nonsexual attributes, behaviors, and feelings that define femininity and masculinity, including such things as predominant interests, mannerisms, speech, emotional responsiveness, aggressiveness, and countless others. Although its roots are laid down in the first years of life, gender identity continues to develop well into adulthood and, even when established, still fluctuates. It is a dynamic (or functional) self-representation, a measurement of performance, which varies with the motivation and capacity to behave in accordance with the prescribed gender role at any given time.

The development of gender precedes that of sexuality and in large part organizes it (3, 4). Only by learning their gender and identifying with the appropriate parent can children proceed into the Oedipal period. To say that gender orders sexuality is not to detract from the autonomous qualities of sexuality (such as intensity) or from interactions between sexuality and gender. This formulation emphasizes that gender, itself the result of postnatal events, organizes object choice (5) and sexual fantasies, which then become linked to the experience of genital pleasure.

Because sex and gender are developmentally intertwined, any problem in sexuality causes anxiety about the adequacy of gender identity, and likewise, any problems in the consolidation of gender will be reflected in difficulties in establishing a firm sexual identity. More important, the content of femininity and masculinity, as culturally dictated, can shape the expression of sexuality or even inhibit it.

LATE ADOLESCENT YEARS IN DEVELOPMENTAL PERSPECTIVE

One major task is the achievement of both a degree of autonomy and social success (6). However, as pointed out by May (6) and Douvan and Adelson (7), these tasks are emphasized differently by females and males. Females are more committed to achieving interpersonal competence, males to achieving autonomy. According to Douvan and Adelson:

> For the girl development of interpersonal ties—the sensitivities, skills, ethics, and values of object ties—forms the core of identity, and it gives expression to much of developing feminine eroticism. Feminine sexuality, consciously inhibited from active and direct expression, seeks more subtle, limited, and covert expression. (7: p.347)

Though the differences between the sexes noted by Douvan and Adelson were based on interviews conducted with adolescents in the mid-1950s, their observations appear to be true today. The difference now is that many young women are simultaneously committed to achieving autonomy in terms of work, while their dedication to interpersonal competence continues undiminished. The size of their burden is thus doubled.

When their insight is applied to the realm of sexuality, it becomes clear why females overemphasize their role as the desired object rather than the role of desiring subject. "Being chosen" is central not just to the female's sexual identity but to her total gender identity as well.

A second task is the consolidation of a sexual identity and the linkage of sexuality into an intimate relationship. Blos (8) has described the difficulties of achieving a coherent sexual identity and suggests that a somewhat ambiguous sexual identity is the rule rather than the exception prior to adolescence. He postulates both the existence of homosexual conflict in relation to adolescent sexual identity formation as part of normal development and a specific adolescent response to it—the Oedipal defense. Blos makes the important point that "sexual activity per se is no indication of normal adolescent closure and offers no assurance that gender-specific sexual identity has been attained" (8: p.419). He points out that the expression of pre-Oedipal attachments by the adolescent are most often denied or silenced both in life and in treatment by diversionary heterosexual activity.

Consequently, the achievement of an authentically articulated sexual identity may be impeded by too abrupt an assumption of a sexual role. While Blos implicates homosexual conflict and pre-Oedipal attachment as the main motivations in premature sexual activity, these are not the only causes.

The older adolescent, by virtue of separating from the family either symbolically or concretely (e.g., going to college), may experience a revival of separation anxiety as well as dependency yearnings generated by the knowledge that she or he will soon be independent. Late adolescence, then, is often a time of generalized anxiety during which longings for the restitution of security and certainty are paramount. Establishing a sexual relationship is sometimes felt as extremely urgent, not primarily for sexual reasons or simply as a reaction-formation against homosexual or incestual impulses, but for reasons of security, dependent gratification, self-esteem, or vicarious strength in countering assorted insecurities, anxieties, and loneliness.

The enactment of a sociosexual role is often used to confer adult status on the self or to form a dependent relationship and thus may serve to override or defer underlying problems, but it certainly does not ensure that a mature sexual identity has been achieved. On the contrary, the achievement of a secure sexual identity is complicated by sexual activity that is laden with so many nonsexual purposes in addition to those sexual conflicts normally encountered.

For the young woman, the temptation to use sexuality for nonsexual purposes may be even greater because of the common cultural demand already alluded to, that she achieve autonomy by coupling. Young women, in order to confirm gender identity, are so dependent on maintaining relationships that they may enter into sexual relationships prematurely and may be tempted to sacrifice erotic gratification to intimacy. Paradoxically, then, the demand of establishing a coherent feminine gender identity through coupling creates problems in the expression of sexuality for its own sake.

While a number of authors warn against premature sexuality (9, 10), they focus almost exclusively on the dangers of perpetuating unconscious fixations or conflicts, stressing either pre-Oedipal object fixations or an unresolved Oedipal conflict as the limiting factor. For many women, such problems are compounded by a low pleasure yield in their early sexual encounters. Inadequate sexual gratification itself then becomes the starting point for a new set of problems that may disrupt sexuality for the remainder of the life cycle.

NORMATIVE PROBLEMS IN THE CONSOLIDATION OF SEXUAL IDENTITY

For the majority of young women, consolidation of sexual identity is not problematic in any serious sense, that is, in the sense of intrapsychic conflict or individually disordered psychosexual development. Even so, consolidation is difficult because of the difficulty young women encounter in achieving a gratifying interpersonal sexual life (qua sex) and integrating it into the context of a relationship.

The best contemporary evidence shows that adolescent girls, although they engage in more sexual activities, have problems of the same nature and scope (relative to pleasure, not behavior) as those that were present prior to "sexual liberation." Like generations before them, they still have considerable difficulty in realizing gratifying sexual lives. The immediate cause can be attributed to difficulties in achieving orgasms in heterosexual intercourse, still the "prescribed" way of achieving sexual gratification.

Sexual difficulties in young women are easily overlooked because most studies of adolescent sexuality focus on sexual behavior instead of the subjective experiences accompanying the behavior, especially pleasure or lack of it. But although behavior has certainly changed, the same cannot be said of the subjective experience. The few studies on adolescent sexuality clearly indicate changed sexual behaviors in response to the sexual revolution. Sorensen (11) documents that among his population of adolescents ranging in age from 13 to 19 years, 59 percent of the boys and 45 percent of the girls had experienced intercourse. This is in contrast to Kinsey's study (12) in which the incidence of premarital intercourse among girls was only 3 percent until the age of 15 and 20 percent from the age of 16 to 20.

Significantly, however, Sorensen's data on the differential response of females and males to first intercourse, while extremely revealing, is cited less frequently than his statistics on changes in behavior (for an exception, see Kalogerakis [13]). It would seem that psychologists and scientists share the underlying assumptions of the sexual revolution, namely, that what counts is behavior, not subjective experience. In fact, if one examines Sorensen's figures, one sees that 46 percent of the boys and 26 percent of the girls reported they were excited in response to first intercourse. But only 17 percent of the boys, contrasted with an astounding 63 percent of the girls, reported that they were afraid. In general, the percentages of adolescent boys reporting happy, affirmative, self-confident feelings is much higher than that of girls. Conversely, the percentage of girls reporting negative, pessimistic, anxious, and self-doubting feelings about first intercourse is much higher.

CLINICAL EXAMPLES OF SEXUAL PROBLEMS IN YOUNG WOMEN

The following descriptions of sexual life by young women patients may serve to illustrate the continuing problem of low pleasure yield for many women, particularly sexually inexperienced ones, despite their participation in sex and the absence of any serious intrapsychic conflict about sex.

S.R., 24 years old when first seen, gave the following account of her sexual life. Never orgasmic prior to treatment by any route whatsoever, she had nevertheless enthusiastically entered into a series of heterosexual relationships and had extensive experience with intercourse in her late high school and college years. Her aim in life, as she saw it at that time, was to have an affair with a man and ultimately get married. The excitement of new relationships was enough to sexually stimulate her. She invariably romanticized a series of sexual relationships though she had no actual orgasmic release in any of these. It was only later that she came to focus on the fact that she did not have orgasms and began to feel that something was wrong with her. Romance had taken priority over sexuality. Therefore, while S.R. readily adopted an "appropriate" sociocultural role, her sexuality remained undeveloped and undefined.

The fact that anorgasmia is a common experience is reported by Toolan (14: p.261): "There has been a definite pressure on the female not only to be involved sexually, but also to achieve orgasm. Not infrequently the therapist is consulted by young women who are very concerned about their sexual adequacy because they are unable to achieve orgasm with any regularity."

In addition, although there are many young women who can achieve orgasm regularly through masturbation or through manual or oral stimulation in an interpersonal situation, many are nonetheless unable to effect orgasm during coitus. A 20–year-old college junior illustrates this not infrequent pattern:

A.D. had a long masturbatory history and was able to reach climax quite easily. In ongoing sexual relationships she could achieve orgasm either through manual or oral manipulation but was not orgasmic during coitus. She was initially excited by single sexual encounters. Despite her intense arousal, she experienced no physical release because those encounters did not focus on foreplay. Gradually, she began to restrict her sexual life to ongoing relationships in which her partner was educated to her orgasmic requirements.

Among the contemporary generation of young women, sexual behavior, sexual responsiveness, and orgasmic competence are all extremely variable. Some young women have difficulty achieving orgasm and may not even have a history of masturbating (let alone masturbating to orgasm), while some others are readily orgasmic on manual or oral stimulation and a significant minority experience orgasms during coitus. For those who do achieve orgasm during intercourse, it is most often facilitated by specific fantasies, by direct clitoral stimulation simultaneous with intercourse, or by assuming the female-superior position.

L.H. is a 20–year-old gifted art student now involved in a long-term relationship with another artist. She experiences a readiness to feel rejected by him over minor slights. On the surface they have a "good" sexual relationship. However, she feels compelled to have an orgasm first, because if he has one first she assumes that sexual encounter is terminated. She often achieves orgasms when stimulated orally but may be orgasmic during intercourse if in the superior position. She is puzzled by her automatic assumption that the sexual encounter lasts as long as his excitement, but has always felt that way. It is interesting that she never masturbates.
L.H. began having sexual intercourse at the age of 13. In retrospect, it appears "all fucked up" because there was no pleasure for her. The

point of sex, in early adolescence, was to appear grown up and to be in a relationship.

SOME REASONS WHY

How are we to account for these continuing difficulties in young women (and older women) once we observe that the lifting of some cultural inhibitions has not resolved them? Must we revert to traditional psychoanalytic explanations of female "hyposexuality"? These would have us believe that female sexuality is inherently debilitated because of two prerequisites to normal female psychosexual development: the necessity of switching the organ from clitoris to vagina and the necessity of switching the object from mother to father.

The first hypothesis was nullified by the work of Masters and Johnson (15), which demonstrated the central role of the clitoris in female sexuality. Very few now believe that the shift in organ can or ought to take place. The second hypothesis, the necessity of switching the object, would better explain a tendency for homosexual potential among many women than any tendency toward hyposexuality, particularly since homosexual women (those who theoretically did not make the shift from mother to father) are neither more nor less sexual than other women.

Both popular and psychoanalytic assumptions have proved inadequate to explain female sexual problems and so-called female hyposexuality. Sexual problems in women do not seem to result primarily either from strictures implicit in female psychosexual behavior or from cultural inhibition alone.

It seems, instead, that the nature and habit of heterosexual practice, particularly in adolescence, is not geared to ensure orgasm for women. Yet difficulties in realizing sexual pleasure must of necessity diminish sexual self-esteem in women.

Women's sexual problems appear to originate in pronounced sexual and social differences between the sexes, particularly prominent during adolescence. They are further exaggerated by the different priorities incumbent in establishing culturally appropriate "femininity" or "masculinity." The ongoing power of these differences is reflected in the inability of the two sexes to incorporate what they "know" about sex into their actual sexual behavior. Moreover, the revision of cultural attitudes toward sexuality is not as extensive as some assume; the ongoing strictures still act selectively against the expression of sexuality in women.

Divergent Sexualities

The relative lack of female enthusiasm for initial intercourse and for coital experience in general has been misunderstood. Instead of being correctly perceived as stemming from a discrepancy between the typical heterosexual practice (intercourse) and the preferential route of satisfaction of many women (manual or oral), it is commonly ascribed to individual frigidity. Many women defer to what they and their female and male peers regard as sexual "normality" and therefore inadvertently preclude the possibility of sexual pleasure and orgasm. As Campbell (16) puts it, "Women's nostalgia for pre-fucking sex, rather than the unmemorable first fuck, seems to be for the rampant sensuality of those adolescent fumblings and gropings. When the agonized decision about whether to go the'whole way'or not was resolved into 'doing it' the fun seemed to stop." Sexuality that concentrated on foreplay was more pleasurable than normal "grown-up" sex.

While the majority of women most easily have orgasms with manual or oral stimulation, the minority (reported as up to 30 to 40 percent in different studies) achieve orgasm either sporadically or regularly during heterosexual intercourse, but this often depends on assumption of a special position (most often female superior), an obligatory fantasy, or concomitant clitoral stimulation. Therefore, although intercourse is still considered to be the normative sexual encounter for heterosexuals, it is more reliably sexually gratifying for men than for women. This is not to say that women who do not have orgasms during coitus do not like penetration or intercourse; it is to say that intercourse does not seem to provide the surest route to orgasm for the majority of women. These differences in mode of orgasmic discharge are not indications of any differences in maturity and do not reflect the presence or absence of psychological conflict.

Sorensen's tentative interpretation of the different response to intercourse his data revealed was that "boys responded more positively than girls because they clearly felt less anxiety-ridden at the time of first intercourse" (11: p.206). But the difference is not solely attitudinal or conditioned by negative affect. It also derives from the fact that the pleasure component in these early experiences is far less developed in the female than it is in the male. Anxiety is pervasive in both sexes, for reasons of continuing cultural restraints as well as problems inherent in intrapsychic development. But the pleasure component in sexual encounters may be great enough in boys to override feelings of anxiety or guilt. Girls do not necessarily have more anxiety or guilt, but they may not have the same pleasure component in casual encounters that would counteract any accompanying negative affect.

Thus, one might justly reverse Sorensen's (11) hypothesis that boys experience more excitement because they are less anxious. On the contrary, they are less aware of anxiety because erection, ejaculation, and pleasure come so easily in the "prescribed" form of heterosexual encounter.

Divergent Masturbatory Histories

I have emphasized the finding that heterosexual males, whatever their preferential route of orgasmic discharge, can easily come to orgasm through intercourse, whereas this is not true of most heterosexual females. This discrepancy, not generally confronted in either the popular literature or the scientific literature, is compounded by the fact that the two sexes come together sexually in adolescence and young adulthood with different masturbatory histories. The difference in masturbatory practices (almost always more extensive in the male) ensures that males generally have greater sexual experience than females prior to first intercourse.

In males, adolescence is characterized by the beginning of overt sexual activity. The hormonal activity causes body changes that focus attention on emerging sexuality and frequently result in spontaneous arousal and orgasm. Many young adolescent males are troubled by their seemingly perpetual erections. In contrast, spontaneous orgasm is relatively rare in adolescent girls, and although they may be caught up in romantic yearnings, relatively few young girls are perpetually sexually aroused. For most females, menstruation is the key event of adolescence, compared with ejaculation in males. Menstruation may tend to inhibit sexual exploration both for symbolic reasons and because it carries not just the promise but also the threat of pregnancy. It is not surprising, then, that sex is organized differently by the two sexes.

There may be some small shift in recent years toward greater female masturbation, but most studies reflect an ongoing predominance of masturbation in males. Males typically achieve arousal and orgasm earlier. In Kinsey's studies, in males, over 80 percent had masturbated to orgasm by age 15, whereas only 20 percent of females had done so (12, 17). This discrepancy was still apparent in data collected 20 years later (17), according to which masturbation in females is more erratic than it is in males. In females only about two-thirds ever masturbate to orgasm, and of those, half discover masturbation after being introduced to orgasm in an interpersonal context.

Sorensen (11) found 58 percent of boys and 39 percent of girls of all ages had masturbated at least once and that boys masturbated more frequently. Arafat and Cotton (19) conclude, "The percentages of both males and females who masturbate appear to approximate the figures given by Kinsey et al." Hunt (20) suggests that his figures approximate Kinsey's but that there may be a small overall increase. In contrast to coital behavior (age and incidence), in which the sexual difference has tended to disappear, the difference in masturbatory behavior has persisted. Females may eventually demonstrate as much or more sexual interest or drive as males, but for many this is consolidated later and remains tied to relational preoccupations. Thus, while interpersonal sexual patterns have changed, adolescent masturbatory patterns have not.

Because of their relative lack of sexual experience and lack of knowledge about how to achieve orgasm (even through self-stimulation), adolescent girls are often unable to specify to themselves or to their partners what is required sexually. The differences in masturbatory histories make this problem almost inevitable and exaggerate the difficulties in achieving orgasm. Consequently, girls often feel diminished during the sexual encounter because they know less about sex than the male does, and because they do not achieve orgasm as readily. They worry about making themselves appear adequately sexual, internalize responsibility for their failure to achieve orgasm, and fail to insist on sexual pleasure, sometimes out of ignorance, sometimes out of a sense of inadequacy, sometimes out of interpersonal intimidation. One girl said she felt as though she ought to be able to exhibit prowess she did not have. Many young women worry about having an orgasm and about how long it takes. Many believe the male will be insulted if she does not have an orgasm.

Female Deference in Sexual Interaction

Given two major realities—that females generally have less sexual experience than their partners and that the normative heterosexual practice is less gratifying for women than for men—it is obvious that many young women will experience difficulties in incorporating sexual gratification into their sexual relationships. This is intensified by the socialization of women to preserve relationships even by deferential behavior when necessary. Whereas boys are free to seek sexual pleasure per se as a confirmation of gender identity, the girl seeks approbation of her femininity through the formation and perpetuation of a relationship.

It should come as no surprise, then, that adolescent girls caught in the struggle to ensure their autonomy and personal identity may of necessity put sexual gratification at a relatively low level of priority. Confirmation of their gender identity through behaving as a social-sexual person frequently takes priority over the achievement of sexual gratification. Insofar as the adolescent girl experiences sexual anxiety, it is often more a fear of rejection than a fear of sex per se.

Because young women often recognize (or fear) that their need to form relational bonds is greater than that of males, they are sometimes tempted to be submissive in order to secure more permanent relationships. This tendency reveals itself both in the feeling adolescent girls have that they must have sex before they really want to in order to preserve a relationship and, once in bed, in the tendency to sacrifice their needs and pleasure to that of the male. Even among young women who achieve orgasmic competence relatively early, priority is still given to the male's sexuality. This is evident in the widespread assumption that male ejaculation terminates the sexual encounter.

Although intercourse may be used to consolidate sociosexual role and guarantee adult status even when unaccompanied by orgasm, the very lack of orgasmic gratification eventually exacts a price. That price does not stem from "the ravages of repression" but reflects a loss of sexual self-esteem. The feeling that one must be deferential, even to the extent of sacrificing one's own sexuality, subverts subjective feelings of self-esteem, perhaps irrevocably.

A sexual encounter in a relationship can be experienced simultaneously as an interpersonal defeat vis-à-vis the partner, while it confers the feeling of social confidence and social success, fulfillment in the larger social sphere. Sexual identity is sacrificed to gender identity. Thus, there may be ambivalence at the heart of relationships that are formed in order to negotiate gender-role identity and social-sexual role. This is particularly poignant for young women because the conflict takes place at the same time of life when another important developmental task—at odds with so much deference—is to seek a sense of autonomy vocationally and personally.

Inasfar as the male achieves gratification and the female does not, the young woman inevitably begins to resent her subordination to the sexual needs of the male. Any pervasive sense of inadequacy, particularly if compared with the male, conflicts with the phase-specific adolescent need to feel important, independent, and autonomous.

Adolescent girls have devised a number of different strategies to preserve their self-esteem despite the felt need for sexual and relational deference. Some girls overcome the ambivalence in relationships, seeking to normalize deference by initiating relationships with older men in which deference appears to have more to do with age than with gender. Some girls turn the dilemma around, playing the role of little girl as a covert method of manipulation. Others develop a compensatory contempt for the purported social immaturity of boys just as many women maintain a contempt for the purported male insensitivity to emotional nuance.

TOWARD A RESOLUTION

Despite these female-male differences with their inherent problems, particularly prominent during adolescence, some resolution must be sought. Fortunately, there is more dissemination of accurate sexual information among the current generation of young people, more sexual experimentation, and more knowledge among both sexes about the requirements for female orgasm.

Portrayal of noncoital sex, particularly oral sex, has become common in films and television, yet this is still a recent development. The first commercial or general-release film portrayal of sex other than coital sex in the missionary position that I recall was the erotic relationship depicted in the movie *Coming Home* between a young woman (Jane Fonda) and a paraplegic (Jon Voight). The film was transitional in the sense that oral sex was requisite to the plot because coital sex was biologically impossible. Since that film, paraplegia has not remained a requirement for portraying noncoital sex. When intercourse is suggested in films, it is now frequently with the female in the superior position.

If I stress film, it is because this medium is uniquely suited to the wide transmission of information about sexuality and undoubtedly plays a major role in the evolution of new normative practices. In part, the importance of film rests on its intrinsic and immediate emotional and sensual impact. By and large, silence prevails regarding the specifics of sexual encounters in other mediums. The individual continues to talk more about partners and encounters than about orifices, lubrication, strokes, and so forth. Once more, we observe that sexual liberation is extremely selective. Scientifically and personally, we are still under the constraints of prudery to a much greater degree than the rhetoric of sexual liberation would lead us to believe.

Yet greater dissemination of information will not totally resolve the sexual difficulties between women and men because the problems do not derive simply from lack of information. Cultural inhibition of female sexuality still continues, though in less obvious forms. The lower rate of masturbation in women relative to men may in part be a product of different biologies, but it also appears to be a product of strictures still engendered in socialization. That this may well be the case is suggested by the presence of masturbatory freedom in a significant minority of girls, a freedom that seems to be linked to later ease in sexuality. Nonlabeling of female genitals, different conventions for the excretory functions, and other subtle discriminations against acknowledgment of the female body and sexuality may inhibit the female freedom for erotic self-exploration.

Just as there are still inhibitions against female sexuality, the perpetuation of gender role stereotypes also serves to limit sexual pleasure and competence. The persistence of women's sexual deference reveals that sexual liberation is not the same thing as gender-role liberation and that the latter, still unrealized, may have to be achieved first. Both sexes still seem to agree that male sexuality dominates the conduct of heterosexual encounters. This is the assumption that underlies the belief that the sexual encounter is terminated when the male reaches orgasm. Here one must look not just at female deference but also at male complicity. The male reluctance to understand the requirements of female sexuality reflects the desire many men have to believe that when a woman gives pleasure she automatically experiences pleasure. Even so, the inability of both sexes to use what they "know" is a complex and crucial question that remains to be explored.

INTRAPSYCHIC IMPEDIMENTS TO THE CONSOLIDATION OF SEXUAL IDENTITY

Thus far I have focused on normative problems in the consolidation of gender identity. In addition to those factors already discussed, other experiential factors unrelated to deep psychological conflicts may contribute to sexual dysfunction and thereby interfere with consolidation of sexual identity. These include misinformation, painful past experiences, cultural and religious strictures, and aspects of the relationship to the partner (some already alluded to). For young women, fear of pregnancy, anxiety about birth control, and fears of venereal disease (particularly herpes) play a central role. But problems consolidating sexual identity sometimes have their roots in intrapsychic conflict rather than in the context of late adolescent sexual life. It is only because these conflicts are more widely discussed in the mental health literature that I have chosen to emphasize contextual problems.

To reiterate, establishing a sexual identity means to incorporate the sense of oneself as a fully sexual person into one's identity, and it depends upon the successful resolution of the Oedipus complex. The Oedipus complex is normally resolved to some degree during the years before puberty and has an important impact on the child's future character, relationships to others, sexual identity, and sexual patterns favored in later life. The inability to resolve the Oedipus complex may derive from either pre-Oedipal or Oedipal conflict. Pre-Oedipal problems may distort sexual expression and result in distortion of sexual identity. For example, sexual promiscuity or excessive masturbation, while they appear to be of a sexual nature, usually derive from pre-Oedipal conflicts.

Pre-Oedipal conflicts arising before the age of 3 may have profound effects on the course of development and the resolution of Oedipal conflicts. Inhibitions of future sexual development may begin following pre-Oedipal parental intimidation of a child's early assertiveness and undergo intensification during the Oedipal phase of development. If childhood intimidation is severe and persistent, normal resolution of the Oedipus complex may be seriously impaired. Childhood fantasies can remain intrusive and may not recede; sexual impulses may then be experienced as dangerous enough to demand either total renunciation or at least a severe degree of inhibition or distortion of sexual expression.

In general, however, the inability to consolidate a sexual identity in young women is usually based on one of three major dynamics referable to the Oedipal period: the avoidance of identification with a despised mother, competition with the mother and fear of her retaliation, or fear of the paternal or male figure. If, in development, her view of her mother is too demeaned, the girl will form a compensatory identification with her father. Many such women can function extremely well in most feminine activities and may even be completely orgasmic. Yet some of these women seek to avoid sex even though they are orgasmic, not because it is unpleasurable but because it reminds them of their femininity and their underlying identification with a demeaned female. Some women, able to negotiate an active sexual life, nonetheless find themselves threatened if pregnancy and childbirth confirm the dreaded female identification.

More typically, Oedipal conflicts arise when the aims of sexual union are opposed by fears of retaliatory punishment from the rival parent. Conflicts of passivity and activity then develop, as well as a confusion about masculine and feminine identifications. Women have a special problem resolving the Oedipus complex. Because the Oedipal rival of the girl is also the chief supplier of early love and dependency gratification, rivalry with the mother sets up a double jeopardy. The girl is threatened not only with the equivalent of the castration anxiety seen in boys and men but also with the broader fear of losing the rival mother's love and subsequently suffering alienation and separation from her, a depressing and oppressing danger. In my experience, when penis envy emerges as a major inhibitory factor, it is usually in conjunction with one of the dynamics already alluded to. (For a good summary discussion of penis envy, see Chodorow [21].)

If the Oedipus complex is incompletely resolved, one sees either fear of injury from the male or fear of loss of love from the female. Most often, fear of loss of love is manifested by a fear of loss of the male partner. However, the underlying fear usually relates to fear of loss of the mother, a fear that has been transposed to the male figure during development.

In analyses and psychotherapies, these various conflicts are not manifested separately but appear intricately interwoven, as shown by the case below.

Case Example

With most young adult women, problems involving sexual dysfunction and sexual identity emerge in the course of treatment initiated for other reasons. The following case illustrates the complexity of untangling the different conflicts impeding consolidation of a mature sexual identity.

A.W. is an attractive 19–year-old woman who was referred to treatment because of poor school performance that eventually resulted in her dropping out. She is the second child, first daughter, in a professional family. Even though during A.W.'s adolescence her mother was revealed to have a major depressive illness requiring hospitalization and shock therapy, A.W. recalls her childhood as uneventfully happy. She initially reported she received great love and support growing up from her mother, but had a violent relationship with her father, particularly in early adolescence.

As with so many adolescents, the treatment focused for many months on her current situation with peers, not on the family or on her earlier years. Her most immediate problem involved an adjustment to starting school in a new location while most of her friends were elsewhere. She talked about her feelings of loneliness and subjective isolation. She longed desperately to have a boyfriend. Those contacts she did have with young men did not result in any enduring relationships. Occasionally, she would engage in sexual activity but was unwilling to say too much about it. Her self-confidence gradually increased as her performance in school got better and she began to establish a social life, first with girls, then with an extended group of both sexes.

About a year and a half into treatment, she formed a relationship with a young man. It was only in this context, after the relationship had lasted for some three months, that her sexual fears emerged. She became frightened of having intercourse. The simplest explanation for her reluctance to have intercourse seemed to be to ascribe it to the negative association of an earlier abortion and the trauma about the abortion, emotionally and with her family. By this time, however, she had developed the capacity for considerable insight and began to recall that the abortion merely served as a convenient rationalization for a long-standing sexual inhibition.

Although she had extensive sexual experience, it was usually accompanied by great anxiety, and she preferred men of a lower social status than her own. Her choices, rationalized in terms of rebellion from the family background, concealed an attempted restitution to what she regarded as an unequal power relation between the sexes. This feeling was unconscious and unconnected to any feminist ideology, which she abhorred, but it derived from a defensive masculine identification with her father. Sex clearly disrupted that identification.

While unconsciously disliking and fearing her father, she had formed a compensatory identification with him. Underneath her near worship of her mother was a heavily disguised contempt of her mother's submissiveness to her father and inability to protect A.W. from her father's whims. This was accompanied by a growing awareness of her mother's serious psychological disability. Her identification with her father in part represented her flight from an identification with her mother.

A.W.'s many arguments with her father reflected the similarity in their personalities. While identifying with him defensively, she also feared him. Her fear of men was evident in her fears of injury during the sex act and her fears of an erect penis.

Underneath her identification with her father, she still maintained an underlying identification with her mother, whom she perceived to be inadequate and submissive. The low regard in which she held her mother was first revealed in her low regard of other women. But she began to see how she avoided "stereotypic" female behaviors in order to avoid the dreaded identification with her mother. In her behavior she was one of the boys, quite proficient athletically, liking to socialize and drink with them.

Gradually, her sense of rejection by her mother was revealed. She felt that females might abandon her. Not only were they too weak to help her, but she believed that they all preferred men. Her unconscious male identification was in part derived from penis envy and the hope of reconciliation with her mother. Ambivalent relationships with women revealed fear of them. This attitude first emerged in a fantasy she had whenever she first went out with a boy: she feared that when she met his parents the father would accept her but the mother would be extremely disapproving. She became conscious of the fact that she did not trust girls and expected them to betray her. She became aware of her own Oedipal rivalries only after being struck by the overt competition between her aunt and her cousin.

This case illustrates four major dynamics: the experience of maternal rejection and penis envy, fear of identification with a demeaned female image, fear of the rivalrous mother, and fear of a threatening male imago.

SUMMARY

Achievement of sexual gratification in an interpersonal relationship is a precondition for realizing a fully consolidated sexual identity. While sexual identity may be disrupted in young women for reasons stemming from disordered psychosexual development, more often any disruption stems from normative, contextual problems. Orgasmic sex is difficult for women to achieve because of sexual and social differences between the sexes. This is particularly true in adolescence, but the adolescent experience has profound effects on subsequent sexuality. Differences in socialization, in sexual preferences, and in masturbatory histories and female sexual deference pertain to the problems of low pleasure yield for women in "normative" sexual encounters. In addition, neurotic conflicts may impede the consolidation of sexual identity.

ACKNOWLEDGMENTS

The author wishes to thank Dr. Eleanor Schuker and Mrs. Ilene Lefcourt for reading an earlier version and making many valuable corrections.

REFERENCES

1. Shulman, A. K. Sex and power: sexual bases of radical feminism. In: Stimpson, C. R., and Person, E. S., eds., Women—Sex and Sexuality. Chicago: University of Chicago Press, 1980.
2. Coons, F. W. The developmental tasks of the college student. In: Feinstein, S. C.; Giovacchini, P.; and Miller, A. A., eds., Adolescent Psychiatry, Vol. I: Development and Clinical Studies. New York: Basic Books, 1971.
3. Person, E. S. Sexuality as the mainstay of identity: psychoanalytic perspectives. In: Stimpson, C. R., and Person, E. S., eds., Women—Sex and Sexuality. Chicago: University of Chicago Press, 1980.
4. Person, E. S., and Ovesey, L. Psychoanalytic theories of gender identity. J. Am. Acad. Psychoanal., 11(2):203–226, 1983.
5. Baker, S. Biological influences on human sex and gender. In: Stimpson, C. R., and Person, E. S., eds., Women—Sex and Sexuality. Chicago: University of Chicago Press, 1981.
6. May, R. Sex and Fantasy: Patterns of Male and Female Development. New York: W. W. Norton, 1980.
7. Douvan, E., and Adelson, J. The Adolescent Experience. New York: John Wiley and Sons, 1960.
8. Blos, P. The Adolescent Passage: Developmental Issues. New York: International Universities Press, 1979.
9. Klebanow, S. Developmental readiness and dependency in adolescent sexuality. In: Adelson, E. T., ed., Sexuality and Psychoanalysis. New York: Brunner/Mazel, 1975.
10. Kestenbaum, C. J. Some effects of the "sexual revolution" on the mid-adolescent girl. In: Adelson, E. T., ed., Sexuality and Psychoanalysis. New York: Brunner/Mazel, 1975.
11. Sorensen, R. C. Adolescent Sexuality in Contemporary America. New York: World, 1973.
12. Kinsey, A. C.; Pomeroy, W. R.; Martin, C. E.; and Gebhard, P. H. Sexual Behavior in the Human Female. Philadelphia: W. B. Saunders, 1953.

13. Kalogerakis, M. G. The effect on ego development of sexual experience in early adolescence. In: Adelson, E. T., ed., Sexuality and Psychoanalysis. New York: Brunner/Mazel, 1975.

14. Toolan, J. Sexual behavior in high school and college students. In: Adelson, E. T., ed., Sexuality and Psychoanalysis. New York: Brunner/Mazel, 1975.

15. Masters, W. H., and Johnson, V. E. Human Sexual Response. Boston: Little, Brown, 1966.

16. Campbell, B. A feminist sexual politics: now you see it, now you don't. In: Feminist Review No. 5. London, England, 1980.

17. Kinsey, A. C.; Pomeroy, W. B.; and Martin, C. E. Sexual Behavior in the Human Male. Philadelphia: W.B. Saunders, 1948.

18. Gagnon, J. H., and Simon, W. Sexual Conduct: Social Sources of Human Sexuality. Chicago: Aldine, 1973.

19. Arafat, I. S., and Cotton, W. L. Masturbation practices of college males and females. In: DeMartino, M. F., ed., Human Autoerotic Practices. New York: Human Sciences Press, 1979.

20. Hunt, M. Changes in masturbatory attitudes and behavior. In: DeMartino, M. F., ed., Human Autoerotic Practices. New York: Human Sciences Press, 1979.

21. Chodorow, N. The Reproduction of Mothering. Berkeley and Los Angeles: University of California Press, 1978.

New Sex Codes in Adolescence

For therapists treating adolescents and postadolescents today, the traditional approaches to sexuality no longer serve as reliable guides. Recently accumulated data about sexual attitudes and conduct have fewer unassailable reference points within existing psychosexual development schedules. The concept of orderly developmental sequences leading to a coming-of-age sexually and to clear-cut sexually differentiated patterns of masculine and feminine behavior are now being critically questioned. In a society of rapidly and radically changing sexual mores, sexual practices once considered aberrant have now become condign. The various sociological and interpersonal events, in addition to the internal ones that inform sexual communication, tend to impart an idiosyncratic quality to sexual behavior that vitiates practical application of a concept of normal behavior.

Of the many sociosexual changes that have occurred in the past few decades, several facts are readily discernible: biological maturation has been occurring at increasingly earlier ages, the age of first intercourse has been getting increasingly lower, increasing numbers of adolescents are engaging in sexual intercourse, and approximately equal numbers of males and females are having coitus. This latter is in marked contrast to former statistics for rates of intercourse which have been consistently two to three times greater for males than females. The occurrence of sexual intercourse at an earlier age by equal numbers of males and females parallels the larger changes in sex-role behavior and affects sexual-identity concepts. With the loss of socially sanctioned ways of behaving sexually, with the erosion of so many sexual taboos, and with the loss of the "meaning" of certain sexual behaviors, today's adolescent has an added obstacle in the normally difficult task of evolving a coherent outlook both in terms of actual sexual behavior and male and female gender-role behavior.

In line with the foregoing depiction of "yesterday's" sexual behavior and ideology as obsolescent, this chapter highlights the changes in adolescent patterns of sexuality. It reviews a series of studies pointing up changes in both sexual attitudes and sexual conduct over the past several decades and discusses the challenge these newly emerging patterns present to commonly accepted notions of adolescent sexual activity and to previously held beliefs of predictable and stable sexually differentiated male-female behaviors. The conclusion addresses the need for therapists to confront the confusions and anxieties engendered by the erosion of standards of sexual conduct and by the lack of clear-cut expectable sexually differentiated male and female patterns of behavior in light of the ongoing emergence of nongender-coded behaviors.

STUDIES ON SEXUAL ACTIVITY

Although sex has been a perpetual source of conflict permeating all reaches of inner and outer life, it did not receive scientific attention until the turn of the century. With the emergence of sexual theoreticians, thinking about sex became "explicit and systematic," marking the beginning (according to historian Paul Robinson) of the birth of sexual modernism, with Freud as its most prominent proponent. The early sexual investigators concentrated on sexual conduct per se and less on the related concepts of gender role and identity, and like Freud they accepted the prevailing view that men and women differed greatly in their sexuality. Experimental psychologists after Freud considered sex differences as polar opposites up until Kinsey's time. Kinsey, with his more systematic approaches, sought to measure behavior objectively rather than by inference, as his predecessors had. He sidestepped the meaning of the differences in behavior by defining sexual behavior in operational terms, thereby confining his study of sex to more objective measurement. In the decades since Kinsey's time there has been a return to concentration on sex differences in behavior and on the sexual attributes of masculinity and femininity that differentiate the sexes and define the core of masculine and feminine personalities. A major concern of sex researchers has been with those processes by which individuals come to correspond in their behavior to the expected male-female patterns of their cultural group and with those factors that facilitate or interfere with adopting ostensibly appropriate patterns of behavior. Complicating today's research is the expanding repertoire of behaviors that are not gender coded and that are a source of confusion for adolescents and investigators alike (1–12).

Much of the challenge to traditional assumptions regarding adolescent patterns of sexual behavior has come from surveys that employ a sociocultural perspective. These surveys vary in methodological sophistication and comparability. Researchers concentrating on sexual activity, specifically rates of premarital intercourse, used survey data mainly from college-student populations. Varying statistics were published on a wide range of population sizes (100 to 1,000) in five surveys from 1929 to 1947 prior to publication of the landmark Kinsey report. These surveys reported figures roughly in agreement with one another showing that approximately twice as many males as females had engaged in premarital intercourse (13–17). In 1948 Kinsey reported on 5,300 college-level male subjects, finding that 49 percent had engaged in premarital intercourse (18). His 1953 study of college-level females found a range of 20 to 27 percent among 3,000 subjects (19).

Subsequent studies have shown that since the mid-1960s there has been a marked increase in the trend toward sexual liberalism that began in the 1950s (20–25). Between 1967 and 1974, premarital intercourse rates for white female senior high school and college students rose by 300 percent and for comparable males by 50 percent (26). Today approximately equal numbers of adolescent males and females are having coitus, in contrast to former statistics showing two to three times greater activity for males than for females. For this generation, there is hardly any practical distinction in behavior between males and females (27).

STUDIES ON SEXUAL ATTITUDES

The progression of sexual surveys in roughly ten-year increments, culminating in the Kinsey reports, helped promote a climate that encouraged more open discussion of sexual behavior and ultimately more intensive study. Research gradually shifted from a focus on sexual activity alone toward a broader range of sexual behavior which included the study of sexual attitudes.

Pronounced double standards of premarital intercourse were found in various studies from the 1930s to the 1960s. In the mid-1950s Landis (28) found that a majority of college students on 11 campuses nationwide believed sexual abstinence to be the proper premarital standard. By the end of the 1950s, change began to be apparent. A 1959 survey of high school and college students in five New York and Virginia institutions by Reiss (22) found that although the majority still disapproved, a considerably larger percentage endorsed premarital intercourse if it was accompanied by love or engagement. Christensen and Gregg's sample of students in a midwestern university in 1959 and again a decade later found a marked increase in "qualified permissiveness" (24). In subsequent studies among college-age individuals in the 1960s, Reiss found further evidence that, within the context of a love relationship, "permissiveness with affection" was acceptable to a broad range of college-educated people (29, 30).

In all these studies, males were consistently more approving than females. In the early 1970s, however, Hunt (32) found extensive changes from earlier studies and a greatly increased acceptance of the idea of premarital intercourse for women as well as men in situations of emotional commitment. If the relationship was one of love, 90 percent of young females said that coitus was acceptable for women. DeLamater and MacCorquodale (33), in their 1979 study of 963 college students at the University of Wisconsin and 511 noncollege students of comparable age in the local town, found that the double standard, in the strict sense of accepting premarital coitus for men but not for women, had virtually disappeared. The ideologies of males and females were essentially the same—that is, standards did not differ as a function of gender.

In addition to the large number of studies on sexual activity and attitudes, there have been several studies on cohabitation among college students. By 1975 it was estimated that roughly 25 percent of undergraduates across the United States were living or had lived in a cohabitation relationship, and only another 25 percent were said to oppose the arrangement. The majority of students who accepted cohabitation did so in the context of an affectionate and preferably monogamous relationship, with male students said to be more accepting than females and with women who approved of cohabitation more likely than their peers to characterize themselves as independent, outgoing, and aggressive (34).

OVERVIEW AND ANALYSIS

Sifting out cause and effect in any sociosexual arena is an almost impossible task. The trend toward greater equality between the sexes both was stimulated by and itself stimulated clinical research in comparability between the sexes. Without question, the sexual revolution and the women's and gay liberation movements have been instrumental in bringing into question some basic tenets of established theory and practice. Many aspects of sexual behavior formerly considered deviant have become the norm, with premarital intercourse for young people of both sexes and extramarital joint living arrangements almost commonplace. These changes have coincided with the growth of equality in sex roles, employment for women, and postponed marriage and family.

Until recently there has been an assumed interrelationship of biological gender, masculine and feminine sex-role behaviors, and psychological attributes of masculinity and femininity. The implicit assumption of a tie between masculine-feminine characteristics and sex-role identity, the view that had dominated behavior research literature, was brought under sharp scrutiny by the feminist movement's vigorous attack on discriminatory social institutions. This, coupled with the growing awareness of novel clinical findings, forced investigators to question and reappraise such premises. The new trend in thinking about the psychological dimensions of masculinity and femininity has rapidly become one of distinguishing these from sex roles. Now masculine and feminine attributes are considered not as bipolar opposites but as separate and essentially "orthogonal" dimensions within each sex, only "weakly related to the broad spectrum of sex role behavior" (35).

A number of impressionistic reports, again on college students, attest to the quality of openness between sexual partners, to an increased sense of mutual responsibility for the relationship, and to a more serious and determined exploration of ways to establish a firmer sexual identity within its confines. Female students are making more demands for affection and caring—but not commitment—that are nonsexual and are at the same time more overt in their expression of sexual enjoyment. Male students seem more free to explore their nonsexual and affectionate feelings.

The changes in sexually differentiated behavior that have occurred in the past 100 years, most notably in the past 10 to 15 years, have made for sex-role broadening, permissiveness for women, participation of women in the labor force, and alterations in traditional conceptions of marriage and family. Such diverse phenomena as vocational interests, interpersonal reactions, and personality characteristics cannot always be readily differentiated sexually. Even though significant correlations are still to be found and psychological implications of masculine and feminine remain crucial to particular sexual feelings and behavior, a blurring of distinctions between the sexes is rapidly becoming evident and may presage much greater neutralization of gender-related phenomena in the future.

Current research interest focuses on the gender similarities in sexual conduct as well as on the relationship between differences and similarities, the way they develop and are maintained, and their degree of reversibility in both individuals and culture. As the public perception of the content of gender-role differences and sexual behavior continues to change, through both politicization and scientific investigation, it is becoming apparent that the interrelatedness of gender role and sexual behavior may be more a result of historical and cultural conditioning than biological conditioning and that some long-cherished assumptions about gender role are no longer tenable. As more information on sexual behavior is accumulated, the deterministic Freudian view of rigidly unfolding stages loses credibility; the notion of discrete and sequential stages of development determining gender role and sexual behavior is no longer a wholly viable construct. Assigning more-or-less specific ages to each developmental stage does not take into account either the impact of changing social phenomena or individual differences in the rate of growth and development. As the ages of sexual maturation, awareness, and experimentation are progressively lowered, increasing numbers of adolescents engage in sexual intercourse (by 1973 some 25 percent of white males and females had had intercourse by the age of 16 [36]). With accelerated biological maturation and social advance, the interchange between inner and outer experience is altered. In a condensed timetable, internalizing the new social reality becomes a formidable task for adolescents. The asynchrony of levels of biological, psychological, and social development imposes demands on the adolescent's adaptive capacities. With a foreshortened opportunity for cognitive development, reality appraisals are too often narrowed to the immediate present, with the result that the adolescent fails to give proper consideration to the long-range effects of his or her sexual behavior. Such shortsightedness has had negative consequences well-known to the population at large in undesired pregnancy, repeated abortion, and an increase in venereal disease.

In a number of studies between 1968 and 1974, only about 50 percent of sexually active college-age women were found to use contraceptives consistently, and figures for those aged 19 or younger were 20 percent (37). Close to 50 percent of sexually active young females depended on male methods of contraception; a majority of adolescent males were held to be markedly unconcerned about contraceptive use (38). Several studies dealing with cognitive development stress the young adolescent's limited ability to conceptualize the effects of present sexual behavior on the future and point up the adolescent's unwillingness to allow any interference with spontaneity (39–42). Knowledge about the relationship between the physiology of reproduction and contraception was found to be minimal if not wholly nonexistent (43). Although adolescents understood the principles of ovulation, they neither incorporated this knowledge nor used it to further awareness or acceptance of the practical implications of intercourse (44, 45).

As for emotional development, vitiated parental authority over the adolescent results in premature autonomy, a spurious sense of independence. This in turn leads to a distorted expectation of help from the sexual partner in affirming identity, an expectation of either too much or too little help, which cannot benefit the relationship. Then too the clash between the expectations of parents and those of peers is accentuated as the adolescent becomes increasingly aware of the social world and of current sexual mores to which parents are generally less attuned. Thus, given the foreshortened sexual maturation and the lack of a corresponding cognitive and emotional advance, outside influences take on particular significance.

As the ever-changing environment imparts a disconnected quality to sexual behavior at both the individual level and the societal level, adolescents have to form new cognitive assessments of a world in which the past has lost its relevance for future behavior and in which male and female patterns of sexual behavior have become increasingly similar. By taking into account the many environmental influences, the perspective of the "new learning theory" avoids sex-role stereotyping, thereby allowing for greater equality in sexual behavior. It also allows for flexibility in adaptation during different phases of development by assuming direct responsiveness of individuals to their immediate environments. Sexual behavior and identity will therefore reflect environments that may differ from one stage to another, over and above any intrapsychic changes.

Adolescents' sexual attitudes are acquired from a number of sources—parents, peers, dating partners, religious institutions, and so forth. It can be a considerable source of anxiety for many, perhaps most, adolescents that each of these sources holds a belief system about what is appropriate behavior which may conflict with the others. Researchers have found that the degree of guilt adolescents feel about their sexual behavior is associated by and large with the attitudes of their peer group. While peer group influence is generally of great consequence for adolescents, who almost invariably seek to conform to the male-female patterns of their particular youth culture, the new code of individuality makes simple conformity impossible. In addition, with parents dismissed as being out of touch and increasing numbers of postadolescents caught up in the sexual confusions of freedom, adolescents have fewer adults to look to as role models. From their perception of current events, adolescents seem to have adopted the idea that sexual behavior, as long as it hurts no one, is more a matter of personal choice than of morality; the sexual ethic is thus more situation-specific than society-wide.

One of the most comprehensive and carefully designed studies on premarital sexuality in college-age individuals is that of DeLamater and MacCorquodale (33). Based on an integration of the best previous research in the field, this study set up an explicit theory of what the authors considered constituted the basis for management and control of sexuality outside marriage, and then tested that theory on a stratified random sample of 432 male and 431 female university undergraduates and an age-matched sample of nonstudent residents of the community. Combining a sociological approach, which related sexuality to social institutions, with a sociopsychological one, which emphasized interpersonal and individual sources of sexual behavior, they constructed their model of the determinants of current sexuality. This model encompassed a developmental perspective as well as influences in the immediate social environment and identified six classes of variables: three sources of social influence or socializing agents (peers, partners, and parents); two sets of individual characteristics (previous sexual experience and sociopsychological characteristics, e.g., body image, self-esteem, gender-role orientation, internal and external controls); and current sexuality, which had two components, sexual activity and attitudes or standards (ideology). This exploration of the complex interconnecting links among sexual ideology, emotional intimacy of the relationship, lifetime sexual experience, sociopsychological characteristics, and peer standards and behavior showed four major determinants of current sexuality: sexual ideology, emotional intensity of the relationship, peer standards, and peer behavior. The study also showed that differences in sexual behavior associated with education were declining and that no strongly consistent relationship existed between an individual's social class and religion, and his or her sexual ideology. This report points up the importance of the immediate environment on premarital sexual behavior, particularly its influence on the nature of the dyadic relationship.

CONCLUSION

The need for clarity in regard to sexual behavior and sex differences is most acute during adolescence. Sexual self-differentiation at that stage is often accompanied by idealized versions of maleness and femaleness that allows for little if any deviation from those ideals. For the adolescent, there can be many and great misguided assumptions about the inevitability and sanctity of certain sex differences or absences of difference. Compounding adolescent confusion and uncertainty over gender and sex role are potential negative consequences of early sexual activity. Aside from the physical manifestations mentioned earlier—undesired pregnancy, repeated abortion, increased venereal disease rates—are such less readily discernible effects as conflict with and estrangement from parents, lack of sexual enjoyment, a sense of pressure to keep up with peers, and sexual dysfunction. All these contribute to a widening gap between the culturally prescribed joy of sex and the burdensome reality.

Without agreed-on societal standards and with an undercurrent of social ideology which decrees that most forms of censorship are deleterious to individual growth, the issue of which freedoms and which limits improve the quality of sexual life continues unresolved if not chaotic. The data from a multitude of sex surveys, all in basic accord about changing attitudes, standards, values, and actual behaviors, the choice of diverse theoretical constructions, and the adolescent's need for clarity and consistency in order to organize perceptions and beliefs and to structure his or her psychic universe—taken together, these create extraordinary problems for therapists who work with patients in an age-range especially vulnerable to changing mores. Feeling their way, therapists need to address the new "pluralism" in sexual choice and the replacement of the "Protestant ethic" by the "situational ethic," along with the many other novel sexual experiments possible in a society in transition (46).

The new sexual morality advocating pluralistic choice and freedom has not automatically led to increased satisfaction in the realm of sexual enjoyment (47). If anything, it has created new problems for the many young people who are barely equipped with the degree of self-determination required to deal with the major value conflicts to which they are exposed. The therapeutic process, intrinsically a method of examining and learning to deal with facts, feelings, and prejudices while maintaining critical judgment, is as good a means as any to help disentangle the confusion and conflict generated by "liberation."

REFERENCES

1. Gagnon, J., and Simon, W. Prospects for change in American sexual patterns. Medical Aspects of Human Sexuality, 4:100–117, January 1970.
2. Reiss, I. How and why America's sex standards are changing. Transaction, 5:26–32, 1968.
3. Sorensen, R. Adolescent Sexuality in Contemporary America. New York: World, 1973.
4. Zubin, J., and Money, J., eds. Contemporary Sexual Behavior: Critical Issues in the 1970's. Baltimore: Johns Hopkins University Press, 1973.
5. Edwards, J. N., ed. Sex and Society—An Overview: The Sociocultural Perspective and Sex Research. Chicago: Markham Publishing Co., 1972.
6. Hunt, M. Sexual Behavior in the 1970's. Chicago: Playboy Press, 1974.
7. Packard, V. The Sexual Wilderness. New York: David McKay Co., 1968.
8. Yankilovich, D. The New Morality: A Profile of American Youth in the 1970's. New York: McGraw-Hill, 1974.
9. Bell, R. and Gordon, M. The Social Dimension of Human Sexuality. Boston: Little, Brown, 1972.
10. Katchadurian, H., and Lunde, D. Fundamentals of Human Sexuality, 2nd edition. New York: Holt, Rinehart and Winston, 1975.
11. Robinson, P. The Modernization of Sex. New York: Harper and Row, 1976.

12. Spence, J. T., and Helmreich, R. L. Masculinity and Femininity: Their Psychological Dimensions. Austin: University of Texas Press, 1978.
13. Hamilton, C. V. A Research in Marriage. New York: Albert and Charles Boni, 1929.
14. Bromley, D., and Britten, F. Youth and Sex. New York: Harper, 1938.
15. Terman, L. M. Psychological Factors in Marital Happiness. New York: McGraw-Hill, 1938.
16. Porterfield, A., and Ellison, S. Current folkways of sexual behavior. American Journal of Sociology, 52:209–216, 1946.
17. Finger, F. Sex beliefs and practices among male college students. Journal of Abnormal and Social Psychology, 42:57–67, 1947.
18. Kinsey, A. C.; Pomeroy, W.; and Martin, C. E. Sexual Behavior in the Human Male. Philadelphia: W. B. Saunders, 1948.
19. Kinsey, A. C.; Pomeroy, W.; Martin, C. E.; and Gebhard, P. H. Sexual Behavior in the Human Female. Philadelphia: W. B. Saunders, 1953.
20. Burgess, E., and Wallin, P. Engagement and Marriage. New York: J. B. Lippincott Co., 1953.
21. Ehrmann, W. Premarital Dating Behavior. New York: Holt, Rinehart, and Winston, 1959.
22. Reiss, I. Premarital Sexual Standards in America. Glencoe, Ill.: Free Press, 1960.
23. Bell, R., and Chaskes, J. Premarital sexual experience among coeds, 1958–1968. Journal of Marriage and the Family, 32:81–84, February 1970.
24. Christensen, H., and Gregg, C. Changing sex norms in America and Scandinavia. Journal of Marriage and the Family, 32:616–627, November 1970.
25. Robinson, I.; King, K.; and Balswick, J. The premarital sexual revolution among college females. Family Coordinator, 21:189–194, April 2, 1972.
26. Chilman, C. S. Adolescent Sexuality in a Changing American Society. National Institute of Health Publication No. 80:1426. Washington, D.C.: U.S. Department of Health, Education, and Welfare, January 1980.
27. What's really happening on campus. Playboy, 23:166–169, October 1976.
28. Landis, J., and Landis, M. Building a Successful Marriage. New York: Prentice-Hall, 1953.
29. Reiss, I. The Social Context of Sexual Permissiveness. New York: Holt, Rinehart, and Winston, 1967.
30. Reiss, I. How and why America's sex standards are changing. Transaction, 5:26–32, 1968.
31. Croake, J., and James, B. A four-year comparison of premarital sexual attitudes. Journal of Sex Research, 9:91–96, 1973.
32. Hunt, M. Sexual Behavior in the 1970's. Chicago: Playboy Press, 1974.
33. DeLamater, J., and MacCorquodale, P. Premarital Sexuality. Madison: University of Wisconsin Press, 1979.
34. Chilman, C. S. Adolescent Sexuality in a Changing American Society. National Institute of Mental Health Publication No. 80:1426. Washington, D.C.: U.S. Department of Health, Education, and Welfare, January 1980.
35. Spence, J. T., and Helmreich, R. L. Masculinity and Femininity: Their Psychological Dimensions, Correlates, and Antecedents. Austin: University of Texas Press, 1978.
36. Vener, A., and Stewart, C. Adolescent sexual behavior in middle America revisited, 1970–73. Journal of Marriage and the Family, 36:728–735, November 1974.

37. Kantor, J., and Zelnick, M. Sexual experiences of young unmarried women in the United States. Family Planning Perspectives, 4:14–17, October 1972.

38. Fujita, B.; Wagner, N.; and Pion, R. Contraceptive use among single college students: a preliminary report. American Journal of Obstetrics and Gynecology, 109:787–793, March 1971.

39. Bauman, K., and Wilson, R. Sexual behaviors of unmarried university students in 1968 and 1972. Journal of Sex Research, 10:327–333, November 1974.

40. Sittlage, D.; Baroff, S.; and Cooper, D. Sexual experience of younger teenage girls seeking contraceptive assistance for the first time. Family Planning Perspectives, 5:233, 1973.

41. Finkel, M., and Finkel, D. Sexual and contraceptive knowledge, attitudes, and behaviors of male adolescents. Family Planning Perspectives, 256–260, November/December 1975.

42. Cobliner, G. W. Pregnancy in the single adolescent girl: the role of cognitive function. Journal of Youth and Adolescence, 3(1):17–29, 1974.

43. Cvelkovich, G. On the psychology of adolescents' use of contraception. Journal of Sex Research, 11:256–270, August 1975.

44. Miller, W. Relation between the intendedness of conception and the wantedness of pregnancy. Journal of Nervous and Mental Diseases, 59:396–406, December 1974.

45. Minsour, K., and Stewart, B. Abortion and sexual behavior in college women. American Journal of Orthopsychiatry, 43:804, October 1973.

46. Rubin, I. Transition in sex values. Journal of Marriage and the Family, 27:185–189, May 1965.

47. Comfort, A. Directiveness in psychotherapy and the sexual revolution. Psychiatry, 44(4), November 1981.

PART TWO

GENDER-ROLE IDENTITY AND PSYCHOPATHOLOGY

Extreme Boyhood Femininity: Overview and New Research Findings

The past decade has witnessed a marked increase of interest in behaviorally feminine boys, that is, boys who display cross-gender behavior, fantasies, and preferences. This interest has been stimulated in part by the findings of Money, Ehrhardt, and the Hampsons (1–3) that sex of assignment during the first three years of life is the critical determinant of gender identity, instead of chromosomes or hormones. They found that in hermaphrodites, when biological sex was incorrectly diagnosed at birth and later reversed due to a subsequent correct identification of the biological sex, the sex of assignment could be switched without untoward effects within the first 18 months to three years of life. In cases where it was discovered later and sex was reassigned, children were often subsequently gender confused and behaviorally and emotionally disturbed. This pointed to the first three years of life as a critical period for the development of gender identity.

One important strategy for exploring the roots of early gender-identity formation which has grown out of this work has been to identify and study very young children who display atypical gender-identity development. One such group has been the behaviorally feminine boy, who can develop this syndrome as early as the first two years of life (4–7). Studying very young children and their psychological environment provides a unique opportunity to explore factors that contribute both to the formation of normal gender identity and to atypical gender identity. Another factor that has contributed to a burgeoning of interest in the behaviorally feminine boy has been the report that adult male transsexuals, transvestites, and homosexuals often recall a childhood history of cross-gender behavior (6–9).

This chapter will selectively review major results of research on boyhood

Research for this chapter was supported by Bio-medical Research Support Grant No. 1–So7–RR05840 from the National Institute of Health.

femininity and some recent findings from the Childhood Gender Identity Project at Roosevelt Hospital in New York City (5). It will include an update of findings on the behavior of feminine boys, the age of onset, and long-range follow-up. The last half of the chapter will evaluate existing etiological theories by reviewing studies of psychopathology in feminine boys and emerging findings on the family matrix.

The Childhood Gender Identity Project is a unit within the Division of Child and Adolescent Psychiatry at Roosevelt Hospital, a voluntary hospital in New York City. This unit has focused its attention on establishing a psychological profile of the feminine boy, exploring the family matrix in which boyhood femininity arises, and treating gender-confused children and their families. Data reported in this chapter was gathered by two senior psychologists, six predoctoral candidates in clinical psychology, and one fellow in child psychiatry, all under the supervision of Dr. Susan Coates. Children evaluated in the Childhood Gender Identity Project are seen for six to seven sessions, during which they receive clinical interviews, are observed during play sessions, and receive extensive psychological testing. Mothers (and fathers when available) were interviewed to attain an extensive developmental history of the child which focused on perinatal history, early temperament, separation experiences, behavior problems, and medical history. In addition, parents were interviewed to obtain a detailed history of the family matrix during the child's early years of life.

EXTREME BOYHOOD FEMININITY: AN OVERVIEW

The *DSM*-III (10) criteria for gender-identity disorder of childhood for boys are as follows:

A. Strongly and persistently stated desire to be a girl, or insistence that he is a girl
B. Either 1 or 2
    1. Persistent repudiation of male anatomic structures as manifested by at least one of the following assertions:
        a. That he will grow up to become a woman (not merely in role)
        b. That his penis or testes are disgusting or will disappear
        c. That it would be better not to have a penis or testes
    2. Preoccupation with female stereotypical activities as manifested by a preference for either cross-dressing or simulating female attire, or by a compelling desire to participate in the games and pastimes of girls
C. Onset of disturbance before puberty

Results reported here from the Roosevelt unit are based on the first 25 boys who were extensively evaluated. All 25 boys received a *DSM*-III diagnosis of gender identity disorder of childhood. One-hundred percent expressed the wish to be a girl, 100 percent displayed female behavior, and 50 percent expressed dislike of their male anatomy (5).

Boys referred to gender-identity units usually display some or all of the following behavior: (a) express a wish to be a girl or wish to grow up to be a girl; (b) have an intense interest in cross-dressing in female clothes; (c) have an intense interest in female stereotypical activities such as playing with dolls, playing house, or playacting the role of mother; (d) display a preference for female peers; (e) display female mannerisms; (f) avoid rough-and-tumble play; and/or (g) express a dislike for their penises (11–13, 6, 14–17). Cross-gender behavior in boys has a consistency that appears to be quite compulsive and has been described by Zucker et al. (17) as rigid and inflexible. These boys do not show the range of interests that normal boys typically display. The results of a normative study of cross-gender behavior in boys have led Zucker et al. to conclude that "frequent cross-gender behavior is never a normal phase of development" (18).

Patterns of behavior similar to those described above were displayed by boys referred to the Roosevelt Hospital Childhood Gender Identity Project. Mothers' descriptions of their sons often took the following form:

He always loved my scarves, high-heeled shoes, dresses, jewelry, and cosmetics. He would put them on and spend hours primping, posing, and dancing in front of the mirror.

He always preferred Barbie dolls to Ken dolls and liked to play house and jump rope with girls in the neighborhood.

He liked to watch me put my makeup on in the morning and would pick out my clothes for me to wear if I would let him.

Boys who present with extreme cross-gender behavior have an ambiguous gender identification that includes elements of masculinity and femininity. In their behavior and in their fantasy play they present with hyperfeminine stereotypical preoccupations. However, both in behavior and in fantasy they are easily distinguished from girls because their behavior shows the rigidity described previously and their feminine preoccupations are caricatures of female interests and mannerisms. Despite the intensity of their feminine preoccupations, they are invariably aware that they are biologically male. In many boys, one sees evidence of female preoccupations only. In some, masculine interests such as playing with cars are evident, even though their overriding interests are typically female.

In the playroom, cross-gender boys typically prefer to play with Barbie dolls and female superheroes such as Wonder Woman or the Bionic Woman. Much of their play is spent changing costumes, wigs, shoes, and combing the dolls' hair. Their favorite stories from early childhood are most often Snow White and Cinderella.

Many feminine boys spend hours playacting and impersonating females (15). Often they are remarkably convincing in these roles, displaying an outstanding ability to "act." One boy in our study spent much of his time impersonating female singers and would repeatedly sing the following lines from popular songs:

"You made me love you, I didn't want to do it" and "Here she comes, She's a maneater." Clearly the content of these songs had personal meaning to him, but his ability to act was remarkable as well.

Feminine boys often function as mothers' helpers. Several boys were described by their mothers as "neatniks" who constantly helped keep the house in order. They washed dishes, cleaned bathrooms, kept their own rooms clean, and involved themselves extensively in housekeeping functions. Many were involved in direct caretaking of their mothers as well. One boy served his mother breakfast in bed on weekends. Others liked to comb and style their mothers' hair. Some would give their mothers back rubs.

Some boys expressed direct dislike of their male anatomy, saying that they did not like their penises and found them to be disgusting. Several boys liked to urinate sitting down, pretending that they were girls. One boy taped his penis back between his legs so he could pretend he was a girl. Despite the wish of some boys to be rid of their penises, none believed that anatomically they were girls. Of the boys who had ideas of what they would like to be when they grew up, their choice most often was a hairdresser, an actor, an interior designer, or a fashion designer.

Femininity in Psychological Testing

Femininity also emerges in systematic psychological testing. In an attempt to study masculine and feminine preferences, Green (6) evaluated his sample of feminine boys using the It-Scale for Children (19). On this test the child is given a gender-neutral figure (It) and is asked to choose which of several pairs of pictures It prefers. Each pair of cards depicts stereotypically masculine or feminine toys, activities, and boy or girl playmates. Results showed that feminine boys had far more stereotypically feminine responses than their masculine cohorts. Furthermore, their responses were comparable to those of typical girls reported in the standardization sample.

Several researchers have studied human figures drawn by feminine boys. Studies of normal children demonstrated that most children draw their own sex first when asked to draw a picture of a person (20, 21), but feminine boys are more likley to draw a girl first (22–24). Feminine boys draw a female first more often than masculine boys (22), than school-problem boys (23), than normal boys, than boys referred to a psychiatric clinic, and than siblings (24). These results suggest that for boys, drawing a female first is a specific indicator of gender problems. Feminine boys also draw the female figure taller than the male figure (23, 24), which may reflect the "general salience" of the opposite sex for feminine boys. In the Roosevelt sample, cross-gender boys most often drew females first and females larger. Several also drew the female in greater detail. These details usually involved stereotypical female attributes such as long eyelashes, contoured lips, earrings, necklaces, bracelets, pocketbooks, ribbons, barrettes, and lace and ruffles.

On the Rorschach test the records of feminine boys were often filled with stereotypical female responses. Women were seen as ballerinas, belly dancers, cheerleaders, Ms. Piggy, superheroes such as Wonder Woman or the Bionic Woman, and so on. Women's accessories, such as dazzling dresses, fans, bras, and high-heeled shoes, were common. Several children reported images of women or animals as pregnant or in the process of giving birth (25).

Thus, in behavior, in play, and in fantasies, feminine boys display stereotyp-·ically female interests.

Social Competence

Virtually all clinicians and researchers who have worked with feminine boys report disruption in their peer relations. Feminine boys are rejected, ridiculed, and scapegoated by their cohorts (6, 26–28). Our own clinical findings verify these reports. Feminine boys are described by their teachers, mothers, and themselves as isolated, rejected, and at times abused by their peers. Close peer relationships rarely exist.

Feminine boys avoid contact with male peers. They have a minimal interest in competitive athletic activities or group functions typical of their male cohorts (14), which may stem in part from the fact that they are less athletically competent than their peers (29). On the rare occasions that they have contact with other males, it is usually with boys of a much younger age. When friendships are formed, it is usually with girls who are willing to allow them to participate in traditional female activities. These friendships also are not typically described as being particularly close or lasting over significant periods of time.

During adolescence feminine boys suffer to an even greater degree than during the school-age years. Pressures to begin dating and increased pressure to participate in competitive athletic pursuits often drive them into increased isolation. Verbal abuse, particularly from male peers, is common. They are often taunted, being called a "sissy" or a "faggot." During adolescence, gym class becomes particularly stressful for them, and often they outright refuse to attend. They appear to be worried about exposing their incompetence at athletic pursuits and are both frightened and humiliated at the thought of undressing in front of other boys in the locker room.

In the Roosevelt study, a similar pattern of difficulties emerged in a study using the Social Competence Scale of the Revised Child Behavior Profile (30) as rated by the boys' parents. This scale includes three subfactors: 1) Activities; 2) Social; 3) School, each of which is rated for the amount of involvement and for the quality of participation. Activities include participation in sports, jobs and non-sport activities, while Social includes involvement with friends and organizations. School assesses overall school performance. In our sample of 25 feminine boys on the overall Social Competence score, 64 percent had a total score in the clinical range. At all age levels the lowest scores were on the Social subfactor that primarily assesses competence in the realm of peer involvement (5).

Age of Onset

In Green's (6) study of 50 feminine boys, all displayed a compelling interest in dressing in women's clothes by the time they were 6 years old, and two-thirds of the sample displayed this interest by the time they were 4. The results of the Roosevelt study are similar. Cross-gender behavior, including an intense interest in mothers' clothes and cross-dressing, emerged clearly by age 3 in 21 out of 25 boys (84 percent). In 56 percent an interest in mothers' clothes was evident by age 2. For one boy it emerged at age 8, which was later than the others. Thus, our findings closely parallel those of Green.

Demographic Findings

The most extensive demographic study of feminine boys was conducted by Green (14). In his study of 60 boys, boyhood femininity was found to be unrelated to ethnic background, to religion, to the educational level of either parent, to the age of parents at the time of referral to the project, or to the age of the parents at the time they gave birth to their son. It was unrelated as well to the number of children in the family, to the birth order of the son, or to the age difference between the next oldest and youngest sibling.

Findings of the Roosevelt study are similar to those reported by Green (14). Boyhood femininity was unrelated to socioeconomic status as measured by the Hollingshead revised scale (31) and was unrelated to ethnic background, religion, or birth order.

Intelligence and Cognitive Style

Three studies have reported ten scores for preadolescent feminine boys. Green and Fuller (32) report a mean IQ of 106 for 35 boys with an average age of 7.3; Money and Epstein (33) report a mean IQ of 112 for 19 boys with an average age of 11.3; and Finegan et al. (34) report a mean IQ of 109 for 13 boys with an average age of 6.5. In the Roosevelt study the mean IQ for 25 boys with an average age of 7.4 was 103. Thus, our results are comparable to those reported in previous studies.

In their early study (33), Money and Epstein raised the question of whether feminine boys had a higher IQ than normal boys. They acknowledged the possibility that this may have resulted from a referral bias because they did not have controls. In a recent study from the Clarke Institute in Canada (34) using sibling controls, no differences in overall IQ were found between cross-gender boys and their masculine brothers. Although the mean IQ of 109 for their feminine group is higher than the national norm, the finding that it does not differ significantly from siblings suggests that the earlier report may well have reflected a referral bias.

Money and Epstein (33) also suggested that feminine boys had higher verbal ability compared with their perceptual organization ability. They argued that this cognitive style may have facilitated the development of feminine interests. A replication of these findings with appropriate controls by the Clarke group has failed to confirm this finding (34). They suggest that the failure to do so may be attributed to the differences in the ages of the children studied. Money and Epstein's sample had an average age of 11.3, while their own sample had an average age of 6.5 The Clarke group points out that if enhanced verbal ability emerges only at older age levels, it must be considered a consequence of boyhood femininity and not an antecedent.

Despite the Clarke group's failure to find significant differences in verbal and perceptual organization ability, they did find that feminine boys did more poorly on Block Design relative to Vocabulary than psychiatric or sibling controls. In our unit we have been unable to replicate this finding. This discrepancy is not surprising given the fact that the effect size in cognitive style sex differences is small. Thus the emergence of sex differences is particularly vulnerable to sample size and sampling fluctuation.

In normal populations, girls tend to do better than boys on a variety of verbal tasks, while boys do better than girls on spatial tasks (35). Block Design is a test of spatial ability that is highly correlated with measures of field-dependence (36, 37). Sex differences demonstrating greater spatial ability and field independence in men are among the most widely established cognitive sex differences.

Sherman (38, 39) argued that experience with spatial tasks is linked to sex-typed activities, with boys traditionally participating in more activities involving spatial skills. She reasons that the acquired experience and learning that takes place over time has a cumulative effect on the development of spatial ability. Viewed from this perspective, the Clarke group's finding of a lowered Block Design score suggests that the feminine boys' preference for feminine activities may decrease their cumulative experience with spatial tasks and in turn affect their cognitive style.

Results on cognitive style patterns of feminine boys appear to be complex and inconsistent and are in need of more research before any general conclusions can be reached.

Genetic and Physical Studies

Genetic and physical studies of feminine boys have typically found no abnormalities. In Green's study of 60 boys (14), buccal smears revealed no genetic abnormalities. Rekers et al. report similar results on a sample of 12 gender-disturbed boys (40). Neither genetic nor gross physical abnormalities, such as hermaphroditism and/or hypospadias, were found. One child had an undescended testicle. Although these studies provide evidence that gross genetic and physical abnormalities are not associated with the development of boyhood femininity, they do not rule out the possibility that subtle hormonal influences not yet readily detectable may be identified in the future.

Follow-up Studies

It has been assumed by researchers of boyhood femininity that this syndrome is the childhood precursor of adult transsexualism (6, 41, 7), but theoreticians (42, 43) have identified three groups of transsexuals, all of whom express the desire to be the other sex: primary transsexuals, transvestic transsexuals, and homosexual transsexuals. On the basis of retrospective reports, homosexual transsexuals most clearly resemble feminine boys in their desire to be a girl, in their effeminacy, in their cross-sex interests, and in their peer preferences.

Few systematic studies in the literature report long-range follow-up for boys identified in childhood as having a gender-identity disorder, and those that exist are difficult to interpret. The clearest follow-up data is presented by Money and Russo (44). Of 11 boys diagnosed with prepubertal gender identity discordance, 5 were available for follow-up. All the men at the time of follow-up were in their 20s, and all five considered themselves homosexual or predominantly so. Green (45) reports a mid-adolescent follow-up of his "feminine boy" sample. He found that two-thirds of his group were either homosexually or bisexually oriented. Zuger (46) evaluated a group of 16 children first seen between the ages of 4 and 16 years. This group consisted of children who were involved in long-term psychotherapy and others who had no treatment at all. At the time of follow-up, subjects ranged in age from 16 years to 29. Zuger concluded that 75 percent presented an atypical outcome at the time of follow-up. The overwhelming proportion were homosexual, and the others were transsexual and transvestic. Lebovitz (47) identified a group of boys whose chief complaint was boyhood femininity. They were children who also had varying degrees of treatment intervention. Age at the time of follow-up was 16 to 30 years. Lebovitz concludes that at the time of follow-up 37.5 percent exhibited "serious gender identity disturbances" including homosexuality, transvestism, and transsexualism.

The major limitation of the Green, Zuger, and Lebovitz studies is that at the time of follow-up either all or several of the subjects were still adolescents. The only follow-up that included subjects who were all above age 23 is that of the small sample of Money and Russo (44). In adolescence it may still be difficult to predict the final outcome of either gender identity or sexual orientation. We believe that the end point should be around age 25–30 if one hopes to be reasonably confident that gender identity and partner choice has stabilized. Furthermore, in both the Zuger study and the Lebovitz study, children had varying forms of psychological interventions, which would necessarily change the natural history and developmental course. Intervention may well have reversed behaviors that would have occurred without psychotherapy.

It seems clear from the studies cited above that boyhood femininity is correlated with a high incidence of homosexual object choice and/or atypical gender behavior in later life. The first evidence that is emerging suggests that boyhood femininity may not primarily be the precursor of transsexualism, as originally assumed, but may more commonly be a precursor of homosexuality. However, we are unable at this time to predict the outcome in any given patient or predict the percentages of heterosexuality, homosexuality, transvestism, or transsexuality in treated and untreated boyhood patient populations.

Theories of Etiology

There are two major theories of the etiology of boyhood femininity: an imprinting theory (7) and a reinforcement theory (6). Stoller (7) states that there are five conditions, all of which must exist for extreme boyhood femininity to develop: a mother who is chronically depressed; a mother who has a bisexual identity with severe penis envy and an only partially suppressed desire to be a male; a distant, passive, physically and psychologically absent father; a beautiful and graceful son; and a period of several years in which mother and son enjoy a blissful symbiosis during which time the mother's femininity becomes imprinted on the boy. Stoller believes that femininity is transmitted by conditioning or imprinting. He states, "These boys do not seek femininity but rather receive it passively via excessive impingement of the too-loving bodies of their mothers" (7: p.55). Furthermore, Stoller believes that in extreme boyhood femininity (which he views as the precursor of adult transsexualism) the dysfunction is specific only to gender identity and not part of a more pervasive ego dysfunction. "These mothers do not cripple the development of ego functions in general or even body ego, except in regard to this sense of femaleness. . . . None of these boys has shown the slightest evidence of psychosis or precursors of psychosis" (7: p.55).

Green (6) draws heavily on Stoller's theory but views social reinforcement as the major factor in the development of extreme boyhood femininity. He states that the prerequisite for the emergence of boyhood femininity is "no discouragement of the behavior by the child's principal caretaker" (6: p.238). He proposes a composite etiologic pattern that he says approximates Stoller's etiologic theory: The mother views her son as unusually attractive; she devotes considerable attention to him; as he begins to explore the environment and plays with her jewelry, shoes, and cosmetics, she thinks this is cute; the father is a less significant person in the boy's life and is often not present physically or psychologically; when present, the father also thinks that his son's playing with feminine objects is cute; girls primarily are available as playmates, and as a result socialization into female activities continues; the father anticipates a time when his son will be able to participate in traditional rough-and-tumble, father-son play, but his son seems unresponsive and more in tune with maternal activities; and early socialization of feminine skills interferes with integration with same sex peers during school-age years. Green's theory, like Stoller's, is based on the notion that the child does not have an inherent psychopathology, although he acknowledges that secondary difficulties arise for the child as a result of peer rejection.

Stoller's and Green's theories were developed on the basis of very incomplete data. Stoller's theory was based on a small number of clinical cases. Although Green studied a large sample of children, he did not systematically evaluate psychopathology in the children, nor did he evaluate the family matrix in depth.

The remainder of this chapter will review research evidence that focuses on the following questions: Is boyhood femininity a disorder that is restricted to gender identity only, or is there evidence of a more pervasive disorder? What is the pattern of relationship between mothers and sons? Is there evidence of a blissful symbiosis, simple reinforcement, or psychological disruption? and What is the pattern of relationship between fathers and sons?

PSYCHOPATHOLOGY OF EXTREME BOYHOOD FEMININITY

Three systematic studies, all from the Gender Identity Unit at the University of California at Los Angeles (UCLA), have explored the relationship between boyhood femininity and behavioral disturbances. In a study of 29 gender-disturbed boys based on clinical ratings of intake evaluations comparing effeminate and noneffeminate boys, it was found that effeminate boys had greater evidence of behavior associated with maternal overprotectiveness (12). This included greater passivity, harm-avoidance, lack of assertiveness, and being compulsively neat. In a second study, 15 gender-referred boys were compared with 175 normal controls on an extensive behavioral questionnaire that was rated by the boys' mothers (11). Feminine boys were rated by their mothers as being less extroverted and more behaviorally disturbed than their normal peers. Items on the extroversion scale included the following: is popular among other boys; tries to make new friends; is the leader in games that he plays with other children; is physically aggressive; is curious and explores things; will keep playing even with torn clothes; likes children's company more than adults' company; and so on. Items on the behavioral disturbance scale included: is defiant when given orders; has temper tantrums; lies to his mother; is restless and overactive; is bossy; cries easily; whines and whimpers; is disobedient; is not easygoing; fights; and so on. Finally, in a third study that compared feminine boys with normal and clinical controls, it was found that "gender-problem" boys scored similarly to clinical controls in terms of behavior disturbance. The authors concluded, "Gender-problem boys evidence a general personality or behavioral disorder rather than simply a narrow set of deviant gender-attitudes or gender behavior tendencies" (29).

A major finding of the Roosevelt study has been the identification of an association between cross-gender behavior in boys and the presence of separation anxiety. Mothers reported that their sons would follow them around the house endlessly, would go into panics and rages when left, were worried that they would never return, were worried that catastrophes would befall the mother when she left the house, and were frequently school reluctant and school avoidant. Of the 25 boys studied, 15 (or 60 percent) had a DSM-III separation-anxiety disorder

(5). Of the separation anxious group, 8 were also school avoidant. Three children who had a separation anxiety disorder had a history of chronic asthma. This raised the question as to whether asthma in these cases may have served as a symptom substitution for separation anxiety or whether it was a predisposing factor to boyhood femininity. Two children without separation anxiety also had a history of asthma.

Further evidence of psychopathology of this sample came from results of the Behavior Problem Checklist of the Revised Child Behavior Profile (30) as rated by the children's parents. The Child Behavior Checklist is a questionnaire based on responses to 118 behavior problems that are rated on a 3–point scale for frequency of occurrence. When compared to the large standardization norm, extremely feminine boys displayed a significantly greater degree of behavioral disturbance than normal controls from the standardization sample (5). Their scores differed dramatically from the non-referred standardization sample. In 84 percent of feminine boys the total mean T-score was in the clinical range (90th percentile or above) for behavioral disturbance. The scales with scores on which 50 percent of the boys fell within the clinical range varied from one age group to the next. At ages 4 and 5, these were social withdrawal, depression, sex problems,* immaturity; at ages 6–11, social withdrawal, schizoid behavior, depression, obsessive-compulsiveness and uncommunicativeness; at ages 12–14, somatic complaints, schizoid behavior, uncommunicativeness, immaturity, aggressiveness, obsessive-compulsiveness and hostile withdrawal, and hyperactivity.

Results consistent with these have been reported by Bradley et al. (48) with the Behavior Problem Checklist using the original norms of the Child Behavior Profile. As has been mentioned earlier, this was a mixed group of cross-gender boys and girls. The Clarke group found no difference in behavioral disturbance between their cross-gender group and a group of psychiatric controls.

Further evidence of psychological disturbance comes from studies of the Rorschachs of feminine boys. Bradley et al. (48), again reporting a sample of mixed sexes, found that 10 out of 15 protocols reflected a borderline personality organization as determined by global clinical ratings.

Tuber and Coates (25) systematically compared the Rorschachs of 14 feminine boys to the standardization data reported by Ames et al. (49). Using the Blatt scale, they found considerable evidence of boundary disturbances, fluidity of thinking, and thought disorder. On structured tests, such as the WISC-R, there was no evidence of thought disturbances in most of our sample. The pattern of thought disturbances emerging on unstructured tasks, such as the Rorschach, but not on a structured task, like the WISC-R, is one of the hallmarks of borderline psychopathology as seen on psychological testing (50).

---

*The items with the highest loadings on the sex problems factor are: (1) wishes to be the opposite sex; and (2) acts like the opposite. Thus the name "sex problems" for this factor is misleading and fails to reflect the cross-gender nature of the behaviors that are rated.

The Rorschachs were also used to evaluate the object relations of the feminine boys (25). Representations of people and animals in the Rorschach have been linked to interpersonal relatedness and conflict (51, 52). In the protocols of feminine boys, when people were seen in interactions with each other the interactions were often malevolent. Themes of malevolent influence, malevolent control, casting spells, and torture, as well as other images of control and destruction, occur frequently.

The major anxiety that emerged in the content of feminine boys' Rorschachs involved fears of dehumanization through malevolent control by others, and fears of annihilation and disintegration. The object-relations representations that were characteristically seen in the records of feminine boys are typical of those found in the records of persons with borderline personality disorders (53). Tuber and Coates (25) conclude that "the severity of distortions of thought organization and object relations seen in these records could only have arisen in the context of a severely disturbed mother-child relationship in the first few years of life. . . . "

Taken together, the results of the UCLA, Clarke, and Roosevelt childhood gender-identity studies do not support Stoller's observation that extreme boyhood femininity is a disorder specific only to the area of gender-identity formation. The studies cited above point to a more pervasive disturbance in ego-functioning and to the presence of significant psychopathology in addition to gender dysfunction in this population.

FAMILY MATRIX

Investigators of boyhood femininity agree that father absence either physically or psychologically occurs with great frequency (12, 5–7). Green (6) reports that in his predominantly white sample 34 percent of the boys were separated from their fathers by divorce, abandonment, or death. Separation through divorce and abandonment occurred with greater frequency in our sample. By the time the boys were 3 years old, 63 percent of the parents were either separated or divorced (5). By the time of referral to our unit, 85 percent of the fathers were no longer physically present in the home. All children remained with their mothers, none of whom remarried. Although we do not yet have the appropriate control data with which to compare this, the 1981 census (54) for children under age 6 reports that 86 percent of children from white families live with both parents. Among our white families, only 25 percent of the children lived with both parents until age 3. Father absence by age 3 was 75 percent for this subgroup. (U.S. Census statistics for Spanish-speaking families are not reported separately, preventing us from comparing this group.) In our study we have too few black families to make a census comparison. Thus, at least for our white sample, the incidence of father absence appears to be unusually high.

Green (6) reported that, in nearly every family, boyhood femininity was not discouraged. In many of his cases, cross-dressing was initiated by a mother, grandmother, or sister. He found that 50 percent of his families sought help for their sons because of pressure from the outside community. We share with Green a similar impression that in many families femininity was not discouraged. In most of the cases in the Roosevelt study, an outside party, such as the school or a physician, first identified the cross-gender problem and put pressure on the family to get help for their son. In our study, family initiation into cross-dressing was not reported, although in some cases, once it occurred, it was not discouraged. In several families cross-dressing was actively discouraged by beatings and other severe disciplinary measures. It is striking that in the cases where femininity was actively discouraged it had little impact on reducing cross-gender behavior. Mothers reported that they had succeeded in stopping a public display of cross-gender behavior but that it continued to go on behind closed doors. Several mothers described walking into their son's room unexpectedly and finding him dressed up as a girl, primping and posing in front of a mirror.

A few reports have linked actual early separations to gender-identity disturbances. In their study of ten adult transsexuals, Person and Ovesey (42, 43) found that 50 percent reported that they were hospitalized for physical illnesses before age 4. Green (14) reports that 22 percent of his sample of feminine boys were hospitalized in the early years of life. This was a significantly greater frequency of hospitalization than his normal controls had experienced. In addition, he found that feminine boys were more frequently separated from their biological fathers before the age of 5. The UCLA study (12) reports an association between boyhood femininity and greater frequency of "early emotional trauma (e.g., divorce)" and a greater frequency of adoption than in a control group of less-feminine but gender-referred boys.

In the Roosevelt study, during the first three years of the child's life 20 percent of the children and 48 percent of the mothers were hospitalized (5). The children were hospitalized for various physical problems. Six of the mothers were hospitalized for physical problems, three for psychiatric problems. When one considers the child and mother hospitalizations jointly, 52 percent of the sample had physical separations due to the hospitalization of either son or mother within the first three years of the child's life.

Maternal State

Stoller (7) cites maternal depression as a prerequisite for development of boyhood femininity. Systematic studies of maternal depression have not been previously reported in the literature. In our unit, mothers described the first year or two of their sons' lives as a time that they felt depressed, overwhelmed, emotionally depleted, and barely able to hold it together (5). Several mothers described themselves as being so depressed that they slept much of the day, leaving the child alone and unattended. One mother was so depressed that she would leave her son for an entire day in soiled diapers, which resulted in his developing a severe rash. One mother described herself saying, "I'm a child trying to raise myself, and there's not enough of me to go around." Another mother described being overwhelmed, depleted, and ambivalent: "I have intense feelings of love and hate. I hate him when he gets hurt. I hate him when he cries. I hate him when he has to eat. But I also love to feed him and hold him. It's half and half. I love him, but I don't feel strong enough mentally and physically to do the things he needs" (55).

Systematic results on depression in mothers come from a study in our unit conducted by Marantz (55). Using the Beck Depression Inventory, Marantz found that mothers of feminine boys were significantly more depressed than a closely matched group of mothers of normal boys. In addition, she found more evidence of borderline psychopathology as measured by the Diagnostic Interview for Borderlines (56, 57) in mothers of feminine boys when compared with normal control mothers. Three subscales distinguished the two groups. Mothers of feminine boys had more difficulty in interpersonal relations, displayed more evidence of transient psychotic phenomena, and had more difficulty with affects. These mothers were characterized as having volatile, intense relationships; they made excessive demands on people, had problems with devaluation, manipulation, and hostility, and displayed more evidence of separation anxiety. In addition, they had difficulty establishing a reliable connection to reality, were more depressed, and reported more chronic feelings of emptiness, loneliness, and boredom (55).

Maternal Trauma

Evidence of severe disruption in the lives of mothers comes from our finding of an unusually high incidence of maternal trauma during the child's first three years of life. In nine, or 45 percent, of the cases such events were described (5). In one case a mother was seriously physically injured when she tried to stop two neighbors from fighting. The neighbor threw lye on the mother while her son observed the entire incident. She subsequently required multiple operations, at times involving long hospitalizations, in order to recover from severe burns from the lye. Another mother lived in terror with a heroin dealer for the first four years of her son's life. She was frightened of drug-related burglaries when her husband was out of the house, and frightened of drug traffic when her husband was home. Another mother was sexually assaulted and suffered serious physical injury. She described experiencing episodes of fear and terror that lasted at least a year after this experience. In another case a 6–month-old daughter died, which precipitated a severe depression in the mother and resulted in a psychiatric hospitalization. In four cases, the mother discovered within weeks of the birth of her son that her husband was having an affair with another woman. Mothers reported developing significant depression in reaction to this discovery. In one case it appeared to be the precipitating factor in a depression that led to a psychiatric hospitalization. Finally, one mother reported having a psychiatric hospitalization for depression during the first year of her son's life but was unable to reconstruct any precipitating events.

Maternal Devaluations of Men

Bradley et al. (48) have noted that many mothers of feminine boys expressed hostility toward men. In our study as well, many mothers of our feminine boys expressed covert or overt devaluation of men and contempt and anger toward men (5). Mothers frequently commented on how nice their feminine sons were and how unlike other boys, who in contrast were mean, aggressive, bullies. Mothers were unable to distinguish between assertive, rambunctious play (rough-and-tumble play) and aggressive or destructive behavior. Several discouraged their children from having any involvement with other boys, telling us that the boys in their neighborhood were too rough and violent. Others stated that they were proud that their sons were not rough and violent like other boys. They saw them as special and better than other boys because of their gentle and nonviolent qualities. They clearly tried to interfere with normal, assertive boyishness and devalued the "regular boys" in front of their sons.

Several mothers remarked on the intensity of their anger toward men during the child's early years of life. Some mothers saw this as a problem that they struggled with over a period of a few years, others saw it as a long-standing issue. One mother remarked that she had been angry at men during the early years of her marriage and of her son's life. She resented her husband's moving ahead in work and her being left at home in a role for which she felt completely unprepared. The same mother found herself constantly screaming at her son "for no reason at all." When she was asked if she had any thoughts about why this happened, she said, "I think I hate him when he reminds me of myself." In their descriptions of their husbands, mothers often viewed husbands as peripheral to their lives and to the lives of their sons. Husbands were often seen as inadequate partners and as intrusions in their lives.

Patterns of Mothering

The UCLA Gender Identity Unit reported an association between parental *overprotectiveness* and boyhood femininity (12). In a systematic study of ratings of clinical evaluations of boys and their families, they found that within a population of gender-referred boys the most effeminate boys came from over-protective families.

In the Roosevelt study, a similar pattern of overprotectiveness was seen in many cases (5). Mothers often overresponded to minor physical illnesses or prevented their sons from playing with other children out of fear that they would be exposed to germs and become ill. Mothers discouraged children from partic-ipating in rough-and-tumble play or active sports in which they would risk getting hurt or dirty. Another pattern observed in the Roosevelt study was for parents to use harsh and *authoritarian and punitive forms of discipline*. Minor and age-typical transgressions were often responded to with withdrawal, with severe and inappropriate threats of abandonment, and with corporal punishment. Mothers would punish their sons for getting their clothes, even jeans, dirty. One mother went into a violent rage and began beating her son, then sent him to his room for a day, when he broke an ashtray that was in "her" living room. The same mothers were at other times overprotective. Many mothers had great difficulty *setting limits*. They were often intimidated by the child and would permit the child to take over and control their lives. These were often the same mothers who were harsh disciplinarians.

Earlier we noted another pattern revealed in the Roosevelt study: many mothers encouraged their sons to become *mother's helper*. With great pride, mothers described their sons as helpful with household chores. They were proud that their sons were fastidious, and they referred to them affectionately as "neatniks." Mothers also encouraged their sons to be attentive and nurturing and caretaking to them. One mother proudly described her son's sensitivity in bringing her breakfast in bed whenever she was "under the weather." Several mothers described their son's sensitivity to their moods and depression. Others enjoyed their son's attention and sensitivity to their dress and looks. Although the sexualized aspect of the mother-son involvement has been emphasized by Stoller (7), we have been struck instead with the mother's wish to have her son function in a maternal role to her. One mother went so far as to call her son "Ma."

In our unit, Marantz (55) systematically studied aspects of symbiosis in the mother-child relationship. As reported earlier, she compared the mothers of feminine boys with a well-matched sample of mothers of normal boys. Using the Summers and Walsh (58) symbiosis scale, she found that mothers of feminine boys differed significantly from control mothers in that: (a) they were more dependent on their sons; (b) they had more difficulty separating from their sons; (c) they were more undifferentiated from their sons; (d) they were intrusive and controlling; (e) they were more disapproving of their son's relationships with people other than themselves. These results provide systematic evidence that mothers of feminine boys have more difficulty than controls in fostering autonomy and age-appropriate differentiation in their sons.

Many of these mothers were overinvolved with their sons based on their own personal needs. Marantz (55) reports several examples of statements from mothers demonstrating this.

I enjoy having him around because he helps me with cleaning and asks me how I'm feeling.

He's my reason for living. He's the only person I really have besides my mother, and I'm the only person he has.

All my relationships have been disastrous, and so I've been putting all my hopes on my relationship with my son—*this* would be the one relationship that would prove me fit to be human.

I miss him when he's in school. It's lonely. I don't enjoy the idea of his doing things apart from me. When he's in school, I go shopping. Then I wait the rest of the day in the parents' room at school. I never really want to be away from him.

Again, these overinvolved and symbiosis fostering mothers were also mothers who were harsh and punitive disciplinarians.

Fathers

As we have already mentioned, most researchers report that father absence occurs with great frequency. In the fathers who were present, Green observed a pattern of psychological absence and at times overt rejection (6). Fathers were uninvolved with their sons and rarely spent time either taking care of or playing with their sons. Green reports that in cases where a father had a masculine son also, a strong preference for the masculine son emerged.

In our study, mothers described fathers and fathers described themselves as remote, violent, and sometimes alternatingly remote and violent. One middle-class father, prone to rages, would smash holes in the wall of his home when upset by even minor slights or disappointments. He was extremely sensitive to personal insult and was ready for a street brawl at the drop of a hat. His son repeatedly witnessed these violent incidents. Another father, during an embittered separation, bashed the front door of his home down with a baseball bat when his wife had locked him out. His son was in the house and witnessed his rampage. When this same father was asked whether his son ever had temper tantrums he said, "No, I have the tantrums. If he had one, I'd drown him in the pool." Another father was prone to violent rages during alcoholic binges and would enlist his son in tearing up and destroying his wife's (the child's mother's) possessions.

Several fathers used harsh discipline with their sons. One would throw his son against a wall when he was angry, another would destroy one of his son's toys whenever his son violated a rule. Other fathers were remote and uninvolved in the ongoing functioning of the family. One father knew before his wife's delivery that he planned to leave her. In an effort to prevent himself from experiencing the loss of his son as well, he consciously and deliberately kept as much emotional distance from his son as possible in order to protect himself. Another father reported disliking his wife and family to such a degree that he would invent reasons to stay late in his office in order to avoid contact with them. Another father began a pattern, soon after his son was born, of living with another woman on weekends. Since, in addition, he worked late into the evening during the week, he never saw his son and rarely saw his wife. This arrangement continued until the son was well into the school-age years. Another father refused to participate in the evaluation of his son, saying that he has known since his son was two that he would be a homosexual and that he believed his son was hopeless; he dismissed his son as not being worthy even of the time involved in the evaluation.

SUMMARY AND DISCUSSION

From the data presented above, there is growing evidence to indicate that extreme boyhood femininity is not a disorder restricted to gender identity alone but is part of a more pervasive psychological disorder. Extremely feminine boys appear to be as behaviorally disturbed as other children referred to psychiatric clinics. Clinically they most often present as children with borderline psychopathology. There is evidence that many have separation-anxiety disorders and impaired object relations. Internally these children view their world and others as devouring, malevolent, and annihilating.

The pattern that emerges with mothers is complex. Like their children, many of these mothers have a borderline personality organization. Their relationships with people are intense, volatile, and demanding. They are often hostile and manipulative and devalue others while they at the same time are overly dependent on others. Many of these mothers devalue men in particular. They suffer from depression and separation anxiety and are prone to brief, limited distortions of reality. They report chronic feelings of emptiness, loneliness, and boredom. In their patterns of mothering they appear to be overprotective and intrusive and impair the child's development of autonomy. Their overprotectiveness seems to stem from a phobic appraisal of the environment as a dangerous place. They are also harsh and severe disciplinarians who put great pressure on the child to behave like a little adult and to become a mother's helper. Their inability to set age-appropriate limits is noteworthy. The mother's overinvolvement with her son is based on her own needs and psychopathology and not on the age-appropriate needs of her son. Thus, although she appears to be overinvolved, she is paradoxically inaccessible because she is responding not to the needs of her son but to her own needs. Her psychopathology and her patterns of mothering are further complicated by the frequency of traumatic experiences occurring to her early in the child's life. Actual physical separations due to hospitalizations, and father absence, create further disruptions. These multiple forces both within the mother's own personality and in her actual life experiences combine to make her inaccessible and insensitive to her son's needs during his early years.

There are no systematic studies reported in the literature that have confirmed Stoller's view that extreme boyhood femininity arises in a matrix of "blissful symbiosis." In the Roosevelt study, in cases where the mother initially presented a "blissful" picture of her relationship with her son when he was a baby, this view, as we have described, did not subsequently hold up. Further interviewing invariably revealed severe disruption in the mother's life and in her relationship with her son. Although we did see evidence of symbiosis, we did not see even one case of a "blissful symbiosis." This does not rule out the possibility that this may be a rare syndrome that did not emerge in our sample. A pattern of findings similar to our own has been reported by Meyer in his studies of adult transsexuals. He states, ''Abandonment, disregard and psychological misuse rather than extraordinary symbiosis marked the histories'' (59). In sum, our work does not provide support for the most critical aspect of Stoller's theory, the ''blissful symbiosis'' hypothesis.

Fathers emerged in our study as most often physically absent; and when they were present they were psychologically absent or violent. In either case, they were not available to their spouses to offer support during the times that they were most psychologically disrupted, nor were they available to their sons to make up for their mothers' withdrawal and depression. Furthermore, their absence made them unavailable to counteract the mothers' overinvolvement, overprotectiveness, inability to set limits, or punitiveness. In effect, the father, by his absence, physical or psychological, did not make up for the loss the child experienced, nor did he present another alternative in parenting, nor was he present as a masculine role model. Thus our studies support the findings of Stoller (7) and Green (6) that father absence is an important precursor of boyhood femininity.

In summary, our findings support the view that extreme boyhood femininity occurs in the context of a more pervasive psychological disorder. Furthermore, our results provide evidence that extreme boyhood femininity arises in a family matrix of severe psychological disruption where the mother is emotionally inaccessible and insensitive to her child's age-appropriate needs.

As for the issue of reinforcement, we think it may be one factor that plays a role. In our study we were struck with the finding that mothers often reinforced their sons' interest in their looks and their dress but did not report that they reinforced their sons' feminine behavior. We also think that mothers discouraged the expression of assertion and aggression (e.g., in rough-and-tumble play). We believe that Green (6) made an important contribution to an understanding of boyhood femininity, but we do not share his view that reinforcement is a necessary condition for its development.

One important question that our research raised is why a history of father absence, separations, trauma, and maternal inaccessibility and depression should be associated with the development of boyhood femininity in particular. We know from the child psychiatric literature that these factors are predisposing to a wide variety of childhood psychiatric disorders. It may be that this constellation of factors must be combined with highly specific other factors, such as maternal devaluation of men, for it to lead to boyhood femininity. Or it is possible that we will find clusters of precursors that are specific not to boyhood femininity but to a spectrum of disorders. More refined and sophisticated studies using normal and clinical controls are needed to shed light on the precursors that we and others have begun to identify.

We studied a group of boys with extreme femininity that have been referred to a clinical setting. The results reported in our own study may be generalizable only to this group of *DSM*-III diagnosed boys. We do not know if feminine boys not referred to clinical settings have a different psychological profile and family history. Nor do we know how boys who experience themselves as feminine but do not display it in their behavior would compare.

Although the accruing evidence suggests that extreme boyhood femininity is often a precursor of homosexuality and/or atypical gender development in adulthood, the end point of the longitudinal studies is still too early for a definitive answer to emerge. It is striking that the original assumption of researchers in this area, that boyhood femininity was the precursor of adult transsexualism, may not in fact be correct. The evidence available suggests that it is most often a precursor of homosexuality. Currently, however, we are unable to predict outcome either of gender development or of partner choice in individual cases.

Finally, we think that in-depth psychotherapy of feminine boys will help us understand the meaning of the symptom and what psychological purposes it serves. This is an area that is just beginning to be explored. Our initial impressions suggest that the meaning of the symptom may differ from one boy to the next. For example, for some it may be a means of handling separation/annihilation-anxiety, for others a means of warding off aggression, or both. Based on the in-depth psychotherapy of several children in our unit, we believe that for some boys femininity is a variant of identification with the lost object. The boy confuses having Mommy with being Mommy and in so doing takes on her femininity. This closely resembles the findings on cross-gender adults that have been retrospectively derived by Person and Ovesey (42, 43, 60–62). Their research identified the critical significance of maternal inaccessibility in adult cross-gender disorders that we now see emerging in our systematic data on mothers of extremely feminine boys. Furthermore, they identifed the meaning of the symptom in cross-gender adults as a variant of identification with the lost object which is emerging in our work with young boys as well. One question we have raised is whether the meaning of the symptom during childhood may be predictive of later outcome.

In our first study we looked at boyhood femininity as a unitary group. Since not all boys displayed identical patterns of behavior, we suggest that, as larger numbers of feminine boys are evaluated, subclusters need to be defined. Future studies should focus on defining and correlating different patterns of boyhood femininity as it is seen in behavior, with its meaning (or meanings) as it emerges in in-depth psychotherapy. Although studies of hormones and genes have not provided evidence of a biological contribution, we believe that studies of temperament will help answer the question of whether early characteristics of the child may interact with experiential and environmental factors in a way that predisposes some children to the development of this syndrome. Finally, in-depth studies of mothers, fathers, and the parenting dyad are needed to shed light on what patterns of parental precursors lead to what kinds of boyhood femininity.

ACKNOWLEDGMENTS

Special thanks are due to Dr. John Fogelman, Director of the Division of Child and Adolescent Psychiatry at Roosevelt Hospital in New York City, for his encouragement and generous support of the project upon which this chapter is based.

I would also like to express my deep appreciation to others whose stimulation and encouragement have facilitated this work: Ross Clinchy, Dr. James Meltzer, Dr. Ethel Person, Dr. Nancy Schultz, and Dr. Steven Tuber.

I wish to thank Penny Donnenfeld, Sonia Marantz, Dr. Bernd Meyenburg, Toby Miroff, and Robert Sherman for their assistance in carrying out this study.

REFERENCES

1. Money, J., and Ehrhardt, A. Man and Woman, Boy and Girl: The Differentiation and Dimorphism of Gender Identity from Conception to Maturity. Baltimore: Johns Hopkins University Press, 1972.

2. Money, J.; Hampson, J. G.; and Hampson, J. L. An examination of some basic sexual concepts: the evidence of human hermaphroditism. Bulletin of the Johns Hopkins Hospital, 97:301–310, 1955.

3. Money, J.; Hampson, J. G.; and Hampson, J. L. Hermaphroditism: recommendations concerning assignment of sex, change of sex, and psychological management. Bulletin of the Johns Hopkins Hospital, 97:284–300, 1955.

4. Coates, S. Extreme Boyhood Femininity. In: Medical Aspects of Human Sexuality. In press, Hospital Publications, Inc.

5. Coates, S., and Person E. Extreme Boyhood Femininity: Isolated Finding or Pervasive Disorder? In press, J. Am. Acad. Child Psychiatry.

6. Green, R. Sexual Identity Conflict in Children and Adults. New York: Basic Books, 1974.

7. Stoller, R. J. Sex and Gender, Vol. II, The Transsexual Experiment. New York: Jason Aronson, 1975.

8. Saghir, M. T., and Robins, E. Male and Female Homosexuality: A Comprehensive Investigation. Baltimore: Williams and Wilkins, 1973.

9. Whitman, F. Childhood indicators of male homosexuality. Archives of Sexual Behavior, 6:89–96, 1977.

10. American Psychiatric Association. Diagnostic and Statistical Manual of Mental Disorders, 3rd edition. Washington, D.C.: APA, 1980.

11. Bates, J. E.; Bentler, P. M.; and Thompson, S. K. Measurement of deviant gender development in boys. Child Development, 44:591–598, 1973.

12. Bates, J. E.; Skilbeck, W. M.; Smith, D. V. R.; and Bentler, P. M. Gender role abnormalities in boys: an analysis of clinical ratings. Journal of Abnormal Child Psychology, 2:1–16, 1974.

13. Bentler, P. M.; Rekers, G. A.; and Rosen, A. C. Congruence of childhood sex-role identity and behavior disturbances. Child: Care, Health, and Development, 5:267–283, 1979.

14. Green, R. One-hundred ten feminine and masculine boys: behavioral contrasts and demographic similarities. Archives of Sexual Behavior, 5:425–446, 1976.

15. Green, R., and Money, J. Stage-acting, role-taking, and effeminate impersonation during boyhood. Archives of General Psychiatry, 15:535–538, 1966.

16. Zucker, K. J. Childhood gender disturbances: diagnostic issues. Journal of the American Academy of Child Psychiatry, 21:274–280, 1982.

17. Zucker, K. J.; Doering, R.W.; Bradley, S.; and Finegan, J. K. Sex-typed play in gender-disturbed children: a comparison to sibling and psychiatric controls. Archives of Sexual Behavior, 11:309–321, 1982.

18. Zucker, K. J.; Bradley, S. J.; Corter, C. M.; Doering, R. W.; and Finegan, J. Cross-gender behavior in very young boys: a normative study. In: Samson, J., ed., Childhood and Sexuality. Montreal: Editions Etudes Vivantes, 1980.

19. Brown, D. Sex role preference in young children. Psychological Monographs, 70:14 (whole no. 1421), 1956.

20. Jolles, K. A study of validity of some hypotheses for the qualitative interpretation of the H-T-P for children of elementary school age, I: sexual identification. Journal of Clinical Psychology, 8:113–118, 1952.

21. Tolor, A., and Tolor, B. Children's figure drawings and changing attitudes toward sex roles. Psychological Reports, 34:343–349, 1974.

22. Green, R.; Fuller, M.; and Rutley, B. It-scale for children and Draw-a-Person Test: 30 feminine vs. 25 masculine boys. Journal of Personality Assessment, 36:349–352, 1972.

23. Skilbeck, W. M.; Bates, J. E.; and Bentler, P. M. Human figure drawings of gender problem and school problem boys. Journal of Abnormal Child Psychology, 3:191–199, 1975.

24. Zucker, K. J.; Finegan, J. K.; Doering, R. W.; and Bradley, S. J. Human figure drawings of gender-problem children: a comparison to sibling, psychiatric, and normal controls. Journal of Abnormal Psychology, 2:287–298, 1983.

25. Tuber, S., and Coates, S. Interpersonal phenomena in the Rorschachs of feminine boys. In press, Psychoanalytic Psychology.

26. Green, R.; Newman, L.; and Stoller, R. Treatment of boyhood "transsexualism." Archives of General Psychiatry, 26:213–217, 1972.

27. Rekers, G. A.; Bentler, P. M.; Rosen, A. C.; and Lovaas, O. I. Child gender disturbances: a clinical rationale for intervention. Psychotherapy: Theory, Research, and Practice, 14:1–8, 1977.

28. Stoller, R. J. Psychotherapy of extremely feminine boys. International Journal of Psychiatry, 9:278–281, 1970.

29. Bates, J. E.; Bentler, P. M.; and Thompson, S. K. Gender-deviant boys compared with normal and clinical control boys. Journal of Abnormal Child Psychology, 7:243–259, 1979.

30. Achenbach, T. M., and Edelbrock, C. Manual for the Child Behavior Checklist and Revised Child Behavior Profile. New York: Queen City Printers, 1983.

31. Hollingshead, A. B. Four Factor Index of Social Status. Unpublished manuscript (available from Department of Sociology, Yale University), 1975.

32. Green, R., and Fuller, M. Family doll play and female identity in preadolescent males. American Journal of Orthopsychiatry, 43:123–127, 1973.

33. Money, J., and Epstein, R. Verbal aptitude in eonism and prepubertal effeminacy— a feminine trait. Transactions of the New York Academy of Science, 29:448–454, 1967.

34. Finegan, J. K.; Zucker, K. D.; Bradley, S. J.; and Doering, R. W. Patterns of '

intellectual functioning and spatial ability in boys with gender identity disorder. Canadian Journal of Psychiatry, 27:135–139, 1982.

35. Maccoby E. E., and Jacklin, C. N. The Psychology of Sex Differences. Stanford, Calif.: Stanford University Press, 1974.

36. Coates, S. Field dependence and intellectual functioning in pre-school children. Perceptual and Motor Skills, 41:251–254, 1975.

37. Goodenough, D. R., and Karp, S. A. Field dependence and intellectual functioning. Journal of Abnormal and Social Psychology, 63:241–246, 1961.

38. Sherman, J. A. Problem of sex differences in space perception and aspects of intellectual functioning. Psychological Review, 74:290–299, 1967.

39. Sherman, J. A. Sex-related Cognitive Differences. Springfield, Ill.: Charles C. Thomas, 1978.

40. Rekers, G. A.; Crandall, B. F.; Rosen, A. C.; and Bentler, P. M. Genetic and physical studies of male children with psychological gender disturbances. Psychological Medicine, 9:373–375, 1979.

41. Stoller, R. Sex and Gender: On the Development of Masculinity and Femininity. New York: Science House, 1968.

42. Person, E., and Ovesey, L. The transsexual syndrome in males, I: primary transsexualism. American Journal of Psychotherapy, 28(1):4–20, 1974.

43. Person, E., and Ovesey, L. The transsexual syndrome in males, II: secondary transsexualism. American Journal of Psychotherapy, 28(1):174–193, 1974.

44. Money, J., and Russo, A. J. Homosexual outcome of discordant gender identity/role in childhood: longitudinal follow-up. Journal of Pediatric Psychology, 4:29–41, 1979.

45. Green, R. Childhood cross-gender behavior and subsequent sexual preference. American Journal of Psychiatry, 136:106–108, 1979.

46. Zuger, B. Effeminate behavior in boys from childhood: ten additional years of follow-up. Comprehensive Psychiatry, 19:363–369, 1978.

47. Lebovitz, P. S. Feminine behavior in boys: aspects of its outcome. American Journal of Psychiatry, 128:1283–1289, 1972.

48. Bradley, S.; Doering, R.; Zucker, K.; Finegan, J.; and Gonda, G. M. Assessment of the gender-disturbed child: a comparison to sibling and psychiatric controls. In: Samson, J., ed., Childhood and Sexuality. Montreal: Editions Etudes Vivantes, 1980.

49. Ames, L. B.; Metraux, R.; Rodell, J. L.; and Walker, R. N. Child Rorschach Responses. New York: Brunner/Mazel, 1974.

50. Singer, M. T. The borderline diagnosis and psychological tests: review and research. In: Hartocollis, P., ed., Borderline Personality Disorders: The Concept, the Syndrome, the Patient. New York: International Universities Press, 1977.

51. Urist, J. The Rorschach test and the assessment of object relations. Journal of Personality Assessment, 41:3–9, 1977.

52. Tuber, S. Children's Rorschach scores as predictors of later adjustment. Journal of Consulting and Clinical Psychology, 51:379–385, 1983.

53. Leichtman, M., and Shapiro, S. An introduction to the psychological assessment of borderline conditions in children: manifestations of borderline phenomena on psychological testing. In: Kwawer, J. S.; Lerner, H. D.; Lerner, P. M.; and Sugarman, A., eds., Borderline Phenomena and the Rorschach Test. New York: International Universities Press, 1980.

54. U.S. Bureau of the Census. Current Population Reports, U.S. Government Printing Office, 1981.
55. Marantz, S. Mothers of extremely feminine boys: psychopathology and childrearing practices. Ph.D. dissertation, New York University, 1984.
56. Gunderson, J., and Kolb J. Discriminating features of borderline patients. American Journal of Psychiatry, (135:7): 792–796, 1978.
57. Gunderson, J.; Kolb, J.; and Austin, V. The diagnostic interview for borderline patients. American Journal of Psychiatry, (138:7):896–903, 1981.
58. Summers, F., and Walsh, F. The nature of the symbiotic bond between mother and schizophrenic. American Journal of Orthopsychiatry, 47(3):484–494, 1977.
59. Meyer, J. K. The theory of gender identity disorders. Journal of the American Psychoanalytic Association, 30:381–418, 1982.
60. Ovesey, L., and Person, E. Gender identity and sexual psychopathology in men: a psychodynamic analysis of homosexuality, transsexualism, and transvestism. Journal of the American Academy of Psychoanalysis, 1:(1)53–72, 1973.
61. Ovesey, L., and Person, E. Transvestism: a disorder of the sense of self. International Journal of Psychoanalytic Psychotherapy, 5:219–236, 1976.
62. Person, E., and Ovesey, L. Transvestism: new perspectives. Journal of the American Academy of Psychoanalysis, 6:301–323, 1978.

JULIANNE IMPERATO-McGINLEY,
RALPH E. PETERSON,
TEOFILO GAUTIER, and
ERASMO STURLA

7

The Impact of Androgens on the Evolution of Male Gender Identity

Sex differences in behavior from infancy through adulthood have been documented in humans (1, 2) and animals (3, 4). In animals, sexually dimorphic behavior is secondary to sex-steroid-induced differentiation and activation of the brain at critical periods. In humans, however, controversy exists as to whether gender-identity formation is influenced by sex-steroid "imprinting" of the brain at critical periods.

In man, pseudohermaphrodites were studied and conclusions were made concerning the supremacy of the sex of rearing as compared to biologic factors in the formation of gender identity (5–15). However, most of the studies were conducted without adequate knowledge of the subjects' hormonal milieu (i.e., androgens) and therefore the conclusions which emphasized the dominant role of the sex of rearing were merely speculative.

Male pseudohermaphrodites with steroid 5a-reductase deficiency (16–18) are unique, since the biosynthesis and peripheral action of testosterone is normal and thus prenatal and neonatal testosterone exposure of the brain proceeds as in the normal male. However, because of deficient 5a-reductase activity resulting in decreased dihydrotestosterone production in utero, there is such severe ambiguity of the external genitalia of the affected male fetus that many affected male subjects are believed to be female at birth and consequently raised as girls. At puberty, however, masculinization occurs under the influence of normal

This chapter was developed from work supported by Research Career Award (R.E.P.), K6-AM 14241–15, Clinical Investigator Award NIAMDD (J.I.-McG.) K08–AM 00615–01, Clinical Research Center Grant RR-47, Research Grant HD0921, from the National Institutes of Health, National Foundation Research Grant 6-52, Shorr Fellowship Fund, and a grant from Gulf and Western (Dominican Republic). The chapter originally appeared in S. J. Kogan and E. S. Hafez, eds., *Pediatric Andrology* (Hingham, Mass.: Kluwer, 1981). It is reprinted here by permission of Martinus Nijhoff Publishing, Boston.

plasma testosterone levels (16, 17). Thus, male pseudohermaphrodites with 5a-reductase deficiency raised as females are extraordinary experiments of nature for evaluating the relative influences of testosterone and the sex of rearing in the determination of gender identity in man.

CLINICAL DESCRIPTION

At birth the affected subjects have a scrotum that is markedly bifid, appearing more labial-like. The phallus is clitoral-like, and they have a urogenital sinus with a blind vaginal pouch. The testes are in the abdomen, inguinal canal, or scrotum (16, 17).

With puberty, a dramatic change occurs, mediated by the normal to high plasma levels of testosterone. The voice deepens and the affected subjects develop a muscular habitus with substantial growth of the phallus (4–6 centimeters). The scrotum becomes rugated and hyperpigmented, and in the majority of cases the testes descend if they are not already in the scrotum. There is no gynecomastia. The subjects have erections and there is an ejaculate from the urethral orifice on the perineum. They are capable of intromission but because of the position of the urethra are not capable of insemination (16, 17). The postpubertal affected males have a scant to absent beard and decreased body hair. The prostate is small or absent (16, 17).

METHODS AND RESULTS

There are 38 known male pseudohermaphrodites with a 5a-reductase deficiency from 23 interrelated families spanning four generations in three rural villages in the southwestern region of the Dominican Republic. The condition is inherited as an autosomal recessive trait (16, 17). Five of the affected subjects are deceased; two died in infancy and three in adulthood. Thirty-three males are living; 25 are postpubertal, 3 pubertal, and 5 prepubertal.

Interviews concerning the psychosexual development of the affected subjects were carried out in Villages A and B. Historical data were obtained by interviewing the living affected male subjects who were raised as females and those who were raised as males. Other males in the villages were interviewed as controls. Parents, siblings, wives, girlfriends, and neighbors of the affected subjects were interviewed when possible. The interviews were conducted in Spanish by members of our research group known to the community since 1972 and were independently translated into English by another member of the group. (Six of the affected subjects are now living and working in the hospital in Santo Domingo with which a member of the research team is affiliated. In addition, numerous trips to the community have been made since 1972 by various members of the team, and the villagers are now quite familiar with most of the team members. Also, eight affected subjects and a father and sister of an affected subject have been hospitalized at The New York Hospital for a minimum of six to eight weeks. Presently eight affected subjects are residing in New York. Thus, in addition to the formal interview sessions, we have been able to observe these subjects over a protracted period of time and have become quite involved with both the subjects and their families.) The interviews were designed to determine any ambiguity in the female sex about rearing the affected subjects and the validity of the change in those that appeared to adopt a male gender identity and gender role. (Gender identity is the sense of being male or female, the self-awareness of knowing to which sex one belongs, the private experience of gender role. Gender role is the public expression of one's gender identity. This is manifested by what one does or says that indicates to others or to oneself the extent of being male or being female, or ambivalent.) Data were obtained concerning the age of the affected subjects who were raised as girls began to doubt their female gender. Information concerning their postpubertal male psychosexual orientation and behavior was also obtained. The social practices within the villages were investigated to discern the influence of cultural factors on the change in gender identity of the subjects.

From the interview data, 19 of 33 affected subjects from Villages A and B were found to have been unambiguously raised as females (39). Adequate postpubertal psychosexual data were obtained on 18 of 19 subjects. Sixteen of the 18 subjects successfully changed to a male gender identity and a male gender role. The two exceptions are Subject 4 and Subject 25 (see Table 7.1). Subject 4 from Village A adopted a male gender identity, but continues to dress as a female. Despite dressing as a female, this subject has the affect and mannerisms of a man and does man's work (see Addendum) as a farmer and woodsman. Subject 4 lives alone but engages in sexual activity with village women. Subject 25 (age 37) from Village B is the only postpubertal affected subject who has maintained a female gender identity and female gender role. She was "married" at the age of 16 to a man in Village B, and they lived together for one year. He left her, and she left the town shortly thereafter. Since moving to the capital she has been living alone and working as a domestic. She has not been sexually involved with other men and denies ever being attracted to women. Since puberty she has been wearing false breasts, yet despite this her build and mannerisms are quite masculine. She states that she wants surgical correction of the genitals so that she can be a normal woman.

Between 7 to 12 years of age, those interviewed affected subjects raised as girls (with the exception of Subject 25) began to realize that they were different from other girls in the village when they did not develop breasts. Serious self-concern was raised over their gender as they began to "feel like men" and as they noted that their bodies began to change in a masculine direction, with masses noted in the inguinal canal or scrotum. A male gender identity evolved as they passed through stages of no longer feeling like girls to "feeling like men" and finally to the self-realization that they were indeed men. In all instances, there was a lag period from the time they began to realize differences from other girls their age until the time they finally changed gender role from

Table 7.1
Male Pseudohermaphrodites with 5a-Reductase Deficiency Who Were
Unambiguously Raised as Females

VILLAGE A

Subject	Age 1978 (years)	Age of Gender Role Change
1	59 (* 59)	16
2	58	17
3	58	24
4	55	No change, male gender iden-tity, and female gender role
5	53*	Puberty
6	50	15
7	49	16
8	45 (* 74)	21
9	44	16
10	40	15
11	36	15
15	24	16

VILLAGE B

Subject	Age 1978 (years)	Age of Gender Role Change
24	40	20
25	37	No change, female gender iden-tity and female gender role
26	35	Left town at 20 (no follow-up)
27	28	14
28	26	15
29	26	15
30	23	17

*Deceased

female to male (see Table 7.1). The change in gender role occurred either during puberty or in the postpubertal period after the affected subjects were convinced of their maleness and were experiencing sexual interest in girls and having morning erections and masturbating. In a few instances, the change in gender role was delayed until they were confident of their ability to defend themselves if necessary. The average age of the gender role change was 16, although in three subjects the change to a male gender role did not occur until they were in their 20s, and in Subject 4 the change did not occur at all (see Table 7.1).

When the ages of initiation of morning erections, nocturnal emissions, masturbation, and first sexual intercourse were compared, there were no significant differences between those subjects raised as girls and those raised as boys. The time of first sexual intercourse was 15 to 18 years of age for those raised as girls, 15 to 17 years for those raised as boys, and 14 to 16 years of age for 20 normal male controls in the village.

In the postpubertal subjects unambiguously raised as girls, the manifestations of male sexual behavior were evaluated according to the four patterns of sexual behavior differentiation: *sexual patterns* (sex-related behavior)—which for males includes direct aggressiveness, assertiveness, large motor activity, occupation; *sexual gender identity*—the sex to which an individual ascribes; *sexual object of choice*—the sex of the individual chosen as an erotically interesting partner; and *sexual mechanisms*—the features of sexual expression over which an individual has little control, which for males includes the ability to obtain and maintain an erection and to achieve orgasm. With the exception of Subject 25, all affected subjects perform male work in a society where there is a definite division of labor according to sex. All except Subject 25 have a male gender identity, and all except Subjects 4 and 25 have adopted a male gender role. All subjects have erections and have chosen females as their sexual object of choice, with the exception of Subject 25, who continues to live an identity as a female (see Table 7.1). The adequacy of sexual intercourse depends upon phallic size and the severity of the chordee.

Fifteen of the 16 subjects who changed to a male gender role are either living in common-law marriages with women or have lived with women in a common-law relationship in the past. They enjoy their role as head of the household (see Addendum). Three of these subjects are presently living with women who have had children from previous unions. In a domestic setting, the women take care of the household activities while the affected male subjects work either as farmers, miners, or woodsmen, as do the normal males in the town. The one exception is Subject 24 from Village B, who lives alone in the hills where he works as a farmer since changing to a male gender role at age 20 (see Table 7.1).

Subject 28 in Village B has been living with the same woman for nine years. During this time the woman has had three pregnancies and has four living children. Although this subject knows the children are not his, he now accepts them. His wife states that although she loves him she wants children and therefore becomes pregnant with other men. Subject 1 started living with his wife when he was 35 years old and she was 13 years of age. She stated that she loved him and was sexually satisfied by him. She remained faithful to him until he died at age 59 after 24 years of marriage. Only when she remarried did she realize that his genitalia were abnormal. Subject 2, a prominent man in Village A, is both respected and feared. Everyone in town knows of his condition, but it is never discussed openly. He is married to a woman who has had three children from a previous union.

Although these subjects behave unequivocally as males, they experience certain insecurities because of the abnormal appearance of their genitalia. They view themselves as incomplete, and this saddens them. They fear ridicule by members of the opposite sex and initially feel quite anxious about forming sexual relationships. They wonder why God made them this way but feel that they cannot question what God has done.

Two postpubertal subjects, Subjects 12 and 13, from Village A were initially raised as girls and later in childhood were changed to a male sex of rearing by their parents and have remained males. They are not considered to have been unambiguously raised as females. Subject 19 from Village A was raised as a girl by her parents despite their knowledge that an older brother had changed gender identity and gender role at puberty and despite the fact that they were raising two affected younger siblings as boys. Thus, Subject 19 was not unambiguously raised as female. Likewise, Subject 33 from Village B is being raised as a girl despite family awareness of the situation. Subject 23, whose parents are descendants of the inhabitants of Village A, was born in Santo Domingo and raised as a female. When she was hospitalized for a hernia repair at age 18 months, her parents were told of her condition. They continued to raise her as a female, however, until she was 5 years old, when the father decided to raise the child as a boy.

Thus, the affected subjects in Villages A and B were raised as girls until the townspeople became aware of the condition, that is, recognizing it at birth and realizing that despite their female sex of rearing the affected subjects would change to a male gender identity and male gender role with the events of puberty. Subsequently, the villagers have either raised the affected subjects as males from birth or have changed the sex of rearing to males as soon as the problem is recognized. As previously mentioned, two families opted to raise two prepubertal affected subjects as females despite complete knowlege of what would transpire with puberty.

Now that the villagers are familiar with the condition, the affected children and adults are sometimes objects of ridicule. The villagers refer to them as *guevedoce*, *guevote* (penis at twelve), and/or *machihembra* (first woman, then man). The affected adult males are quite capable of defending themselves when necessary, since they are as tall and generally more muscular than the rest of the male community. Their comparative strength and ability to gain respect by physical force if necessary enables them to exist in the community.

DISCUSSION

Androgens administered prenatally and/or postnatally to either female animals or male castrate animals can induce both adult male sexual and nonsexual behavior and inhibit female sexual response. Although the amount of administered androgen and the critical period for treatment differ from species to species, comparable effects on the development of male sexual behavior have been obtained in the rat (19, 20), guinea pig (21), mouse (22), rabbit (23), hamster (24), dog (25), sheep (26), and rhesus monkey (27). The critical period for induction of male sexual response varies with the animal species, for example, the dog requiring both pre- and postnatal exposure for optimal effect (25). Conversely, depriving the male animal of testosterone at a critical period will inhibit male sexual behavior and augment female sexual behavior in adulthood (25).

In addition to behavioral differences, androgen-induced sex differences in brain morphology and function are well documented. In rats, perinatal androgen administration produces structural differences in brain areas associated with masculine sexual behavior (28–31). In rats, under the neonatal influence of androgens, the preoptic suprachiasmatic area of the hypothalamus "differentiates" to regulate a tonic release of gonadotrophins from the pituitary, whereas in the absence of neonatal androgen exposure a cyclical release of gonadotrophins will occur (32). In canaries (*Werinus canarius*) and zebra finches (*Poephila gutata*), three vocal control areas in the brain are strikingly larger in males than in females (33); a fourth area is absent in female zebra finches and less well developed in female canaries. These differences correlate well with differences in singing behavior, as only males usually sing. In the squirrel monkey, sex differences have been found in the nuclear size of neurons in the medical amygdala which may be related to sex differences in the control of pituitary gonadotrophin secretion (34). The androgen effects on the brain causing sexual dimorphism in animals may be mediated either directly through androgens (i.e., testosterone) and/or through aromatization of androgens to estrogens in the brain (35).

In man, the basic question of the relative influences of hormonal factors and environmental factors in the determination of gender identity remains unanswered. In 1955 the theory of sexual neutrality at birth was proposed (6, 7). It stated that in man sexuality was undifferentiated at birth, becoming differentiated as either masculine or feminine in the course of various experiences of growing. Later the concept of sexual neutrality at birth was broadened to recognize that human male and female infants express sexually dimorphic behavior from birth. However, it was postulated that such sexually dimorphic behavior could be incorporated into either a male or female gender identity pattern and was not the exclusive property of either sex (36). To test this hypothesis, pseudohermaphrodites were matched so that they were "chromosomally, gonadally, and otherwise diagnostically the same." The "matched pairs" were said to differ only in their sex of assignment and therefore their sex of rearing. The studies appeared to show that the gender identity of the individuals was concordant with the sex of rearing and not with the chromosomal or gonadal sex. Therefore, it was concluded that the sex of rearing predominated in establishing gender identity in man.

Although the subjects of those aforementioned studies may have been matched chromosomally and gonadally, they were not matched for a similar hormonal milieu as the methodology for adequate plasma steroid evaluation was not available at that time. Thus the amount of androgen exposure was assumed to be similar for the "matched pairs" of pseudohermaphrodites but not known to be so. Therefore, in these studies the issue of nature (i.e., androgen) versus nurture (i.e., sex of rearing) in the determination of a male gender identity cannot be adequately resolved due to lack of sufficient hormonal data. Furthermore, since the etiology of most cases of male pseudohermaphroditism is secondary to either inadequate testosterone production or action, many of the subjects described were probably testosterone deficient (37) and are inappropriate models (as are female pseudohermaphrodites) for determining the relative importance of the sex of rearing versus nature (i.e., androgen) in determination of male gender identity in man. Also, in most cases studied, where the gender identity was concordant with the sex of rearing and discordant with the chromosomal and gonadal sex, castration and sex hormone therapy were usually initiated to coincide with the sex of rearing, thereby interrupting the natural sequence of events (6, 7, 36).

In this study of human male pseudohermaphrodites with 5a-reductase deficiency, 18 subjects were unambiguously raised as girls. Despite the female sex of rearing, 17 subjects changed to a male gender identity and 16 subjects changed to a male gender role during or following puberty. These events occurred in a setting without physician intervention and/or other social factors which might have acted to interrupt the natural sequence of events. Intervention by a physician—that is, reassurance, surgical correction of the external genitalia to coincide with the female sex assignment, or administration of hormone therapy concordant with the female sex of rearing—did not occur. Parental attitude when the change was occurring was one of amazement, confusion, and finally acceptance, rather than hostility and prevention. Social pressure, that is, embarrassment and possible harassment afterward by the other villagers, was the cause of the major anxieties the affected males experienced, which may have led them to hesitate for a time. However, with the exception of Subject 4, the pressures were not strong enough to prevent the change to a male gender role from occurring in all 17 subjects who had adopted a male gender identity with puberty. The one affected subject (Subject 25) who retained her female gender identity postpubertally is a complete exception to this general phenomenon of pubertal gender identity change in these subjects. This highlights the fact that in humans, because of higher cognitive processes and the multifactorial input in forming gender identity, there will always be exceptions to a general rule.

Normally the sex of rearing and testosterone imprinting of the brain act in unison to determine the complete expression of the male gender (see Figure 7.1). However, the subjects of this study demonstrate that in a laissez-faire environment, when the sex of rearing (female) is discordant with the testosterone mediated biologic sex; the biologic sex prevails if normal testosterone activation of puberty is permitted to occur (see Figure 7.2).

From the data it appears that the extent of testosterone exposure of the brain in utero, in the early postnatal period, and at puberty has greater impact in determining male gender identity than the female sex of rearing. Theoretically,

Figure 7.1
Schema Depicting the Hormonal Factors and Environmental Factors, i.e., Sex of Rearing, Acting in Unison to Form Male Gender Identity in the Normal Male

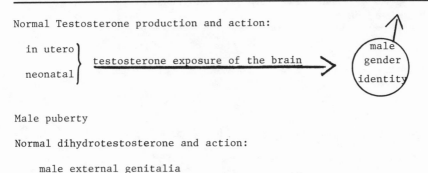

```
Normal Testosterone production and action:

  in utero ⎫
           ⎬  testosterone exposure of the brain   >     male
  neonatal ⎭                                            gender
                                                       identity


Male puberty

Normal dihydrotestosterone and action:

     male external genitalia

     male sex of rearing
```

"masculinization" of the brain occurs under the influence of testosterone, and together with the activation of a testosterone-mediated puberty, male gender identity develops, overriding the female sex of rearing. This experiment of nature emphasizes the importance of androgens, which act as inducers and activators in the evolution of male gender identity in man (38, 39). We recently investigated a 65–year-old male pseudohermaphrodite with 5a-reductase deficiency born in southern Italy and raised as a girl. The subject emigrated to the United States at age 16. Psychosexual evaluation shows that the subject gradually changed to a male gender identity with puberty and presently has a male gender identity but because of family pressure has retained a female gender role.(45)

In pseudohermaphrodites with inadequate testosterone production or action, it is understandable that gender identity might coincide with the sex of rearing. Adequate androgen imprinting has not occurred, and therefore the sex of rearing becomes the predominant factor. Such individuals are a testimonial to the malleability of human beings in the acquisition of gender identity but in no way approximate the normal sequence of events (40). (See Figures 7.3 and 7.4.)

It has been proposed that gender identity becomes fixed by 18 months to 4 years of age, around the time of language development (6, 7, 36). At this time a child becomes aware of his or her gender. However, being aware of one's gender and being unalterably fixed in that gender are two separate issues. From this study, it appears that the development of gender identity in man is continually evolving throughout childhood, becoming fixed with puberty.

Since the evolution of a male gender identity is initiated with early puberty in subjects with 5a-reductase deficiency, it is not surprising that either prepubertal or pubertal castration with the initiation of female hormone therapy might abort its development (18, 41, 42). The time course for the development of a male

Figure 7.2
Schema Depicting the Dominance of Testosterone Imprinting and Activation in the Evolution of a Male Gender Identity, Completely Overriding the Unambiguous Female Sex of Rearing in Male Pseudohermaphrodites with 5a-Reductase Deficiency

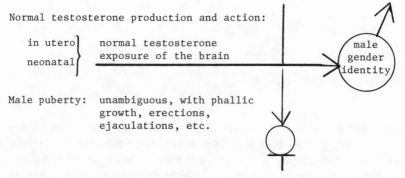

```
                              Deficient dihydrotestosterone production:

                                 marked genital ambiguity

                                 female sex of rearing

Normal testosterone production and action:

   in utero ⎤      normal testosterone                         male
            ⎬      exposure of the brain                      gender
   neonatal ⎦                                                identity

Male puberty:    unambiguous, with phallic
                 growth, erections,
                 ejaculations, etc.
```

*No reinforcement of the female sex of rearing by a physician

*No surgical correction of the external genitalia or castration

*No hormone therapy concordant with the female sex of rearing

gender identity with puberty appears to be unique to each individual (see Table 7.1). Thus, the age when successful interruption (castration, sociocultural factors, and so on) can be initiated to prevent the complete evolution of a male gender identity and/or the change to a male gender role will differ for each affected subject.

There are many reported cases of male pseudohermaphrodites, with successful changes in gender from female to male occurring after the proposed "critical period" (5, 8–13, 43). In many of these cases, the change in gender role occurred during adolescence. Adequate hormonal evaluation would be important in these cases, as they also appear to challenge both the theory of the immutability of gender identity after the age of 3 or 4 and the sex of rearing as the major factor in determining male gender identity.

The data from this study show that, in humans, environmental or sociocultural factors are not solely responsible for the formation of a male gender identity. Androgens make a strong and definite contribution. Analogous to the induction of the male phenotype from the inherent female phenotype, the formation of a male gender identity in man also appears to be at least partially induced by

Figure 7.3
Schema Depicting the Predominance of Female Sex of Rearing in
Pseudohermaphrodites with Deficient Testosterone Production

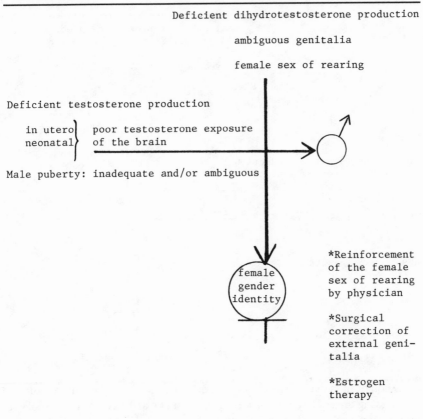

androgens from an undifferentiated and/or inherently female nervous system (Figure 7.5).

ADDENDUM: THE TOWNS AND SOCIAL PRACTICES

Villages A and B are in a remote and rural area in the southwestern section of the Dominican Republic. Both villages were virtually geographic isolates, with access only via dirt roads. However, approximately 20 years ago the government paved the road to Village A in order to bring workers to the salt mine from a neighboring village. The access road to Village B is unchanged. The population of Village A is approximately 5,000 and the population of Village B is 2,500. The houses on the main street of the villages are constructed from woven palm leaves. The homes consist of two bedrooms and a living area. The

Figure 7.4
Schema Depicting the Predominance of the Female Sex of Rearing in Subjects
with the Complete Androgen Insensitivity Syndrome (Testicular Feminization)
Who Were Raised as Females

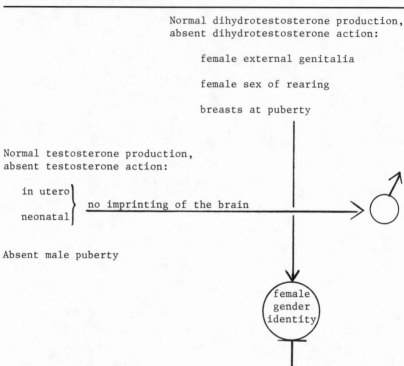

other homes in the villages are huts with only two rooms: a community bedroom and a living area. They are constructed with sticks and have thatched roofs. In all the homes, the kitchen is separate and located behind the house. Very few homes have an outhouse, and even fewer have shower facilities. The inhabitants of the towns, both adults and children, bathe in the river.

The family unit consists of a mother and father, who have not been married in either a legal or religious ceremony, and their offspring. The men earn a living either farming, mining, or by chopping down trees to provide fuel (carbonero activity) for cooking. The farms are small agricultural plots and are worked individually by the head of the household (the father) or collectively by immediate male members of the family and other male kin. On the outskirts of Village A there is a salt and gypsum mine. Some of the men from the village are employed in the mine, but the majority of the miners are brought in by truck from a larger village nearby.

The women generally do not help in the carbonero activities or in cultivating the agricultural plots. They maintain the household, take care of the children, and cultivate small gardens in back of the house. Female relatives of the mother

Figure 7.5
Schema Depicting the Critical Factors Involved in the Evolution of a Male
Gender Identity in Man

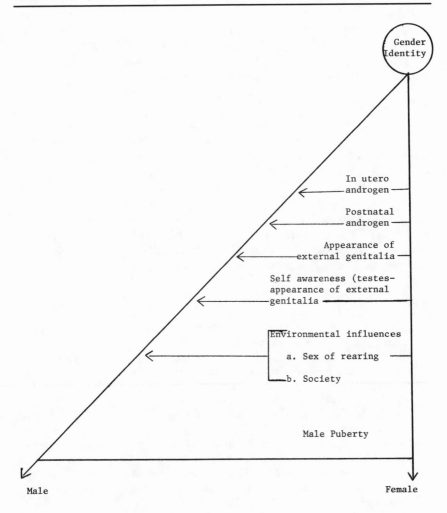

usually come over during the day to participate in such household activities as cooking, cleaning, washing, and babysitting. The children are taken care of by the mother or the grandmother, older sisters, and other female relatives.

There is a definite socialization of the children according to sex. The boys are also allowed to go naked until the seventh or eighth year of life. However, the girls wear underpants from the time they are toilet-trained. The boys and girls play together until the age of 6; between the ages of 6 and 11 the children are encouraged to separate according to sex. From approximately the age of 7, the girls help their mothers with the household activities while the boys help their fathers during the planting and harvesting season or with the carbonero activities. In general, however, the boys have more freedom to romp and play. The girls are encouraged to stay with their mothers or play in close proximity to the house.

There is a primary school in the town, and the children start their education at about 7 or 8 years of age. Boys and girls attend school together, with no segregation according to sex. Most of the children, however, do not go to school, either because the parents do not have money to buy them books and pencils or because of lack of parental interest. Very few children in the town attend school beyond the third grade.

From the age of 11 or 12, the boys seek entertainment at the bars and attend cockfights. The girls, on the other hand, stay home and help with household chores and only occasionally go to the local bar to dance and socialize. In general, the girls marry earlier, between the ages of 13 and 20, and the boys between the ages of 18 to 25. Fidelity is demanded from the women but not from the men.

There are no laws in the town against homosexuality, but there is strong social pressure against it and thus it is practiced furtively in both villages. Female prostitution also exists and is accepted as a fact of life. The boys in the town start going to prostitutes from the age of 14.

REFERENCES

1. Ounsted, C., and Taylor, D. C. Gender Differences: Their Ontogeny and Significance. Baltimore: Williams and Wilkins, 1972.
2. Hutt, C. Males and Females. Harmondsworth, Eng.: Penguin Education, 1977.
3. Reinish, J. Fetal hormones, the brain, and human sex differences: a heuristic, integrative review of the recent literature. Arch. Sex. Behav., 3:51, 1974.
4. Goy, R. W., and Goldfoot, D. A. Hormonal influences on sexually dimorphic behavior. In: Greep, R. O., ed., Handbook of Physiology, Section 7, Vol. II, Part 1. Washington, D.C.: American Physiological Society, 1973.
5. Chapman, A. H.; Saslow, G.; and Watson, F. Pseudohermaphroditism, a medical, social, and psychiatric case study. Psychosomat. Med., 13:212, 1951.
6. Money, J.; Hampson, J.; and Hampson, J. L. Hermophroditism: recommendations concerning assignment of sex, change of sex, and psychologic management. Bull. Johns Hopkins Hosp., 97:284, 1955.
7. Money, J.; Hampson, J.; and Hampson, J. L. An examination of some basic sexual concepts: the evidence of human hermaphroditism. Bull. Johns Hopkins Hosp., 97:301, 1955.
8. Burns, E.; Segaloff, A.; and Carrera, G. M. Reassignment of sex: report of 3 cases. J. Urol., 84:126, 1960.
9. Ghabrial, F., and Girgis, S. Reorientation of sex: report of two cases. Int. J. Fertil., 7:249, 1962.
10. Berg, I., and Leeds, M. B. Change of assigned sex at puberty. The Lancet, ii:1216, 1963.
11. Brown, J. B., and Fryer, M. P. Plastic surgical correction of hypospadias with

mistaken sex identity and transvestism resulting in normal marriage and parenthood. Surg. Gynecol. Obstet., 118:45, 1964.

12. Teter, J. and Boczkowski, K. Errors in management and assignment of sex in patients with abnormal sexual differentiation. Am. J. Obstet. Gynecol. 93:1084, 1965.

13. Dewhurst, C. G., and Gordan, R. R. Case histories involving re-registration of sex. In: The Intersexual Disorder. London: Ballieri, Tindall, and Cassall, 1969.

14. Money, J. and Ogunro, C. Behavioral sexology: ten cases of genetic male intersexuality with impaired prenatal and pubertal androgenization. Arch. Sex. Behav., 3:181, 1974.

15. Lev-Ran, A. Gender role differentiation in hermaphrodites. Arch. Sex. Behav., 3:391, 1974.

16. Imperato-McGinley, J.; Guerrero, L.; Gautier, T.; and Peterson, R. E. Steroid 5a-reductase deficiency in man: an inherited form of male pseudohermaphroditism. Science, 186:1213, 1974.

17. Peterson, R. E.; Imperato-McGinley, J.; Gautier, T.; and Sturla, E. Male pseudohermaphroditism due to steroid 5a-reductase defiency. Am. J. Med., 62:170, 1977.

18. Walsh, P. C.; Madden, J. D.; Harrod, M. H.; Goldstein, J. L.; MacDonald, P. C.; and Wilson, J. D. Familial incomplete male pseudohermaphroditism, type 2: decreased dihydrotestosterone formation in pseudovaginal perineoscrotal hypospadias. New Engl. J. Med., 291:944, 1974.

19. Harris, G. W. Sex hormones, brain development, and brain function. Endocrinology, 75:627, 1964.

20. Pfaff, S. W., and Zigmond, R. E. Neonatal androgen effects on sexual and nonsexual behavior of adult rats tested under various hormone regimens. Neuroendocrinology, 7:129, 1971.

21. Phoenix, C. H.; Goy, R. W.; Gerall, A. A.; and Young, W. C. Organizing action of prenatally administered testosterone propionate on tissues mediating mating behavior in the female guinea pig. Endocrinology, 65:369, 1959.

22. Edwards, D. A., and Burge, K. C. Early androgen treatment and male and female sexual behavior in mice. Horm. Behav., 2:49, 1971.

23. Beyer, C.; de la Torre, L.; Larsson, L.; and Perez-Palacio, G. Synergistic actions of estrogen and androgen on the sexual behavior of the castrated male rabbit. Horm. Behav., 6:301, 1975.

24. Paup, D. C.; Goniglio, L. P.; and Clemens, L. G. Masculinization of the female golden hamster by neonatal treatment with androgen or estrogen. Horm. Behav., 3:123, 1972.

25. Beach, F. A. Hormonal modification of sexually dimorphic behavior. Psychoneuroendocrinology, 1:3, 1975.

26. Clarke, I. J. The sexual behavior of prenatally androgenized ewes observed in the field. J. Reprod. Fertil., 49:311, 1977.

27. Goy, R. W.; Wolf, J. E.; and Eisele, S. G. Experimental female hermaphroditism in rhesus monkeys: anatomical and psychological characteristics. In: Husaph, H., and Money, J., eds., Handbook of Sexology. Amsterdam: Excerpta Medica, 1977.

28. Pfaff, D. W. Morphological changes in the brain of adult male rats after neonatal castration. J. Endocrinol., 36:415, 1966.

29. Dorner, G., and Staudt, J. Structural changes in the preoptic anterior hypothalamic

area of the male rat, following neonatal castration and androgen substitution. Neuroendocrinology, 3:136, 1968.

30. Raisman, G., and Field, P. M. Sexual dimorphism in the neuropil of the preoptic area of the rat and its dependence on neonatal androgen. Brain Res., 54:1, 1973.

31. Gorski, R. A.; Gordon, J. H.; Shryne, J. E.; and Southam, A. M. Evidence for a morphological sex difference within the medial preoptic area of the rat brain. Brain Res., 148:333, 1978.

32. Barraclough, C. A. Modification in the CNS regulation of reproduction after exposure of prepubertal rats to steroid hormones. Rec. Prog. Horm. Res., 22:503, 1966.

33. Notterbohn, F., and Arnold, A. P. Sexual dimorphism in vocal control areas of the songbird brain. Science, 194:211, 1976.

34. Bubenik, G. A., and Brown, G. M. Morphologic sex differences in primate brain areas involved in regulation of reproductive activity. Experientia, 29:619, 1973.

35. Reddy, V. V. R.; Naftolin, F.; and Ryan, K. J. Conversion of androstenedione to estrone by neural tissues from fetal and neonatal rats. Endocrinology, 94:117, 1974.

36. Money, J., and Ehrhardt, A. A. Man and woman / boy and girl—the differentiation and dimorphism of gender identity from conception to maturity. Baltimore: Johns Hopkins University Press, 1972.

37. Imperato-McGinley, J., and Peterson, R. E. Male pseudohermaphroditism: the complexities of male phenotypic development. Am. J. Med., 61:251, 1976.

38. Imperato-McGinley, J.; Peterson, R. E.; Stoller, R.; and Goodwin, W. E. Male pseudohermaphroditism secondary to 17b-hydroxysteroid dehydrogenase deficiency: gender role change with puberty. J. Clin. Endocrinol. Metab., 49:391, 1979.

39. Imperato-McGinley, J.; Peterson, R. E.; Gautier, T.; and Sturla, E. Androgens and the evolution of male gender identity among male pseudohermaphrodites with 5a-reductase deficiency. New Engl. J. Med., 300:1233, 1979b.

40. Diamond, M. A critical evaluation of the ontogeny of human sexual behavior. Q. Rev. Bio., 40:147, 1965.

41. Saenger, P.; Goldman, A. S.; Levine, L. S.; Korth-Schultz, S.; Muecke, E. E.; Katsumata, M.; Doberne, Y.; and New, M. I. Prepubertal diagnosis of steroid 5a-reductase deficiency. J. Clin. Endocrinol. Metab., 46:627, 1978.

42. Fisher, L. K.; Kogut, M. D.; Moore, R. J.; Goebelsmann, U.; Weitzman, J. J.; Isaacs, H., Jr.; Griffin, J. E.; and Wilson, J. D. Clinical, endocrinological, and enzymatic characterization of two patients with 5a-reductase deficiency: evidence that a single enzyme is responsible for the 5a-reductase of cortisol and testosterone. J. Clin. Endocrinol. Metab., 47:653, 1978.

43. Stoller, R. A contribution to the study of gender identity. Int. J. Psychoanal. 45:220, 1964.

44. Zuger, B. Gender role determination: a critical review of the evidence from hermaphroditism. Psychosomat. Med., 32:449, 1970.

45. Imperato-McGinley, J.; Peterson, R. E.; Leshin, M.; Griffin, J.; Cooper, G.; Draghi, S.; Berenyi, M.; and Wilson, J. D. Steroid 5-reductase deficiency in a 65-year-old male pseudohermaphrodite: The natural history, ultrastructure of the testes, and evidence for inherited enzyme heterogeneity. J. Clin. Endrocrinol. Metab., 50:15, 1980.

Male Homosexuality Reconsidered

The interrelations between the events of life, the happenings to which the individual has been subjected, and the transformations of those events into inner experience, or lived history, compose much of what is most interesting to psychoanalysis. In general, we have laid principal importance on the interrelations that we can help our patients recover from the early years of life. Equally erroneous caricatures of psychoanalysis arise from the misconception, on the one hand, that the personality is entirely shaped by external events and, on the other hand, that the personality develops without the constituting effects of experience in the world. When we undertake to look psychoanalytically at male homosexuality, we ordinarily study the case history of the patient with the presumption that the sexual preference itself demands an explanation: What happened to these individuals to cause them to deviate from the norm? For reasons that should become apparent, I am undertaking to examine the history of homosexuals from another point of view, and to begin with I should like to reflect a bit on what kind of world the homosexually disposed boy enters. I am postponing the question of the nature of this disposition.

It is by necessity a heterosexual situation that not only conceived his existence but also surrounds his early days. A mother and a father—or some surrogate for either of them or both—are present. The dualities boy/girl, man/woman, male/female are built into the structure of any society that has children, pervading the social and cultural milieux. There are boys' rooms and girls' rooms, boys' names and girls' names, blue and pink clothing, boys' toys and girls' toys, games, and even words. This is a nearly endless list which remains valid even during the present feminist era, when we recognize the claims of girls to privileges, re-

©1983 by S. A. Leavy. This chapter originally appeared in the 1985 edition of the *International Journal of Psychoanalytic Psychotherapy*.

sponsibilities, and capacities hitherto reserved for boys, and the liberal-minded may even encourage boys to take part in traditionally girls' activities—usually halfheartedly. But the structural elements in the sexual division go much deeper than this and into the heart of the expectations of parents and grandparents.

What is more, distinctions of prescribed roles of action are early apparent too. There are things boys do that are different from the things girls do. Not only do parents impart them but, more significantly, contemporaries teach them, such as most of the games that have acquired the immortality of childhood. Games never become obsolete, because the world of childhood perpetuates them jealously long after the individual child outgrows them. Ball games of all sorts are predominantly boys' games (and woe unto the boy who does not care for them), but so too ways of walking, sitting, standing—let alone urinating—all are sexually defined. Girls who adopt boys' ways may be admired for a while, but while they are eventually declared misfits they are not in such danger of ostracism as boys who adopt whatever are considered to be girls' ways. That too is understandable, since the female is usually if tacitly held to be the inferior.

All this is as nothing in the future experience of the homosexual youth. The sex difference qualifies all the relations projected into the future of the growing child, heterosexuality being the unquestioned norm, literally so since the question is not open to discussion. Boy will meet girl, boy will live with and marry girl (or boy will do neither and will get into all sorts of trouble with or on account of girls), and boy and girl, married, will as man and wife become parents and renew the cycle. Animals and plants even are drawn into the paradigm, and most valuably, since their sexuality is relatively fixed and the ambiguities that follow from the state of being human are not often met with, certainly not in plants, of which neither the monoecious nor the dioecious can qualify as homosexual.

Emphasizing the binary discrimination male-female (or better, masculine-feminine, since it is behavior and experience and not biology that is there in question) is a means of avoiding anxiety. Whatever falls into the overlap between the expected sexual patterns is in a potentially taboo area. To be sure, the polarity only moves the question a step further: Why does blurring of the distinctions provoke anxiety? But that is one of the questions that really concern psychoanalysis, which is probably also the only instrument that can show whether or not the recent social trend toward the blending of superficial sexual characteristics might reflect a mitigation of anxiety and so encourage permissiveness toward homosexuality, which is associatively linked with androgyny.

In any case, the homosexual boy under the best of circumstances grows up in a milieu for the most part silent about what concerns him very much. Silence can be far more powerful than obloquy. Indeed, silence promotes repression like nothing else, what is not mentioned becoming nonexistent, except in the unconscious that never forgets—and in the consciousness of the homosexual. The homosexual, boy and youth, is not confronted by any normalizing let alone celebrating presentation of homosexuality. This stream of erotism, sensuality, and fantasy runs in a dark cavern of secrecy. The conversation of parents and teachers makes no open mention of it, while it may abound in comment about ordinary family life and make at least indirect reference to the joys and sufferings of heterosexual love. Even the ridicule that boys of "latency" age may undergo about their real or fancied interest in girls is only briefly painful because it is a foreshadowing of praise for the aggressive sexuality of later adolescence. The homosexually disposed boy has no such encouragement, and one of the commonest experiences is believing that he is the only such variant in the world. He needs to make adjustments in his speech and mentally interpret the speech of others in order to effect conformity to accepted discourse. The fate, passions, conflicts, heroism, even the desperation of the homosexual are not significantly present in the literature taught in schools. Even in the avant-garde subject of sex education homosexuality is mentioned only warily, lest anxious parents get the idea that it is being promoted.

This state of mental solitude may be the best available when we consider the alternative, which is steeped in the language of obloquy, for all the terms presenting homosexuals and homosexuality are strung on a gamut of contempt or worse. Neutrality is virtually unknown. The boy's first apprehension of homosexuality as a reality in others often, maybe usually, consists of warnings to beware of "strange" men, the notion of sexual arousal through seduction becoming thereby condensed with the threat of kidnapping or murder. In another category, that of sexual play, he is warned against "sissy" behavior; in this way the persistent denigration of girls and women is pressed into the service of the defense against homosexuality. The feminine identifications of many boys likewise encounter formidable opposition, and attempts are made to suppress them by enforced participation in masculine play.

Words of obloquy usually enter the vocabulary of youth long before their meaning becomes plain. There are mysterious allusions to queers, queens, fags, fairies, pansies, nancy-boys (their name is legion)—but rarely as signifiers designating members of the intimate or familial social situation. The bearers of these ignominious names abide supposedly only on a remote periphery, carrying out their shady and sinister existence as at best figures of fun, at worst corrupters and criminals. If it is remotely possible to attach one of these names to an otherwise hateful personage, that is unfailingly done. The homosexual youth, despite frantic attempts to meet the requirements of the social order held to be "straight" while knowing that he is deviant, succumbs to the injunctions that attack his sexual disposition root and branch: he becomes hypocritically censorious of the qualities in others that he secretly suppresses in himself. In the analysis of homosexuals, the profound self-loathing of many (interpreted by some analysts as an autonomous judgment proceeding from the healthy desire to be heterosexual) reveals itself first in belittling talk about other homosexuals. In any case, it is an internalized judgment, fulfilling the purpose of reducing estrangement of the boy or man from the unthinkingly but anxiously heterosexual society of which he is a part—as much as he is part of any society. But the deeper effect is one of inner alienation, as he forms an important superego identification in abasing his own desires or constricting them into a narrowly sexual sphere. The universal human problem of the abasement of love here finds an especially revealing form. Whereas public approbation abounds to uphold heterosexual love despite the explicit derogation of sensuality, no such ennoblement attaches to homosexual love. Another outcome of the identification with the heterosexual superego is the disposition to elevate or depreciate one or another mode of sexual expression in order to retain or regain self-respect. It can now be further predicted that homosexual boys will turn the present threat of the acquired immune deficiency syndrome to the purpose of self-derogation rather than that of rational sexual life.

Although in more sophisticated quarters it seems to be mitigating its adverse judgments, religion is not of much comfort to the young homosexual. It has always provided a background for secular obloquy, in both Testaments, from the dire punishment of the men of Sodom to St. Paul's pronouncement that "no homosexual shall inherit the kingdom of God." Professor Boswell's account (1) of the transformations in Christian attitudes over the centuries is highly persuasive, but living as we do in the terminal moraine of a puritan glacier, the atmosphere for any unblessed sexuality remains chilly. Nor is Judaism more lenient than Christianity. Church and synagogue continue to be for many people principal dispensers of effective symbols; they are very poor in their positive symbolism of homosexuality.

I have sketched in only faint outlines the universe of the homosexual man. Ironically some of the more compassionate views of the nineteenth and twentieth centuries have complicated the situation, and not for his peace of mind. Humanitarians balked at the criminalizing and pillorying of homosexuals as wicked, dangerous, evil, corrupting enemies of the family, heirs of Sodom and Gomorrah, and the social legislation of our time in many democratic countries has been remarkably effective in depenalizing homosexual conduct. But such compassion has a price too—the acceptance of medical diagnosis as a way of classifying and supposedly understanding these irregular people. They are supposed to be inherently sick, by the fact of their deviation, although not necessarily contagiously so, and need treatment, whether they want it or no. Diagnosed, the homosexual is to believe that what he feels so intensely throughout his being— and sexuality is, in health, diffused throughout the person—is symptomatic in nature, either the euphoria of an intoxication or the ominous prodrome of a malignant disorder. Unlike "the way of a man with a maid," it is never what it seems to be.

The diagnostic judgment too has to be assimilated into the homosexual's concept of hmself, whatever the mitigating effect of *DSM-III* may be in the world of psychiatry. The cost of participation in the mind of the consensus, always high because it necessitated yielding to a conspiracy of silence and secrecy, includes the additional tally of psychopathology. Psychoanalysis contributes to this heavy freight. It seems to have the last word in psychopathology because it investigates unconscious meanings. No state of mind is, in theory, inaccessible to psychoanalytic inquiry. If we accept the method, we cannot disown its consequences; whatever is exposed "behind" or "within" or "beneath" the manifest content of consciousness belongs to its motivational scope, whether it be a symptom, a declamation, a nightmare, a sexual act, a creative work, a criminal deed, a self-sacrifice, or a vision. Psychoanalytic revisionist systems do not waver in intending this exposure, although they may extend or narrow the field of desires and meanings included in their focus.

Nevertheless, it is arbitrary to infer from the analysis of homosexual acts, fantasies, desires, and relationships that they are symptomatic in nature in themselves, whether or not their protagonists, our patients, find them so. We must go further and, on the basis of what I have here described as the mental universe in which homosexuals are thrown, question their symptomatic nature, even when they are so qualified by our patients, dominated as they often are by the public significations of homosexuality. A symptom of homosexuality that does stand in need of treatment is the judgment imposed by the agent on the act. This treatment is distinctly not an absolution but, in the most classical Freudian terms, an analysis of the superego. In these patients, a whole range of experience has been allowed, or even forced, to develop outside the synthesizing, symbolizing realm of ethical life. When there is *no* right way to do something that needs to be done, the possibility of a good conscience is negligible.

It is self-evident that these ideas have a bearing on the analysis of the transference. I have found it useful to look on the transference as an emergent part of a psychoanalytic dialogue (2). Transferences are repetitions, but what they repeat in this dialectical situation is the elaborate complex of earlier dialogues. Accordingly, both the patient as speaker and the analyst (man or woman) as the one addressed are continually misrecognized under the masks of earlier distortions. I should like to apply this principle to the analysis of homosexuals. Whatever else their transferences may be, they are sure to repeat the earlier dialectic in which their homosexuality as a signifier of evil comes under condemnation. That happens regardless of the attitude that the analyst presents in reality, but the analysis of the transference—that is, of the masochistic-depressive reproduction of earlier exchanges—is impossible so long as the analyst sticks consistently to his conception of homosexuality as defense or deficiency. (I introduce the word "consistently" because there are occasions when this defensive posture is indeed paramount.) In fact, the progress of the analysis under such prejudicial conditions will only confirm the prejudice over and over again: stuck in the primitive anti-instinctual state of sphincter morality, the analysand will dredge up acknowledgments of the evils of his sexual life—to bolster his anxious unity with the analyst—whenever the analyst interprets his sexual strivings as something to overcome. The analyst may maintain scrupulously neutral views on the morality or even the normality of homosexuality, but so long as he interprets it primarily as a defensive function, or treats it as a defect to be surpassed, he cannot himself be separated analytically from the voice of an anguished parent.

Practically all psychoanalytic studies of homosexuality take as their point of departure the assumption that it is a developmental deviation of the individual originating in sources that can be hypothetically reconstructed in the transference (3, 4). Freud claimed that homosexuals (and he referred mainly to males) reveal in analytic treatment the positive Oedipus complex as an invariable part of their history (5). Like others, these boys were passionately attached to their mothers and had patricidal fantasies. Also like them, they went through a negative Oedipus complex, with sexual subordination to their fathers and abandonment of their mothers as love objects, but unlike the normals they remained fixated at this stage, their attachment being both stronger and more permanent. Homosexuality in its manifest form was thus ostensibly derived from a developmental fixation, in which perhaps oral and anal libidinal structures also exercised dominant roles. Constitutional predispositions might exist too, but were hardly stressed.

Later studies modified the first Freudian account (3), but it has essentially prevailed. The centrality of the Oedipal development yielded to a focus on pre-Oedipal elements, the Oepidal serving, as so often in psychopathological development, as a decisive turning point, in which precursor states become definitively summated. The fixations and the regression undergone to the fixation points were variously accounted for, and other elements were uncovered. Sadomasochism, for example, appeared to be one of them, with roots not only in the pregenital ambivalence but also in an intense sibling hatred that was defensively transmuted to the love of boys. Homosexuality was related to narcissism— the obvious choice of a mirrored love object being extended to generalized narcissistic character formation, a category of immense amplitude if one includes all the definitions assigned to it (6).

All these elements of deviant sexual orientation were inferred in psychoanalysis through direct recall of memories, through conscious fantasies, or through the reconstruction of unconscious fantasies, especially in the transference. The pre-Oedipal background, for example, emerged to help account for the overdevelopment of the negative Oedipus complex; at the same time, the exposure of very primitive antecedents implied, in the minds of some analysts, a general psychic disturbance of far more serious nature than had been realized, suggesting a psychotic or pre-psychotic background for most homosexual men (7, 8)—all the phenomenological evidence to the contrary being ignored. The rigidity of the boy's tie to his mother, both as phallic woman and as the one with whom the symbiotic relation was permanent, facilitated feminine identification on the one side and severe castration anxiety on the other. It was not difficult to postulate convincingly the interpersonal patterns that paved the way to the homosexual outcome: actual dominance of mothers, absence of effective fathers, early incestuous seductions leading to homosexual defenses, self-abasement in the presence of attacking older brothers. Various students of the subject arrived at different hypotheses of the basic vulnerability that could await such a wide variety of deviating experiences.

The relation between manifest male homosexuality, which is my principal topic, and latent homosexuality has been the focal psychoanalytic concern. Freud's nearly mathematical formula "The neurosis is the negative of the perversion" presents the idea aphoristically (5). While Freud did not say in so many words that the formula was exhaustive, the implication is that there is nothing unique about homosexuality in its manifest form, particularly since a wide spectrum of homosexual attitudes, fantasies, and impulses emerges in the analysis of heterosexual patients. Conversely, the analysis of homosexuals usually revealed latent heterosexual attitudes, fantasies, and impulses. In fact, the treatment of homosexuals could be justified by assuming that under the conditions of psychoanalysis hitherto submerged or "blighted" (9), heterosexual tendencies would come to the conscious surface, leaving the patient free to follow a new and presumably preferable path of fulfillment. That homosexuals can be neurotic enough to suit any nosological pattern did not invalidate the formula, since it was obvious that the expression of ordinarily unconscious "perverse" impulses can never be complete; enough is always left behind as potential for neurotic compromise. On the other hand, Freud, far from disparaging *latent*homosexuality as itself pathological, saw in it the energic source of philanthropic action. The brotherhood of man, to the slight extent that it is enacted, rests on this homoerotism, the love between the two sexes, latent or manifest, being apparently too productive of aggressive competition to support this more diffuse form of erotism (10).

So the argument runs, briefly summarized. It is based on a clear if not always stated assumption that heterosexuality being normative for reproductive life was generally normative too. The biological fact of the sexual difference—so immensely widespread throughout the natural world, arising as a convergent phenomenon through parallel evolutions, and so variously and ingeniously adapted to the same end of sexual reproduction, the seemingly universal biologically structured attraction of the two sexes for one another, and the overwhelming if not quite unanimous judgment of moral tradition—militates in favor of the heterosexual norm and, correspondingly, of homosexual disorder. Although psychoanalytic writers often initiate their discussions by admitting that this extended normative role of heterosexuality is arbitrary, they customarily proceed as though it were self-evident. Much of what I have to claim in this chapter will question this position.

I do not refer primarily to questioning from outside psychoanalysis, although a really comprehensive view of the subject does demand information from outside, including biological knowledge, sociological knowledge, and even literary sources, and I shall make some explicit references to them in the proper places. I would like first to call attention to an alternative psychoanalytic view of sexual norms and deviations. Robert and Ilse Barande (11) have written a critical review of the whole idea of perversion, including homosexuality. How in the first place, the Barandes ask, can we speak after Freud of "normal sexuality"? To do so is simply to reinstate the pre-Freudian designation of morally stigmatized behavior as perversions. It is true that Freud did use the term, and true that he postulated sexual norms, but he did not follow the social consensus. Once we recognize that human desire comes to life in an essentially immature, even fetalized being (*néoténique*), we can see that its ineluctable fate lies in an endless quest for the lost object from whom birth separated it in all its immaturity. All real objects, without exception, merely interrupt the quest, so that the individual perpetually mistakes his or her hunger for its fulfillment (*sa faim comme sa fin*). As the Barandes put it, "It is the task of the 'néoténique,' being separated from its original union by its fall into life and into time, to invent detours for itself, deviations of object as well as of means and aims. Its condition is inexorably perverse—if perversions must be." Or, as they go on to say, perversions do not exist, and we are all perverse.

With evident irony, the Barandes account for our psychoanalytic adherence to the concept of sexual normality as "the promotion of counter-transference to the rank of theory." This is indeed a kind of ad hominem argument that might easily be fired back at its proponents. But as we shall see later, the acceptance of a traditional value as a relatively unquestioned psychoanalytic tenet surely calls for the query "Is this too a defense against anxiety?"

It is plain that although they do not say so in so many words, the Barandes' position is influenced by Lacanian theory, although they are avowedly not Lacanians. The many deviations of desire follow the symbolic route; their origin is biological but the route is defined by meanings. *Néoténie* is a useful concept to describe at once the immaturity of the human infant and the potential for its development to be influenced by imaginary or symbolic representations. Lacan supposed that human desire (in contrast to biological need) found its origin in the loss of the mother-child unity, experienced throughout life as a "lack of being" made up for through the agency of the network of objects of desire that signify, but *are not*, the lost object (12). We too do not have to accept the whole of Lacan's system to see in this hypothesis a different way of proceeding from that provided by a more strictly epigenetic hypothesis, according to which the pathways of desire are outlined by the essentially biological unfolding of the individual. I shall present an alternative at a later point, supplementary rather than contradictory in nature.

For analysts who follow the traditional diagnostic system, homosexuality results from a failed heterosexuality. This conviction is not merely a theoretical one. Trying to understand it, we must add the subjective bias of the analyst, for whom personally the kind of sexual experience that homosexuals claim to enjoy would be grotesque as well as unsatisfying. The analyst, along with the layperson, might see in the reported forms of homosexual union only frustrated mimicking of the intercourse "normally" practiced by men and women. Consequently, since both partners are of the same sex, one at least must be engaging in an alien activity and holding to a spurious representation of himself. This judgment springing uncritically from a heterosexual position does not suddenly become a neutral one when the analyst reports confirmatory data from the patient's associations; selective emphasis may skew the data toward the side of the symptomatic and away from the side of gratification. Nor, as we shall see, does the revelation of latent homosexuality in heterosexual analysands, incuding the analyst as candidate, facilitate neutrality. Here, if anywhere, a miss is as good as a mile.

Notwithstanding, as analysts we have reason to know that our patients do suffer, since no one comes to be treated for happiness. Yet the inference that our homosexual patients are suffering from their sexuality itself demands critical reappraisal. Practically any kind of sexuality may be accompanied by suffering in the presence of neurotic disorder, and yet we do not always attribute the suffering to the sexuality. And even if the homosexual sufferer himself lays his troubles at the door of his sexuality, that is not a psychoanalytic explanation. We need to learn about the complaint in the context of its presentation in the analytic discourse to discover its unconscious interrelations, and this is an intricate process, hard to keep uncontaminated by deep-seated convictions often shared unconsciously by analyst and patient.

Attempting a different orientation in our psychoanalytic attitudes toward male homosexual patients, I propose that we take as their unique differentiatingcharacteristic the conscious and persistent choice of members of the same sex as objects of love and desire. Whether this choice is effectuated or not, whether it is even accepted or not, it is to be contrasted with unconscious homosexual preferences revealed in the analysis of heterosexual patients. *This* man desires another man as his sexual partner however the choice may be masked—nor do I exclude the bisexual instances in which heterosexual desires also occur.

I suggest that we define the constitutive, elementary, and *unconscious* nucleus of homosexuality as the search for the narcissistic object, the specular image of oneself discovered or revived outside oneself. I am prepared to meet the objection that this definition, while indisputable, is hardly new from a theoretical point of view, since it would be only tautological to state that the sexual object of the homosexual man is a fellow male. Indeed, there is little new here, but that little may be basic: if we take narcissism—very narrowly understood, as I shall go on to show—as the regulatory mode of homosexuality, we proceed on a different terrain from the traditional approaches, which at once elaborate the concept of narcissism and take it as only a single and undecisive factor in homosexuality.

I must therefore first try to distinguish carefully some of the meanings of ''narcissism.'' Freud at the outset associated a group of concepts with a seeming resemblance and attributed deep ties to them. In his ''On Narcissism'' (6) Freud claimed to unite such disparate phenomena as narcissism with the schizophrenic flight from the world of external objects to the cathexis of the ego, the hypochondriacal state, megalomania, even the characteristic erotic position of women, as if their resemblances presented a fundamental accord. True, in all these cases the individual ''looks'' at himself in some sense of the word, and this fact became for Freud the key to narcissism, the signified for all these diverse signifiers. I must hold it to be a misunderstanding at a deep philosophical level, even if it was meant to be a clinical generalization. It is part of the notion of mental substances that Freud adhered to without always recognizing it as such. If mental substances like libido, anxiety, aggression, and so on, are distributed among psychic structures in ways at least analogous to physical principles, why not then hypothesize a narcissism present whenever the subject turns "an allocation of the libido" toward his own being? The poet's involvement with words, the mother's with her children (her "offspring"), any mental effort, any interest of the individual not outwardly directed, merits the term "narcissism" with or without psychopathological connotation.

This expansion of the concept needs to be abridged (and not only for the sake of the argument that I am now pursuing), or rather the many definable "narcissisms" need to be distinguished, rather than conflated. It is also misleading to suppose that they occur in a kind of epigenetic series, so that the presence of one supposes the potential presence—or absence—of another. Clinical experience does not reveal that the narcissism of homosexuals implies an outstanding degree of egoism, a disposition to hypochondriasis or to megalomania, and so forth, although it does not exclude any of these either. It is a narcissism that literally conforms to that recognized by Lacan in the "mirror stage" without being necessarily marked by the negative characteristics of that stage as Lacan defined it. The homosexual man has chosen as the object of his love and desire his own specular image; it may be enlarged, reduced, made powerful or powerless, reversed or identical, blanched or darkened, disguised or transparently represented. Here too, as elsewhere, individual tastes exist, but basically it is the mirror image (or the photographic image, since the mirror necessarily reverses) that provides the other (with a small "o," as in Lacan's usage).

Some of the transformations of "mirroring" in the body narcissism of a young homosexual man may be illustrated by the following abridged analysis of a dream:

He is in a war, not really *in* uniform, but occupying a uniform, together with someone else. The other person was behind him—no, in front of him. It reminds him of those comic stage horses made up of two people. Was the other one a man or a woman? At first it seemed to be a woman, but when the person emerged it was a naked man, white skinned. After he woke up he phoned a couple of friends.

My own thoughts while listening went to Plato's *Symposium*, to Aristophanes' mythical account in it of the origins of sexual life in the division of the bisexual unity, a subject we had talked of not long ago. But also, in the last session, he had surprised me by talking about his desire to have a child, which led to the thought that gay men "reproduced" themselves by wearing similar clothing "like a uniform," and on a similar occasion he had jokingly referred to them as "clones." Being unable to reproduce themselves the usual way, they reproduced by looking all alike. I understood him to be talking about mirror images and twinning.

The "war" had to do with the deeper, hostile levels of the transference. Bringing in dreams always bothered him, because my supposed expertness would be evident there if anywhere, and he tended to take a defensive, judicious posture toward dreams, and indeed toward all my interpretations, and where he could, dismiss them as intellectualizations. The war also had to do with his anxiety lest I stop him from his search for the other self, from whom he obtained renewal in sexual relations. At the same time also, war pervaded his more lasting sexual relationships because they exposed to him the imaginary nature of his quest for the mirror image. Sexual acts with men simultaneously united him with the body of an idealized companion, reassured him of his own desirability, and left him once again disappointed that he was not changed.

Two additional comments are in order. Surely the traditional point of view is correct that the patient was attempting to find reparation for his defective, "castrated" state. But the castration complex is not the fate of homosexuals alone, and what is unique here is the attempted mastery of it through the reproduced image of the body, the doubling. This patient's sexual life was neurotic (that is, unsatisfying) because he was unable to compromise with reality and accept the complementarity of a lover who was not himself the ideal. The thought in the manifest dream that the other might have been a woman represents the patient's still more useless efforts to fulfill his desire with women partners. The second comment is that homosexual normality probably is not very different from heterosexual normality—the capacity to accept the limits of the fulfillment of desire. There is no historical reason to be sure that monogamy, although ethically preferable, is universally the norm in either case.

The narcissism of male homosexuals is, then, not a diffusely characterological universal. Absorption of sexual desire in the contemplation of the physical self mirrored in another does not bespeak the absence or loss of object love. The capacity for the love of another person does not depend on the sexual orientation. Everyone knows of heterosexual men whose sexual goals are unqualifiedly "normal" but who treat their wives or lovers as extensions of themselves, or as more or less valuable property. Conversely, homosexual men are capable of love and esteem for the subjectivity of their partners; attainment of that goal is as difficult for one as for the other. It would be false, to be sure, to claim that homosexual love and heterosexual love follow parallel lines, even aside from the social and historical influences that we have already discussed. With the different possibilities for family life go differences in the kind of real responsibility of the partners for one another. Even when the homosexual relation is deliberately modeled on the family, the prospects for permanence must be still less hopeful than in modern heterosexual marriage.

What is the origin of this specific narcissism magnified to the degree of an object choice that deviates radically from the common form? In an early study, Freud outlined a theoretical sequence that has more or less stood up to later inquiry, although its details have been extensively amplified. Interestingly for our present appraisal, Freud postulates an "organic factor favoring the passive role in love" (13). It is worth keeping this in mind, since most later writers omit the "organic" consideration—and in the way that Freud puts it, little wonder:

while passivity in one partner might bring two persons together, passivity in both would stall the acquaintance indefinitely. (It helps not at all that the passivity intended here might be unconscious, since that trend is equally likely to be present in heterosexual love on the side of each partner.) Be that as it may, Freud makes much more of the intrapsychic process, of course, further postulating an unusual attachment to the mother that yields to identification with her. The narcissistic object choice—here Freud seems to use the term in the narrow limits that I follow—"is easier to put into effect than the move towards the opposite sex," which again raises a serious question: if easier, why not pursued by a larger number of boys than it is? Perhaps the implied response would be that it is the organically passive who take the easier way. Next, the castration complex is the dominant influence. Freud introduces it here by way of the manifestly high value set on the penis by the male homosexual, and his corresponding inability to tolerate its absence. Women are depreciated as sexual objects by the early discovery that they have no penis. The narcissistic overvaluation of the penis is then an essential element to account for homosexual development. (I must point out again that castration anxiety originating in the discovery of the seemingly castrated other sex will not do as an explanation of it, since castration anxiety is a universal crux, the overcoming of which can follow a variety of pathways, none of them necessitating homosexual choice.) Another constitutive element early recognized by Freud is fear of the father, so experienced as to lead to the renunciation of the mother, and all females as well, in order to avoid further rivalry. Real seduction then results in permanent fixation of the libido and—the new contribution in this paper of Freud's—sibling rivalry may defensively induce the first homosexual objects by a reversal of the cathexis from hate to love.

Later additions to the theory add significantly in pushing behind the castration complex and the Oedipus complex to pregenitality. I suppose that the overattachment to and identification with the mother raises the question of how it came to be, since all babies are attached to their mothers, and in the pregenital stages, at least, are likely to be identified with them in the sense of not being differentiated from them, regardless of gender. Some trauma, usually irretrievable, must be reconstructed from the evidence to be found in an unconscious fantasy such as that of persistent intrauterine residence, the interior of the mother's body as an ambivalently longed for space, for example. The supposed trauma comes down suspiciously to an all-too-familiar explanation: maternal rejection and/or oversolicitude.

A brief aside is relevant here. After the writing and presentation of the material in this chapter, Paul Moor, a journalist, called to my attention the work of Fritz Morgenthaler of Zurich. In his book *Homosexualität, Heterosexualität, und Perversion* (1984), Morgenthaler (14) elaborates a theory of the origins of homosexuality, in both normal and neurotic development, with certain striking resemblances to what I have proposed here. He sees a primary infantile distinction between the need for identity, or "the achievement of knowing who one is," and "the need for autonomy, the assurance of being able to decide and act independently." Emphasis on the latter, the need for autonomy, stimulates autoerotic activity aimed at the regulation of the psychic equilibrium through a diffuse feeling of well-being. In later homosexual development, regulation of self-esteem, maintenance of differentiated human relations, capacity for love, and so on, remain dependent on the autonomic functions of the personality. The tie between autoerotism and strivings for autonomy persists in the sexual organization of homosexuals, and accordingly sexual interest is directed to the self and to others of the same sex. "Curiosity is directed to that which one can experience by oneself or with others like oneself." Morgenthaler seems to imply a traumatic origin for the development of either identity or autonomy, but it is in the latter instance that the heightened autoerotism issues in the homosexual orientation. Nevertheless, the later homosexual development need not be more neurotic than the heterosexual, since the capacity for love is equally present. Morgenthaler's theoretical discussion (which is greatly influenced by Heinz Kohut's thought) significantly amplifies my proposal of a specific body-narcissism as structurally essential for male homosexuality. Why the way of "autonomy" is chosen over that of "identity" remains a mystery, unless the biological predisposition that I postulate resides there. Morgenthaler does not seem to have any opinion about this.

I suggest that the account of the development of homosexuality offered by Freud and many others suffers from a certain factitiousness, for it does seem that the underlying fantasies, when they truly exist, either are not specific to homosexuals or, if they are specific, appear to arise out of intrafamilial situations that are themselves not unique. If the analyst takes recourse in the "complementary series" proposed by Freud, he ordinarily reduces the series to its postnatal aspects, that is, to the reciprocal influences of trauma and fixation. Unconscious fantasies produced in the transference are interpreted as revelatory of traumatic experiences along certain predictable lines. I want to return—and I am not the first—to the most primitive aspect of the complementary series, the innate or biological, or constitutional, assuming that the essential nucleus of the narcissism I have described is to be found in the individual at birth. That this argument will be speculative and inferential I would concede from the start.

Every analysis, regardless of the diagnosis, if pursued deeply enough, reveals a basic mental structure that cannot be entirely distinguished from the constitutional nature of the person. We sometimes merely allude to it when we remark in our case histories about peculiarities in the lives of other members of our patients' families. It is usually impossible in psychoanalysis to pick out what is part of the biological given (obviously handedness, hereditary gifts, etc., would be exceptions not requiring much argument), because familial interaction not only immediately inaugurated the conditions of life of the newborn but has long preestablished those conditions, maybe generations ago. But we know from extensive and increasingly persuasive studies that babies are not the passive receptive internalizers we have often made them out to be. They also evoke in the caring persons actions on them that do not so much set psychological tendencies into motion as they keep going what has been there from the start. Even the structures of archaic fantasy are probably biologically organized (15).

It is easy to understand our customary refusal to consider the biological structure in an analysis: psychoanalysis is circumscribed by the symbolic horizon barring our passage outside the realm of meaning and interpretation to that of neurological and endocrinological data. It is to them, presumably, that we would have to have access to investigate the biological origin of homosexuality or any other mental state. It has also been implied that recourse to biological explanation of the mental states we encounter in analysis betrays a lack of trust in our theory and method. With such recourse, we allegedly give up hope of curing the patient; this would, it is said, be fatalism or laziness, or yielding to the propaganda of homosexual politics. A less invidious objection to the hypothesis of the inborn nature of homosexuality has in the past also come from the side of evolutionary biology: it is at first encounter hard to see how a trait leading to reproductive sterility could itself be reproduced—an objection that demands our attention, although of course it is equally unanswerable from the psychoanalytic evidence.

One can be sympathetic with these objections to a point, because there is truth in them. Yet they seem mainly to hinge on the implication that an essential innate trait entails inevitability and irreversibility. That is plainly illogical, because an innate mental trait cannot remain unaffected by experience. Moreover, the trait or traits here in question probably would contribute only indirectly to homosexual preference. With respect to irreversibility there is no entailment either, since degrees of preference exist. On the matter of resistance to change, may I call attention to that profound resistance arising from the conviction of many patients, including homosexuals, that their parents are "to blame" for their misfortunes? It is not likely to check progress toward change if it is even just surmised that a dispositional factor exists which parents cannot have introduced either consciously or unconsciously.

I put forward as a hypothesis in search of confirmation that the male homosexual does indeed start life differently. Something about his constitutive psychic reality shapes him as the Other of the heterosexual unconscious; he is already in some way what heterosexuals fear so much to become. Subsequent development from such roots may be subjected to traumatic or, for that matter, progressive influence, but it is a different psychosexual development. Does this mean that the unconscious homosexual impulses manifested in all neurotics differ from this peculiar nucleus? I so postulate, and furthermore I think it can be shown that latent homosexual impulses never lead to manifest homosexuality except either incidentally or in those instances called "facultative," or *faute de mieux*, despite their power to generate enormous anxiety and to institute powerful neurotic defenses. They are part of the Oedipus and castration complexes, while the innate nucleus would exist independently of those complexes but be able to modify them to its own ends. Goethe's marvelous phrase here applies: "Geprägte Form, die lebend sich entwickelt."

It is on clinical grounds that I prefer such speculative notions to the accepted idea that the elementary nucleus of the narcissistic object choice found in homosexuals is the product of one or another family constellation or of neonatal experience. How many accounts have we heard of the inhuman-superhuman mother who has robbed her son of his "masculinity" either brutally or by the more subtle instrument of seduction, or of the more or less well-meaning father more impressive by his absence than his presence? Such histories have been broadcast widely and form a part of what by now is popular psychology, but I do not find that they illuminate our clinical instances. Contrary to such claims, I have found that the dynamic constellations of the families of homosexual men cannot be distinguished from those of heterosexual men, if we observe the two structures neutrally; that is, without foregone conclusions relating genesis to outcome. Likewise, I can show the opposite: instances of severely traumatic family settings that ought (according to paradigms of that sort) to predestine the boys inevitably to homosexuality, whereas in reality the victims of such mishandling loved women exclusively. Very complicated Oedipal conflicts arose, with ensuing neurotic symptoms and distortions of character, but not manifest homosexuality, even in suppressed or delayed expression.

It is impressive how often when we think through the analyses of heterosexual men we find that they have had the kind of attachments to their parents that are allegedly prescriptive for homosexuality. Their mothers played with them erotically, have disparaged their unsuccessful fathers, or the boys have been victimized by older siblings—yet all to no avail so far as support for the theory goes, since with puberty the drive toward the female body easily prevailed. The narcissistic attachment of a kind that I consider here to be essential to the homosexual choice yields to the advance of puberty, and the youth becomes permanently heterosexual, although still able to recognize homosexual impulses as acceptable but fleeting and readily subordinated desires.

A young man first seen in his late teens was the only child of parents who were divorced when he was 2 years old. He lived with his mother, a far more lively, successful, and gifted person than his father (by the boy's account, of course), who saw him rarely and never became an active figure in the boy's conscious life. Unconsciously, to the contrary, he was omnipotent: the boy's depression and rage were based on his persistent conviction that his life had been ruined by his parents' divorce. He had the unconscious fantasy, based on his father's declaration that he would never be a real man as long as he lived with his mother, that he was totally controlled, dominated, and ultimately to be destroyed by his father. His father "rode" him. He had rage enough against his mother too, but he depended fully on her unstinting love and devotion. To make matters worse, so to speak, he inherited a soft, girlish face and wore an abundance of wavy blond hair. But while the usual undercurrent of latent homosexuality made itself all too clear in his symptoms and his self-destructive acting out, his sexual longings were totally directed toward beautiful young women, and he had at least his share of success in fulfilling them.

I know that such examples—and anyone could find them in his or her practice—prove nothing. All they are intended to do here is to make us less confident of those conventional case histories of homosexual men which are supposed to define the traumatic origins of the sexual preference.

In order to account for deviations from the reproductive norm, we have to be able to offer cogent reasons. Something very important must happen to bring about the homosexual variation, taking place in about 6 to 10 percent of the male population (although this does not imply that the 6 to 10 percent are all nonreproductive). The psychoanalytic causal explanations so far offered become persuasive only when we take less warning than we ought about the dangers of the genetic fallacy. The discovery of a significant unconscious fantasy exposes a meaning of any conscious preoccupation, concern, or activity, but it does not thereby disclose an essential link in the causal chain. The primitive or archaic nature of the fantasy may indeed be an index to the inner history of the patient's sexuality, without being an index to a causal sequence. A fantasy of this kind is the psychical record of the encounter of the infantile mind with the world. It is not a passively experienced tracing, but a personal rendition of the encounter. Take, for example, the symbiotic fantasy that has been discovered fairly often in the analysis of homosexual men (and in other men too). It may be variously interpreted, depending on the circumstances, but at least some of the time it appears to be a solution to the problems of separation and loneliness, through the imaginary duplication of the self.

While on the subject of fantasies, I want to add that many of what pass as the unconscious fantasies ''explaining'' homosexuality are in reality quite conscious. The acquisition of masculine strength and beauty through taking the genital of the other into oneself is an example. That is in fact a fairly common conscious fantasy reported by homosexual men, and even one that is expressed without embarrassment and as a matter of course. That it is also a fantasy of women is important, but only in the obvious parallelism, that some women and some homosexual men want to acquire the strength and the beauty that they behold outside themselves. It will not do to protest that, unlike men, women desire it justifiably because they lack just that, which is to resume the outworn opinion that penis envy is what really matters in female sexuality. A strong and beautiful woman feels stronger and more beautiful because of a man's recognition of her and his loving entrance into her. So apparently does a homosexual man. It also adds little to explain this homosexual fantasy as a feminine identification, since such identifications exist in both homosexual and heterosexual men. Likewise, the discovery that the unconscious source of the fantasy is the desire for union with the father is expectable enough, but once again we meet with that desire very often in the analysis of those heterosexual men who never have the conscious fantasy of taking another man's genital into themselves.

I have not gone very far toward establishing any specific hypothesis covering just what it is that is innate in male homosexuality. There are difficult problems here. The fact of the very early disposition to homosexuality demands an influence that, while specific and orientating, is not grossly equivalent to postpubertal object choice. I have raised questions, I hope, but maybe the most important one is this: What might we learn in the psychoanalysis of homosexual men in which neither the hypothesis of disorder nor the aim of transformation to heterosexuality is assumed?

Is such a neutrality compatible with the position from which I have worked in this chapter, namely, that an essential component of homosexuality is innate, and not universally distributed, so that no combination of experiences, no overdetermining influences, can bring about a final common path of homosexuality in the absence of the innate disposition (which does not imply that such experiences may not be also essential in its presence)? This hypothesis, it might be claimed, also slants the investigative and therapeutic position of the analyst. I admit that we ought to reckon with this danger, but I contend that it is less of a danger than our traditional stance: the danger of unnecessary pathologizing and the concomitants of excessive interpretation of defense, that easily and unaware arouses the sadistic power of the superego. The usual approach to the treatment is to increase or even induce splitting, in the effort to render the homosexuality yet more dystonic than life experience has already done. Predicated there is the assumption that the desire to be free of one's homosexuality proceeds from a more, not less, autonomic source. I urge consideration of the opposite view, that the patient's seeming cooperation with this normalizing interest may be a part of his deepest immaturity, his fight against self-acceptance for the purpose of retaining parental love, even in its symbiotic state.

There are problems in the point of view that I am urging. If the innate takes precedence over the traumatic, why then the aversion for or at least indifference to the female as a sexual object? Or, if we do not posit a developmental arrest, why does the specular image as the object of love *exclude* the opposite sex? That there are intermediate grades of sexual responsiveness to the same or to the other sex is another problem. These are no idle questions. Many homosexuals want to be able to love women and beget children, even when they accept and enjoy homosexual relations. In fact, quite apart from any interest in being analyzed, many do love women and do beget children. The personal and social complications that may ensue are obvious enough, although prejudiced report— sometimes from homosexual sources too—exaggerates their gravity. At this point we may need to look outside our science and our method for a clearer picture while at the same time maintaining the insights into meaning that only psychoanalysis can obtain.

REFERENCES

1. Boswell, J. Christianity, Social Tolerance, and Homosexuality. Chicago: University of Chicago Press, 1980.
2. Leavy, S. The Psychoanalytic Dialogue. New Haven: Yale University Press, 1980.

3. Wiedeman, G. Survey of the psychoanalytic literature on overt male homosexuality. JAPA, 10: 386–409, 1962.

4. Hunt, S. Homosexuality from a contemporary perspective. Connecticut Medicine, 42(2): 105–108, 1978.

5. Freud, S. Three essays on sexuality. Standard Edition, Vol. VII, p. 125, 1905.

6. Freud, S. On narcissism. Standard Edition, Vol. XIV, pp. 67–102, 1914.

7. Bychowski, G. The ego of homosexuals. Int. P. P. 26:114–127, 1945.

8. Socarides, C. The Overt Homosexual. New York: Grune and Stratton, 1968.

9. Freud, S. Letter to Mrs. N. N. In: Briefe, 1873–1939. Frankfurt am Main: S. Fischer, 1960.

10. Freud, S. Psychoanalytic notes on an autobiographical account of a case of paranoia (dementia paranoides). Standard Edition, Vol. XII, pp. 3–82, 1911.

11. Barande, I., and Barande, R. Antinomies du concept de perversion et epigénèse de l'appétit d'excitation. 4ᵉ Congrès des psychanalystes de langue française. Montréal, 1982.

12. Lacan, J. Écrits: A Section. Translated by A. Sheridan. New York: W. W. Norton, 1977.

13. Freud, S. Some neurotic mechanisms in jealousy, paranoia, and homosexuality. Standard Edition, Vol. XVIII, pp. 221–232, 1922.

14. Morgenthaler, F. Homosexualität, Heterosexualität, Perversion. Mit einem Vorwort von Hans-Jürgen Heinrichs. Frankfurt am Main: Qumran, 1984.

15. Laplanche, J., and Pontalis, J. B. Fantasy and the origins of sexuality. Int. J. Psa., 49(1):1–18, 1968.

Disturbances in Sex and Love in Borderline Patients

> Once more he had found her out, got through the barrier and seen her for what she was, a beautiful woman who could not believe in her own beauty or accept love without casting every conceivable doubt upon it. Now and every other time that they quarreled, she was merely seeing how far she could go, leading him to the edge of the pit and making him look down, threatening their common happiness in order to convince herself of its reality.
>
> William Maxwell, *Time Will Darken It*

Since borderline conditions are situated either expressly (within the broad definitions of Kernberg [1], Vanggaard [2], or Bergeret [3]) or indirectly (within the syndromal definitions of Gunderson [4] or *DSM*-III [5]) in between the neuroses and the psychoses, it should not be surprising that, alongside the characteristic disturbances in identity, impulse control, and mood regulation, disturbances in intimate relationships are encountered with some regularity. Within the borderline domain, Freud's bipartite division of life into *Liebe* and *Arbeit* finds partial expression under the heading "poor sublimatory channeling" (Kernberg) (6) or "work below capacity" (Gunderson) (4). Less attention has been paid to the other half of life in borderline patients, though some authors have alluded to their chaotic sexuality. Hoch and Polatin (7), for example, spoke of "pan-sexuality" in their pseudoneurotic schizophrenics, many of whom would be considered borderline by contemporary diagnostic standards. Included in that no longer popular term were such manifestations as promiscuity, "polymorphous perverse practices," and rapid fluctuations between homosexuality and heterosexuality.

Our examination of the problems experienced in this realm of life by borderline patients will be facilitated if we divide Freud's *Liebe* once again into sexuality and love. Such a division is all the more relevant when speaking of borderline patients, insofar as these attributes are less often integrated in this group than in normal or "neurotic" persons. Feelings of love (including the components mentioned by Erich Fromm: tenderness, concern about the welfare and personal growth of the beloved, etc.) regularly coexist with lustful feelings in those that have the capacity to integrate these strong emotions. In those whom we call "borderline" this integrative capacity is, for a variety of reasons, either lacking or seriously enfeebled. The borderline's general disturbance in identity-sense may contribute to this lack, or the borderline person may have been reared in an environment where striking inconsistencies and deficiencies in the parents' ability to love simply left their children with no template, no pattern, for mature, integrated loving with which to identify and utilize later. As a result, when one examines the intimate relationships of borderlines, one may find sex unaccompanied by love, compulsively and throughout the life cycle (even in long-term partnerships, where ideally these elements are blended), or else sex and love combined, but in a way that seems immature, a grotesque caricature of the ideal state: a stifling possessiveness within the context of a symbiotic partnership, rather than a sexual love between two people who respect and foster each other's needs for continued individuation and evolution.

The sources from which my impressions are derived consist of borderline patients seen over the past 17 years in private practice and less methodically studied samples of inpatient borderlines seen, over a 20–year period, at the three hospitals where I have been affiliated (New York State Psychiatric Institute, New York Hospital/Westchester Division, and the University of Connecticut Health Center). In the office sample there are, as of this writing, 54 patients, all "borderline' by Kernberg criteria (6) (poor identity integration, yet with adequate capacity for reality testing), of whom 39 are female and 15 are male. Homosexuality has not been particularly common in this group, having been noted only in one male and in three of the female patients. Among the latter, one was exclusively homosexual, one was predominantly homosexual, and one was episodically homosexual. These figures did not differ significantly from the equally low incidence of homosexuality among the neurotic patients seen in private practice for psychotherapy over the same period of time.

We would like to be able to answer such questions as whether homosexuality is more common in borderline patients than in better-integrated patients, and whether female borderlines would be any more prone to develop along homosexual lines than female neurotics. One is tempted to ask these questions, partly in relation to the popular theories concerning the psychodynamics of borderline development (6, 8–10), stressing, as they do, serious problems in effecting emotional separation from the maternal figure (which could, speculatively, predispose borderline-to-be females to remain excessively attached to or yearning for closeness with motherly females) and also problems that are conducive to narcissistic object-choice (which might predispose future borderlines of either sex to remain fixated at the "homosexual level," as the latter is envisioned by psychoanalysts who espouse a linear model of psychosexual evolution).

The homosexual community is a large one, and granted that within it males considerably outnumber females, there is little convincing evidence that its emotional health is appreciably lower than what one finds in the heterosexual population. Psychiatrists and psychoanalysts see a skewed sample, naturally: those who suffer and seek help (11). It is for the epidemiologists, not for us, to say whether a systematic survey of male or of female homosexuals, where those not seeking psychiatric help were also included, would turn up a higher proportion of emotionally ill persons than would be expected in the general population. I am not acquainted with any such survey, let alone one measuring the prevalence of "borderline" conditions according to some commonly accepted criteria.

One's impressions about the relative mental health of homosexuals would be influenced by the particular system one chose for arriving at a borderline diagnosis. Psychoanalysts, for example, tend to regard human nature with normative lenses, according to which homosexuality is *eo ipso* a deviation (some analysts do not share this view; Judd Marmor, for example, or Robert Stoller or Richard Friedman). Those who exhibit homosexuality tend to be regarded as manifesting a problem in gender identity more often than might be the case if viewed by a clinician without psychoanalytic training. But "identity disturbances" is the hallmark of borderline personality organization in Kernberg's (psychoanalytic) schema. I know of some homosexual patients who, despite their not being impulsive, angry, or given to suicidal gestures, get labeled "borderline" by Kernberg criteria, even while they would not be considered Gunderson, or *DSM-III*, borderlines. In the absence of hard data, I am inclined to adopt the more conservative position—that borderlines, at least as defined by the narrower criteria of Gunderson, may not be overrepresented in a population of homosexuals.

In my private practice series, among 39 female borderlines there were 3 who were homosexuals (7.7 percent); of the 15 males, 1 was homosexual (6.6 percent). The incidence in the female subgroup may be higher than what is found in the general population, but from a small, nonrandom sample of that sort one is not entitled to draw conclusions. Among the 29 inpatient *DSM* borderlines at the University of Connecticut Health Center who were part of our diagnostic research project, there were no homosexuals.

In general, it is difficult to create a representative sample of borderlines within a particular community, in order, for example, to evaluate the incidence of homosexuality. It is likewise difficult to select a "random" sample of homosexuals within which to study the incidence of borderline psychopathology. Both tasks would require a broad epidemiological survey.

PROMISCUITY

By *promiscuity*, I refer not so much to the number of sexual partners, to the brevity of relationships, or to the rapidity with which partners are exchanged in favor of others as to the drivenness and dehumanization, or impersonality, that characterizes the sexual patterns of those whom we may meaningfully regard as "promiscuous." One sees not only compulsive seeking of one partner after another but also the joylessness accompanying this process, along with a general handicap in forming a deep and integrated relationship with another person.

The correlation between borderline psychopathology and sexual promiscuity seems impressive in contrast to the situation with homosexuality. More than 25 percent of my office-practice borderline patients exhibited this trait: 2 of the 15 males, 12 of the 39 females. Promiscuity was rare among their neurotic counterparts. I recall only one analysand within my experience to whom this label could be said to apply. She was a lonely, narcissistic graduate student given to seducing men met casually in the elevator of her apartment building or at work or at the musical events she was fond of attending, and inviting them to enjoy with her what she called, adopting the phrase from Erica Jong's *Fear of Flying*, a "zipless fuck." But this combination of loneliness, hunger for attention, indifference to social convention, and impulsivity was common among the borderline women especially. Other manifestations of their drivenness and affect hunger included alcoholism and abuse of various drugs. A significant difference, for example, emerges when the borderlines with promiscuity and those without are compared with respect to substance abuse. In the nonpromiscuous group, 8 out of 40 abused drugs or alcohol (20 percent), while substance abuse and promiscuity were found in common in 9 of 14 instances (64 percent).

A number of factors appear to converge in creating the emotional environment in which promiscuity is likely to occur. This "overdetermined" system is found in patients, most of whom are female, who show a particularly low and self-denigrated self-image. Often they have been called "tramps" by fathers who, unable to deal more maturely with their daughters' burgeoning sexuality during adolescence, protect themselves from their own incestuous impulses toward the latter by a projective mechanism, where the girl rather than the father is seen as the tramp. Subjected to this interaction long enough, the daughters often live out their fathers' unconscious yearnings and become "whores."

In another subgroup of borderline women, incest has indeed been acted out and not merely defended against (12). This was so in 16 percent of my female office-practice borderlines, and in over 50 percent of a sample of inpatient borderline women at New York Hospital/Westchester Division. Probably the majority of the nonpsychotic hospitalized girls with a history of incest, as described by Emslie and Rosenfeld (13), were functionally borderline. One may compare these figures with those noted for the general population, where about 1 woman in 20 in the United States has had incestuous experiences with a brother or an older male relative.

Side by side with a low self-image, and especially in those who have either experienced incest or been raised by overtly seductive fathers, is a morbid fascination with sex as well as a pronounced tendency toward "sensation-seeking." Ambivalence toward men is marked: idealization is intertwined with contempt and hatred for having been misused. In the casual sexual encounters with strangers, there is opportunity to live out these contradictory attitudes. The stranger is viewed as mysterious, powerful, protecting, loving (as with Mr. Goodbar), but he is also viewed (perhaps more accurately) as inconstant and unfaithful, as exploitative but paradoxically easily exploitable, by the woman who lures him with the promise of sexual favors.

Inability to postpone gratification is characteristic of the promiscuous group, almost by identification; their capacity for sublimatory activities is almost invariably impaired (6). The sexual drive in borderlines is often intense to start out with, owing to constitutional factors, of which the most important is predisposition to hypomania (where all the drives are intensified—hence the pacing, rapid speech, overspending, impulsive planning, and so on). Add to this the extra measure of intensification through sexual overstimulation by family members during childhood or adolescence, and one can appreciate how the trait of promiscuity becomes an all-but-inescapable outcome.

In many borderlines with this trait, rapid alterations in attitude are often discernible in relation to their sexual partners. These oscillations, taken together, can be seen as a manifestation of the "splitting," both in self-image and in the internalized representations of others, that is characteristic of the borderline patient (6). The following vignette is illustrative:

Promiscuity as Paradoxical Fidelity

A woman in her late 20s entered psychotherapy following hospitalization for suicide gestures and abuse of alcohol following a romantic disappointment. She came from an upper-class New England family, consisting, besides two siblings, of a father whom she idealized and a mother whom she experienced as perfectionistic, hypercritical, and intrusive. Though of average appearance and refined manners, she saw herself as ugly. Longing for acceptance and approval by men, she would, especially when lonely, either place herself in situations where she could get "picked up" by strangers or would accept dates with men who, though they had been "properly introduced," did not really appeal to her. In either case, she could not say no to either advances and invariably ended up in bed. During the beginning moments of sexual play, she would feel exhilarated, basking in the admittedly illusory enthusiasm of her partner, feeling for these few minutes that she was pretty, desirable, and as capable as the next woman of "getting a man." But this euphoric mood would dissipate shortly before orgasm, to be replaced by a mood of self-denigration and hostility. She would vilify her partner (not usually out loud) as a manipulative cad who was just out to "get laid" and who would scarcely remember her name the next morning. Herself she would vilify as a pathetic tramp, a stain on the family escutcheon, and so forth.

Much more hidden from her view was another set of attitudes toward these one-night stands, which emerged only from prolonged and meticulous work with her dreams—wherein the men were prized never for themselves but only to the extent they could become symbols to her of the cherished father. She could not love a man for himself without relinquishing something of the excessive attachment to her father, and that she was unwilling to do. In this sense, *promiscuity* with unimportant strangers was, as is so often true with borderline women, the reverse side of the coin, on whose obverse was a pathological *fidelity* to the all-important father.

In this case, the father had not behaved in a particularly seductive manner, nor had the woman experienced incestuous advances or play. Perhaps because of this her sexuality, although disturbed, was not as grotesque or chaotic as what one often observes in those who have experienced incest (see below). Her quasi-delusional conviction of being ugly is something one encounters often among borderline women. The psychodynamics are not always the same. This symptom, which has received some attention in the literature under the disarming rubric "dysmorphobia," deserves a closer look and will be discussed in detail later.

HYPERSEXUALITY

Despite the frequency of promiscuity in borderline women and in some borderline men, it is less common to see hypersexuality, if by this term we refer to a morbid and incessant craving for sex and a preoccupation with this topic throughout almost all one's waking moments. The three patients in this category, with whom I have worked, consist of two females and a male. All had incestuous relationships throughout much of their childhood (through adolescence). The male, a homosexual, was masturbated by his mother, who presided over his nightly bath until he was 15. He became "obsessed" with sex; as a young adult, he would supplement what he could not get in the context of a relationship with encounters with strangers in subway men's rooms. One of the women, who thought about sex all day long and would never "get enough," despite intercourse with her husband three or four times a day, had had an incestuous relationship (involving oral sex) with her father from the time she was 6 until she was 16. The other woman, a divorced schoolteacher, would be desolated if her fiancé failed to make love to her in the morning, even if they had had sex two or three times the evening before and if he were exhausted or else worried because he was late for some important business meeting. She would become convinced he no longer loved her. During her younger years, she had incestuous involvements with both parents—the only patient I have heard of so far where this was true—the mother masturbating her under the pretext of checking to see if her organs were "all right," her father engaging in intercourse from about the time she was 11.

It is perhaps relevant that in these three patients there had been no physical cruelty in the parent-child relationship (instead, the psychological cruelty of so grossly misusing one's child in the first place). The balance between sexual excitement and hostility toward the older person was tipped much in favor of the former, at least in the women: overstimulated as youngsters, they became hypersexual as adults, but always with the view of sex as something natural and joyful. The male patient reacted against his seductive mother in repudiating his heterosexual impulses (which were still a part of his fantasy life until his late 20s), reaching out instead to men, though with the same compulsive and insatiable quality noted in the two female patients.

That there could be a constitutional component to hypersexuality (nymphomania), of a sort similar to what we speculated could be operative in certain promiscuous patients, seems likely in some instances. Here again a predisposition to hypomania seems the most probable factor. Isolated cases of this sort have been described in the earlier literature, the most noteworthy example being that of Voisin (14), a portion of which (concerning a 3–year-old girl who grew up to become a nymphomaniac) I have translated elsewhere (15).

Kraepelin (16) was aware of hypersexuality as one possible accompaniment of "manic temperament," by which he referred to the constellation of personality traits one sees often either in true bipolar patients or in their close relatives. In fact, it is the hallmark of manic psychopathology that one is excessive in everything: besides hypersexuality, common manifestations are verbosity, overspending, a diminished need for sleep, hyperactivity, and aggressiveness. Some nymphomaniacs are, so to speak, nympho*manics* (and responsive to lithium).

INCEST: ITS IMPACT ON PSYCHOSEXUAL DEVELOPMENT

We have already alluded to several instances of incestuous involvement among borderline patients with specific sexual problems. The topic deserves further mention, not only because of the profound effects on psychosexual development that incest regularly brings about but also because of the unusual frequency with which a history of incest will be elicited in a borderline population. Although I have encountered isolated instances of father-son incest in borderline men, the overwhelming majority of cases concern young women who have had some form of sexual involvement with a male relative. Even if the latter were a stepfather or some other non-blood-related male living within the close family circle, the example should be counted as incestuous, if for no other reason than that the *emotional* impact would approximate the traumatic level engendered by incest with an actual blood relative. Estimates of incest frequency in women, chosen randomly from the normal population, converge around the 5 percent level (17). The frequency noted among my private practice borderline women was three times this figure (16 percent); in a hospitalized sample of 39 borderlines at New York Hospital/Westchester Division, over half the females had experienced incestuous relations either occasionally or over protracted periods of time throughout childhood (12). When I have presented this material at symposiums on borderlines, in various communities throughout the United States or in Europe (chiefly the Scandinavian countries and France), therapists who do any considerable work in this diagnostic domain have shared with me their perceptions, namely, that incest is remarkably common in the anamneses of their female borderlines also.

If one thinks about the characteristics of borderline organization as Kernberg (1) has described it, and compares these features with the typical attitudes engendered in young persons who have participated in incestuous relations, it will not be difficult to see the close correspondence between them. The defense pattern in borderlines consists largely of primitive mechanisms such as denial, disavowal (refusal to acknowledge verbally what one is already consciously aware of), splitting (coexisting contradictory attitudes, only one of which is conscious at any given moment), devaluation, idealization, and omnipotent control. But the actualization of sexual feelings toward a parent, or submission to the incestuous impulses of an older, more powerful family member, leads quite predictably to excitement by, idealization toward, and passionate infatuation with the older relative-turned-sex-object, but at the same time contempt, revulsion, and hatred toward this same person as having taken unfair advantage, as having betrayed a trust, violated a taboo, interfered with one's development, and so on. The ambivalence, in other words, that is inherent in all human relations, and certainly in the Oedipal situation, becomes unavoidably magnified and intensified to levels far in excess of what the average young person has to cope with. Because daughters are far more apt to become incest victims than sons, the theme of incest is mostly relevant to women, whose image of men is often distorted beyond the powers of psychotherapy to rectify. As the incest victim grows up, men become for her cherished persecutors to be alternately adored and vilified. To make matters worse, the early fixation of sexual interest on the father or other male relative renders all newcomers ultimately less fascinating, less appealing—such that even the most suitable man (judged by realistic standards) will after a time be scrapped as the woman returns emotionally to the original figure. To a far greater and grossly pathological extent (compared with what is true of normal women) her heart belongs to Daddy—forever. But it is just this tendency to oscillate between adoration and vilification that the clinician recognizes as a form of "borderline" splitting. Likewise, the incest victim sees her own self in conflicting and sharply drawn images: she is at once outraged victim and, to the extent that she found the forbidden experiences exciting and gratifying, perfidious whore. Particularly in instances of father-daughter incest, the girl sees herself as having mocked and betrayed her mother; the ensuing guilt is often overpowering. As she matures, she fears inordinately the tables being turned on her—by her own daughter.

Her attitude about motherhood is vitiated by this anticipation of betrayal and abandonment, as life finally exacts its vengeance for having betrayed her mother. Vengefulness and scorn may become extreme in relation to men. It appears common for incest victims (at least those who come to the attention of psychotherapists) to become borderline, and not only that but to develop the character traits of spitefulness and jealousy to extreme degrees. This is all the more true when the sexual relations with the family member were highly sadomasochistic in nature, where hatred of men would become an inevitable outgrowth.

The aftereffects of incest are often shattering with respect to psychosexual development. Incest can, I believe, create "borderline" psychopathology, even in the absence of constitutional predisposition to psychosis (a factor otherwise important, in many other borderlines, as I have underlined elsewhere [18, 12]), and probably helps account in no small measure for the lopsided female preponderance (2:1 to 4:1) in most borderline patient samples.

In the following clinical example, the "splitting" and storminess are particularly striking:

Chaotic Marital Relationship in a Borderline Woman with a History of Incest

A 36–year-old woman had been married for 15 years to a man of conventional habits and placid temperament. She kept the emotional atmosphere tense, however, and at times explosive, owing to rapid shifts in mood (from adoration to hostility and vindictiveness toward her husband, from possessiveness to indifference toward her children). Throughout the marriage she made repeated suicidal gestures, always staged to coerce her husband into gratifying some impulse of the moment. When in a happy frame of mind, she would be sexy and loving, but suddenly and with no or only slight provocation, she could become verbally abusive, humiliating him in front of family friends, with such remarks as "I'd like to cut off your dick!"

While growing up, from age 7 to 17, she had sexual relations with her four brothers, who forced themselves on her at first in a kind of gang rape. She developed, and maintained on into adult life, intensely ambivalent relationships with her brothers as well as intensely sadomasochistic relations with men in general.

As her daughter entered puberty, the woman became convinced that her husband "had designs" on their daughter in the same way her brothers had taken advantage of her. For weeks at a time she would take her daughter and go into hiding. When they returned, she would taunt her husband with innuendos about her having developed a sexual interest in various women; their own sexual relationship deteriorated. Finally, she sued for divorce and tried to prevent him from having any access to his daughter, who she was still convinced was the object of his "incestuous desires." Even toward her daughter, however, her behavior was inconsistent, fluctuating between the inappropriate protectiveness just described and aloofness or cruelty. Once when her daughter tearfully complained to her mother, "You don't love me," she slapped the girl's face. But the next night, confronted with a similar complaint, she would console the girl with hugs.

As a final comment on this issue, it is worth noting that borderline incest victims were reared without adherence to the ordinary boundaries—between blood relatives, between the generations—that are respected and that create the foundation for social integration by the vast majority of people. They become, and almost invariably view themselves as, pariahs. They expect the worst from all human relationships (particularly that marital bonds will not be honored) and are quite prepared to extract revenge at any price for wrongs done them either in fact or in fancy. Some avoid intimacy altogether (in a few cases known to me vows of celibacy have been taken in connection with a religious order). But others may live out a pattern of seduction, betrayal, cruelty, and abandonment, inflicting on relatively innocuous men the hurt inflicted on them by their not so innocuous relatives. As a result, their love relationships fail. Worse still, the expectation of betrayal is so ingrained, having been engendered by a breach of trust within the home itself, that therapeutic relationships are also undermined. Trust either never develops or, in the rare instances where the doctor-patient relationship is satisfactory, the problems in everyday living remain insurmountable. Most borderline women with this history find it impossible to adapt to a world where the majority of people (men included) are acknowledged as fundamentally wholesome and fair. Their psychic machinery has been too distorted to permit this view, and in addition their deviant assumptions and behavior patterns would not allow them to become comfortably integrated into conventional society. It remains easier to see everyone as corrupt and despicable, which conforms with life as the incest victim "knows" it. Besides, if everyone is basically corrupt, then father (or whoever) was not really so bad after all. In other words, the gloomy world-view becomes, paradoxically, a view compatible with the incest victim's loyalty and continuing love toward her original sexual object.

UNUSUAL AVOIDANCE OF SEX

Unlike the patients described in the preceding sections, some borderline patients avoid sex altogether. In the absence of studies bearing directly on this issue, the precise frequency of this phenomenon is difficult to estimate. Among my borderline patients in private practice, about 1 in 8 (7 out of 54), ranging in age from 20 to 45, had never had a sexual experience progressing to orgasm with another person. One instance concerned a man in his late 20s who had been used sexually by his father; this schizotypal borderline man showed pronounced paranoid features, mistrusting people of either sex (as wanting only to "hurt" him in some way) and eschewing the company of others almost entirely. The oldest patient in this group had been reared in a wealthy home where the parents were often away for long periods; several family members, including her mother, were schizophrenic. The patient formed fantasy relationships with homosexual men, for whom she would bake cookies and send cards but who showed no interest in her even as a friend. Dynamically, these homosexual acquaintances served as mother surrogates, whom she hoped would compensate for the extreme deprivation she experienced from her own mother. But as one might expect, all that happened was that she reduplicated the early deprivation through her choice of men who returned none of her affection. Another woman was a hostile and infantilizing woman who made clear her intolerance of any moves toward independence on the part of her daughter. The younger woman complied to the extent of avoiding romantic involvements of any kind; her negative feelings toward her mother were acted out against her own person, however, in the form of self-induced illnesses (culminating in her putting out one of her eyes with a pencil). Several other asexual patients had been brutalized by a parent throughout their childhood, so that they now choose to live more or less as hermits rather than risk further humiliation and hurt from other people.

"Sins of commission" (incest, child abuse) involving quite real pain or humiliation are probably harder for a child to overcome than "sins of omission" (neglect), unless the latter are extreme. Many of these asexual borderlines, having been abused (beaten, locked in closets, tortured) as children, were just as overwhelmed, and rendered to the same extent outcasts from society, as were the victims of incest. Their improvement in psychotherapy was meager or negligible, as with the incest group. Only a few established a close friendship, and none has thus far formed a sexual relationship with anyone.

DYSMORPHOPHOBIA

Originally used to denote, in persons of average appearance, a delusion of ugliness (19, 20), the false conviction usually centering on the face or the breasts, the term *dysmorphophobia* has also come to be used in reference to certain even more paradoxical situations where an unusually attractive woman imagines herself ugly (21). Some of the patients in the original descriptions were presumably schizophrenic, but it seems that this phenomenon is quite common in borderline patients, more so in women but occasionally in males as well. Recent authors have emphasized only the exaggerated nature of the patient's perception, taking at face value the supposition that the patient would wish if at all possible to be rid of the ugly self-image. At times that may be so, but in my experience at least, the "dysmorphophobia" is a rank misnomer (to say nothing of the fact that ugliness is not an external object of which one could have a true phobia). The patient is often a beautiful woman who clings paradoxically but desperately to the notion of being "ugly" by way of minimizing what is to her way of thinking murderous envy on the part of other women—or else the conviction of ugliness serves dynamically to "protect" her from the emotionally unmanageable advances of men. I have noted this surprising dynamic particulary in beautiful women who have had incestuous relations with a father or older brother: to be "pretty" means to be the target of illicit desire, to be "ugly" means to be safe. Their complaint of being ugly acquires the force of delusion, masking the far worse fear of being (what they actually are) beautiful. I have even encountered one male patient, extraordinarily handsome, who imagined himself to be of insect-like repugnance to others. As a child of 8 or 9, he had been sodomized by his father. To think of himself as ugly was his way of neutralizing the leering stares of homosexual men or the envious glances of heterosexual men whom he would pass in the street.

In the more common cases where women of average appearance feel ugly, there is often another paradoxical dynamic related to the father. These women complain as if their ugliness disqualifies them for romantic attachment to a potential lover or husband. They feel "condemned" never to marry, but underneath they are extraordinarily closely attached to their fathers, not because of incestuous involvement but because their mothers were rejecting and their fathers were warm and accepting. Through their distorted self-image they remain permanently unattached to any new men an permanently close to the one safe object of their earlier years.

Recently I worked with two borderline women, each of a markedly "infantile" personality (6), where their attempts to achieve any closeness in a love relationship were frustrated not only by a "father fixation" of the sort just described but also by an emptiness, an impoverishment of personality. Both tended to be critical, intolerant, and impatient of any shortcomings in the men who courted them. They had no real interests in life (and were therefore boring) and no real interests in the men as individuals. As a result, each woman, despite her pleasing appearance, was unattractive as a long-range prospect for any man. The patients spoke as though they had some inchoate awareness of where the real trouble lay, but to recognize that one is undesirable because of having "no personality" (and because of one's contemptuousness) is terrifying: these are not qualities one can easily modify or control. Instead, each dwelt to a morbid degree on her looks, becoming "dysmorphophobic." This was, to be sure, an unpleasant symptom, but one that seemed amenable to ordinary measures: the hairdresser, the gym, the plastic surgeon. To remedy the real problem—the *inner*ugliness— was, as each patient intuitively recognized, an almost insuperable and much less well defined task.

Occasionally, one will discover a somewhat different dynamic theme in a borderline woman with "dysmorphophobia." I have worked with a few, for example, where their attractiveness was denied and their appearance chronically derogated by their fathers, all throughout adolescence. In these instances it emerged during the course of psychotherapy that the father was struggling with incestuous impulses toward a very attractive daughter, sometimes within the context of a deteriorating marriage. The defense the father utilized was that of denying his impulse and then criticizing the daughter's looks, as though she were the last woman on earth who could stir up in him a sexual feeling. The advantage in these cases was that no incest occurred; the disadvantage was that it gave a shattered self-image to a young woman, who began to feel not only unattractive but also unlovable and worthless. As they enter adult life, these women, if handicapped further by functioning at the borderline level, are extremely sensitive to the mildest disappointments, let alone criticisms, in a love relationship. It is impossible to reassure them sufficiently to keep the relationship afloat and smooth-sailing. Their lives are characterized by one broken romance after the other, until in their late 30s or early 40s they give up on men entirely. This gloomy prospect is sometimes reversible with psychotherapy, but the task requires many years.

As a final comment on this intriguing condition, it is worth mentioning that one will encounter from time to time a borderline "dysmorphophobic" woman whose conviction of ugliness stems mainly from an inchoate realization of having an "ugly" nature. Their conviction of this becomes the concrete expression ("my face is ugly") of a figurative turn of phrase ("my personality is ugly"). Sometimes the personality will have become deformed owing to external circumstances—incest, sadistic treatment, verbal humiliation—of which the future borderline woman started out as a victim. Or constitutional aberrations, including perinatal brain damage, may even in the absence of adverse parental influences predispose her to insatiable drives, affect hunger, uncontrollable rage, and a grotesque abrasiveness of personality, noticeable from earliest childhood. In either event, a true ugliness of personality develops (with contemptuousness, mendacity, manipulativeness, hostility, and other socially offensive qualities), which causes alienation and loss of friends, as well as the dysmorphophobia—here consisting of a secret ugliness that corrodes the attractive exterior until the latter, too, is experienced as "ugly."

JEALOUSY

Freud (22) spoke of three varieties of jealousy: The *competitive* or "normal" type; the *projected* type, where one's own impulses toward infidelity are projected onto one's partner, as though the latter is untrustworthy rather than oneself; and the *delusional* type, where unresolved homosexual feelings are dealt with via a mechanism where (to take the case of a male patient) the subject claims, "*I* do not love him; *she* loves him") and consciously experiences jealousy toward the often nonexistent other male. Freud adds that in the delusional cases jealousy is not restricted to this last type but involves all three mechanisms.

Considering the frequency with which serious disturbances in psychosexual development and in interpersonal relations are encountered in borderline patients, one might expect to find in them the more severe forms of jealousy also. Delusional jealousy remains, nevertheless, an uncommon phenomenon, at least in the borderline patients whom I have treated or seen in consultation. Nor has the theme of homosexuality been prominent in every case. Granted that many of Freud's so-called neurotic analysands would be considered *borderline* today (namely, the Wolf-Man [23], with his strong latent homsexuality, seduction by a sister, dysmorphophobia regarding his nose, etc.), his clinical experience seldom included the near-psychotic end of the borderline spectrum. It may also be that in our day less stigma attaches to homosexuality impulses than in Freud's era. At any rate, some cases of pathological jealousy known to me involve intense fear of betrayal and separation and only secondarily, if at all, homosexuality. One such patient, a man of 22, was preoccupied with the fear that his fiancée would take up with another man. Though domineering, athletic, and free of any difficulties in sexual performance, he would become enraged by the most trivial sign of friendliness on the part of his fiancée toward another man, even though she was never seductive or flirtatious with other men and was totally devoted to the patient. His mother had been intrusive, infantilizing, and extremely seductive toward him for many years, barging into his room when he, or even she, would be undressed, ostensibly to chat or to lay out his clothes for the next day. He found his mother's behavior at once repugnant and exciting. He began to develop a view of women according to which they were all whorish Jezebels whom God condemned men to fall in love with, even though they were destined to desert their men just as surely as his mother deserted, at least emotionally, his father in favor of her son.

Another borderline man of 23, married with two children, had been given up at age 4 to foster care by his parents, who were unable financially to support their three sons. His foster parents, their demonic sadism subsequently corroborated by the courts, subjected him and his brothers to grotesque brutalities under the pretext of teaching them obedience. He was forced to kneel on rice for hours at a time, whipped to the point of bleeding, knocked unconscious, and so on. In response to this systematic torture, he developed a paranoid personality; his extreme touchiness about his personal "space" was a reaction not to fear of homosexual assault but to fear of purely physical assault. Wary of people in general, he had few friends and was extremely dependent on and possessive of his wife, whom he suspected of infidelity from time to time, not on account of any proclivities in that direction on her part but simply because he expected the worst from everybody, including her.

Jealousy, in a hospitalized borderline woman named Donna, took the form of extreme overattachment to her therapist (a woman) and violent reactions to the inevitable interest shown by the latter in relation to other patients in her case load. Once, when her therapist was assigned a new female patient, Donna ran off the hospital grounds and made deep gashes in both wrists, creating an emergency that she hoped would preempt her therapist's time, rendering her unavailable for the new "sister." As with the preceding patient, maternal deprivation and possessive love were the wellsprings of the pathological jealousy, to a much greater extent than any repressed homosexual longings. But Donna did express some homosexual interest in her therapist, and it may be that maternal deprivation in a *female* patient predisposes, via subsequent erotization (in adolescence) of the yearning for closeness, to a homosexual interest such as might *not* develop in a male patient with a similar dynamic constellation. In a few instances known to me, borderline women with delusional jealousy have been bisexual, their homosexual tendencies not repressed at all. In any event, it is easy to appreciate how the more severe forms of jealousy interfere with romantic relationships, disrupt marriages, and so forth, since (a) the jealous person is incapable of distinguishing between a trustworthy partner and one whose behavior would truly merit his suspiciousness; (b) the jealous person will tend to torment the partner with unfair accusations until the latter is driven away, and (c) partners are usually chosen, albeit unconsciously, for conformity to the jealous person's unrealistic anxieties—meaning that the partner with whom one falls in love *really is* unfaithful, so of course the relationship is stormy and ultimately unworkable.

This last point relates to a curious facet of the "assortative mating" that brings one possessive person together with another. Naively, one might guess that the best antidote to pathological jealousy is extreme trustworthiness and devotion in the partner, but this is not so. Those qualities are the attributes of fairly integrated, emotionally healthy persons, but healthy people have friends, even nonsexual friendships with the opposite sex. They live in the world. Their emotional organization is not symbiotic. All this is immensely threatening to a jealous borderline person, for whom anything less than exclusive round-the-clock possession of the "important other" causes unbearable anguish. If the borderline person has also been an incest victim, he (or, as is more often the case, she) will assume that all human relationships end up in bed, so that innocent friendships become resented not only as sources of inattention, which is bad enough, but as potential sources of infidelity, which is intolerable. Hence, it more often happens that a possessive, jealous, symbiotically organized borderline will fall in love with someone who is quite similar and equally friendless, whose own inordinate need for an exclusive relationship is in harmony with that of the borderline person. But the latter, having avoided the Scylla of a partner's friendships, now turns into the Charybdis of the partner's immaturity, irascibility, and so forth. The comfort of choosing someone as ill as oneself endures only a short time and then collapses. Particularly with the delusionally jealous borderline, whose hidden agenda is not to forge a harmonious relationship with another person but primarily to seek revenge for wrongs (real or imaginary) once suffered, inflicting similar torment on the partner, relationships are doomed from the beginning. Worse still, the tendency to externalize and distort, and the generally poor capacity for reality-testing about people, render psychotherapy with jealous borderlines unrewarding. The success rate is low.

It may be that some of the confusion and controversy surrounding the theme of homosexuality in delusional jealousy stems from the failure to distinguish between latent and conscious homosexuality. This is the point raised and later resolved by Frosch (24) in his lucid discussion of the issue as it relates to patients (some of them "borderline") who partake of what he terms the *psychotic process*. The delusionally jealous are only occasionally overt homosexuals; not many are even latently so, in the sense that "latent" refers to a tendency not yet lived out in behavior but about to be, or one that could eventually be acted on. These patients, instead, are (like Schreber) heterosexuals who are preoccupied nonetheless by uncertainty regarding gender or by repressed yearnings for closeness with the same sex, not accompanied, however, by sexual excitement in relation to persons of the same sex (as would characterize the true homosexual). Frosch notes that the delusionally jealous, as with other markedly paranoid patients, have often been victims, as children, of one or another sort of humiliation. Frosch's comments are not directed to the borderline case specifically but are strikingly exemplified in the jealousy of a borderline "hysteroid dysphoric" woman whose unconscious homosexuality manifested itself in several unusual ways.

This woman, recently divorced and in the midst of a new relationship, would frequently manipulate the old and the new lover so that they would encounter each other. After sex with her new partner, she would sometimes submit to oral sex with her ex-husband, who was eager to suck out the semen of his rival. She thus made herself the instrument of a homosexual act. Having been abandoned by her mother as an infant, she was left with an inordinate (though repressed) longing for physical closeness with a woman, and it was this that expressed itself indirectly in her delusional jealousy. Another form taken by her preoccupation with women was her encouragement of her lovers—as if that is what they wanted—to engage in a *ménage à trois* with herself and another woman. She thus served, sandwich fashion, as the pretext for two men to indulge their "homosexuality," or made of her male partner the pretext to indulge hers. Psychotherapy was able to unearth these themes, but it had only a minimal effect on attenuating the force of her jealousy.

SADOMASOCHISM

Here we speak of a clinical phenomenon that needs some separate discussion, as though it were an entity entirely apart, despite the close interrelationships that often exist between sadomasochism and, say, jealousy, promiscuity, homosexuality, or incest. There is a difference, however, between the psychological sadomasochism implied when a borderline person subjects a love partner to mental cruelty, as it is aptly known in the courts, via jealous taunts or promiscuous behavior, and the more direct forms of this perversion, where sexual excitement is intertwined with the literal infliction or suffering of bodily pain.

My clinical experience in this area is not broad enough to permit me to make even an educated guess as to whether couples given to whipping or bondage necessarily contain at least one member who is "borderline" by one or another definition. Since extremism—all-or-none thinking, all-or-none behavior—is of the essence of borderline pathology, it stands to reason that, almost by definition, people whose sexual excitement depended on whips, ropes, and chains, to say nothing of more bizarre or sophisticated instruments of torture, would tend to be acting out very primitive, "pregenital" fantasies and often turn out to be "borderline." Similarly, borderlines might be overrepresented among people who subject their sexual partners to acts whose social meanings signify something disgraceful—eating feces, for example—or among those who actively crave submission to such practices. In my practice I know of no neurotics, and only two borderlines, in this category.

By the same token, my clinical experience with the physically painful forms of sadomasochism is confined to borderlines, whereas I have seen some of the less exaggerated or painful forms of "unusual" sexual practices (voyeurism, exhibitionism) in my neurotic patients. A homosexual borderline man of 21, admitted to New York Hospital because of a suicide gesture, was involved in a sadomasochistic relationship with a man who used to beat him with whips as a prelude to sex. At a certain point the patient's lover abandoned him, whereupon the patient strangled to death his lover's pet German Shepherd (how this was effected without suffering further bodily injury was never made clear). When his rage subsided, giving way to loneliness and despair, he made a suicide gesture, cutting his wrists superficially with a razor.

The one instance of bondage known to me involved an obsessive and somewhat sadistic but reasonably well integrated man and his fiancée, a delusionally jealous and frequently promiscuous borderline woman of 20, who abused marijuana and who subjected her lover to humiliating arguments in public. His retaliation consisted of tying her to the bedposts with ropes, whipping her, engaging in intercourse, and then leaving for a number of hours without telling her when, or whether, he would return.

MASOCHISM: MORAL VS. SELF-MUTILATIVE ASPECTS

Even within the realm of borderline conditions it is not common to find sexual arousal dependent primarily on physical pain. Much more common is the pattern of "moral masochism," when intimacy and, particularly, sexual pleasure are purchased at a price of displeasure, often at the level of mental anguish, within the context of a self-defeating relationship. Several paths are open to the "moral masochist" with respect to self-defeat. One could choose a partner with whom a lifetime relationship is possible but where the lifetime of togetherness is punctuated by episodes of extreme unfairness, unfounded accusations, humiliation, and psychological cruelties of every sort. The partner, alternatingly loving and cruel, brings about oscillations in the relationship as a whole, such that each period of intense pleasure is "paid for" by the anguish that unaccountably but predictably follows, each period of anguish made tolerable by a happy reconciliation. Characteristics of the partner who creates this kind of roller-coaster existence include extreme jealousy and perfectionism, but one may also encounter a markedly ambivalent attitude toward closeness. For example, one borderline patient, a female homosexual in her early 20s, became enamored of a somewhat older woman who, though not taunting her with the wish to seek other partners, would nevertheless torment the patient by suddenly disappearing for hours, days, or a week without provocation or reason. The patient, running the gamut of painful emotion from frenzy to despair, would be near the point of making a suicide gesture when, with equal suddenness, her lover would turn up again, as loving and seemingly devoted as before. The lover, herself borderline, had suffered the rejection and disappearance of her mother on multiple occasions throughout her childhood. The patient saw in her lover the embodiment of her parents' own stormy relationship: her "long-suffering" (read "masochistic") mother and her alcoholic, alternately passionate and sadistic (and chronically unfaithful) father. Despite, or perhaps because of, these episodes of abandonment and reunion, the patient felt completely "at home" with her lover, as the two busied themselves with the unconscious living out of the only patterns of intimacy either had ever witnessed or experienced.

Another self-defeating pattern involves the choice of partners, one after the other, with whom only a brief relationship is possible—and that stormy and ultimately ungratifying. Sometimes the partners are selected, unconsciously of course, for some cruel or menacing quality, which has the effect of expiating the guilt engendered by the borderline's sexual activity. Typifying this pattern was an attractive 22–year-old college student who had been admitted to New York State Psychiatric Institute for globus hystericus, depressive symptoms, and two superficial wrist-cuttings. This woman had a series of brief involvements with older men, many of whom were crude, abusive, and from the wrong side of the tracks socially, in contrast to her artistocratic background. All these elements—the cruelty, the brevity, the indifference—were of special significance when viewed against the backdrop of her own family history: her father had abandoned her mother when she was three and a half and had not spoken to her since. Attracted only to cruel and inconstant men, she was cruel and inconstant herself to the "nice" men who fell in love with her.

Overlapping with the already mentioned themes of dysmorphophobia, jealousy, and masochism is another form of painful relationship encountered frequently among borderlines, though it is hardly unknown within the broader realm of neurotic individuals. I speak of a sadomasochistic trend, directed ostensibly at the sexual life, whose primary purpose centers around the "pregenital" concern over separation. This trend manifests itself as an unending, outrageous testing of the partner's continuing devotion. A typical example concerns a borderline woman with chronic worries about her attractiveness and a tendency to disbelieve compliments about her beauty, who will subject her spouse or partner to unnecessary separations, social humiliations (such as spoiling a dinner party by suddenly absenting herself from her guests without any explanation), sexual rebuffs, and the like—all by way of seeing whether her partner "still loves her." If a husband imploringly professes his undying adoration after his wife made an embarrassing scene in front of his boss, the case is much more "convincing" than if similar remarks were as pillow talk after a lovely day. Many of the acts and assertions of the borderline caught up in this pattern have a half-conscious and therefore gamelike quality, as with the taunt "You never really loved me." The beautiful woman who acknowledges her own attractiveness "loses" (to the extent that she may be borderline and woefully lacking in self-esteem) a valuable weapon with which to extract reassurances from the men in her life. The mechanism I allude to is well known, and more tellingly described, by literary authors than by psychiatric authors: Murray Shisgal in his play *Luv* stages a hilarious battle between the two lover-protagonists, each of whom torments the other with a series of escalating insults (she kicks him in the shins, he slaps her in the face, she breaks his glasses, he throws her mink coat over the bridge . . .)—each insult followed by the urgent question, " 'Ya still *luv* me?!' "

Recently I became aware of still another unusual masochistic dynamic. Pain is endured not so much as expiation for sexual guilt but rather as a necessary by-product of a relationship whose main effect is to shore up a negative self-image (through the choice of a partner who is truly inferior in some important way). Thus, a schizotypal borderline woman who was herself markedly gauche and irritating in social situations began to date a man who was considerably more disrespectful of social convention than she was. For example, he was crude, his hygiene was poor, and he would flaunt his interest in other women in front of her. All this she complained of as immensely annoying, yet she clung to the relationship. At first this seemed inexplicable, but gradually it emerged that she felt for the first time a kind of social and moral superiority over someone, whereas in relation to just about everyone else she had become used to the uncomfortable image of being the obnoxious one, the less poised one, and so on. According to the calculus of her particular psychic economy, this feeling of moral superiority, along with the surcease from loneliness and the mild sexual pleasure he afforded, weighed heavier in the balance than the suffering she endured on account of his shabby treatment.

Self-damaging acts constitute one of the diagnostic items for the *DSM*-III diagnosis of borderline and are important in the Gunderson schema as well. Though such acts are neither necessary nor sufficient for the diagnosis, many borderlines exhibit them from time to time, often flamboyantly. Whereas only one in six of my office-practice borderlines indulged in wrist-cutting, burning, or other self-mutilative acts, these acts figure almost invariably among the precipitants of hospitalization, such that any sample of inpatient borderlines (particularly of the affective variety) will contain very few who have *not* engaged in self-mutilative acts just prior to admission. In female borderlines these acts will often be found to have taken place premenstrually (25), especially if there had been a recent disruption in a romantic relationship. Psychodynamically, these self-damaging acts are frequently intertwined with sexual themes, or else are part and parcel of an exploitative attitude toward the loved one, as manifestations of a desperate, not to say outrageous, effort to control the latter's psychological freedom.

Pregenital themes may be fused with strictly genital themes, but to such an extent that the various motifs that underlie the self-mutilative act cannot easily be pried apart. For example, a 22–year-old depressed and hospitalized borderline woman, having heard of her therapist's impending vacation, broke a light bulb and scratched her wrists. The more obvious meaning of her act concerned anxiety about separation, but she also experienced herself as in love with her therapist, whose vacation she interpreted as personal rejection. Implicit in her act was the taunt "If you really loved me, you'd drop what you're doing and minister to my wounds."

ADORATION AND HATRED, AS THE BORDERLINE FALLS—AND FAILS—IN LOVE

As we hinted above, if one is borderline the extremes are "average," and average behavior, average attitudes, are almost unknown. Falling in love has been compared by such diverse groups as poets and psychiatrists to psychosis. This is a bit unfair to love, because even though love draws its strength from unconscious and irrational forces, it is too common an experience and is too often conducive to stable, gratifying relationships lasting years to qualify truly as a brand of madness. The early stage of most love relationships is characterized by "infatuation," two of whose characteristics are idealization and uncritical acceptance of the loved one. Everything is "perfect," or what imperfections the lover permits himself to notice—a tooth out of line, a few hairs where they shouldn't be—only add to the individuality and charm of the beloved. This reverential attitude toward the beloved is often accompanied by the spontaneous assertion "I adore you." The adoration resembles the adoration of the religious ecstatic and indeed may constitute one's sole experience of this intense and blissful emotion—especially in our era, when for most people, religious fervor has become unfamiliar and passé.

But adoration may also be seen as the counterpart to the symbiotic mode of interrelatedness—whether encountered, under quite normal circumstances, in the mother-infant relationship (8) or in abnormal situations, such as the attitudes prevailing in the early transference relationship between a schizophrenic patient and his therapist. Borderlines too, with their intolerance of separation and their predilection for possessive, symbiotic attachments, are also more prone than better integrated people to fall into and remain in the state of adoration. If they love at all, they adore.

If borderlines were able to sustain feelings of adoration for long periods, or if their reactions to the inevitable shortcomings, negative qualities, social gaffes, and so on—of which their loved ones will sooner or later be "guilty"—were less drastic, all would be well. But precisely because borderlines cannot construct an integrated and blended view of other people (no more than they can of themselves), the first recognition of an unpleasant trait in the loved one, the first glimpse of the hair under the nose, as it were, tends to be shattering. Minor blemishes that ordinary folk would scarcely notice may provoke a disappointment so keen as to be insuperable, leading in turn to dissolution of the relationship. The beloved has indeed been placed on a pedestal, but the pedestal was balanced on a pin. I think in this regard of a couple I once worked with, where both members were borderlines, a plastic surgeon and his wife, who was "Miss— ————"in the Miss America contest. Despite her being unusually attractive, her husband had a catalog of objections: her jawline was not straight enough, her incisors jutted down too far, her nose "needed a little work" (all of which he himself was eager to perform on her until I forbade it), and so forth. Whenever he would castigate her for these anatomical deficiencies, she would burst into tears, then rage, and would lock herself in the bathroom to scarify her wrists with a razor. The situation did not right itself until I prescribed for her a therapist of her own and for him the reading of Hawthorne's "The Birthmark." Fortunately this powerful tale of a man who destroys his beloved wife in the process of trying to extract her insignificant birthmark struck home, and he was able to understand the grotesqueness of his perfectionistic standards. Behind these standards were the important dynamic layers having to do with a hostile symbiotic attachment to his own ambivalently loved mother, compared with whom every other woman, even a beauty queen, had to be rejected. This marriage happened to succeed, since both partners were amenable to therapy and were motivated to remain together. But the more typical story involves a partnership that is severed, when the phase of adoration is abruptly replaced, on recognition of the first "fault," by an equally intense and irrational hatred—either that, or the borderline person begins to oscillate between adoration and hatred, with the inevitable consequence of wearing down the patience of the loved one until he or she finally breaks off the relationship.

In the more successful cases, psychotherapy is eventually able to elevate the borderline patient from the plane of primitive adoration/vilification to the plane of mature love and acceptance. Psychosexually, this would equate with an advance from an early "oral," symbiotic mode of relatedness to a nearly "genital" mode of mature interdependence.

IDENTITY-DISTURBANCE AND THE LOVE RELATIONSHIP, WITH A NOTE ON DON JUANISM

A serious disturbance in the sense of a self, in "identity," is a necessary element in the Kernberg (1) definition of borderline and an almost universal feature of borderlines diagnosed by checklist criteria (26, 18). What are the implications for such a disturbance with respect to the capacity for love? The implications are profound, and they affect the love life in at least two important ways.

The extremely low self-esteem routinely encountered in borderline patients contributes to their suspicion that the love others may claim to feel toward them cannot be genuine (along the lines of Groucho Marx's famous quip that he would not wish to be a member of any club that was willing to accept him). This conviction, analogous to dysmorphophobia, may contribute to pathological jealousy inasmuch as a cripplingly low self-esteem robs one of the feeling of lovability: in comparison to oneself, *any* outsider would "therefore" be preferable in the eyes of one's beloved. The borderline patient with an esteem problem of such dimensions requires inordinate reassurance, which vitiates the love relationship, exhausting, worrying, and ultimately offending the partner (who cannot help but wonder, Why is my sweetheart so down on himself? Maybe he knows something I don't know).

In the more restrictive situation where gender identity is grossly disturbed, as it is in a fairly large subgroup of borderlines, there may be another source of impairment in a love relationship, stemming from uncertainty about the very sex of one's potential partners. It is unclear to me whether bisexuals are apt to be borderline or whether borderlines contain more than their share of bisexuals, but where these situations coexist it is easy to see how one could never be happy in a relationship of long duration with either a man or a woman. This plight was portrayed with considerable effectiveness in Harvey Fierstein's recent play *The Torch-Song Trilogy* (in which a bisexual man cannot at first make up his mind between a transvestite and his "straight" wife). Even bisexual borderline patients who feel relatively unconflicted and comfortable (I have only worked with one) often have troubled relationships: if they marry, they still maintain their homosexual interests, and partners, discovery of which is usually impossible for the spouse to accept with nonchalance.

Not unrelated to the foregoing is the phenomenon of Don Juanism (27, 28), somewhat related to promiscuity and seen usually in males, whose dynamics have been ascribed to unconscious homosexual impulses defended against by a compulsive display of heterosexuality.

Actually, conventional usage makes subtle distinctions between promiscuity and Don Juanism, based partly on sociocultural differences between the sexes, partly on biological differences. Some men engage compulsively in making sexual conquests. Mozart's Don Giovanni racked up just over a thousand in Spain alone, if we are to believe his valet, Leporello. These conquests do not represent the warding off of intolerable loneliness, as is the usual dynamic underlying promiscuity, so much as the less primitive dynamic concerning a reaffirmation of one's gender identity and sexual prowess. For a man to pick up a woman in a bar and have sex with her is still (in his eyes) a bit of a conquest; for the women it is more often than not an act of desperation. However, a woman can be a Don Jaun if she uses her attractiveness (an unprepossessing woman could never be a Don Juan) to make repeated conquests of men whom she views as ordinarily out of her reach, not the anonymous fellow on the adjoining bar stool but men of prominence, power, and fame. Most borderline women are intensely lonely, and if inclined toward driven sexuality, they tend to be promiscuous (rather than female Don Juans). The character of Blanche in *Streetcar Named Desire* is a prototype of the latter. Nevertheless, a few borderline women flaunt their beauty in an effort to "conquer" men of social prominence, often by way of seeking revenge against hurts suffered earlier at the hands of an important male figure from early life. One may correctly consider these women female Don Juans. Numerically there is good reason to suppose there are more males than females who exemplify this phenomenon. Not all Don Juans are borderline, but the more extreme cases probably are, especially where the component of contemptuousness toward women is disproportionately great. The highly narcissistic Don Juan who murdered his wife and daughters, as described in McGinnis's recent book (29), is a case in point and was very likely borderline by Kernberg criteria. Since it is not in the nature of the Don Juan type to admit faults of any kind, let alone worries over sexual prowess, he seldom seeks psychotherapy. I have worked, briefly and unsuccessfully, with only one, a man in his mid-30s forced by his wife to get help, alongside the treatment she was in the midst of, because of his compulsive womanizing. Far from feeling any guilt over subjecting his wife to the details of his escapades, he was proud of being able to juggle so many women at once. He was asymptomatic and quit therapy after seven or eight sessions. Another instance I am familiar with concerns a clearly borderline graduate student in his late 20s who exhibited, in addition to his promiscuity, pseudologia fantastica—making up the most preposterous stories about his sexual exploits. One New Year's Eve he announced to his buddies at school that he was about to go to his engagement party, his fiancée allegedly being the daughter of a famous European nobleman. Dressed in tuxedo, tails, and top hat, he waved ta-ta to his friends, cradling a box with 12 American Beauty roses ostensibly for the delight of his betrothed. Followed surreptitiously by a fellow student, he was observed dumping the roses in a trash bin at the end of the street and then entering a nearby pool-hall to while away the evening with the local hustlers. His roommate noted that he did not once use their bathroom during the entire year, performing his ablutions in some other locale, presumably to preserve the illusion that he was somehow above the smells and noises to which the remainder of humankind is prone. Unusually handsome and dapper, he was adept at getting dependent girls to fall in love with him, only to humiliate them shortly thereafter, often with exquisite cruelty. Don Juans of this type are borderline in personality organization, but they are also largely psychopathic and as such incapable of warm and mutual relationships with anyone: sex is compulsive, love is nonexistent.

DISTURBANCES IN EMPATHY AND COMPASSION IN BORDERLINES

If one thinks in normative terms of the "narcissistic path of development," in contrast to the object-relational path, then every borderline person must exhibit some narcissistic abnormalities, for this path concerns, ideally, awareness and realistic appraisal of one's personality traits, of the impression one makes on others, and of one's potential, self-worth, self-regard, and the like. Borderlines, by virtue of their impaired sense of identity, represent one kind of failure, of deviation, in this path, since their self-image is full of contradictions and distortions. In addition, many but not all borderlines show a constellation of abnormal personality traits that we also call "narcissistic," no longer in the normative but in the pathological sense. Kernberg (6, 30) has outlined the salient features: excessive self-absorption, superficially smooth social adaptation, intense ambition and envy, grandiosity, feelings of inferiority, craving for acclaim, a sense of emptiness, deficiency in empathic capacity, an incapacity to love, and exploitativeness, even ruthlessness, toward others. The presence of this pathological narcissism in a borderline patient augurs poorly for social recovery, let alone for success in love relationships. It should not be difficult to grasp why this is so, since psychotherapists have ample opportunity to discover how easy it is to dispel various (egodystonic) symptoms, yet how hard it is to bring about constructive changes in character formation. Empathy and compassion, if they are seriously lacking, cannot be taught even by the most skilled and patient therapist, although in some persons a rudimentary compassion may be "released" when certain neurotic traits have been modified through analysis. The Wolf-Man (31), in fact, spoke of how his analyses with Freud and Mack Brunswick freed him up to become, in his later years, much more sympathetic and kind to those around him than he had been at the height of his neurosis.

If I divide the borderline patients with whom I have worked in private practice into three groups—those with dramatic recoveries, 11; those with modest improvement, 19; and treatment failures, 21—I notice that empathy and compassion were well developed in all but one of the highly successful cases and in three-fourths of the middle group, but only in half the treatment failures.

How seriously self-absorption and lack of compassion may interfere with love and intimacy can be surmised from the following vignette:

An unmarried borderline woman of 34 was referred for therapy because of an eating disorder. Two subjects preoccupied her mind to the exclusion of all else: her food and her figure. She hungered for testimonials to her beauty, eschewed the company of her (few) friends unless her weight and shape were "perfect," and even then was in a state of high anxiety lest a waiter, a passerby, or some other stranger in a restaurant appear to be more in awe of her girlfriend's looks than of her own looks. Sex frightened her; she had had only a few brief affairs. Though she craved the attention of men (actually only of handsome men), she had no interest in them as individuals; they were simply machines from which she could, under the right circumstances, extract an approving stare. The idea of having to *relate* to one, to express genuine concern as to how his day went, what his insecurities and worries were, and so on, was incomprehensible to her. When she did accept a date, she would spruce up for hours and emerge as a "fashion plate," to *stun* him (literally) with her attractiveness. Once he shook off the effects of being stunned in this way and began to talk to her, she was out of her element. After it became clear to the man, two or three dates later, that she did not care much about him as a person, his enthusiasm cooled. It is interesting that she came from a family where hardly any attention was focused on this or that family member's humanity, but rather on how each one looked. Her own lack of compassion may have come about as a result of her hostility at being so neglected, except as a "package," as well as out of her general lack of practice, coming from such a family, in learning and enjoying learning what makes other people tick.

Empathy and compassion do not travel on quite the same tracks; it is possible to read others' feelings correctly (i.e., to possess *empathy*) but yet to lack compassion. Many borderlines who are also (pathologically) narcissistic lack both and, to the extent that mature love depends on genuine concern for the beloved, are capable at most of lust but not of love. Some schizotypal borderlines have a measure of compassion but so woefully misread the feelings of others as to render lasting relationships impossible. Because of their lack of empathy, they are constantly misconstruing the intentions of others, incorrectly estimating their affections, and so on. Worse still, they cannot easily understand why someone considered their responses off the wall, so they tend to pursue, without self-correction, a jarring and inappropriate attitude (e.g., cracking a joke at a funeral to cheer up the bereaved). Unempathic but compassionate schizotypes of this sort can sometimes maintain a relationship wth someone else of a similar nature, whose emotional insensitivity renders the schizotype's out-of-tune comments less irritating.

Where compassion and empathy are both in short supply, relationships could endure only to the extent that the partner could tolerate sex without affection. But here one is usually dealing with a coldly exploitative borderline who is not only incapable of love but scarcely able to gratify the sexual needs of another person.

FINAL COMMENT

I am aware, as I complete this catalog relevant to the borderline domain of impediments to love and gratifying sexuality, that I have painted a dreary picture. Happily, however, there is more to the picture than the masochism, jealousy, narcissism, and so forth, on which I have dwelt. Among my borderline patients with the more successful outcomes, half were able to form quite satisfactory love relationships of a lasting nature. Two female homosexuals were in this group. These patients had predominantly affective rather than schizotypal traits, although several schizotypal borderlines also functioned at this high level. All were orgastic without difficulty (several began treatment with complaints of unresponsiveness, but they grew less inhibited as treatment progressed). In a few instances, hypomanic personality features were present, including a marked degree of intensity in all their behavior. In the same way manic patients tend to be "augmenters" in their response to stimuli of whatever kind, the borderlines with these traits sometimes reacted to orgasm with exhilaration rather than post-coital drowsiness, such that while their partners would be trying to sleep they would spring out of bed and engage in exercise and all sorts of activities, including another round of lovemaking. Apart from dyssynchronies of this sort, their relationships were for the most part harmonious.

It is also worth noting that, despite the prevalence of empathic difficulties in this category of patients, some borderlines are unusually capable of reasoning with those around them, including their love partners, as though whatever combination of constitutional and experiential factors rendered them overly sensitive to the actions of others, left them, as a compensatory advantage, so to speak, better able than average to sense the hidden feelings of those with whom they are close. Their knowledge of what it is to suffer, and the lengths they go to in order to put their love partners at ease, helps to solidify their intimate relationships. The gratitude and love inspired by their attentions makes it much easier for their loved ones to endure and to remain supportive during the emotional crises to which these borderline persons are periodically subject.

Among borderline patients in general, based on my private practice experience, I have the impression that adequate sexual performance and enjoyment is more common than the capacity for mature love. The patients with the best outcomes did well in at least one of these two areas. Half functioned well in both sex and love. In the intermediate- and poor-outcome groups, adequate sexual performance was present in half, the capacity for love in only a few. One-third of the patients in these two groups demonstrated serious deficiencies in both.

The inability to love was often related to chronic mistrustfulness. This is very much in line with a personal communication from a well-known analyst, Henriette Klein: "Where there is no trust, there is no love." We have already examined one form that this mistrust takes, namely, jealousy. But some borderline patients, even without being particularly prone to jealousy, were mistrustful of and angry at their sexual partners. They were often hypercritical, in a manner suggesting that they foisted onto their partners (via "projective identification") the harsh criticisms with which they, consciously or otherwise, regarded themselves. This issue of *basic trust*, though of fundamental importance in understanding borderline pathology (especially in the realm under discussion here), has its elusive aspects. For example, the patient who had incestuous experiences with both parents, though hypersexual and schizotypal, was orgastic and had the capacity to love, even though her life story at first glance would have led one to suppose she had no reason to develop trust. Some favorable if less dramatic elements in her relationship with her parents must have offset the effects of the sexual abuse. In another instance, a schizotypal borderline woman had unusually warm and supportive parents and seven normal siblings. There was no history of physical or sexual abuse, yet she became hostile, paranoid, referential, and irascible as she entered her 20s. Could these traits be the reflection of her (apparent) constitutional defect alone?

While there is much that is blatant and simple—as we attempt to understand the borderline's difficulties in sex and love—there is still much that is subtle and puzzling. In the meantime, one can summarize the borderline's plight by stating that, among borderlines, one often sees sex without love, or love without sex, or else both sex and love—but with a partner that is unsuitable. In other words, sex and love remain unintegrated.

REFERENCES

1. Kernberg, O. F. The structural diagnosis of borderline personality organization. In: Hartocollis, P., ed., Borderline Personality Disorders. New York: International Universities Press, 1977.
2. Vanggaard, T. Borderlands of Sanity. Copenhagen: Munksgaard, 1979.
3. Bergeret, J. La Dépression et les États-Limites. Paris: Payot, 1975.
4. Gunderson, J. G., and Singer, M. T. Defining borderline patients: an overview. Am. J. Psychiat., 132:1–10, 1975.
5. Diagnostic and Statistical Manual of Mental Disorders (DSM-III). American Psychiatric Association, 1980.
6. Kernberg, O. F. Borderline personality organization. J. Am. Psychoanal. Assoc., 15:641–685, 1967.
7. Hoch, P. H., and Polatin, P. Pseudoneurotic forms of schizophrenia. Psychiat. Q., 23:248–276, 1949.
8. Mahler, M. S. A study of the separation individuation process, and its possible application to borderline phenomena in the psychoanalytic situation. Psychoanal. Study of the Child, 26:403–424, 1971.
9. Masterson, J. F. The Narcissistic and Borderline Disorders. New York: Brunner/Mazel, 1981.
10. Rinsley, D. B. Borderline and Other Self Disorders. New York: Jason Aronson, 1982.
11. Friedman, R. C. Review of "Homosexuality" by C. W. Socarides. J. Amer. Psychoanal. Assoc., 31:316–323, 1983.
12. Stone, M. H. Borderline syndromes: a consideration of subtypes and an overview, directions for research. Psychiatric Clinics of North America, 4 (1):3–24, 1981.
13. Emslie, G. J., and Rosenfeld, A. Incest reported by children and adolescents hospitalized for severe psychiatric problems. Am. J. Psychiat., 140:708–711, 1983.
14. Voisin, F. Des Causes Morales and Physiques des Maladies Mentales. Paris: J. B. Baillière, 1826.
15. Stone, M. H. Child psychiatry before the 20th century. Internat. J. Child Psychother., 2:264–308, 1973.
16. Kraepelin, E. Manic-Depressive Insanity and Paranoia. Edinburgh: E. and S. Livingstone, 1921.
17. Finkelhor, D. Sexually Victimized Children. New York: Free Press, 1979.
18. Stone, M. H. The Borderline Syndromes: Constitution, Adaptation, and Personality. New York: McGraw-Hill, 1980.
19. Morselli, E. Sulla dismorfofobia e sulla tafefobia. Boll. Acad. della Scienze Med. di Genova, 6:110, 1866.
20. Koupernik, C. Psychopathologie de l'adolescence. In: Koupernik, C.; Loo, H.; and Zarifian, E., eds., Précis de Psychiatrie. Paris: Flammarion, 1982.
21. Hay, G. G. Dysmorphophobia. Brit. J. Psychiat., 116:399–406, 1970.
22. Freud, S. Some neurotic mechanisms in jealousy, paranoia, and homosexuality. Standard Edition, XVIII, 223–232, 1922.

23. Freud, S. From the history of an infantile neurosis. S.E., 18:1–122, 1914.
24. Frosch, J. The Psychotic Process. New York: International Universities Press, 1983.
25. Stone, M. H. Premenstrual tension in borderline and related disorders. In: Friedman, R. C., ed., Behavior and the Menstrual Cycle. New York: Marcel Dekker, 1983.
26. Spitzer, R. L.; Endicott, J.; and Gibbon, M. Crossing the border into borderline personality and borderline schizophrenia. Arch. Gen. Psychiatr., 36:17–24, 1979.
27. Pfister, O. Donjuanismus und Dirnetum. In: Die Liebe vor der Ehe und ihre Fehlentwicklung, Almanach, 13:190–200, 1931.
28. Robbins, L. L. A contribution to the psychological understanding of the character of Don Juan. Bull. Menn. Clinic, 20:166–180, 1956.
29. McGinnis, J. Fatal Vision. New York: G. P. Putnam's Sons, 1983.
30. Kernberg, O. F. Further contributions to the treatment of narcissistic personalities. Int. J. Psychoanal., 55:215–240, 1974.
31. The Wolf-Man. In: Gardiner, M., ed., The Wolf-Man. New York: Basic Books, 1971.

PART THREE

MEDICAL AND PHYSIOLOGICAL ASPECTS OF SEXUAL BEHAVIOR

Acquired Immune Deficiency Syndrome: Interaction of Viral, Genetic, Environmental, and Sociological Factors

In 1908, Paul Ehrlich (1) postulated that cancer cells arise frequently and bear surface alterations that could be recognized as foreign antigens by the host. Fifty years later, Lewis Thomas (2) and F. M. Burnett (3) argued that the evolutionary development of cell-mediated immunity was driven by the need for immunologic surveillance of such newly arising malignancies. The immune system is known to hold a crucial role in resistance not only against incursions by neoplastic cells but also in reaction to microbal invaders and altered or foreign tissues. Four main components assist in this defense: T lymphocyte dependent immunity; antibody mediated, B lymphocyte dependent immunity; mononuclear phagocytic cells; and the series of complement serum proteins. Minor and accessory cell populations, some of which lack the immunologic hallmarks of memory and specificity, are also involved in immune interactions. Each system may act independently or in concert. Selective breakdowns in this network include congenital syndromes secondary to embryological or enzymatic defects (4, 5) as well as immunosuppression related to cancer chemotherapy or drugs administered in preparation for organ allografting. Naturally developing perturbations of the immune system also occur. These processes, of variable severity and physiologic consequence, include aging, pregnancy (6), psychological stress (7), severe malnutrition (8), and acute and chronic viral infections (9). In certain of these diverse settings, individuals are at risk for the development of cancers of the skin and the hematopoietic system, as well as rare "opportunistic" neoplasms and infections, disorders commonly recognized only in the milieu of immune dysfunction (10, 11). The relatively low incidence of primary or acquired immune deficiencies is not an accurate measure of their scientific importance. They have provided valuable models applicable to an understanding of the pathophysiology of a variety of diseases, from common allergies and diabetes mellitus through complex autoimmune disorders such as systemic lupus erythematosus.

Over the past four years the frequency and nature of acquired immune deficiencies has dramatically changed. In June 1981 the Centers for Disease Control (CDC) in Atlanta, Georgia, reported the unprecedented occurrence of a rare malignancy, Kaposi's sarcoma, a pneumonia caused by the parasite *Pneumocystis carinii*, and other severe infections (12, 13). Because of the profound disturbances of immune function underlying these illnesses, they were categorized by the term acquired immune deficiency syndrome (AIDS). Viral, genetic, environmental, and sociological factors interact in combinations resulting in devastating immune abnormalities. Initially there was a concentration of cases among previously healthy, sexually promiscuous homosexual and bisexual men in New York City, San Francisco, and Los Angeles (see Figures 10.1 and 10.2). By April 30, 1985, 10,000 instances were reported from all 50 states, and as of January 1985 there were 762 additional patients from 21 countries of the European region of the World Health Organization (14). The populations in which AIDS is now recognized have expanded to include intravenous drug abusers (15), hemophiliacs and other frequent recipients of blood or blood products (16), native Haitians (17) and recent Haitian immigrants to the United States (18), natives and emigrants from central Africa (19, 20), female sexual partners of men with AIDS (21), and infants born to parents with risk factors for AIDS (22, 23). (See Table 10.1.) Cases have been diagnosed in all primary racial and ethnic groups in the United States. Some 57 percent of those reported to the CDC have been white, 26 percent black, 14 percent Hispanic, and 3 percent other (including Oriental). Seventeen percent of all patients are female. Approximately 50 percent of AIDS patients are 30–39 years old at diagnosis; an additional 22 percent are 20–29 and 40–49 years old, respectively. The age of drug-abuse patients clusters more closely, with 81 percent being 20–39 years of age (24). Most cases continue to be found among residents of large cities. The New York City metropolitan area accounts for 42 percent of all cases, San Francisco for 11 percent, Los Angeles for 7 percent and Miami for 5 percent.

There is no evidence that AIDS can be acquired through casual social contact with an AIDS patient or with persons in population groups with increased incidences of AIDS. Four cases have been uncovered among health-care personnel not known to belong to a recognized risk group (25). The source of disease in these individuals is unclear, but none had documented contact with another AIDS patient. The fact that AIDS is not highly infectious and cannot be transmitted by casual exposure is emphasized by the constancy of the types of groups at risk for its development. There is also no epidemiologic support for such vectors as food, water, air, or environmental surfaces. Rather, its pattern of spread is reminiscent of hepatitis B viral infection and suggests that AIDS involves a biologic agent requiring sexual or blood-borne transmission. This agent has recently been identified as a virus, and will be discussed in detail later. With a mortality of over 40 percent per year and an average of three to four new cases diagnosed daily, compared with a mean of a single case per day in 1981, AIDS has become a public-health problem of epidemic proportions.

As presently defined by the CDC, however, AIDS probably signifies a very

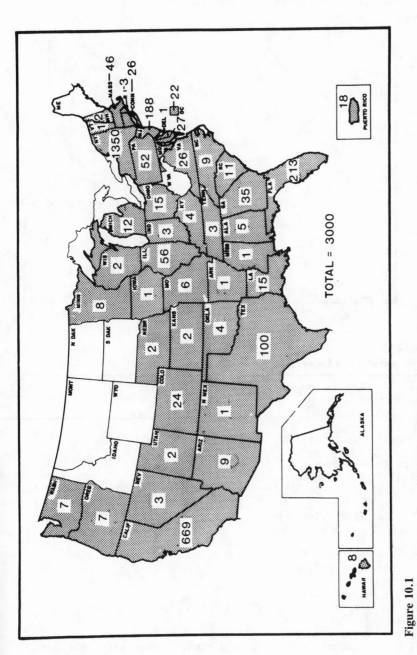

Figure 10.1
AIDS Cases Reported to the Centers for Disease Control by State, as of December 19, 1983

Figure 10.2
AIDS Cases in the United States by Quarter of Diagnosis

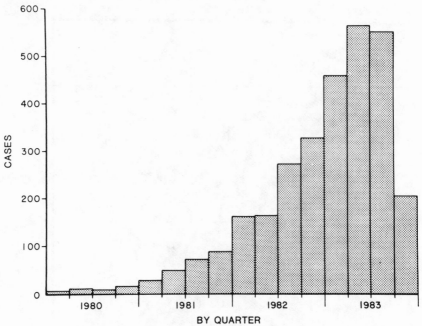

Table 10.1
Distribution of AIDS Cases by Risk Factors

	Risk Group	Incidence (%)		
		Males	Females	Total
1.	Homosexual or bisexual	75.9	0	71.1
2.	Intravenous drug abuser (no history of homosexuality)	14.7	53.3	17.1
3.	Haitian (not belonging to Risk Group 1 or 2)	4.9	9.8	5.2
4.	Hemophiliac (not belonging to Risk Groups above)	0.9	0	0.8
5.	No apparent risk group or unknown*	3.7	37.0	5.7

*Includes immigrants from central Africa, female sexual partners of male intravenous drug abusers, and individuals who died before adequate sexual and social histories could be obtained. Does not include cases in children.

small segment of potential cases. Since October 1981, increasing instances of persistent, generalized lymphadenopathy have been found among otherwise asymptomatic members of the risk groups described above (26). Histologically these nodes show an intense hyperplasia of the follicular or germinal centers, containing primarily B-lymphocytes, together with depletion of the paracortical regions of T cells (27). These findings are of special concern as a spectrum of disorders, leading from nodal hyperplasia accompanied by systemic symptoms such as unexplained fever, night sweats, weight loss, and chronic diarrhea to development of AIDS, is postulated to occur among susceptible groups. These conditions are often referred to as pre-AIDS, prodromal AIDS, or the AIDS-related complex (ARC), although as will be illustrated later the great majority of patients with these symptoms do not progress to development of clinical AIDS. It also implies that the reservoir of people capable of transmitting an infectious AIDS agent is much greater than the present number of recorded cases. Investigation of a cluster of AIDS cases involving a chain of sexual contacts among homosexual men in southern California (28) defined an incubation period of from several months to over two years between estimated first exposure and clinical illness and suggested that transmissibility precludes obvious signs or symptoms. These concepts are supported by the occurrence of AIDS in an infant who received multiple blood and platelet transfusions during the first few days of life for Rh disease. He became ill with recurrent opportunistic infections when six months old and died of *Pneumocystis carinii* pneumonia at two years of age (29). One of the blood donors, who was well at the time of blood collection, died 17 months later with multiple opportunistic infections and acquired immunodeficiency.

The common denominator in patients with AIDS is a marked but selective abnormality of immunoregulation. Experiments by Henry Claman et al. (30) in 1966 demonstrated that the antibody response to complex antigens is dependent on the presence of both thymus-drived T lymphocytes and bone-marrow-derivedB cells. This provided some of the first evidence that the expression of immunity requires cooperative interactions among distinct cell populations. Subsequent studies by many investigators indicated that development of cell-mediated and humoral (antibody) immune reactivities are founded on communication, by way of cell-to-cell contacts and soluble substances, among many cell types. This collaboration results in alteration of the ultimate immune response, as represented by some product or phenomenon of the participating units (see Table 10.2). Such modulation may be either positive (help), or negative (suppression), or more likely involves a synthesis of both. Virtually all AIDS patients show a defect in cell-mediated immunity. This is manifest *in vivo* by anergy to intra-dermally introduced antigens in the delayed type hypersensitivity reaction, and *in vitro* by a decreased DNA synthetic response on exposure of peripheral blood mononuclear cells to antigen or mitogen (31, 32). This defect may be further defined by exploring the four main attributes characteristic of the T cell: its specificity, function, state of activation, and surface phenotype.

Table 10.2
Immunologic Abnormalities in AIDS

Cellular

Cutaneous anergy
Lymphopenia
Reduced total number of mature, circulating T cells
Decreased percentage and absolute number of helper/inducer
   (Leu 3 or T4 +) T cells
Increased percentage and variable absolute number of suppressor/
   cytotoxic (Leu 2 or T8 +) T cells
Reduction in T helper: suppressor ratio
Reduced T cell proliferative responses to antigens and mitogens
Depressed natural killer (NK) cell activity
Variable autologous and allogeneic mixed lymphocyte culture
   (MLC) responses
Normal macrophage function (bactericidal killing, lymphocyto-
   toxin production, antigen presentation, interleukin 1
   synthesis)
Normal dendritic cell function

Humoral

Normal numbers of circulating B lymphocytes
Elevated serum IgA and IgM levels
Elevated titers to EBV and CMV viral antigens
Elevated circulating immune complexes
Increased α -1-thymosin in serum
Increased α -2-acid labile interferon in serum
Increased spontaneous elaboration of immunoglobulin, coupled
   with depressed responses to pokeweed mitogen in vitro

Systematic recognition of T lymphocyte subsets with functionally different roles in the normal immune response was facilitated by isolation of monoclonal antibodies directed against discrete T cell membrane antigens. Using monoclonal T cell markers prepared by the hybridoma techniques developed by Kohler and Milstein (33), Reinherz et al. (34) established three stages of T lymphocyte ontogeny. Stage I thymocytes normally comprise only 10 percent of thymic cells and bear the antigen T10. Monoclonal antibody against T10 also reacts with a high percentage of peripheral T lymphocytes obtained from individuals following viral infection and immunization and in certain acquired immunodeficiencies. Most thymocytes belong to Stage II, where molecules characteristic of T cells exhibiting positive (the helper/inducer T4$^+$ subset) or negative (the suppressor/cytotoxic T8$^+$ subset) influences on immune reactivity are simultaneously expressed. As these cells mature further, the distinct subpopulations of Stage III develop. These cells are phenotypically distinguished by an antigen characteristic of mature T cells, T3 as well as either T4 or T8.

The distribution of these markers normally differs, depending on the tissue or organ examined. The T4$^+$ subset represents 60 percent of the peripheral T cell pool and is also the predominant T cell in lymph nodes. The T8$^+$ suppressor cell comprises 20 percent of circulating T lymphocytes yet is the major thymus-drived cell in bone marrow and intestinal epithelium. The complexity of this system is reflected in functional interactions among these subsets. For example, T4$^+$ cells are primarily responsible for the induction of antibody responses to T cell dependent antigens. Within this subset, however, there are likely to be subpopulations that selectively regulate cell-mediated as opposed to humoral responses. The effector role of the T8$^+$ suppressor cell also requires activation by a T4$^+$ "inducer."

Perturbations of the relative proportions of helper to suppressor T cells occur transiently in many disease states. The usual ratio of T4$^+$: T8$^+$ circulating lymphocytes is $1.8 + 0.6$, indicating the preponderance of helper T cells. This ratio is depressed, because of a relative or absolute increase in T8$^+$ cells, during the acute and immediate convalescent phases of viral infections, particularly influenza, hepatitis A and B, and those of the herpesvirus family, including Epstein-Barr virus (EBV) and cytomegalovirus (CMV) (9, 35). The finding of a lack of mature T3$^+$ cells, an increase in circulating immature Stage II T lymphocytes, and a selective depletion of the T4$^+$ cell resulting in reversal of the helper : suppressor T cell ratio in favor of suppression is consistent in AIDS (32). Recently one fraction of the T4$^+$ subset, designated TQ1$^+$/Leu-8$^+$, has been determined to be specifically affected in AIDS (36). Some of these findings are also apparent, albeit to a less pronounced degree, in homosexual men with lymphadenopathy (27) and hemophiliacs receiving therapeutic doses of Factor VIII or IX concentrates, clotting substances prepared from the plasma of thousands of donors (37). (In addition, in some studies, ostensibly healthy homosexual men were found to have evidence of *in vitro* abnormalities similar to that seen in AIDS [38, 39]. These defects were not prominent in other series examining similar individuals, however [40]. Whatever agent or agents, acting independently or synergistically, are involved in the catastrophic immunosuppression observed in AIDS, this remarkable selectivity for a specific T cell subset must be explained. Clues as to its cause have arisen from an exploration of mechanisms for the observed blockade of cellular immune interactions.

The basic vocabulary used in communication among cells in the immune system includes two major classes of self-determinants: major histocompatibility antigens and idiotypes. The major histocompatibility complex (MHC) in humans is a closely linked group of genes on the short arm of Chromosome 6. It codes for the structure of certain cell surface molecules and plasma proteins as well as for factors regulating immune responses to antigen. The human histocompatibility (HLA) antigens directed by this region comprise the most polymorphic antigen system known. This diversity implies an as yet poorly understood biologic advantage. The MHC does have a pivotal role as a barrier to effective allogeneic organ transplantation. Recent evidence also implicates its involvement in determining susceptibility or resistance to a wide spectrum of diseases (41).

The coding sequences for these antigens are known as Class I and Class II segments. Class I genes code HLA-A,B,C determinants, glycoproteins displayed on the membranes of all nucleated cells. These antigens elicit strong antibody and T cell proliferative responses when introduced into genetically disparate recipients. Class II genes code for the HLA-D specificities, define by lymphocyte typing. This technique utilizes the capacity of allogeneic lymphocytes from HLA-A,B,C identical individuals to elicit DNA synthesis by T cells in the mixed lymphocyte culture (MLC) reaction. Human alloantisera or monoclonal antibodies may also be utilized to detect these specificities on cell surfaces, describing the HLA-DR (D-related) determinants. Such molecules are structurally similar to the mouse immune response region-associated (Ia) antigens found on B lymphocytes, macrophages, sperm, endothelial cells, and immature and activated T cells (42). Ia molecules physically associate with antigen on the surface of certain cells capable of presenting antigen in a manner suitable for recognition by T lymphocytes.

Although an organism can respond to many diverse antigens, individual T cells, like B cells, can recognize only one or a few. In the case of the B lymphocyte, this restriction is imposed by membrane immunoglobulin. Functional studies of the basis for T cell specificity have revealed a remarkable connection between T cell antigen recognition and the MHC. This dual specificity of T lymphocytes is termed "MHC restriction," as alleles of the MHC appear to determine whether an encounter with antigen will lead to T lymphocyte activation. Disruption of this system appears to be a critical defect in acquired immunodeficiency states, including AIDS.

The T cell subclasses described above differ with regard to the type of MHC-encoded molecules they are capable of recognizing. Cytotoxic T8$^+$ cells usually recognize antigen plus Class I determinants, while helper or cytotoxic T4$^+$ cells classically respond to antigen in the context of a Class II molecule (43, 44). The development of cells capable of killing virally infected targets, and thereby serving to limit virus replication, is dependent on the ability of an individual T cell to identity both MHC and virally specified antigen components (45).

Reinherz and Schlossman (43) have proposed that T cells bear a second recognition unit, a complex composed of the T3 molecule and a clonally unique glycoprotein (idiotype) which binds antigen in association with MHC gene products. Both T cell proliferation to antigen and T helper function for autologous B lymphocytes appear to relate to this complex, the putative T cell receptor (43, 46). That portion of an immune response involving cells capable of presenting antigen to T-lymphocytes appears to function normally in many AIDS and pre-AIDS patients (47), although some abnormalities have been reported among some of these individuals (48). Defects in T cell recognition are prominent, however, and cannot be explained solely on the basis of a quantitative T cell deficiency.

Two *in vitro* assays for the competency of T cell antigen recognition and the capacity for development of effector T cell functions are the autologous and allogeneic MLC. In the former, T cells proliferate on exposure to autologous non-T cells or $T8^+$ cells. In the latter, cytotoxic T lymphocytes specifically sensitized against foreign target molecules are developed. AIDS patients have defects in both reactions, secondary to a functional abnormality in helper T cells (49). Such lesions could result in the failure of an individual to generate killer T cells capable of reacting with self-HLA determinants and viral antigen, leading to uncontrolled virus replication and perhaps perpetuating the immunodeficient state. In addition, irrelevant HLA specificities may be induced on the T cell membrane in conjunction with viral infections, including one linked to AIDS. This phenomenon, discussed in detail later, may also interfere with appropriate T cell antigen recognition in AIDS.

Class II genes also control the magnitude of cytolytic responses to foreign cells as well as the ability of T lymphocytes to respond to certain antigens in a protective or pathologic manner. For example, chronic administration of CMV (a virus to which most AIDS patients have been exposed) to young mice often leads to immune suppression, but only in select strains. Susceptibility to this viral interaction is genetically dominant and partially controlled by the murine MHC, H2 (50).

The first link between a human disorder and the human MHC was a description of the increased frequency of HLA-B27 among patients with ankylosing spondylitis. This association is quantitated by calculation of the "relative risk": the chance an individual with the disease-linked MHC specificity has of developing the condition, compared with that of a person who lacks that specificity. For HLA-B27 and ankylosing spondylitis, this risk is over 90–fold. The frequency of HLA-DR5 was found to be significantly increased in homosexual men with lymphadenopathy, compared with an ethnic and race-matched control group (27). Many of these individuals also admitted constitutional symptoms, including fever, night sweats, and weight loss greater than or equal to 10 percent of ideal body weight. Of 90 such persons followed for a mean of 18 months, 15 developed an infection or malignancy consistent with the CDC definition of AIDS (27). Similarly, the risk for development of Kaposi's sarcoma, both in AIDS patients and in other individuals, is increased sixfold in the presence of the same HLA determinant (51). It is hoped that identification of such allospecificitiesassociated with a given disease will provide leads as to the genes directly involved in establishing susceptibility or resistance to that condition.

Kaposi's sarcoma is a multicentric neoplasm probably of endothelial lining cells, manifested as vascular tumors composed of proliferating connective tissue cells and capillary vessels (52). It is exceedingly uncommon in the United States, with but one case per 1 million population, but in central Africa it is very common, comprising 13 percent of all malignancies in Zaire (53). It has been associated with CMV, as human CMV DNA homologous sequences as well as CMV-specific RNA and antigen have been identified in tumor biopsies of Kaposi's sarcoma specimens from the United States and Africa (54). The importance of the immune system in its development is illuminated by the high frequency

Table 10.3
Distribution of AIDS Cases in Males by Disease Category and Sexual Orientation

Disease Category	Sexual Orientation (%)		
	Homosexual or bisexual	Heterosexual	Unknown
Kaposi's sarcoma without pneumocystis	34.9	6.7	8.0
Pneumocystis without Kaposi's sarcoma	44.6	69.2	64.0
Kaposi's sarcoma and pneumocystis	11.1	0.01	0
Other opportunistic infection	9.4	24.1	28.0

of this neoplasm among patients given immunosuppressive drugs in preparation for organ allografting (52) and the regression of the sarcoma in 50 percent of patients on cessation of immunosuppressive therapy (55).

It has also been postulated that the secretion of soluble factors by immune cells with angiogenesis-promoting activity is important in the development of Kaposi's sarcoma in immunodeficient patients (56). These substances would enhance capillary proliferation and subsequent transformation of endothelial cells, perhaps involving CMV or other viruses trophic for endothelium and having oncogenic potential. For example, CMV has the capacity to transform human fibroblasts in tissue culture into cells with unlimited growth potential (57). These immortalized cells show a variety of morphologic alterations typical of cancer cells. Endothelial cells can also be transformed by herpesviruses, in the course of which novel membrane receptors and antigens arise (58). This process may be the first part of a proposed two-step model for the malignant transformation of cells (59). Following the change in growth characteristics initiated by the virus, activation of specific cancer-associated cellular genes may be facilitated, as will be discussed later.

The importance of the interplay of genetic and environmental factors in Kaposi's sarcoma is emphasized by the absence of this tumor among a large series of immunosuppressed renal transplant recipients in Australia and New Zealand (60) and by the rarity of Kaposi's sarcoma in Americans of African ancestry or among Europeans living in Africa (52). In addition, homosexual AIDS patients have a markedly increased frequency of Kaposi's, compared with heterosexual AIDS patients, among whom opportunistic infections predominate (61) (Table 10.3). As homosexual men have a much higher carrier rate of CMV than heterosexual controls (62), a two-step model involving this virus could be evoked to explain this epidemiologic observation.

Besides the T cell, the phagocytic macrophage and the B lymphocyte are also involved in the immune dysregulation of AIDS. People at risk for AIDS are bombarded by myriad environmental antigens and common infectious agents: bacterial, parasitic, and viral. Such persistent exposure can elicit selective amplification of suppressor cell networks involving the macrophage (9, 63). Macrophages infected with murine CMV, for example, inhibit both cell-mediated and humoral immunity (64). In man, soluble factors are released by or in collaboration with activated macrophages in the course of fungal infections, leprosy, tuberculosis, and in certain malignancies (9, 63). CMV mononucleosis leads to proliferation of a $T8^+$ cell in man (65), together with the formation of inhibitory adherent mononuclear cells (66).

Working in the laboratory of Henry Kunkel at The Rockefeller University, I recently identified soluble factors released spontaneously during the culture of peripheral blood mononuclear cells from homosexual men with lymphadenopathyand systemic symptoms (67). These substances, known as soluble suppressor factors (SSF), were capable of inhibiting the production of antibody by normal B and T cells stimulated with the plant lectin pokeweed mitogen. They also inhibited the capacity of normal T cells to proliferate in response to a specific antigen, tetanus toxoid. Immune responses which do not require the presence of T cells or accessory cells, such as EBV-mediated antibody synthesis, were not affected by SSF. Cell separation techniques demonstrated that SSF-AIDS was the result of an interaction between T lymphocytes and adherent cells with the properties of macrophages (67).

The effect of SSF-AIDS could be partially blocked by the reducing agent 2–mercaptoethanol. Use of similar compounds capable of abrogating SSF activity *in vitro* may serve as a model for determining whether the SSF-adherent cell network is involved in other immunoregulatory systems linked to soluble inhibitory products with known stimuli for their induction. For example, *in vitro* suppressor molecules have been associated with virally induced tumors in animals. Murine sarcoma virus-transformed mouse fibroblasts produce low molecular weight factors that are potent inhibitors of both T cell stimulation and immunoglobulin production (68). Induction of these substances is independent of virus particle synthesis, although murine sarcoma virus itself is immunosuppressive *in vitro* and *in vivo*. Feline leukemia virus, despite its name, frequently causes death in cats by predisposing the animals to infections by other organisms rather than by consistently inducing a leukemia. This appears to be related to the virus' capacity to depress both cellular and humoral immune responses (69). The envelope protein of the feline leukemia virus may cause this immunosuppression by inhibiting T lymphocyte secretion of and response to a lymphokine known as T cell growth factor or interleukin 2 (70). Lymphokines are proteins made by lymphocytes which transmit growth and differentiation signals among immune cells (35). These hormone-like substances have a central role in immunoregulation and, as discussed below, not only are involved in the immune abnormalities of AIDS but may be therapeutically useful as well.

Marked alterations in B cell activation and immune modulation at the level of the B lymphocyte have also been described in AIDS. The number of circulating B cells in AIDS patients is typically normal. However, these cells are unable to mount a DNA synthetic response following stimulation with T cell dependent or independent polyclonal activators. In addition, the number of B lymphocytes spontaneously secreting immunoglobulin is tenfold higher in AIDS patients than in healthy controls (71). The lack of functional T4$^+$ helper cells, together with an increase in suppressor T cells characteristic of AIDS, places this defect at the level of the B cell. This spontaneous activity is suggestive of viral stimulation or transformation, as is known to occur during the course of both CMV and EBV infections. The ability of AIDS patients to secrete specific antibody, however, is severely restricted. Thus, primary antibody responses to the novel antigen keyhole-limpet hemocyanin were found to be depressed in individuals with AIDS or its prodromes (71).

Descriptions of the functional immune defects typical of AIDS and its prodromes, together with careful virologic culture studies performed by two independent groups working in Paris and at the National Institutes of Health, have led to the isolation of a new human retrovirus with a probable etiologic link to these syndromes. It is conceivable, however, that one discrete factor alone will not be responsible for the complete clinical picture, at least as it arises in adults. Among these groups, exposure to additional environmental immunosuppressive factors may be required. Other models have thus become the focus of intensive research, including the AIDS-like syndromes occurring in immunologically immature infants and juvenile monkeys.

The human fetus has a physiologic T cell deficiency which could facilitate certain viral infections even in the presence of maternal resistance (72). Epidemiologically compelling evidence for AIDS in infants born to parents with AIDS or who are at risk for its development has come from pediatricians in New York City, Newark, New Jersey, and San Francisco (22, 23, 29). These infants often succumb to the same opportunistic infections and Kaposi's sarcoma described in adults with AIDS. Exposure to an "AIDS agent" must have occurred early in life, as several infants were but six months old at the time an opportunistic infection developed. Many of these children were also free of those viral agents postulated to be of importance as co-factors in adult AIDS: CMV, EBV, and hepatitis B.

Immature monkeys and mice are very susceptible to opportunistic pathogens following exposure to CMV. In adult mice, chronic viral infection must be combined with a second stimulus, either a foreign cell, another virus, or an immunosupressive compound (such as azathioprine, used in renal transplant recipients), in order to induce susceptibility to opportunistic infections or the lymphadenopathy and B cell malignancies typical of AIDS (73). This scheme implies than an immune deficit, whether it be an early consequence of or unrelated to an "AIDS agent," may be a prerequisite in adults for subsequent infection by the AIDS-inducing factor. It also predicts that should AIDS spread beyond the currently defined risk populations it will begin to appear next in patients undergoing organ allografts or cancer chemotherapy, or in the chronically ill, elderly, and patients with autoimmune disorders.

Outbreaks of "simian AIDS" at the New England Primate Research Center in Southborough, Massachusetts (74, 75), and the California Primate Research Center at the University of California at Davis (76) have recently been described. Mortality among *Macaca cyclopsis*, an endangered species, and *Macaca mulatta* (rhesus) Old World monkeys has tripled over the past four years because of infections with *Pneumocystis carinii* and other pathogens typical of AIDS in man. In addition, B cell lymphomas have begun appearing in these animals, all of which were less than 4 years old, had not yet reached sexual maturity, and were housed together in cages. While features of this epizootic do not correlate exactly with AIDS—ony 40 percent of affected animals had depressed helper: suppressor T cell ratios utilizing the human monoclonal reagents, and altered T cell stimulation by lectins was not a consistent finding—it is a provocative model for the human disease. B cell lymphomas, Kaposi-like skin lesions, or opportunistic infections developed in some rhesus monkeys inoculated with cell-free filtrates of tissue homogenates from these animals (77, 78). The development of such transmissible lymphomas, and the known association of a class of RNA tumor viruses or retroviruses with both immune deficiencies and cancer in animals, has intensified the search for a retrovirus etiologically linked to AIDS.

Retroviruses are responsible for many spontaneous leukemias and lymphomas in several animal species (79). One class of these viruses, the actual transforming species, has arisen by substitution of viral genes necessary for replication with discrete segments of host genetic information. When incorporated within the viral genome, such transduced cellular sequences, termed *onc* genes, acquire the ability to induce neoplastic transformation. Some of these cellular genes or proto-onco-genes have been implicated as important targets for a genetic alteration causing normal cells to become cancerous. Another class of retrovirus lacks a definable *onc* gene, does not transform cells directly *in vitro*, and requires long latency periods for disease induction. Most of these agents contain two complete copies of single-stranded RNA. The RNA replicates through a DNA proviral phase in which virus-encoded reverse transcriptase is used. Integration of the proviral DNA thus formed into the DNA of the infected target occurs routinely (79).

Retroviruses appear to represent one of the most efficient ways for the natural activation and transduction of genes in mammalian cells. Activation of cellular *onc* genes provides a potential common mechanism of tumorigenesis by viral as well as nonviral agents (80). Such a process may be the result of or modified by host-specific and environmental factors including age at first infection, route or frequency of exposure, state of prior immunity, or even random events, such as the chance insertion of a viral RNA transcriptional "promoter" at an appropriate site to switch on those cellular genes whose inappropriate expression results in a malignant phenotype.

The search for evidence of retroviral infection in AIDS poses many problems, however. Several of the hallmarks of such an infection, including virus production, complete provirus incorporation into host DNA, and antibody responses to the foreign viral antigens, have not been found in certain known retrovirus-induced neoplasms in animals (79). In a disorder characterized by profound T cell depletion, it may be difficult to sample a patient's lymphocytes during the critical period of virus replication and prior to destruction of that cell population. In addition, AIDS patients have difficulty mounting effective humoral responses to new antigens; their antibody response to an "AIDS agent" may similarly be suboptimal.

One candidate for a human retrovirus in AIDS is the human T cell leukemia virus, HTLV. Currently it is the only known class of retrovirus associated with disease in man. It is found in two related malignancies, adult T cell leukemia and cutaneous T cell lymphoma (79). The neoplastic cells are here usually $T4^+$, but in contrast to their surface phenotype, they function as suppressors rather than helpers of immune reactivity (81). Indeed, patients with HTLV-associated leukemia/lymphoma often succumb to opportunistic infections. The entity was first recognized clinically in Japan, where a high incidence exists in the southwestern part of the main island, Honshu (82). A second geographic focus has been reported in the Caribbean basin (82). This virus appears to occur in the Caribbean and in Africa at rates that may exceed that reported for Japan. These data have made HTLV and its variants a focus of intensive interest in the virologic studies of AIDS, as both Haiti and central Africa have been postulated as possible sources of an AIDS agent. This is based on the migration of natives from western Africa to Haiti, the frequent recreational homosexual contacts between residents of New York City and Haiti over the past several years, and the prevalence of AIDS-linked malignancies and infections in central Africa.

Central Africa has the highest rate of polygamous marriage in the world, with young women married to the tribal elders, each of whom may have as many as 30 wives (53). Men in these villages below the age of 30 are effectively denied female sexual contact and typically engage in frequent homosexual relationships (53). The incidence of AIDS-like disorders in Africa appears to be highly specific. Two villages, located but a few miles apart yet isolated in terms of sexual contacts, may have large differences in the frequency of these diseases. Among the first 267 reported European cases of AIDS, 59 had a connection with Africa, including 45 from Zaire (53).

Robert Gallo and associates at the National Institutes of Health, who first isolated HTLV from tumor specimens in the United States, have been examining lymphocytes from individuals with AIDS or in risk groups for its development for the presence of HTLV genome. Ten percent of such individuals' lymphocytes harbored HTLV proviral DNA, and analysis of the nucleic acid sequences of HTLV isolated from these patients revealed its similarity to the most common HTLV subtype, HTLV-1 (83).

Complementing this evidence, 19 out of 75 AIDS patients or homosexual males with lymphadenopathy, but only 2 out of 336 controls, had antibody to a T lymphoblastoid cell line known to contain HTLV-I (84). Similarly, an increased incidence of this antibody was found in the sera of hemophiliacs who were frequent recipients of clotting products, another population at risk for the development of AIDS (85).

Two problems in the attempt to solidify a link between HTLV-I and AIDS are the long latency period thought to be required for the development of HTLV-related malignancies, and the absence of an AIDS-like disease in at least one HTLV-I endemic area, Japan. Luc Montagnier et al. at the Institut Pasteur in Paris have recently isolated a putative varient of HTLV from the lymph node cells of a homosexual male with immunodeficiency (86) as well as from AIDS patients. This retrovirus, known as LAV, or lymphadenopathy-associated virus, has a core protein slightly higher in molecular weight than HTLV-I. Antibody to LAV appears to be present in certain AIDS patients lacking detectable exposure to HTLV-I and, what is also important, has not been found in HLTV$^+$ sera from Japanese individuals. This isolate is similar to a virus subsequently recovered by Gallo et al. in over 90 AIDS and pre-AIDS patients (87). The latter particle, labeled HTLV-III because of genomic correspondence with HLTV-I and II, is the most probable etiologic agent in AIDS. HTLV-III and LAV are most likely identical since they have the same morphology by electron microscopy, they are both lymphotropic and cytopathic for T4$^+$ cells, isolates from American AIDs patients are immunologically indistinguishable from LAV, and their core proteins are equivalent by competitive radioimmunoassay (88).

Like other members of the HTLV family, HTLV-III/LAV is a type C retrovirus that in mature form exists as a 100 nm particle with a small, cylindrical core. Similar to HTLV-I and II, T cells infected with HTLV-III form syncytia of multinucleated giant cells with large cytoplasmic vacuoles. However, while HTLV-I and II is tropic for all T4$^+$ cells and leads to their immortalization, HTLV-III is tropic for a small proportion of T4$^+$ cells and usually leads to cytopathic changes rather than transformation.

The most widely used serologic technique for detection of IgG antibody to this virus is an enzyme-linked immunosorbent assay (ELISA) with whole disrupted virus or purified p24 core protein as antigen. A variety of investigations are attempting to establish the frequency of exposure of various individuals to HTLV-III, to correlate seropositivity with current infection, clinical signs and symptoms, and soon, to detect carrier states, and to document progression of disease from lymphadenopathy or other prodromal states to AIDS. Initial data indicated that but 38 to 42 percent of AIDS patients evaluated at the Institut Pasteur were positive for anti-LAV antibody (89, 90), compared with at least 86 percent for anti-HTLV-III serum antibodies as evaluated by Gallo's group (91). A more specific ELISA utilizing total LAV protein has raised the rate of postivity in both AIDS and pre-AIDS patients for anti-LAV immunoglobulin (92). (Table 10.4 presents such serologic data). This study (92) also documented the vertical spread of AIDS from mother to child, a transmission pattern which

Table 10.4

IgG Anti-LAV Serum Antibody in Controls, Patients with AIDS, and AIDS Risk Groups

Subject	TH:TS Ratio Mean (range)	Prevalence of Serum Antibody to LAV % (no. +/no. tested)
1. AIDS		
Total cases	0.34 (0.00–2.0)	68.0 (17/25)
Kaposi's sarcoma (KS) or B cell lymphoma	0.22 (0.03–0.26)	100.0 (5/5)
Opportunistic infection (+/- KS), adult	0.18 (0.02–0.72)	50.0 (6/12)
Opportunistic infection, juvenile	0.63 (0.03–2.0)	75.0 (6/8)
2. PRODROMAL AIDS*	0.58 (0.27–1.0)	100.0 (5/5)
3. LYMPHADENOPATHY	0.77 (0.15–1.13)	100.0 (8/8)
4. CONTROLS		
Healthy, + AIDS risk factors+	1.20 (0.50–2.30)	0.0 (0/9)
Sexual contacts of AIDS patients	1.09 (0.59–1.78)	40.0 (2/5)
Healthy mothers of juvenile AIDS‡	1.12: 0.36: 1.14	100.0 (3/3)

Healthy infants of LAV
    negative mothers + AIDS
    risk factors‡
	not done	0.0 (0.2)

Common Variable Immuno- deficiency	1.52 (1.20–2.0)	0.0 (0/5)
IgA deficiency	Not done	0.0 (0/18)

Source: Laurence, J.; Brun-Vezinet, F.; Schutzer, S.E.; et al. Lymphadenopathy-associated viral antibody in AIDS; immune correlations and definition of a carrier state. N. Engl. J. Med. 311:1269, 1984.

*All developed AIDS within 2–11 months of follow-up.
+Six active male homosexuals, 2 male and 1 female former intravenous drug abusers.
‡All mothers were active or former intravenous drug abusers.

did not demand either the presence of clinical signs of symptoms in the maternal "carriers" or, in a few cases, any *in vitro* evidence of a cellular immune deficiency.

The fact that HTLV-III/LAV was introduced into the United States relatively recently, concomitant with recognition of the AIDS epidemic, is supported by an increase in LAV seropositivity from 1 percent (1 in 100) in 1978 to 25 percent (12 in 48) in 1980 and 65 percent (140 in 215) in 1984 among serum samples obtained from homosexual men attending a sexually transmitted diseases clinic in San Francisco (88). In New York City, where AIDS cases among intravenous drug abusers are concentrated, 58 percent (50 in 86) of recent frequent drug abusers without clinical AIDS had antibody to LAV. In contrast, fewer than 10 percent of methadone recipients had such antibody, and all these persons had been in treatment for at least three years, admitting greatly reduced intravenous drug use (88).

These studies further emphasize that exposure to HLTV-III is much more common than either AIDS or generalized lymphadenopathy among members of at-risk groups. Currently available serologic tests also appear to be of sufficient sensitivity and specificity to permit estimates of the frequency of HTLV-III exposure in a population group. Antibody data alone, however, may be of *clinical value* mainly to evaluate infants, blood donors, and heterosexual contacts of at-risk patients, as background anti-HTLV-III titers in these individuals should be very low. The implications of a positive serology for a given individual in a group at high risk for AIDS, that is, the asymptomatic homosexual male, Haitian, or intravenous drug abuser, is much less clear.

HTLV-III has been recovered in both the presence and absence of circulating antibody. This is of special concern because a high percentage of seropositive patients are active secretors of infectious virus, and antibody to HTLV-I (93) and, by analogy, to HTLV-III has minimal or no neutralizing capability *in vitro*. This fact will probably complicate efforts to use passive immunization in the therapy of AIDS and its prodromes, as well as in the development of an effective vaccine.

Such serologic associations and viral isolations do not serve as proof of etiology. HTLV-III, like cytomegalovirus, could be a coincidental passenger in these multiply infected patients. This is very unlikely, however, based on the transmission of AIDS from mother to infant in association with LAV seroconversion (92) and on information on LAV infection of a blood donor-recipient pair and the development of AIDS (94).

Finally, the ethical considerations as to the desirability of a member of a population at high risk for AIDS to undergo testing for anti-HTLV-III antibody must be addressed. It appears that such antibody, at least when present in high titer, implies the presence of infectious viral particles, with probable active secretion not only in blood but also in semen, saliva, tears, and sweat. This is true for AIDS patients as well as for individuals with no obvious signs or symptoms of "pre-AIDS," implying that otherwise healthy individuals are capable of carrying and transmitting the virus. Recent data documenting the very high incidence of anti-HTLV-III seropositivity in homosexual men in New York City and San Francisco render the value of a positive test in such communities for any individual uncertain. Such testing should probably not be encouraged outside a research or blood donor bank setting, where the confidentiality and, most important, immunity to subpoena of such records can be guaranteed.

As discussed in the context of disturbed T cell antigen recognition in AIDS, involvement of human MHC determinants may be important in the development of immunodeficiency and malignancy related to uncontrolled virus reproduction. Cell lines producing HTLV-I express a supernumerary HLA specificity on their surface, coded for by the retrovirus (95). Nucleotide sequence homology has been established for DNA clones of the HTLV envelope gene and the segment coding for the extracellular portion of a Class I, HLA-B determinant (96). Expression of such an inappropriate HLA alloantigen on infected T cells might impair their normal function, leading to a state of altered immunoregulation. The deficit in the autologous MLC seen in AIDS could relate to similar, virally induced membrane alterations, blocking recognition sites by which autologous cells normally interact.

The first event leading to AIDS may thus be a retrovirus infection that disrupts a crucial recognition component in the immune system, presumably on the T4$^+$ lymphocyte. The closer one's life-style or other circumstances, such as frequent exposure to blood products, leads to a chain of viral transmission, the higher the risk of encountering such a virus. Whether immunosuppression alone or a neoplasm results from such exposures may depend on the state of the host's immune system, host genetic factors (e.g., HLA-DR type), subtle variations in the viral genome or viral integration site, and so forth. Thus, a retroviral infection would not automatically lead to disease. In most cases this infection would be clinically insignificant, and only a small population of T cells would integrate the viral genome. This hypothesis is important because in some series 50 to 80 percent of asymptomatic, homosexually active men and 10 to 30 percent of hemophiliacs manifest evidence of *in vitro* immune abnormalities, at least by depression of the T helper : suppressor cell ratio. This large reservoir of people would be susceptible to a secondary phase, during which many antigenic stimuli might be able to affect the immune system, including common bacterial, parasitic, and viral pathogens.

It has also been postulated that cells bearing MHC Class II determinants, such as spermatozoa and lymphocytes, are an important contributory factor for immune deficiency in the male homosexual population (97). Such cells may gain access to the circulatory system by an intestinal route, such as through breaks in the rectal or oral mucosa. Indeed, antisperm and antilymphocyte specific antibodies have been detected in the sera of AIDS patients as well as healthy homosexual men (98). It has also been shown that a single intravenous injection of sperm into mice induces prolonged T cell mediated suppression of cellular immune functions (99). The additional entry of foreign lymphocytes might also initiate a graft-versus-host reaction, particularly if introduced into a preexisting state of immune suppression. The features of this reaction, based on the pathologic response of these lymphocytes to the recipient's cells, include decreased helper T cells, polyclonal elevation of serum immunoglobulins, and depressed T cell mitogen and delayed type hypersensitivity reactions, resembling that seen in AIDS (100). Graft-versus-host reactions are also known to initiate latent viral infections such as CMV (101) and, as previously noted, may serve as a co-factor for the induction of lymphadenopathy or cancer in mice (73).

Human seminal plasma itself is also immunosuppressive, consisting of a variety of molecules, including prostaglandins, anticomplementary proteins, polyamines, and viruses such as CMV, all of which can inhibit immune reactions, at least *in vitro* (102, 103). Normally these factors may serve to protect sperm from immunologic injury and prevent sensitization of females to sperm antigens after insemination. One might then predict development of local immunosuppression in the cervicovaginal or anorectal regions of individuals experiencing frequent vaginal or anal intercourse, respectively. This might promote bacterial, fungal, or viral infections and possibly enhance the growth of neoplasms induced by other agents. Indeed, an increased incidence of cloacagenic and squamous carcinomas of the rectum have been reported in homosexual males with AIDS (104), in male homosexuals in general (105), and possibly in women engaging in regular anal intercourse (105).

It is also known that the mucosal immune system has regulatory mechanisms distinct from the systemic immune system, permitting it to react selectively to many or most substances normally found in the mucosal environment (106). Thus, under some circumstances, oral introduction of an antigen may lead to suppression of serum IgG (systemic suppression) associated with IgA enhancement (mucosal enhancement) (106). Continous oral or rectal introduction of viral or other antigens in male homosexuals may lead to establishment of a state of systemic immune tolerance to those antigens and contribute to the immune deficits.

The above hypotheses are supported by the striking differences observed between homosexual AIDS patients and healthy homosexual controls in the numbers of sexual partners (Table 10.5). The median number of male sex partners per year for AIDS cases was 61 in one study, versus 27 for controls (107). A difference between cases and controls was also noted in the reported number of male sex partners in the 12 months preceding the onset of illness (107). Cases were also more likely to have met their sex partners in bathhouses and to have begun regular (at least once a month) homosexual intercourse at an earlier age than controls (107). Sexual frequency was also highly correlated with the use of "street drugs" and nitrite inhalants. Initially, amyl nitrite attracted great interest as a possible co-factor in the pathogenesis of AIDS, as epidemiologic evidence indicated that this drug, inhaled as a sexual stimulant during intercourse, may alter T lymphocyte helper : suppressor ratios (108). Recently, however, the use of these inhalants has been found to be as prevalent in the male homosexual control population, with more than 85 percent of apparently healthy male hom-

Table 10.5

Frequency of Selected Social Variables Among 50 Homosexual Male AIDS Patients and 120 Age - Matched Homosexual Male Controls

Variable	Patients (n = 50)	Controls	
		Clinic (n = 78)	Private (n = 42)
Sexual activity			
Median male sex partners per year (n)	61	27	25
Median proportion of sex partners from bathhouses in past year (%)	50	23	4
Index of feces exposure in past year (maximum score = 3)	2.3	1.9	1.9
Index of sperm exposure and rectal trauma in past year (maximum score = 3)	2.1	2.0	2.2
Use of illicit substances			
Number of street drugs used (cocaine, heroin, LSD, marijuana, methaqualone, phencyclidine, amphetamines, barbiturates)	6	4	4
Used nitrite inhalants (%)	96	96	95
Previous illness (%)			
Gonorrhea	86	73	74
Syphilis	68	36	36
Hepatitis B	14	14	21
"Mononucleosis"	14	17	7

Source: Adapted from Jaffe, H.W.; Choi, K.; Thomas, P.A.; et al. National case-control study of Kaposi's sarcoma and pneumocystis carinii pneumonia in homosexual men: Part I, epidemiologic results. Ann. Intern. Med. 99: 145, 1983.

osexuals in New York and California reporting such use during the past five years (13).

Certain sexual practices, particularly those leading to exposure to feces or semen or to rectal trauma, were also analyzed among male homosexual AIDS cases and controls (Table 10.5). Cases were more likely than controls to have reported inserting their tongue ("rimming") or hand ("fisting") into a partner's rectum at least once during the year preceding onset of illness (107). The differences were minor between these groups in the frequency of taking a receptive role in "fisting," oral, or anal intercourse, however (107). In another study, 27 pecent of 89 healthy homosexually active men were found to have a T helper : suppressor ratio of 0.08 (normal 1.8 ± 0.6) (109). Those practicing passive (receptive) anal intercourse had a significantly higher mean number of suppressor T cells than did those engaging in active (insertive) anal intercourse or no anal intercourse. As the authors note, these studies need to be confirmed in large series, as only a small number of participants admitted to active anal intercourse or refrained from any form of such activity (109).

Treatment of AIDS patients usually focuses on their life-threatening opportunistic infections or malignancies. Mortality remains high, with almost a 100 percent death rate at two years for those individuals presenting with an opportunistic pathogen. Immunomodulatory agents or procedures, including glucocorticoids, cimetidine, antiprostaglandins, Isoprinosine, androgens, plasmaphoresis, transfer factor, and alpha-interferon have been tried in attempts to mitigate the devastating immune abnormalities associated with AIDS. With the possible exception of alpha-interferon (110), these interventions have shown little efficacy. New therapies are currently undergoing clinical trials, however, based on exciting results *in vitro* with certain immunoregulatory hormones and anti-viral drugs, including suramin (111), HPA 23 (112), and ribavirin (113).

While the immune recognition of foreign antigens described above is highly specific, amplification of the response of a few cells capable of recognizing an antigen to the point at which they can mount an effective immune attack requires a complex interplay of nonspecific chemical signals known as lymphokines and monokines. Exposure to antigen or mitogen alone is insufficient to stimulate T cell division. Accessory cells are required to present the antigen, and macrophages to supply a chemical signal in the form of interleukin 1 (IL-1) (35). IL-1 does not stimulate T cell division directly but rather induces the production of interleukin 2 (IL-2) by activated T cells. It is this latter lymphokine which leads to T cell proliferation. In addition to augmenting the size of a specific T cell population, IL-2 also elicits production by the T cell of immune or gamma-interferon. Gamma-interferon is itself a lymphokine, serving to enhance the cytolytic activities of T cells, macrophages, and a minor immune cell population, the natural killer (NK) cell. NK cells normally represent 5 percent of circulating leukocytes (111). They are defined by their ability to kill tumor cells and virally infected cells spontaneously. These cells appear to function as a defense mechanism against malignant cells, viruses, and possibly other intracellular pathogens (35), and they can be activated before a specific immune response has had a chance to develop. AIDS patients produce normal or exaggerated amounts of IL-1 (112) but have profound deficits in IL-2 production, gamma-interferon (47), serum thymic factor (114), and natural killer cell activity (115). Patients with AIDS and its prodromes also have elevated levels of an unusual acid-labile form of human alpha-interferon (116), serum thymosin α_1 (117), and B_2 microglobulin (118).

Table 10.6
Manifestations of AIDS Other Than Opportunistic Infection or Malignancy

Sign or Symptom	Incidence (%)	
	Patients with Kaposi's sarcoma	Patients with Opportunistic Infection
Unexplained altered mental status	11.1	9.5
Neural radiculopathy	1.4	3.2
Autoimmune hemolytic anemia	1.4	3.2
Nephrotic syndrome	0	4.8
Thrombocytopenia	5.6	0

In vitro a marked reconstitution of AIDS patients' NK and T cell cytotoxic effector function is noted following addition of IL-2 (119), and trials of this lymphokine in AIDS are currently being conducted (120, 121). The use of a genetically engineered preparation of human gamma-interferon is also planned.

Although the prognosis for most patients with AIDS is bleak, epidemiologic evidence suggests that intensive preventive efforts can reduce the spread of this disorder and that individuals with the putative "AIDS complex," *in vitro* immune abnormalities and constitutional symptoms, can improve. In one series, the vast majority of homosexual men with decreased T cell helper : suppressor ratios and depressed lymphocyte proliferation to mitogens experienced normalization of these values (122). Close to 90 percent of all AIDS patients are from two risk categories: homosexual men and intravenous drug abusers. Many of the other AIDS patients also appear to be related to these two groups. Effective prevention may thus be accomplished by attempts to reduce anonymous sexual contacts among homosexual men as well as intravenous drug use (123). Such measures should be attempted in addition to the CDC's guidelines for the protection of health-care workers and allied professionals from the spread of AIDS (124, 125, 126).

Attention should also be directed toward several unusual complications of AIDS and its prodromes, which are ostensibly not connected with any recognized opportunistic pathogen or neoplasm involved in AIDS or the AIDS complex as so far defined. These disorders include neuroradiculopathies, the nephrotic syndrome, and possibly autoimmune syndromes (Table 10.6). Of particular note are neurological and psychological disturbances, including progressive dementia, seizures, syndrome of inappropriate antidiuretic hormone secretion, focal defects, hallucinations, painful paresthesias, and coma (127). There are two general patterns of neurological involvement in AIDS. One is characterized by constitutional and psychiatric symptoms (loss of recent memory, apathy) that lead to suspicion of nonfocal disease. Microglial nodules and Alzheimer type II cells are often found at autopsy in these patients' brains (127). A second pattern involves symptoms of focal neurologic deficit. Meninoencephalitis or abscesses secondary to CMV, *Toxoplasma gondii*, *Cryptococcus neoformans*, *Aspergillus fumigatus*, *Herpes simplex*, or papovavirus (progressive multifocal leukoencephalopathy) are the main causes of such neurological symptoms. However, the neuropathological findings in these AIDS patients do not always explain the clinical symptoms, suggesting that either HTLV-III/LAV or an undetermined agent with neurotropic features is involved.

Professionals dealing with AIDS patients should emphasize the importance of these life-style changes, both from a macrocosmal (community-oriented) and microcosmal (improvement of individual health) viewpoint. Abstinence from all exposures to body secretions, particularly urine, feces, and semen, is mandatory, especially in relation to sexual practices that increase the risk of mucosal abrasions. This is especially true now that infectious HTLV-III particles have been identified not only in blood and serum but also in saliva and semen of patients with AIDS and pre-AIDS as well as of ostensibly healthy homosexual male "carriers." This does not mean avoidance of intimacy, which should be encouraged. Kissing appears not to be an important mode of spread for AIDS, which in light of present epidemiologic data is *not* a highly infectious disorder. Mutual masturbation may also be an appropriate form of sexual release for some individuals. Drugs used to treat the infections and malignancies associated with AIDS may also disrupt sexual desire or performance. Advice for the sexual health care of patients receiving these agents has been published (128). In New York City, the Gay Men's Health Crisis Program publishes valuable information booklets and sponsors social and psychological support groups for AIDS patients and their partners.

In summary, the acquired immune deficiency syndrome represents a disorder in which viral, genetic, environmental, and sociological factors appear to interact in combinations leading to a profound disruption of normal immunoregulatoryprocesses. This alteration may be heralded in some individuals by the development of constitutional symptoms, including generalized lymphadenopathy, fever, or night sweats and laboratory evidence of cellular and humoral immune dysfunction. These defects may be reversible. At the present time, development of an opportunistic infection or certain malignancies in connection with AIDS is ultimately fatal. AIDS thus offers a challenge to public health officials, research scientists, and health-care professionals to attempt to prevent the spread of this disorder as well as to create novel approaches to augment patients' immune defenses.

REFERENCES

1. Ehrlich, P. Über den jetzigen Stand der Karzinomforschung. In: The Collected Papers of Paul Ehrlich, Vol. II. London: Pergamon Press, 1957.

2. Thomas L. Reactions to homologous tissue antigens in relationship to hypersensitivity. In: Lawrence, H. S., ed., Cellular and Humoral Aspects of the Hypersensitivity States. New York: Hoeber-Harber, 1959.

3. Burnett, F. M. The concept of immunological surveillance. Prog. Exp. Tumor Res., 13:1, 1970.

4. Parkman, R. Treatment of human immunodeficiencies. Clin. Immunol. Rev., 1:375, 1982.

5. Reinherz, E. L., and Rosen, F. S. New concepts of immunodeficiency. Am. J. Med., 71:511, 1981.

6. Sridama, V.; Pacini, F.; Yang, S.-L., et al. Decreased levels of helper T cells: a possible cause of immunodeficiency in pregnancy. N. Engl. J. Med., 307:352, 1982.

7. Dorian, B.; Garfinkel, P.; Brown, G.; et al. Aberrations in lymphocyte subpopulations and function during psychologic stress. Clin. Exp. Immunol., 50:132, 1982.

8. Hughes, W. T.; Price, R. A.; Sisko, F., et al. Protein-calorie malnutrition: a host determinant for *Pneumocystis carinii* infection. Am. J. Dis. Child, 128:44, 1974.

9. Ellner, J. J. Suppressor cells of man. Clin. Immunol. Rev., 1:119, 1981.

10. Waldmann, T. A. Immunodeficiency disease and malignancy: various immunologic deficiencies of man and the role of immune processes in the control of malignant disease. Ann. Intern. Med., 77:605, 1972.

11. Penn, I. Depressed immunity and the development of cancer, Clin. Exp. Immunol., 46:459, 1981.

12. Gottlieb, M. S.; Shanker, H. M.; Fan, P. T., et al. *Pneumocystis* pneumonia—Los Angeles. Morbid. Mortal. Weekly Rep., 30:250, 1981.

13. Friedman-Kien, A.; Laubenstein, L.; Marmor, M., et al. Kaposi's sarcoma and *Pneumocystis* pneumonia among homosexual men—New York City and California. Morbid. Mortal. Weekly Rep., 30:305, 1981.

14. World Health Organization. Update: acquired immuno-deficiency syndrome— Europe. Morbid. Mortal. Weekly Rep., 34:147, 1985.

15. Greene, J. B.; Sidhu, G. S.; Lewin, S., et al. Mycobacterium avium-intracellulare: a cause of disseminated life-threatening infection in homosexuals and drug abusers. Ann. Intern. Med., 97:539, 1982.

16. Centers for Disease Control. Update: acquired immunodeficiency syndrome (AIDS) among patients with hemophilia—United States. Morbid. Mortal. Weekly Rep., 32:613, 1983.

17. Pape, J. W.; Liautaud, B.; Thomas, F., et al. Characteristics of the acquired immunodeficiency syndrome in Haiti. N. Eng. J. Med., 309:945, 1983.

18. Vieira, J.; Frank, E.; Spira, T. J.; and Landesman, S. H. Acquired immune deficiency in Haitians: opportunisitic infections in previously healthy Haitian immigrants. N. Engl. J. Med., 308:125, 1983.

19. Pinta, G. O.; Hericord, P.; Jagueux, M., et al. Multiple opportunistic infections due to AIDS in a previously healthy black woman from Zaire. N. Engl. J. Med., 308:775, 1983.

20. Clumeck, N.; Mascart-Lemone, F.; de Maubeuge, J; Brenez, D.; and Marcelis, L. Acquired immune deficiency syndrome in black Africans. The Lancet, 1:642, 1983.

21. Harris, C.; Small, C. B.; Klein, R. S., et al. Immunodeficiency in female sexual

partners of men with the acquired immunodeficiency syndrome. N. Engl. J. Med., 308:1181, 1983.

22. Oleske, J.; Minnetor, A.; and Cooper, R., Jr. Immune deficiency syndrome in children. J. Amer. Med. Assoc., 249:2345, 1983.

23. Rubenstein, A.; Sicklick, M.; Gupta, A., et al. Acquired immunodeficiency with reversed T4/T8 ratios in infants born to promiscuous and drug-addicted mothers. J. Amer. Med. Assoc., 249:2350, 1983.

24. Centers for Disease Control. Update: Acquired immune deficiency syndrome (AIDS)—United States. Morbid. Mortal. Weekly Rep., 32:465, 1983.

25. Rosen, S.; Levin, M.; Berg, R., et al. An evaluation of the acquired immunodeficiency syndrome (AIDS) reported in health-care personnel—United States. Morbid. Mortal. Weekly Rep., 32:358, 1983.

26. Mildvan, D.; Mathur, U.; Enlow, R., et al. Persistent, generalized lymphadenopathy among homosexual males. Morbid. Mortal. Weekly Rep., 31:249, 1982.

27. Metroka, C. E.; Cunningham-Rundles, S.; Pollack, M. S., et al. Generalized lymphadenopathy in homosexual men. Ann. Intern. Med., 99:585, 1983.

28. Centers for Disease Control. A cluster of Kaposi's sarcoma and *Pneumocystis carinii* pneumonia among homosexual male residents of Los Angeles and Orange counties, California. Morbid. Mortal. Weekly Rep., 31:305, 1982.

29. Ammann, A. J.; Cowan, M. J.; Wara, D. W., et al. Acquired immunodeficiency in an infant: possible transmission by means of blood products. The Lancet, 2:956, 1983.

30. Claman, H. N.; Chaperon, E. A.; and Triplett, R. F. Thymus-marrow cell combinations: synergism in antibody production. Proc. Soc. Exp. Biol. Med., 122:1167, 1966.

31. Masur, H.; Michelis, M. A.; Greene, J. B., et al. An outbreak of community-acquired *Pneumocystis carinii* pneumonia: initial manifestation of cellular immune dysfunction. N. Engl. J. Med., 305:1431, 1981.

32. Prince, H. E.; Gottlieb, M. S.; and Fahey, J. L. Acquired immune deficiency syndromes: a review of immunologic aspects. Clin. Immunol. Newsletter, 4:44, 1983.

33. Kohler, G., and Milstein, C. Continuous cultures of fused cells secreting antibody of predetermined specificity. Nature, 256:495, 1975.

34. Reinherz, E. L.; Kung, P. C.; Goldstein, G.; Levey, R. H.; and Schlossman, S. F. Discrete stages of human intrathymic differentiation: analysis of normal thymocytes and leukemic lymphoblasts of T-cell lineage. Proc. Natl. Acad. Sci., 77:1588, 1980.

35. Laurence, J. Lymphocyte markers in health and disease. Disease-a-Month, 31:1, 1984.

36. Nicholson, J. K. A.; Spira, T. J.; Cross, G. D.; Jones, B. M.; and Reinherz, E. L. Immunoregulatory subsets of the T helper and T suppressor cell subpopulations in homosexual men with crhonic unexplained lymphadenopathy. J. Clin. Invest., 73:191, 1984.

37. Landay, A.; Poon, M. C.; Abo, T.; Stagno, S.; and Cooper, M. D. Immunologic studies in asymptomatic hemophiliac patients: relationship to acquired immune deficiency syndrome (AIDS). J. Clin. Invest., 71:1500, 1983.

38. Kornfield, H.; Vande Stouwe, R. A.; Lange, M.; Reddy, M. M.; and Grieco, M. H.

214 Sexuality

T-lymphocyte subpopulations in homosexual men. N. Engl. J. Med., 307:729, 1982.

39. Ammann, A. J.; Abrams, D.; Conant, M., et al. Acquired immune dysfunction in homosexual men: immunologic profiles. Clin. Immunol. Immunopathol., 27:315, 1983.

40. Schroff, R. W.; Gottlieb, M. S.; Prince, H. E; Chai, L. L.; and Fahey, J. L. Immunologic studies of homosexual men with immunodeficiency and Kaposi's sarcoma. Clin. Immunol. Immunopathol., 27:300, 1983.

41. Stastny, P.; Ball, E. J.; Dry, P. J.; and Nunez, G. The human immune response region (HLA-D) and disease susceptibility. Immunological Rev., 70:116, 1983.

42. Winchester, R. J., and Kunkel, H. G. The human Ia system Adv. Immunol., 28:221, 1979.

43. Reinherz, E. L.; Meuer, S. C.; and Schlossman, S. F. The delineation of antigen receptors on human T lymphocytes. Immunol. Today, 4:5, 1983.

44. Pawelec, G.; Schneider, E.M.; and Wernet, P. Human T-cell clones with multiple and changing functions: indications of unexpected flexibility in immune response networks? Immunol. Today, 4:275, 1983.

45. Biddiso, W. E.; Sharrow, S.O.; and Shearer, G. M. T cell sub-populations required for the human cytotoxic T lymphocyte response to influenza virus: evidence for T cell help. J. Immunol., 127:487, 1981.

46. Meuer, S. C.; Cooper, D. A.; Hodgdon, J. C., et al. Identification of the receptor for antigen and major histocompatibility complex on human inducer T lymphocytes. Science, 222:1239, 1983.

47. Murray, H. W.; Rubin, B. Y.; Masur, H.; and Roberts, R. B. Impaired production of lymphokines and immune (gamma) interferon in the acquired immunodeficiency syndrome. N. Engl. J. Med., 310:883, 1984.

48. Kirkpatrick, C. H.; Davies, K. C.; Horsburgh, C. R., Jr. Reduced Ia-positive Langerhans' cells in AIDS. N. Engl. J. Med., 311:857, 1984.

49. Gupta, S., and Safai, B. Deficient autologous mixed lymphocyte reaction in Kaposi's sarcoma associated with deficiency of Leu-3$^+$ responder T cells. J. Clin. Invest., 71:296, 1983.

50. Chalmer, J. E. Genetic resistance to MCMV infection. In: Skamene, E., ed., Genetic Control of Natural Resistance to Infection and Malignancy. New York: Academic Press, 1980.

51. Friedman-Kien, A.; Laubenstein, L. J.; Rubenstein, P., et al. Disseminated Kaposi's sarcoma in homosexual men. Ann. Intern. Med., 96:693, 1982.

52. Templeton, A. C. Kaposi's sarcoma. In: Cancer of the Skin, Vol. II. Philadelphia: W. B. Saunders, 1976.

53. Weber, J. The AIDS connection of central Africa. Proc. Royal Soc. Med., in press.

54. Boldogh, I.; Beth, E.; Huang, E.-S.; Kyalwazi, S. K.; and Giraldo, G. Kaposi's sarcoma, IV: Detection of CMV DNA, CMV RNA, and CMNA in tumor biopsies. Int. J. Cancer, 28:469, 1981.

55. Harwood, A R.; Osoba, D.; Hofstader, M. B., et al. Kaposi's sarcoma in recipients of renal transplants. Am. J. Med., 67:759, 1979.

56. Levy, J. A., and Ziegler, J. L. Acquired immunodeficiency syndrome is an opportunistic infection and Kaposi's sarcoma results from secondary immune stimulation. The Lancet, 2:78, 1983.

57. Nelson, J. A.; Fleckenstein, B.; Galloway, D. A.; and McDougall, J. K. Trans-

formation of NIH 3T3 cells with cloned fragments of human cytomegalovirus strain AD169. J. Virol., 43:83, 1982.

58. Cines, D. B.; Lyss, A. P.; Bina, M., et al. Fc and C3 receptors induced by herpes simplex virus on cultured human endothelial cells. J. Clin. Invest., 69:123, 1982.

59. Land, H.; Parada, L. F.; and Weinberg, R. A. Tumorigenic conversion of primary embryo fibroblasts requires at least two cooperating oncogenes. Nature, 304:596, 1983.

60. Sheil, A. G. R. Cancer in renal allograft recipients in Australia and New Zealand. Transplant Proc., 9:1133, 1977.

61. Detels, R. Epidemiologic perspectives. In: Gottlieb, M. S., mod., The acquired immunodeficiency syndrome. Ann. Intern. Med., 99:208, 1983.

62. Drew, W.L.; Mintz, L.; Miner, R. C.; Sands, M.; and Ketterer, B. Prevalance of cytomegalovirus infection in homosexual men. J. Infect. Dis., 143:188, 1981.

63. Krakauer, R. S., and Clough, J. D., eds. Suppressor Cells and Their Factors. Boca Raton, Fla.: CRC Press, 1981.

64. Loh, L., and Hudson, B. Immunosuppressive effect of murine cytomegalovirus. Infect. Immun., 27:54, 1980.

65. Carney, W. P.; Iacoviello, V.; and Hirsch, M. S. Functional properties of T lymphocytes and their subsets in cytomegalovirus mononucleosis. J. Immunol., 130:390, 1983.

66. Rinaldo, C. R., Jr.; Carrey, W. P.; Richter, B.; Black, P. H.; and Hirsch, M. S. Mechanisms of immunosuppression in cytomegalovirus mononucleosis. J. Infect. Dis., 141:488, 1980.

67. Laurence, J.; Gottlieb, A. B.; and Kunkel, H. G. Soluble suppressor factors in patients with acquired immune deficiency syndrome and its prodromes: elaboration *in vitro* by T lymphocyte-adherent cell interactions. J. Clin. Invest., 72:2072, 1983.

68. Mizel, S. B.; DeLarco, J. E.; Todaro, G. J.; Farrar, W. L.; and Hilfiker, M. L. *In vitro* production of immunosuppressive factors by murine sarcoma virus-transformed mouse fibroblasts. Proc. Natl. Acad. Sci., 77:2205, 1980.

69. Trainin, Z.; Wernicke, D.; Ungar-Waron, H.; and Essex, M. Suppression of the humoral antibody response in natural retrovirus infection. Science, 220:858, 1983.

70. Copelan, E. A.; Rinehart, J. J.; and Lewis, M. The mechanism of retrovirus suppression of human T cell proliferation *in vitro*. J. Immunol., 131:2017, 1983.

71. Lane, H. C.; Masur, H.; Edgar, L. C., et al. Abnormalities of B-cell activation and immunoregulation in patients with the acquired immunodeficiency syndrome. N. Engl. J. Med., 309:453, 1983.

72. Jacoby, D. R., and Oldstone, M. B. A. Delineation of suppressor and helper activity within the OKT4-defined T lymphocyte subset in human newborns. J. Immunol., 131:1765, 1983.

73. Krueger, G. R. F.; Malmgren, R. A.; and Berard, C. W. Malignant lymphomas and plasmacytosis in mice under prolonged immunosuppression and persistent antigenic stimulation. Transplant., 11:138, 1971.

74. Letvin, N. L.; Eaton, K. A.; Aldrich, W. R., et al. Acquired immunodeficiency syndrome in a colony of macaque monkeys. Proc. Natl. Acad. Sci., 80:2718, 1983.

75. King, N. W.; Hunt, R. D.; and Letvin, N. L. Histopathologic changes in macaques

with an acquired immunodeficiency syndrome (AIDS). Am. J. Pathol., 113:382, 1983.

76. Hendrickson, R. V.; Osborn, K. G.; Madden, D. C., et al. Epidemic of acquired immunodeficiency in rhesus monkeys. The Lancet, 1:388, 1983.

77. Letvin, N. L.; King, N. W.; and Daniel, M. D. Experimental transmission of macaque AIDS by means of inoculation of macaque lymphoma tissue. The Lancet, 1:599, 1983.

78. Londo, W. T.; Madden, D. L.; Gravell, M., et al. Experimental transmission of simian acquired immunodeficiency sndrome (SAIDS) and Kaposi-like skin lesions. The Lancet, 2:869, 1983.

79. Gallo, R. C., and Wong-Staal, F. Retroviruses as etiologic agents of some animal and human leukemias and lymphomas and as tools for elucidating the molecular mechanisms of leukemogenesis. Blood, 60:545, 1982.

80. Weinberg, R. A. Oncogenes of spontaneous and chemically induced tumors. Adv. Cancer Res., 36:149, 1982.

81. Hattori, T.; Uchiyama, T.; Toibana, T.; Takatsuki, K.; and Uchino, H. Surface phenotype of Japanese adult T-cell leukemia cells characterized by monoclonal antibodies. Blood, 58:645, 1981.

82. Blattner, W. A.; Blayney, D. W.; Robert-Guroff, M., et al. Epidemiology of human T-cell leukemia/lymphoma virus. J. Infect. Dis., 147:406, 1983.

83. Gelmann, E. P.; Popovic, M.; Blayney, D., et al. Proviral DNA of a retrovirus, human T-cell leukemia virus, in two patients with AIDS. Science, 220:862, 1983.

84. Essex, M.; McLane, M. F.; Lee, T. J., et al. Antibodies to cell membrane antigens associated with human T-cell leukemia virus in patients with AIDS. Science, 220:859, 1983.

85. Evatt, B. L.; Francis, D. P.; and McLane, M. F. Antibodies to human T-cell leukemia virus-associated membrane antigens in hemophiliacs: evidence for infection before 1980. The Lancet, 2:698, 1983.

86. Barre-Sinoussi, F.; Chermann, J. C.; Rey, F., et al. Isolation of a T-lymphotropic retrovirus from a patient at risk for acquired immune deficiency syndrome (AIDS). Science, 220:868, 1983.

87. Gallo, R. C.; Salahuddin, S. Z.; Popovic, M., et al. Frequent detection and isolation of cytopathic retroviruses (HTLV-III) from patients with AIDS and at risk for AIDS. Science, 224:500, 1984.

88. Des Jarlis, D. C.; Marmor, M.; Cohen, H., et al. Antibodies to a retrovirus etiologically associated with acquired immunodeficiency syndrome (AIDS) in populations with increased incidences of the syndrome. Morbid. Mortal. Weekly Rep., 33:377, 1984.

89. Brun-Vezinet, F.; Rouzioux, C.; Barre-Sinoussi, F., et al. Detection of IgG antibodies to lymphadenopathy-associated virus in patients with AIDS or lymphadenopathy syndrome. The Lancet, 1:1253, 1984.

90. Kalyanaraman, V. S.; Cabradilla, C. D.; Getchell, J. P., et al. Antibodies to the core protein of lymphadenopathy-associated virus (LAV) in patients with AIDS. Science, 225:321, 1984.

91. Sarngadharan, M. G.; Popovic, M.; Bruch, L.; Schupbach, J.; and Gallo, R. C. Antibodies reactive with human T-lymphotropic retrovirus (HTLV-III) in the serum of patients with AIDS. Science, 224:506, 1984.

92. Laurence, J.; Brun-Vezinet, F.; Schutzer, S. E., et al. Lymphadenopathy-associated

viral (LAV) antibody in AIDS: immune correlations and definition of a carrier state. N. Engl. J. Med., 311:1269, 1984.

93. Hoshino, H.; Tanaka, H.; Miwa, M.; and Okada, H. Human T-cell leukemia virus is not lysed by human serum. Nature, 309:59, 1984.

94. Feorino, P.M.; Kalyanaraman, V. S.; Haverkos, H. W., et al. Lymphadenopathy associated virus infection of a blood donor-recipient pair with acquired immunodeficiency syndrome. Science, 225:69, 1984.

95. Mann, D. L.; Popovic, M.; Sarin, P., et al. Cell lines producing human T-cell lymphoma virus show altered HLA expression. Nature, 305:58, 1983.

96. Clarke, M. F.; Gelmann, E. P.; Reitz, M. S., Jr. Homology of human T-cell leukemia virus envelope gene with class I HLA gene. Nature, 305:60, 1983.

97. Shearer, G. Acquired immune-deficiency syndrome (AIDS): a consequence of allogenic Ia-antigen recognition. Immunol. Today, 7:184, 1983.

98. Rubenstein, P. Personal communication.

99. Shearer, G. M., and Hurtenbach, U. Is sperm immunosuppressive in male homosexuals and vasectomized men? Immunol. Today, 3:153, 1983.

100. Tsoi, M. S. Immunological mechanisms of graft-versus-host disease in man. Transplant., 33:459, 1982.

101. Olding, L. B.; Jensen, F. C.; Oldstone, M. B. A. Pathogenesis of cytomegalovirus infection, I: activation of virus from bone-marrow-derived lmphocytes by in vitro allogenic reaction. J. Exp. Med., 141:561, 1978.

102. Marcus. Z. H.; Freischeim, J. H.; Houk, J. L.; Hernon, V. H.; and Hess, E. V. In vitro studies in reproductive immunology, I: suppression of cell-mediated immune response by human spermatozoa and fractions isolated from human seminal plasma. Clin. Immunol. Immunopathol., 9:318, 1978.

103. Anderson, D. J., and Tarter, T. H. Immunosuppressive effects of mouse seminal pasma components in vivo and in vitro. J. Immunol., 128:535, 1982.

104. Groopman, J. E. Kaposi's sarcoma and other neoplasms. In Gottlieb, M. S., mod., The acquired immunodeficiency syndrome. Ann. Intern. Med., 99:208, 1983.

105. Daling, J. R.; Weiss, N. S.; Klopfenstein, L. L., et al. Correlates of homosexual behavior and the incidence of anal cancer, J. Amer. Med. Assoc., 247:1988, 1982.

106. Strober, W.; Richman, L. K.; and Elson, C. O. The regulation of gastrointestinal immune responses. Immunol. Today, 4:156, 1981.

107. Jaffe, H. W.; Choi, K.; Thomas, P. A., et al. National case-control study of Kaposi's sarcoma and Pneumocystis carinii pneumonia in homosexual men, I: epidemiologic results. Ann. Intern. Med., 99:145, 1983.

108. Goedert, J. J.; Wallen, W. C.; and Mann, D. L. Amyl nitrite may alter T lymphocytes in homosexual men. The Lancet, 2:412, 1982.

109. Detels, R.; Schwartz, K.; Visscher, B. R.,, et al. Relation between sexual practices and T-cell subsets in homosexually active men. The Lancet, 1:609, 1983.

110. Krown, S. E.; Real, F. X.; Cunningham-Rundles, S., et al. Preliminary observations on the effect of recombinant leukocyte A interferon in homosexual men with Kaposi's sarcoma. N. Engl. J. Med., 308:1071, 1983.

111. Mitsuya, H.; Popovic, M.; Yarchoan, R.; Matsushita, S.; Gallo, R. C.; and Broder, S. Suramin protection of T cells in vitro against infectivity and cytopathic effect of HTLV-III. Science, 226:172, 1984.

112. Rozenbaum, W.; Dormont, D.; Spire, B.; et al. Antimoniotungstate (HPA 23) treatment of three patients with AIDS and one with prodrome. Lancet, 1:450, 1985.

113. McCormick, J. B.; Getchell, J. P.; Mitchell, S. W.; and Hicks, D. R. Ribavirin suppresses replication of lymphadenopathy-associated virus in cultures of human adult T lymphocytes. Lancet, 2:1367, 1984.

114. Dardenne, M.; Bach, J. F.; and Safai, B. Low serum thymic hormone levels in patients with acquired immunodeficiency syndrome. N. Engl. J. Med., 309:48, 1983.

115. Siegal, F. P.; Lopez, C.; Hammer, G. S., et al. Severe acquired immunodeficiency in male homosexuals, manifested by chronic perianal ulcerative herpes simplex lesions. N. Engl. J. Med., 305:1439, 1981.

116. Eyster, M. E.; Goedert, J. J.; Poon, M. C.; and Preble, O. T. Acid-labile alpha interferon: a possible preclinical marker for the acquired immunodeficiencysyndrome in hemophilia. N. Engl. J. Med., 309:583, 1983.

117. Hersh, E. M.; Reuben, J. M.; Rios, A., et al. Elevated serum thymosin α_1 levels associated with evidence of immune dysregulation in male homosexuals with a history of infectious diseases or Kaposi's sarcoma. N. Engl. J. Med., 308:45, 1983.

118. Francioli, P., and Clement, F. Beta-microglobulin and immunodeficiencyin a homosexual man. N. Engl. J. Med., 307:1402, 1982.

119. Rook, A. H.; Masur, H.; Lane, H. C., et al. Interleukin-2 enhances the depressed natural killer and cytomegalovirus-specific cytotoxic activities of lymphocytes from patients with the acquired immune deficiency syndrome. J. Clin. Invest., 72:398, 1983.

120. Flomenberg, N.; Welte, K.; Mertelsmann, R., et al. Immunologic effects of interleukin 2 in primary immunodeficiency diseases. J. Immunol., 130:2644, 1983.

121. Marwick, C. Interleukin 2 trial will try to spark flagging immunity of AIDS patients. J. Amer. Med. Assoc., 250:1125, 1983.

122. Gerstoft, J.; Dickmeiss, E.; Bentsen, K., et al. The prognosis of asymptomatic homosexual men with decreased T-helper to T-suppressor cell ratios. Scan. J. Immunol., 19:275, 1984.

123. Hassell, L. A. Preventing the acquired immunodeficiency syndrome. N. Engl. J. Med., 309:1395, 1983.

124. Centers for Disease Control. Acquired immunodeficiency syndrome (AIDS): precautions for health-care workers and allied professionals. Morbid. Mortal. Weekly Rep., 32:450, 1983.

125. Sande, M. A.; Volberding, P.; Ammann, A., et al. Infection-control guidelines for patients with the acquired immunodeficiency syndrome (AIDS). N. Engl. J. Med., 309:740, 1983.

126. Centers for Disease Control. Prevention of acquired immune deficiency syndrome (AIDS): report of inter-agency recommendations. Morbid. Mortal. Weekly Rep., 32:101, 1983.

127. Gapen, P. Neurological complications now characterizing many AIDS victims. J. Amer. Med. Assoc., 248:2941, 1982.

128. Rosenbaum, E. H.; Rosenbaum, I. R.; Bullard, J. S.; and Bullard, D. How you can help cancer patients solve their sexual concerns. Your Patient and Cancer, 3:45, 1983.

Sexually Transmitted Disease Update

Venereal disease of prior decades was typically represented by five infectious agents: syphilis, gonorrhea, lymphogranulomas venereum and inguinale and chancroid, of which the first two assumed major prominence. The current scope of venereology has broadened considerably beyond these so-called traditional subjects to a long and seemingly limitless list of pathogens whose inclusion as sexually transmitted diseases has only recently been appreciated. These diseases, which presumably date to antiquity but have gained wider recognition both because of improved diagnostic methods that facilitate detection and because of an absolute increase in prevalence secondary to changing sexual behaviors are variously termed "the new generation" (1) or "neglected" (2) sexually transmitted diseases (see Table 11.1). Many of these exist in epidemic proportions throughout the world and assume increasing importance as treatment diminishes gonorrhea and syphilis. Some researchers even contend that the new organisms collectively influence morbidity to a greater extent than the traditional venereal diseases (2).

Discussion of these agents and their myriad associated disorders has already provided sufficient material for several lengthy symposiums and lengthier monographs clearly precluding addressing the list in its entirety in this chapter. I propose to address three of them in depth: chlamydia, the mycoplasmas, and gardnerella, primarily with respect to their presentation in women. Selection was based on their prevalence, recent emergence as major sexually transmitted disease pathogens, and notable though generally unrecognized roles in newer, commonly occurring, sexually transmitted syndromes such as the acute urethral syndrome and perihepatitis, as well as their dominant etiologic roles in familiar clinical entities like cervicitis and salpingitis.

CHLAMYDIA

Although chlamydial genital infections are more prevalent in the United States than any other venereal disease, with an estimated 3 million cases a year and

Table 11.1
Most Important Sexually Transmitted Pathogens and the Diseases They Cause

Pathogen	Disease or Syndrome
Bacterial agents	
Neisseria gonorrhoeae	Urethritis, epididymitis, cervicitis, proctitis, pharyngitis, conjunctivitis, endometritis, perihepatitis, bartholinitis, amniotic infection syndrome, disseminated gonococcal infection, premature delivery and premature rupture of membranes(?), salpingitis and related sequelae (infertility, ectopic pregnancy, recurrent salpingitis)
Chlamydia trachomatis	Urethritis, epididymitis, cervicitis, proctitis, salpingitis, inclusion conjunctivitis, infant pneumonia, otitis media, trachoma, lymphogranuloma venereum, perihepatitis(?), bartholinitis(?), Reiter's disease(?), fetal and neonatal mortality(?)
Mycoplasma hominis	Postpartum fever, salpingitis
Ureaplasma urealyticum	Urethritis, chorioamnionitis, low birth-weight(?)
Treponema pallidum	Syphilis
Gardnerella (Haemophilus) vaginalis	Vaginitis
Haemophilus ducreyi	Chancroid
Calymmatobacterium granulomatis	Donovanosis (granuloma inguinale)
Shigella, Campylobacter	Enterocolitis (among homosexual men)
Group B beta-hemolytic *streptococcus(?)*	Neonatal sepsis, neonatal meningitis
Viral agents	
Herpes simplex virus	Primary and recurrent genital herpes, aseptic meningitis, neonatal herpes with associated mortality or neurologic sequelae, carcinoma of the uterine cervix(?), spontaneous abortion and premature delivery(?)
Hepatitis B virus	Acute, chronic, and fulminant hepatitis, with associated immune complex phenomena
Cytomegalovirus(?)	Congenital infection: gross birth defects and infant mortality, cognitive impairment (e.g., mental retardation, sensorineural deafness), heterophile-negative infectious mononucleosis, cervicitis(?), protean manifestations in the immunosuppressed host
Genital wart virus	Condyloma acuminata, laryngeal papiloma in infants, cervical dysplasia (?)
Molluscum contagiosum virus	Genital molluscum contagiosum
Protozoan agents	
Trichomonas vaginalis	Vaginitis, urethritis(?), balanitis(?)
Entamoeba histolytica	Amebiasis (sexually transmitted especially among homosexual men)
Giardia lamblia	Giardiasis (sexually transmitted especially among homosexual men)
Fungal agents	
Candida albicans	Vulvovaginitis, balanitis and balanoposthitis
Ectoparasites	
Phthirus pubis	Pubic louse infestation
Sarcoptes scabiei	Scabies

Source: K.K Holmes, Introduction: classification of sexually transmitted diseases. In: K.K. Holmes and P.-A. Mårdh, eds., International Perspectives on Neglected Sexually Transmitted Diseases. New York: McGraw-Hill, 1983.

an annual medical cost of more than $1 billion (3), the interesting causative organism *Chlamydia trachomatis* is hardly a household word, having been overshadowed by herpes and AIDS (acquired immune deficiency syndrome). Chlamydiae, which have a unique developmental cycle, are members of their own order (Chlamydiales) and genus (*Chlamydia*) with two species: *C. psittaci*, which causes psittacosis, and *C. trachomatis*, which causes genital infections in the male and female.

Diagnosis

Chlamydia are diagnosed by cytology, serology, and isolation (7). Characteristic intracytoplasmic bodies may be stained with Giemsa's stain iodine, or fluorescent antibody techniques utilizing epithelial scrapings of urethral, conjunctival, or cervical origin, but this is relatively ineffective in diagnosing genital infections (4). Fluorescein-conjugated monoclonal antibody stain, which has been recently introduced, promises rapid and accurate detection of chlamydiae (8, 9) and is purported to approximate the sensitivity of culture (9). Serological tests (5–7) include complement fixation, which detects antibodies to a common polysaccharide cell wall antigen and the microimmunofluorescence test of Wang and Grayston (10), which measures antibodies by immunoglobulin class in sera (IgG and IgM) and secretions (IgA and IgG), the distributions of which have been widely studied (11–13). Serology is of limited diagnostic value because of high background rates (11, 12), the difficulty of obtaining appropriately timed samples to permit the requisite fourfold titer increase (seroconversion), and the evanescence of certain antibody classes. It is useful only in first-episode urethritis (13), in severe systemic infections and in pelvic inflammatory disease where relatively high titers are demonstrable which correlate well with the severity of the disease process, and where alternate diagnostic techniques are invasive and not routinely performed.

Isolation utilizing tissue culture techniques became widely available in 1965. Monolayers of host cells (usually McCoy monkey cells) are pretreated with irradiation or antimetabolites, inoculated with epithelial cell scrapings, incubated, and then stained. Modifications that improve the yield continue to be reported in the literature (14–16).

Incidence

The incidence of chlamydia has been widely studied; rates vary from 1 percent in a nonsexually active group (17), 1 to 16 percent in apparently healthy women (20), 4.6 percent in unselected college women (18), 16 to 38 percent in women attending venereal disease clinics (19, 20), and 45 to 68 percent in female sexual partners of men with chlamydia culture-positive nonspecific urethritis (20), all of which is extensively summarized in tabular form (20). These and other studies

(17, 21) show that chlamydia-positive women are younger, more sexually active, and more likely to use oral contraceptives than controls.

Prevalence studies demonstrate that asymptomatic genital infection may "represent the major form of chlamydial genital infection in women" (20), although retrospective studies of presumably asymptomatic infected women document a small proportion who have genitourinary symptoms (dysuria and vaginal discharge) (19, 20). The magnitude of asymptomatic women is troublesome, because they constitute a significant carrier population and obscure our recognition of *C. trachomatis* as a pathogen; colonization rates of 68 percent, for example, in a given, albeit selected, population are hardly a mandate for treatment. Epidemiology is further complicated by a 10 percent incidence in unselected, asymptomatic men as noted in men undergoing routine army induction physical examinations (22).

Clinical Spectrum

As one author notes, "Hardly a month goes by without a report describing an etiologic role for *Chlamydia trachomatis* in yet another disease" (23). This wide spectrum of chlamydial disorders includes urethritis, cervicitis, salpingitis, endometritis, and perihepatitis (Fitz-Hugh–Curtis syndrome) in the female, nongonococcal urethritis and epididymitis in the male, proctitis in the homosexual male, and inclusion conjunctivitis and pneumonitis of the newborn. Thus chlamydia are a diverse group of pathogens responsible for a number of seemingly unrelated disease entities. The protean nature of these manifestations derives from the organism's predilection for columnar or transitional epithelium in contrast to squamous epithelium; this "limits the target organ specificity of infection" (23). As summarized by Schachter (5), "Although it is perhaps simplistic, a satisfactory way to visualize the pathogenic role of these agents is to consider them pathogens of columnar epithelial cells. They are likely to cause disease in any columnar cells that they may reach."

The Cervix

The infected cervix may be totally normal; high chlamydial isolation rates, however, have been associated with mucopurulent discharge and ectopy (26–28). These changes normalize with tetracycline (29) and are seen to correlate with younger age (27), oral contraceptive use (26), and subsequent trichomonal infection but did not correlate with simultaneous gonorrheal infection. Chlamydial cervical infections would be basically self-limited and benign (28, 32) were it not for their association with Papps abnormalities, which included cervical atypia (28) and dysplasia (31, 32), as well as with cervical biopsy evidence of cervical intraepithelial neoplasia (CIN) (33) and neoplasia (28, 31, 32). Serological studies all document higher antichlamydial antibody titers in women with cervical abnormalities than in controls. Some authors caution that "serioepidemiologic observations do not constitute proof of an etiologic role'' but may simply reflect a sexually more promiscuous population without implying etiologic interrelationships'' (32). Other critics contend that since both antichlamydial antibody titer and cervical atypia vary directly with sexual activity, conclusions about chlamydia's causative role in atypia are erroneous, or at least premature.

Investigators have attempted to control for the variable of sexual activity (28, 33, 34) by evaluating the differences between seropositive and seronegative women with respect to other causes of mild dysplasia (*T. vaginalis, N. gonorrhea*, multiple sex partners) (28) or by concomitantly evaluating colonization with other organisms known to correlate with sexual activity, such as the mycoplasmas (33) or herpes (34). The most noteworthy study, however, utilized specific methodology to obviate the difficulties of earlier investigations (34). Schachter evaluated 883 women with cervical neoplasia and controls and with sophisticated statistical analyses addressed variables of age, number of sexual partners, and age of first coitus (34). He found a higher than predicted rate of antichlamydial antibodies (78 percent) in patients with cervical neoplasia than in a control group with similar sexual activity (61 percent), in contrast to similar rates for antibodies to Herpes Simplex virus II (HSV-II) in the two groups (46 percent vs. 42 percent). The seroepidemiologic results were surprising, even to the investigators, who had initiated the study seeking to establish a causative role for HSV-II and included chlamydia only because of its prevalence as a sexually transmitted disease pathogen with a "sensitive serological test" (35).

Urethritis

While *C. trachomatis* has been well established as a urinary tract pathogen in nongonococcal urethritis (NGU) in the male (13, 36, 37), its role as a causative agent in female urinary tract infections has only recently been elucidated. In his legendary three-part article in the *New England Journal of Medicine* in 1978, Schachter (4) reported that no definitive data existed implicating *C. trachomatis* in the female. The probable basis for this contention is the large number of asymptomatic, urethral culture-positive women reported in many studies (20). However, while chlamydial cervicitis "is often asymptomatic and even inapparent . . . urethral symptoms are not at all unusual complaints among women positive for *C. trachomatis*" (38) and in fact have been reported for several years (39, 40).

Paavonen (38) found urinary symptoms which included dysuria and frequency in over 50 percent of women with positive urethral cultures, in contrast to 21 percent of women with negative cultures, and concluded that *C. trachomatis* "may be a significant cause of abacterial cystitis in sexually active young women" (38). Johannisson (41) studied 583 unselected women and also found high incidences of positive urethral cultures in women with urinary symptoms.

Stamm, in his now classic treatise on the acute urethral syndrome (42), confirmed the role of chlamydia as one of several etiologic agents responsible for a newly described disease entity, the acute urethral syndrome. He evaluated 59 women with dysuria and frequent urination in the absence of "significant bacteriuria" (defined as less than 10^5 organisms per milliliter), 35 women with cystitis, and 66 asymptomatic, presumably noninfected controls and determined that of 32 women with sterile urines, 11 had infections with *C. trachomatis*, as indicated by positive cervical and/or urethral culture, a fourfold rise in IgG antibody titer, or both. The presence of pyuria was seen to correlate well with infection; of 16 women with pyuria, 10 had chlamydia, whereas only one patient with chlamydia was seen out of 16 women without pyuria. Thus Stamm provides convincing evidence in a prospective study of chlamydia's association with urinary symptoms in women (42).

Most recently, Panja (43) found 14 cases of chlamydial urethritis in 107 outpatient women with frequency and dysuria, which is a ratio similar to that of the Barnard Health Service (unpublished data), where approximately 10 percent of the 20 women seen weekly with urinary tract symptoms have totally sterile bacterial urine cultures, and of the subgroup with pyuria virtually all have positive cervical and/or urethral cultures for chlamydia with prompt resolution of symptoms on initiation of appropriate treatment regimens.

Salpingitis/Pelvic Inflammatory Disease (PID)

Of the chlamydial genital tract disorders considered here, the disease state that creates the most diagnostic and epidemiologic uncertainty is salpingitis. Markedly different conclusions reached in studies in Europe and the United States regarding chlamydia's role as a causative organism in this condition are difficult to reconcile even when one accounts for variations in age, parity, contraceptive practices, sexual proclivities, and prevalence of additional bacteria such as gonorrhea or anaerobes in the populations studied, as well as significant differences in the health-care system and employed scientific methodology, all of which influence experimental outcome. Therefore, an elegant prospective Scandinavian study utilizing laparoscopy and biopsy techniques and an analogous American assessment yield divergent, even conflicting, data with respect to the role of chlamydiae (or anaerobes or gonococci or mycoplasmae) as causative agents in salpingitis. Moreover, diagnostic criteria for salpingitis (i.e., the triad of bilateral lower abdominal pain, adnexal tenderness on examination, and either fever, leukocytosis, elevated erythrocyte sedimentation rate, or adnexal mass) are intrinsically unsound, as demonstrated by routine laparoscopy whereby misdiagnosis occurred in 39 percent of the cases where such clinical criteria alone were used.

The role of *C. trachomatis* in salpingitis was first reported by Mardh (44) in Sweden, who recovered the organism from 36 percent of 53 patients seen consecutively for acute salpingitis and from the tubes of 6 out of 7 of those with chlamydia who underwent laparoscopy. Subsequent studies, summarized in Table 11.2, were undertaken in Sweden (11, 45, 49–51), Finland (46, 47), Denmark

Table 11.2
Isolation Rates and Serologic Data in Studies on Salpingitis

Study	No. Pts.	Method of Diagnosis	Source	Culture Results Positive	Antibodies IgM	IgG	Comments
Treharne, Ripa, Mardh, Svenson, Westrom, Darougar (Sweden, 1979) Ref. 45	143	laparoscopy			23%>1:8	62% 1:64	Correlation between severity of tubal inflammation and GMT was significant viz. mild-15, mod.-24 marked-58
Paavonen, Saiku, Vesterinen, Aho (Finland, 1979) Ref. 46	106 (72 c̄ sera)	clinical (adnexal mass, pain, ESR, fever)	cervix urethral	27 (26%) +	single antigen 10 (46%) of 22 CT + 9 (18%) of 50 CT - 19 of 72 (26%) seroconverted total	IFAT	43% of 72 with paired sera had + culture seroconversion; 30% of 27 CT + had GC GMT (219) of CT + pts. higher than other studies (e.g., 84)
Paavonen, (Finland, 1980) Ref. 47	228 consec. ER pts. prospec. study (167 c̄ sera)	clinical divided into 2 grps. AS c̄ abscess 86 (38%) AS s̄ abscess 142 (62%)	cervix urethra	41/142 (29%) s abscess 28/86 (33%) c̄ abscess 69/228 (30%) total	IFAT titer 512 28/69 (41%) CT+ 28/159 (18%) CT- 56/228 (25%) total seroconverted 17/54 (32%) CT+ 15/113 (13%) CT-		GMT of pts. with abscess (192) higher than those without (53) No difference in the 2 groups with respect to isolation rates (33% vs. 29%)

Table 11.2—Continued

Study	No. Pts.	Method of Diagnosis	Source	Culture Results Positive	Antibodies Igm	Antibodies IgG	Comments
Ripa, Svenson, Treharne, Westrom, Mardh (Sweden, 1980) Ref. 48	206	laparoscopy 3 grps. mild mod. severe	cervix	52/156 (33%) 20/58 (34%) 19/56 (34%) 13/42 (31%)	titer 1:8 34/206 (17%) seroconverted 17/80 (21%)	titer>1:64 29/74 (39%) 52/78 (67%) 37/54 (69%) 118/206 (57%) LGTI 8/50 16%	GMT's correlated well mild 72 mod. – 186 severe – 311
	50 controls					controls 12/50 (14%)	
Svenson, Westrom, Mardh (Sweden, 1981) Ref. 49	10	laparoscopy	tubes cervix urethra	10/10 7/10	titer >1:16 1/10 seroconverted 1/10	titer >1:64 9/10 titer 1:128 7/10	2 pts. had GC "neither the failure to isolate CT from the cervix nor a stationery titer of antibodies precludes a chlamydial etiology"
Moller, Mardh, Ahrons, Nussler (Sweden and Denmark, 1981) Ref. 50	166	clinical (lower abdominal pain, cervical tenderness) ESR and fever	cervix	37 (22%) +	titer 1:16 0 pts. seroconverted 3/37 CT+ 0/129 CT-	titer>1:32 27/37 (73%) CT+ 36/129 (28%) CT- seroconversion 20/37(54%) CT+ 14/129(11%) CT-	studied M. hominis and G.C. specimens stored too long; may account for low CT isolation rate

226

Study	No Pts.	Method of Diagnosis	Source	Culture Results Positive	Antibodies IgM	IgG	Comments
Gjonnaess, Dalaker, Anestad, Mardh, Kvile, Bergan (Norway and Sweden, 1982) Ref. 51	65	laparoscopy	tubes cervix hepatic surface (9)	5 (8) 26 (40%)	titer 1:8 0 pts.	seroconversion or titer > 1:256 36 (55%)	0 anaerobic bacteria were isolated 8% had cervical GC
Oser and Person (Sweden, 1982) Ref. 11	209 69 con- trols (s̄ AS)	laparoscopy (80%) clinical	cervix urethra	52/111 (47%) 8/69 (12%) pts. s̄ AS	titer 1:64 25/72	seroconver- sion 25/72 37/72(51%) showed either IgM 1:64 or IgG conversion 20/22CT+ had either 9/24CT- had either (not all had both serology and culture)	11% positive for GC authors conclude "Chlamydia in cervical specimens...most likely involved in the salpingitis "

Abbreviations:

AS = acute salpingitis
c̄ = with
CT = Chlamydia trachomatis
ER = emergency room
GC = gonorrhea

Grp = group
GMT = geometric mean titer
L.G.T.I.= lower genital tract infection
IFAT = immuno flourescence antibody titer

mod. = moderate
pts. = patients
s̄ = without
+ = positive
- = negative

227

(50), and Norway (51) to further elucidate chlamydia's pathogenicity in salpingitis and to devise objective clinical and serological diagnostic criteria. These studies reveal many interesting differences between gonococcal and chlamydial acute salpingitis; patients with chlamydia are younger, have longer duration of symptoms before presenting, have less acute pelvic pain in general (23), and have higher erythrocyte sedimentation rates and more prominent masses than those with gonorrhea (23). In addition, a higher rate of infertility has been associated with chlamydia (23).

Table 11.2 demonstrates lower genital tract isolation rates of 22 to 47 percent, and seroconversion ranges of 32 to 75 percent in chlamydia (cervical) positive women and 11 to 18 percent in chlamydia culture-negative women. The explanation for high titers of various antibodies (11 to 28 percent overall) in chlamydia-negative women is twofold: titers may be indicative of prior infection, or technical difficulty in obtaining cervical cultures may be responsible. Ripa (48) speculated that local antibodies in cervical secretions neutralize the infection of cell monolayers by *C. trachomatis* paradoxically creating false-negative cervical cultures. Geometric mean titers (GMTs) were calculated for various subgroups and were seen to correlate well with the severity of the disease either by clinical assessment (e.g., abscess formation; those with abscess had a GMT of 192 vs. those without, who had 53 [47]) or laparoscopic evalution;''mild,'' '' moderate,'' and ''severe'' corresponded to GMTs of 15, 24, and 58 (control 2), respectively, in one study (45) and 72, 186, and 311 (control 42) in another (48).

Experimental studies wherein tubal secretions from salpingitis patients are inoculated into the genital tract of grivet monkeys and produce pathological changes identical to those of human chlamydial salpingitis biopsy specimens are being undertaken to clarify the pathophysiology of the disorder. Histological changes indistinguishable from those traditionally ascribed to gonococcal salpingitis are reported; some investigators postulate that immunopathologicalmechanisms are responsible for tubal infertility.

Human infertility studies beginning to appear in the literature (53) illustrate dramatically chlamydia's etiologic significance in salpingitis. Henry-Suchet (53) performed laparoscopies on 17 patients with acute PID, 46 infertile women who had no history (except for one patient) or current findings of PID, and 36 controls, and did serologies on 56 (of 63) patients and 28 (of 36) controls and cultures in all 99 subjects. Some 69 percent of the patients with mild inflammation, and 50 percent of those with *no* inflammation, yielded serological evidence of chlamydia infection, compared with 18 percent of the controls and 35 percent of those with mild inflammation; 21 percent of those with no inflammation had positive tubal cultures, in contrast to 0 of 36 controls, strongly suggesting ''that *C. trachomatis* causes silent PID which results in infertility'' (53). These findings are consistent with the view of other authors that chlamydia may represent a quiescent, low-grade, indolent infection with devastating sequelae on the tubes and fertility potential.

Perihepatitis

Perihepatitis as a complication of salpingitis was first reported by Stajano in 1919 and was rediscovered in 1939 by Curtis and Fitz-Hugh, accounting for its current appellation, Fitz-Hugh–Curtis syndrome (FHC). It is characterized by a localized fibrinous inflammation of the anterior hepatic surface and adjacent peritoneum, which produces typical fibrous ("violin string") adhesions between the liver and the diaphragm. The syndrome classically presents with acute onset right upper quadrant pain indistinguishable from that of acute cholecystitis or pancreatitis with or without a history of recent genital tract infection.

Fitz-Hugh's original discovery of gram-negative diplococci resulted in its alternate name, gonococcic perihepatitis, but despite this traditional association, studies confirm gonorrheal etiology in less than half of the evaluated cases (54, 55) directing attention to nongonococcal origins. Evidence for chlamydia's role derives from studies utilizing serology (where high titers of IgG are characteristically present), lower genital tract cultures, and laparoscopy, summarized in Table 11.3.

Geometric mean titers of antichlamydial antibody are significantly higher in the FHC group (1:724) than in the uncomplicated PID group (1:138) or the non-PID group (1:103) (59), and high titers in patients with perihepatitis are uniformly reported in the various studies (50, 57–59) cited in Table 11.3. Also noteworthy is the higher isolation rate of chlamydia compared with gonorrhea in the majority of studies that cultured for both organisms (50, 58, 60), clearly establishing an important causative role for chlamydia in the syndrome.

As familiarity with Fitz-Hugh–Curtis syndrome increases, it is gaining wider recognition as a clinical entity responsible for right upper quadrant pain. Investigators in a recent *Lancet* article speculated that chlamydial perihepatitis may account for more than 10 percent of all admissions for acute cholecystitis in Britain; when they retrospectively analyzed the clinical presentations of 22 hospitalized women seen in a nine-month period who had markedly elevated antichlamydial antibody titers compared with control groups, they found right upper quadrant pain was the presenting symptom in 5, or 23 percent. They concluded that perihepatitis secondary to *C. trachomatis* is a frequent cause of right upper quadrant pain in young women and that failure to diagnose this condition can "subject patients to many expensive and possibly unnecessary investigations and to surgery without relieving the presenting symptoms" (61).

The mechanism for perihepatitis, while not fully understood, is believed to involve ascending pelvic infection from the cervix through the uterine cavity, the Fallopian tubes, and across the peritoneal cavity to the hepatic region. Data also supports an alternative thesis predicating noncanalicular spread, that is, via the lymphatics and the surrounding ligaments. Regardless of pathogenesis, chlamydial salpingitis clearly occurs frequently and must be considered in the evaluation of right upper quadrant pain.

Table 11.3
Isolation Rates and Serologic Data in Studies on Perihepatitis

Study	Year	No. Cases	Clinical Details	Laparoscopy	Findings			
					Culture		G.C.	Serology
					G.T. Tubes	Cervix	Cervix	
Muller-Shoop et al. (Switzerland) Ref. 56	1978	11	not classic FHC, 11 c̄ peritonitis, 2 c̄ AS 7 c̄ perihepatitis	3/11 PH	Not obtained		3	10/11 seroconv.
Paavonen and Valtonen (Finland) Ref. 57	1980	1	first documented case 2 to CT; presented c̄ cervicitis and salpingitis	NR		1/1	0/1	Ig>1024
Wolner-Hansen et. al (Sweden) Ref. 58	1980	4	all had salpingitis 3 c̄ RUQ pain	3/4 PH	0/1	3/3	0/3	3/4 seroconv. 3/4 titer>512 4/4 with either
Wang et al. (U.S.) Ref. 59	1980	23	all had PID and RUQ pain			3/10	7/23	14/23 seroconv. 13/23 IgG titer>1024 11/23 IgM elevation 20/23
Dalaker et. al. (Norway) Ref. 60	1981	4	3 with lower abdominal pain and AS on exam; all 4 had RUQ pain	4/4 PID & PH	2/4	4/4	0/4	N.R.
Gjonnaess (Norway) Ref. 51	1982	65	65 women with laparoscopically verified PID	65 c̄ PID 18 c̄ PH & PID	3/10 PH	7/18 PH 26/65 PID	5/65	10/18 c̄ PM either seroconv. or had IgC titer>256

Abbreviations:

AS = acute salpingitis
CT = Chlamydia trachomatis
GC = gonorrhea
FHC = Fitz-Hugh Curtis syndrome

N.R. = not reported
PID = pelvic inflammation
PH = perihepatitis
RUQ = right upper quadrant

Seroconv. = seroconverted
c̄ = with

Chlamydia in Pregnancy

The role of *C. trachomatis* in postpartum endometritis was established in 1977, when Rees and Tait (30) discovered that two-thirds of the mothers of babies with neonatal conjunctivitis had postpartum infection, and isolated chlamydia from the cervices of all mothers who had not received antibiotics prior to culture (30). Treatment of antepartum chlamydia eliminated this complication (62). Postpartum infectious morbidity was seen in 34 percent of women with antepartum *C. trachomatis* vs. 8 percent of normal women implicating the organism in "late" (2 days to 6 weeks) postpartum endometritis (63).

Postabortal morbidity of women with preoperative, asymptomatic chlamydia has been extensively studied (64–66). Postabortal PID occurred in chlamydia-positive women at a rate of 23 percent (64) and 24 percent (66), in contrast to the usual rate of 3 to 4 percent (64) or at most 10 percent (66). The significance of *C. trachomatis* is well demonstrated in a two-part Danish-Norwegian study. In one group none of 25 chlamydia-positive women who received preoperative doxycycline developed postabortal PID, whereas of 23 chlamydia-positive women in a second demographically comparable group, 22 percent developed PID. Thus, asymptomatic chlamydial cervical colonization is associated with a "significantly higher risk of developing postabortal PID" (66). Presumably instrumentation and/or cervical dilatation produces spread to the tubes of heretofore inconsequential cervical infection. The fact that pretreatment with chlamydia sensitive antibiotics eliminates this complication indicates that prophylactic coverage for individuals undergoing induced outpatient abortion may be appropriate when cultures are unavailable.

The most important effect of untreated maternal chlamydia infection, however, relates to the outcome of pregnancy (67). Perinatal mortality (defined as "fetal and neonatal deaths between the 20th week of gestation and 28 days postpartum) was evaluated in 18 (6.7 percent) of 268 women who were examined before 19 weeks' gestation and had positive endocervical cultures for chlamydia and in 26 culture-negative controls matched for age, marital and socioeconomic status, and pregnancy order. Birth weight and gestational duration were also compared in the 18 chlamydia-positive and 238 chlamydia-negative mothers. Analysis of pregnancy outcome revealed that pregnancy terminated with a perinatal death for 6 (33 percent) of the 18 infected women and 8 (3 percent) of 238 uninfected controls. Matched cohort analysis using the 26 controls revealed 1 perinatal death for a rate of 3.8 percent (vs. 33 percent), and mean birth weights and mean gestational duration for chlamydia-positive women were significantly less than for the 238 uninfected women. Despite the authors' caution against extrapolation because of small sample size, failure to evaluate other causes of prematurity and perinatal mortality, incompleteness of pathological studies, and lack of explanatory mechanisms accounting for mortality data, the fact that stillbirth or neonatal deaths "occurred ten times more often than among" well-matched "uninfected controls" is impressive.

A later study found slightly lower rates of prematurity, stillbirth, and low birth weights in chlamydia-positive women (in somewhat noncomparable experimental groups), but IgM seropositive *C. trachomatis* infected women (i.e., those with presumed primary infection) had more low birth weight infants and premature rupture of membranes than either IgM-negative *C. trachomatis* infected or *C. trachomatis* negative women. Serious sequelae in untreated chlamydia-infected women clearly precludes additional studies of this design, so definitive perinatal mortality data in larger experimental groups will not be forthcoming. The results of the former study, notwithstanding its lack of confirmation, should be addressed and should focus attention on the importance of detection and treatment of maternal chlamydial infections.

Treatment

Fortunately, there are many drugs that will eradicate *C. trachomatis*. Tetra-cyclines, erythromycin, the sulfonamides, and in long-term high-dose courses, even the semisynthetic penicillins are effective (3). The Center for Disease Control (CDC) recommends the following regimens for treatment of culture-proven, uncomplicated urethral, endocervical, or rectal infection or suspected mucorpulent cervicitis or the acute urethral syndrome (69):

First choice:

> tetracycline 500 mg p.o. four times a day (Q.I.D.) for at least 7 days
>
> doxycycline 100 mg p.o. Q.I.D. for at least 7 days

As an alternative and first choice in pregnant women:

> erythromycin 500 mg p.o. Q.I.D. for at least 7 days
>
> erythromycin 250 mg p.o. Q.I.D. for at least 14 days

Specific regimens are not given for other conditions, although the CDC recommends "combination regimens with broad activity against major pathogens in PID."

Studies have most frequently addressed urethritis in the male (20). The efficacy of 6–day courses of rifampin, 7–day courses of minocycline, doxycycline, tetracycline, and rosarimicin, 10–day courses of sulfonamides, and 10–to–14–day courses of erythromycin is demonstrated. (20) Lower genital tract pathology in the female has been successfully treated with 7–day courses of triple tetracycline 300 mg twice a day (B.I.D.) (70) and 10–day courses of doxycylcine 100 mg B.I.D. (71), erythromycin 500 mg B.I.D. (41), trimethoprim-sulfadiazine B.I.D. (41), and lymecycline 300 mg B.I.D. (72). Ampicillin 500 mg. Q.I.D. following a loading dose is effective in 80 percent of cases (73), as was rosarimicin (29, 74), although a significant number of associated abnormal liver function tests account for the latter's withdrawal.

Few studies have evaluated treatment of other female genital tract disorders;

"the optimal dose and duration for treatment of chlamydial endometritis, sal-pingitis, and perihepatitis have yet to be ascertained" (29). Moreover, there is uncertainty about the benefit of antibiotics in acute salpingitis and about "the extent to which it influences the clinical course and frequency of sequelae . . . the only reliable parameter to evaluate the positive effect . . . has been to study the frequency of intrauterine pregnancy in patients who have suffered from this disease . . . so far no such studies have been published" (52). Cure, defined as nonrecurrence in two months, was seen in 95 percent of unselected women with laparoscopically proven acute salpingitis with doxycycline 200, then 100 mg per day for 14 days (75). A subsequent study illustrates that clinical improvement may be misleading since "notable" clinical response was observed with ceph-alosporins, but posttreatment endometrial cultures yielded *C. trachomatis* in 12 of 13 patients biopsied (76). So the fallability of clinical assessment mandates posttreatment cultures preferably from endometrial sources.

Conclusion

Thus, *Chlamydia trachomatis*, a relatively unknown organism, even though it is the most prevalent sexually transmitted disease pathogen in the world today (3), has been seen to produce a wide and varied list of disorders. Except for mucopurulent cervicitis and the acute urethral syndrome, the manifestations of this infectious agent have a remarkably profound effect on morbidity of women and their offspring. The role of *C. trachomatis* in cervical atypica and neoplasia has been postulated by some investigators to outrank that of herpes, which is noteworthy in view of the extensive media hype over the latter organism. Chla-mydia's significance in neonatal morbidity and mortality accounting for a tenfold increase in rate of stillborn infants is equally striking. Finally, the growing number of cases of perihepatitis and acute and chronic salpingitis which are attributable to chlamydia are particularly worrisome in view of the long-range complications of chlamydial pelvic inflammatory disease on tubal infertility. Moreover, the propensity of *C. trachomatis* to cause silent, almost subclinical infection and undetected tubal destruction heightens the importance of early consideration of this organism so that appropriate diagnosis and treatment can be undertaken early and propitiously.

THE MYCOPLASMAS

In continuing to assess the nontraditional sexually transmitted diseases, it is natural to follow a review of *C. trachomatis* with the mycoplasmas. Both or-ganisms have been implicated in many of the same genital tract disorders and are often simultaneously evaluated (40, 48, 53, 68), although the etiologic role of the mycoplasmas is less defined in endometritis, pelvic inflammatory disease, intra- and postpartum feto-maternal complications, and reproductive failure.

The mycoplasmas have a relatively short history. In 1937, Dienes and Edsall isolated mycoplasma from a Bartholin's gland cyst for its first example in human disease; *Ureaplasma urealyticum* was identified by Shepard in 1954, and its association with nongonococcal urethritis was suggested in 1956 (77). Since then, mycoplasma organisms, previously well known in veterinary medicine, have been observed to be common inhabitants of the oropharyngeal and genital mucous membranes (78). *M. hominis* is one of eight recognized human mycoplasma species and a member of the genus *Mycoplasma*. *Ureaplasma urealyticum*, once considered a T mycoplasma, is the only recognized species of the genus *Ureaplasma*. Both genera belong to the family Mycoplasmataceae, characterized by their growth requirement of sterols, and will be considered jointly as "mycoplasmas." Interesting biological properties and differences are reviewed elsewhere (79).

Diagnosis

Although the mycoplasmas are readily demonstrable with Giemsa's stain, slide interpretation is difficult (5) and definitive diagnosis requires isolation of the organisms. Appropriate culture sources include urinary sediment, vaginal or cervical secretions, and endometrial or tubal aspirates, which may be grown on agar or in infusion broth. "Progress in methods for the detection of antibodies has been slow" (5). Indirect hemagglutination, designated "the method of choice" for *M. hominis* in a recent symposium (80), has been questioned as a reliable indicator of infection because of its marked variability in prevalence rates in similar populations (e.g., 9 percent vs. 97 percent). Other conventional antibody tests employed include indirect immunofluorescence, the modified growth inhibition test, and the mycoplasmacidal test, which measures antibodies with a possible protective effect in humans (79). Recently developed ELISA tests are allegedly "more sensitive than conventional tests for detection of antibody to *M. hominis*" and offer "rapidity and economy" (79). Progress in uncovering serologic tests for *U. urealyticum* antibodies in *urealyticum* has been even more limited. Prevalence of antibodies in the general population requires that seroconversion or fourfold titer increase be demonstrated for serologic diagnosis of current infection.

Epidemiology

Widely studied mycoplasma colonization rates (18, 81–85) demonstrate disappearance of the organism presumably acquired during birth canal passage within the first year (81). After puberty, isolation rates rise directly with age and sexual experience and average 50 to 60 percent for *U. urealyticum* and 20 to 30 percent for *M. hominis* in the urogenital tract of asymptomatic adults (77).

Blacks, women from lower socioeconomic groups, jail inmates, and clinic patients are more frequently colonized than, for example, private patients. While more extensive sexual activity is postulated as the basis for these differences, "there is little objective data to support this contention" (78), and studies indicate "that race is predictive of *M. hominis* vaginal colonization independent of sexual experience" (80). Other variables that are significantly predictive of colonization include lifetime number of sexual partners, use of nonbarrier contraceptive measures, and young age (80). Use of oral contraceptives or intrauterine devices, pregnancy, and having a consort with NGU increase isolation rates, whereas use of condoms and circumcision decreases the isolation rates of the two organisms differently (77). Comparison of cultivation sites reveals highest isolation rates from the vagina, while the proximal urethra, bladder, uterus, and Fallopian tubes are normally free of mycoplasmas (78).

Vaginitis and Cervicitis

The role of *M. hominis* in vaginitis is unclear. While earlier, poorly controlled, studies documented a higher rate of *M. hominis* from symptomatic individuals than from asymptomatic individuals, more recent evaluations of large groups of women with symptoms suggestive of vulvovaginitis and asymptomatic controls demonstrate no statistically significant differences in the prevalence of either of the mycoplasmas in the two groups (85). Moreover, the coexistence of the mycoplasmas with other genital tract pathogens obscures the establishment of causality, because it is difficult to exclude the possibility that the presence of mycoplasmas is secondary to favorable growth conditions produced by the coexisting true pathogens. An alternate hypothesis is that two (or more) organisms have a symbiotic relationship accounting for dual causation, as in nonspecific vaginitis, where a majority of women harbor both organisms. Presumptive evidence against a significant role for mycoplasma in this condition derives from the observation that eradication of *H. vaginalis* correlated with clinical improvement, whereas eradication of *M. hominis* alone did not (79). *U. urealyticum* has not been implicated in vaginitis in any reports to date (79).

Pelvic Inflammatory Disease

Following the discovery of the mycoplasmas in the female genital tract, investigators have questioned their role in pelvic inflammatory disease. In 1970 a series of three Swedish studies compared women with both laparoscopically verified salpingitis and lower genital tract infections and noninfected controls (87–89). *M. hominis* was isolated from the tubes of four and *U. urealyticum* from two of the salpingitis patients and from no patients in the other two groups (87). Indirect hemagglutination antibody (IHA) to *M. hominis* were seen in 54 percent of the salpingitis patients, 27 percent of the lower genital tract infected women, and ten percent of the healthy controls (88). IgM titers were markedly elevated (500 percent of the standard [86]) in 34 percent of the salpingitis patients and correlated with both IHA in 17 of 18 patients and positive cervical cultures in 14 of 15 patients (89), suggesting that *M. hominis* "may have a primary pathogenetic role in a... proportion of patients with PID'' (78). Subsequent large studies documented *M. hominis* in cervices of 71 percent and *U. urealyticum* in 80 percent of PID patients (90) and 47 percent of acute salpingitis (AS) patients (49). IHA to *M. hominis* were seen in 40 percent of AS patients vs. 8 percent of age-matched controls (91), with titer changes in 47 percent of cervical culture-positive women in contrast to only 7 percent of culture-negative women (49).

Significant experimental studies include those with grivet monkeys as animal models (52) and organ culture studies of fallopian tube epithelium (92). *M. hominis* inoculation into the Fallopian tubes of five grivet monkeys produced a self-limited acute exosalpingitis and parametritis characteristic of so-called non-gonococcal salpingitis with noncanalicular spread (52, 92) accompanied by four-fold IHA titer rise (52). Organ culture studies wherein normal tubal epithelium was infected with *M. hominis* revealed cilial swelling and diminished ciliary activity, which was worse than analogous infection with *N. gonorrhea* and absent in uninfected specimens. Thus, both clinical and experimental research predicate an etiologic role for *M. hominis* in acute salpingitis.

Diseases of Pregnancy

Postabortal and Postpartum Fever

Studies in the 1960s demonstrated an association between *M. hominis* and postabortal fever, with the organism found in 8 percent and seroconversion in 50 percent of febrile aborters, in contrast to 0 and 14 percent respectively in nonfebrile women (78). The role of antepartum *M. hominis* on the development of *M. hominis* septicemia and postpartum fever remains unclear. Some studies show a higher rate of antenatal cervicovaginal isolations in patients who develop postpartum fever, whereas others do not (78), attributing it instead to prolonged labor and duration of ruptured membranes and vaginal exam prior to parturition, which all predispose to invasion of the bloodstream by *M. hominis* (77) or to low titers of protective mycoplasmacidal antibodies (79). A recent prospective study of 100 pregnant women in which antepartum colonization with *M. hominis, C. trachomatis,* and *U. urealyticum* was evaluated, revealed that only ''*M. hominis* was associated with postpartum endometritis'' (80).

Spontaneous Abortion and Stillbirth

Initial studies failed to confirm the role of the genital mycoplasmas in spontaneous abortion and stillbirth. Subsequent investigators suggested that alternate culture sources than the vagina or cervix might be more productive, and isolated mycoplasmas from the tubes of one cervical culture-negative repeat spontaneous aborter and from the fetal membranes of 18 of 25 women with spontaneous abortion or premature deliveries, in contrast to 1 of 13 women with full-term deliveries or voluntary abortions (78). Stray-Pedersen (94) demonstrated that while no significant differences were observed between recovery of *U. urealyticum* from the cervices of 46 habitual aborters and of 45 normal fertile women, the organism was found in endometrial culture in 28 percent of habitual aborters, in contrast to 7 percent of controls. Doxycycline treatment decreased the spontaneous abortion rate to 9 percent in contrast to 50 percent in the untreated women, indicating that "endometrial Ureaplasma infections may be of some pathogenetic significance" (94).

Quinn (95) found an 84.5 percent prevalence rate of genital mycoplasmas in 71 couples with "pregnancy wastage," compared with 25.4 percent in 51 controls. Among culture-positive women, 96 percent aborted. Titer elevations four times the maternal level were found in 43 percent of 14 infants born to mothers in the pregnancy wastage group, in contrast to only 15 percent of normal infants, and was believed to represent true *in utero* infection. Antibiotic regimens that reduced the 96 percent spontaneous abortion rate included preconception doxycycline (48 percent loss), intrapartum erythromycin (15 percent loss), and combined treatment (16.7 percent loss) (95), which further supports a significant role for the mycoplasmas (or for doxycycline and/or erythromycin-sensitive offending organisms).

Prematurity and Low Birth Weight

Prospective studies of 484 women at the Boston City Hospital associated ureaplasma colonization and low birth weights (79); subsequent studies both confirmed and refuted these findings. The association of *M. hominis* with low birth weights is "less striking" (79). Moreover, "it cannot be concluded that genital mycoplasmas are directly responsible for low birth weight because it is possible that women who have a predisposition to smaller babies are selectively colonized" (79).

Infertility

The least interpretable studies on the sequelae of the genital mycoplasmas are those on infertility. Not only do the problems cited in the previous studies pertain, namely, absence of comparable control groups, incomplete profile of potential pathogens, improper sampling sites for culture, absense of double-blind placebo-controlled treatment protocols, and so on, but other inherent difficulties further compound these errors and render investigative research virtually impossible. These include the multifactorial basis of infertility, the complexity of the interaction of the relevant variables, and the capriciousness of the conception process. Moreover, evaluation of the mycoplasmas is particularly troublesome because they characteristically produce clinically inapparent tubal infection and subtle tubal changes. Despite these vicissitudes, investigators have attempted to implicate the genital mycoplasmas in various phases of reproductive failure in both the male and the female.

Mycoplasmas were first isolated from an infertile couple in 1970; tetracycline treatment of both partners resulted in pregnancy (96). Ureaplasmas were found in 85 percent of the men and 91 percent of the females in couples with "unexplained" infertility of more than five years' duration, compared with 22 percent of female controls and 23 percent of their consorts (97). Prolonged doxycycline treatment yielded a pregnancy rate of 27 percent (98). In other studies, couples treated with doxycycline had conception rates similar to those treated with placebo and untreated couples (99), and no statistically significant difference in ureaplasma isolation rates was found in infertile and fertile couples with equivocal treatment results (97). Stray-Pedersen et al. (100) performed cultures from endometrial sources and found ureaplasmas in 50 percent of 18 women with unexplained infertility of five years' duration, compared with 7 percent of 45 controls in one study (100), and 26 percent of 175 women with unexplained infertility, compared with 8 percent of 40 controls in another study (101), suggesting that endometrial colonization is significant and predictive of infertility.

Toth et al. clearly demonstrated the efficacy of doxycycline in a study of somewhat different design (102). Pregnancy rates of women whose husbands' ureaplasma infections were successfully eradicated, as confirmed by negative cultures, were compared with those of women whose husbands' infections were not eradicated by treatment. The only criteria for admission to the study were a positive mycoplasma culture and the intent to conceive. Variables such as age, length of time spent to conceive, fertility procedures performed, and sperm count were assessed independently by a variety of statistical methods. After treatment, 129 (80 percent) of the 161 men originally positive had negative cultures, and their three-year pregnancy rate was 60 percent, compared with a 5 percent pregnancy rate among the 32 couples in which the men had positive cultures after treatment. Multivariate analysis revealed that the variable most significantly associated with the time until successful pregnancy occurred was the mycoplasma status at the end of treatment. Although understanding of ureaplasma's effect "on infertility may be provided only by a double blind prospective study in which well defined cases of unexplained infertility are randomly assigned to placebo or antibiotic treatment" (102), and although differences in pregnancy rate among mycoplasma culture-negative and culture-positive men may not be "due solely to the successful eradication of mycoplasma or . . . of other . . . bacteria . . . for which doxycycline is an effective antibiotic" (102), the data is nonetheless impressive.

Treatment

Both *U. urealyticum* and *M. hominis* are susceptible to doxycycline, tetracycline, streptomycin, gentamicin, spectinomycin, and choloramphenicol and resistant to sulfonamides, trimethoprim, the cephalosporins, ampicillin, and penicillin (77). *U. urealyticum* can be treated with erythromycin, and *M. hominis* is sensitive to lincomycin (77). Specific recommendations for treatment are lacking because there is no consensus about the appropriateness of treating conditions in which mycoplasma's causative role is yet undefined. CDC references include only ureaplasma treatment in NGU and *M. hominis* coverage in acute PID (69). It is well recognized that standard doses of doxycycline result in "fast disappearance of ureaplasmas from both male and female genital tracts" (97). Few authors, however, will commit themselves to specific indications for therapy (except in PID, where treatment regimens are characteristically imprecise), much less to dosage and duration schedules. Clearly unanimity about treating the conditions described herein will create more definitive therapeutic recommendations.

Conclusion

In the 35 years since their discovery as human genital tract inhabitants, the mycoplasmas have been evaluated in a variety of urogenital infections, intra- and postpartum complications, and reproductive failure. High colonization rates (50 to 60 percent for *Ureaplasma urealyticum* and 20 to 30 percent for *M. hominis*) for asymptomatic adults have complicated the establishment of etiologic relationships with a variety of conditions studied. A table that summarizes the relationship of the organisms with these conditions (79) designates *M. hominis* as having a "strong" association with PID and postabortal and postpartum fever, endometritis, and *U. urealyticum* similarly with respect to NGU in males and low birth weight in infants. Recent additions to the list should include the role of *U. urealyticum* in spontaneous abortion (94, 95) and reproductive failure in the female (101) and the male (102).

As with other infectious agents discussed herein, the many unresolved issues obscure our complete understanding of the role of mycoplasmas in the various delineated disorders. Newer diagnostic tests, such as the ELISA, and insights such as that of the preferability of endometrial over cervical culture sites, should facilitate definition of etiologic role, pathogenetic mechanisms, and optimum treatment courses of these ubiquitous but illusive organisms.

GARDNERELLA

Gardnerella will be discussed here in relation to its association with nonspecific vaginitis (NSV), a condition with which 7.5 million women are currently infected (103). Concepts about this condition have evolved from a series of controversial and contradictory studies, which will be reviewed herein, and only recently has a meaningful consensus been achieved about the exact nature of the interrelationship of the causative agents in which *Gardnerella* figures quite prominently.

Taxonomy and Diagnosis

In 1953 Leopold isolated a nonmotile, nonencapsulated pleomorphic gram-negative rod which he tentatively placed in the *Hemophilus* genus (104). Its relationship to vaginitis was proposed two years later, when the identical organism was isolated by Gardner and Dukes (105) and named *Haemophilus vaginalis*. Because it did not conform to taxonomic criteria for hemophilus, reclassification was suggested, and after interim inclusion in the *Corynebacterium* genus, it was ultimately placed in its own genus, *Gardnerella*, to be known as *Gardnerella vaginalis*. There is little doubt that the trilogy of titles: *Hemophilus vaginalis*, *Corynebacterium vaginale*, and *Gardnerella vaginalis* have contributed to the confusion about the organism; the name *Gardnerella (G.) vaginalis*, or gardnerella, will be used henceforth.

Laboratory diagnosis of the organism is based entirely on isolation, but clinical criteria are more commonly employed in the diagnosis of the associated nonspecific vaginitis in which cultures are not routinely performed. Serologic tests have not been reported to date, and cytological evaluation is unsuitable because of abundant coexisting vaginal organisms. *G. vaginalis* has been isolated on a variety of culture media; isolation rates vary, depending on which selective medium is employed. Most recently a highly selective medium, CNAF, has been developed, yielding much higher isolation rates than prior methods (104).

Incidence and Epidemiology

As with the other organisms reviewed in this chapter, the prevalence of *G. vaginalis* and its relationship to symptoms is controversial. In fact, discrepancies in the prevalence of this organism in symptomatic versus asymptomatic women are at the core of the confusion about Gardenerella's role in NSV. Clearly, if the organism is found in large numbers of asymptomatic women so that it can be considered a normal inhabitant of the vaginal flora, it becomes very difficult to implicate in a disease state.

Isolation rates from various studies are well summarized in tabular form and vary from 30 to 45 percent in asymptomatic women and 33 to 50 percent in symptomatic women (104). McCormack et al. (106) isolated *G. vaginalis* from a total of 150 (32 percent) of 466 university coeds. Colonization was not associated wtih an abnormal discharge ''either as reported by the patient or by the examining gynecologist'' (106). Logit analysis correlated colonization with four factors: nonwhite race, oral contraceptive use, nonmarital status, and history of pregnancy. Isolation rates did not parallel sexual experience, in contrast to analogous studies of *U. urealyticum*, and were interpreted to reflect that Gardnerella was not an exogenous genital organism, that is, one for which ''sexual contact is the primary mode of acquisition,'' like ''*N. gonorrhea* . . . and the genital mycoplasmas'' (106). McCormack (106) concedes ''quantitative evaluation of the vaginal microflora may . . . be necessary. . . . It is possible that . . . it is not the presence per se of the organism but its presence in large numbers relative to the other components . . . that is associated with pathogenicity'' (106). Osborne et al. (86), in a later study of 253 women, isolated *G. vaginalis* from 24 percent of symptomatic women and only 5 percent of controls.

Vaginitis

As already noted, there are many unresolved aspects about nonspecific vaginitis, but our knowledge has clearly transcended the traditional view that it represented that clinical entity which remained after trichomonal and candidal bases for infectious vaginitis were excluded. Our current understanding has evolved from a series of controversial and contradictory studies from which myriad misconceptions derive. These are well summarized in a review article (104) and provide an excellent background for initiating this discussion. In addition to those already noted, they include (a) "an emphasis on the identification of the . . . organism rather than on the identification of the disease entity nonspecific vaginitis," (b) the utilization of culture methods with variable sensitivities for detecting *G. vaginalis* yielding disparate isolation rates in populations studied, thereby creating (c) lack of clarification of that organism's status as a member of normal vaginal flora or as a pathogen, (d) confusion over the significance of coexisting aerobic and anaerobic bacteria, and (e) "a lack of uniform case definition" (104).

Gardner and Dukes defined NSV as a bacterial vaginitis due to a gram-negative bacillus, designated *H. vaginalis*, which they isolated from 92 percent of 311 patients with abnormal discharge and from none of the control patients with normal discharge. Diagnosis was based on very specific characteristics of the discharge: a thin, gray, homogeneous, malodorous discharge that was increased in volume and adherent to the vaginal wall, with a pH of 5 to 5.6, constituted the requisite specimen. "Clue cells," cornified, squamous vaginal epithelial cells that had a stippled, granular appearance with obscured borders due to the adherence of the small bacilli to the cell surface, were first described. The investigators also recovered *H. vaginalis* from the urethra of 96 percent of 47 husbands of women with NSV but not from 20 medical student volunteers (104). Evaluation of the therapeutic regimens revealed the highest cure with vaginal tetracycline (97 percent) (105). Vontver and Eschenbach (104) summarize: "Gardner and Dukes thoroughly investigated the entity of NSV. They described the clinical and laboratory characteristics of NSV, including the description of the clue cell, . . . associated a single organism, *H. vaginalis*, . . . recommended a treatment regimen, and recognized a male role. . . . This research provided a basis for all further NSV study."

Unfortunately, subsequent studies failed to confirm various aspects of the Gardner and Duke investigation. Similar isolation rates of *G. vaginalis* in symptomatic and asymptomatic women caused researchers to seriously question what, if any, role this organism had in NSV. Variations in isolation rates, we now know, derived from using alternate criteria in defining NSV. In fact, "failure to use criteria independent of symptoms in the diagnosis of vaginitis may represent the largest single factor producing discrepancies between the association of *G. vaginalis* in the various studies" (104).

Pheifer and his Seattle co-workers (107) returned to the clinical criteria of

Gardner and Dukes in their assessment of prevalence and treatment in NSV. They found *G. vaginalis* in 91 percent of the symptomatic women with an abnormal discharge, in 80 percent of the asymptomatic women with an abnormal discharge, and in none of the asymptomatic women with normal discharge, clearly correlating the presence of the organism with an abnormal discharge rather than with symptoms. They also demonstrated that anaerobic bacteria were increased in patients with NSV (107).

Spiegel, from the same group, further evaluated the role of these anaerobes in nonspecific vaginitis with quantitative culture techniques and gas-liquid chromatography. Nonvolatile organic acids produced by these anaerobes were analyzed, and specific organic acid patterns emerged as detailed elsewhere 108, which were then predictive of bacterial colonization. Results demonstrated that while *G. vaginalis* was the most prominent organism in NSV (recovered from 52 of 53 patients), bacteroides species and peptococci were also "significantly in 219 creased as shown by quantitative . . . culture" (108). Subsequent in treatment with metronidazole caused return to normal organic acid patterns in 20 of 21 patients, documenting that "anaerobic bacteria do have an important role in the pathogenesis of this disease" because of "the efficacy of metronidazole, which is highly active against anaerobes and only moderately active against *G. vaginalis*" (108).

Amsel et al. (109) studied 397 women presenting for routine exam and attempted to correlate specific combinations of clinical criteria with the recovery of *G. vaginalis* (see Table 11.4). They found that NSV ranged from 12 to 15 percent, as determined by the various diagnostic criteria. Colonization rate for *G. vaginalis* using a highly selective culture medium was 51 percent, and "the prevalence of *G. vaginalis* was significantly higher among patients with NSV" (109) regardless of which criteria for NSV were employed. Only 39 percent of the women from whom *G. vaginalis* was isolated had NSV, for example, using criteria B; also, according to quantitative culture techniques, "those with NSV have a higher concentration of *G. vaginalis* than those without NSV" (109).

Thus, the authors clearly dissociate NSV as defined by Gardner and Dukes and others (107, 108) from the colonization with *G. vaginalis* clarifying the difference and reconciling the various contradictory studies of the past decade. Moreover, while research methodology was employed, the criteria defined in the last two studies are fully applicable to office gynecology, enabling clinicians to diagnose and treat this illusive condition with greater precision.

Treatment

In its guidelines for treatment, the CDC provides an accurate descriptive summary of nonspecific vaginitis or "vaginal discharge associated with *Gardnerella vaginalis*":

This syndrome consists of nonirritating, odoriferous, thin, grayish-white vaginal discharge; elevated vaginal pH (greater than 4.5); and the elaboration of malodorous amines

Table 11.4
Diagnostic Classification of 311 Consecutive Patients According to Various Criteria for Nonspecific Vaginitis

Criteria†	Patients with Nonspecific Vaginitis			Normal Patients		
	No. (%)	Clue Cells Present	G. vaginalis Isolated‡	No. (%)	Clue Cells Present	G. vaginalis Isolated‡
A	36 (12)	35	21/21	275 (88)	37	80/183
B	69 (22)	61	41/44	242 (78)	11	64/160
C	64 (21)	—§	39/40	247 (79)	—§	62/164
D	77 (25)	—§	45/48	234 (75)	—§	56/156

* Excludes 72 patients with other genital infection and 14 patients with incomplete data.
† Criteria sets used for diagnosis of nonspecific vaginitis: **A** = pH above 4.5, nonspecific vaginitis discharge, and positive potassium hydroxide odor; **B** = any three of: pH above 4.5, nonspecific vaginitis discharge, positive potassium hydroxide odor, abnormal amines; **C** = any three of: pH above 4.5, nonspecific vaginitis discharge, positive potassium hydroxide odor, clue cells; **D** = any three of: pH above 4.5, nonspecific vaginitis discharge, positive potassium hydroxide odor, abnormal amines, clue cells.
‡ Isolation on selective medium (HB agar) described in text.
§ Not given; clue cells included in diagnostic criteria.

Source: R. Amsel, et al., Nonspecific vaginitis: diagnostic criteria and microbial and epidemiologic associations. The American Journal of Medicine, 74, January 1983.

from discharge fluid after alkalinization with KOH. Microscopic examination typically reveals the absence of gram-positive rods and the presence of . . . "clue cells." It is now believed that gardnerellae act synergistically with anaerobic bacteria to produce the syndrome (69).

Recommendations for treatment include metronidazole 500 mg p.o. B.I.D. for seven days or ampicillin 500 mg Q.I.D. for pregnant patients or individuals in whom metronidazole is contraindicated, although the latter regimen is "less effective." Other sources recommend ampicillin as the first-line treatment, on the grounds that "the safety of the use of metronidazole for nonspecific vaginitis has not yet been established" (110).

Conclusion

Thus nonspecific vaginitis has been well defined as a clinical entity and its relationship to *Gardnerella vaginalis* and presumably synergistic anaerobic bacteria finally clarified. Clinical criteria for accurate diagnosis have been established and treatment alternatives listed. Further research, if conducted along the guidelines of the last three studies (107–109), should elucidate the role of sexual transmission, the specific mode of interaction between the relevant pathogenic bacteria, and the mechanism of action of effective therapeutic regimens.

REFERENCES

1. Holmes, K. K. Introduction: classification of sexually transmitted diseases. In: Holmes, K. K., and Mardh, P. A., eds., International Perspectives on Neglected Sexually Transmitted Diseases. Washington, D.C.: Hemisphere, 1983.
2. Holmes, K. K., and Mardh, P. A. Preface. In: Holmes, K. K., and Mardh, P. A., eds., International Perspectives on Neglected Sexually Transmitted Diseases. Washington, D.C.: Hemisphere, 1983.
3. Gunby, P. Primary care medicine: chlamydial infections probably the most prevalent of STDs. Arch. Int. Med., 143:1665, 1983.
4. Schachter, J. Chlamydial infections. N. Eng. J. Med., 298:428–435, 490–495, 540–549, 1978.
5. Schachter, J. Chlamydia trachomatis. In: Holmes, K. K., and Mardh, P. A., eds., International Perspectives on Neglected Sexually Transmitted Diseases. Washington, D.C.: Hemisphere, 1983.
6. Sng, E. H. Laboratory diagnosis. In: Holmes, K. K., and Mardh, P. A., eds., International Perspectives on Neglected Sexually Transmitted Diseases. Washington, D.C.: Hemisphere, 1983.
7. Schachter, J. Diagnosis of chlamydia infections. In: Sexually Transmitted Disease, Symposium Proceedings. New York: Science and Medicine, 1979.
8. Scientists develop new test to diagnose V.D. in minutes. New York Times, February 4, 1983.
9. Medical news: two new tests for chlamydia get quick results without culture. JAMA, 250:2257–2259, 1983.

10. Wang, S. P. and Grayston, J. T. Human serology in *Chlamydia trachomatis* infection with microimmunofluorescence. J. Inf. Dis., 130:338–393, 1974.

11. Osser, J. and Persson, K. Epidemiologic and serodiagnostic aspects of chlamydial salpingitis. Obstet. and Gynecol. 59:207–209, 1982.

12. Schachter, J.; Cles, L.; Ray, R.; and Hines, P. A. Failure of serology in diagnosing chlamydial infections of the female genital tract. Clin. Microbiol., 10:647–649, 1979.

13. Bowie, W. R.; Wang, S. P.; Alexander, E. R; Floyd, J.; Forsyth, P. S.; Pollock, H. M.; Lin, J. L.; Buchanan, T. M; and Holmes, K. K. Etiology of nongonococcal urethritis: evidence for *Chlamydia trachomatis* and *Ureaplasma urealyticum*. J. Clin. Invest., 59:735–742, 1977.

14. Johnson, F. W. A.; Hobson, D.; Rees, E.; and Tait, I. A. Quantitative aspects of the growth of *Chlamydia trachomatis* in diagnostic tissue culture procedures. In: Holmes, K. K. and Hobsen, D., eds., Nongonococcal Urethritis and Related Infections, American Society for Microbiology, Washington, D.C., 1977.

15. Ripa, K. T. and Mardh, P. A. Cultivation of *Chlamydia trachomatis* in cycloheximide-treated McCoy cells. J. Clin. Microbiol., 6:328–330, 1977.

16. Embil, J. A.; Thiebaux, H. J.; Manuel, F. R.; Pereira, L. H.; and MacDonald, S. W. Sequential cervical specimens and the isolation of *Chlamydia trachomatis*: factors affecting detection. Sex. Trans. Dis., 10:62–66, 1983.

17. Woolfitt, J. M. G., and Watt, L. Chlamydial infection of the urogenital tract in prosmiscuous and non-promiscuous women. Br. J. Vener. Dis., 53:93–95, 1977.

18. McCormack, W. M.; Evard, J. R.; Laughlin, C.E.; Rosner, B.; Alpert, S. A.; Crockett, V. A.; McComb, D.; and Zinner, S. H. Sexually transmitted conditions among women college students. Am. J. Obstet. Gynecol., 139: 130–133, 1981.

19. Paavonen, J.; Saikku, P.; Vesterinen, E.; Meyer, B.; Vartiainen, E.; and Saksela, E. Genital chlamydial infections in patients attending a gynaecological outpatient clinic. Br. J. Vener. Dis., 54:257–261, 1978.

20. Johannisson, G. Studies on *Chlamydia trachomatis* as a cause of lower urogenital tract infection. In: Acta Dermato-Venereologica, Supplment 93. Stockholm: Almqvist and Wiksell, 1981.

21. Svensson, L.; Westrom, L.; and Mardh, P. A. *Chlamydia trachomatis* in women attending a gynaecological outpatient clinic with lower genital tract infection. Br. J. Vener. Dis., 57:259–262, 1981.

22. Podgore, J. K.; Holmes, K. K.; and Alexander, E. R. Asymptomatic urethral infections due to *Chlamydia trachomatis* in male U.S. military personnel. J. Inf. Dis., 146:828, 1982.

23. McCormack, W. M.; Alpert, S.; McComb, D. E.; Nichols, R. L.; Semine, D. Z; and Zinner, S. H. Fifteen-month followup study of women infected with *Chlamydia trachomatis*. N. Eng. J. Med., 300:123–125, 1979.

24. Holmes, K. K. The chlamydia epidemic. JAMA, 245:1718–1723, 1981.

25. Ghadiran, F. D. and Robson, H. *Chlamydia trachomatis* genital infections. Br. J. Vener. Dis. 55:415–420, 1979.

26. Tait, I. A.; Rees, E; Bryng, R.; and Tweedie, M. C. K. Chlamydia infection of the cervix in contacts of men with nongonococcal urethritis. Br. J. Vener. Dis. 56:37–42, 1980.

27. Hobson, D; Karayiannis, P.; Byng, R. E.; Rees, E.; Tait, I. A.; and Davies, J. A.

Quantitative aspects of chlamydial infection of the cervix. Br. J. Vener. Dis., 56:156–162, 1980.

28. Cevenini, R., and LaPlaca, M. Chlamydial infections in Italy. Sex. Trans. Dis., 8:349–352, 1981.

29. Brunham, R. C.; Kuo, C. C; Stevens, C. E.; and Holmes, K. K. Therapy of cervical chlamydial infection. Ann. Int. Med., 97:216–219, 1982.

30. Rees, E.; Tait, I. A.; Hobsen, D.; and Johnson, F. W. A. Chlamydia in relation to cervical infection and pelvic inflammatory disease. In: Holmes, K. K. and Hobsen, D., eds., Nongonococcal Urethritis and Related Infections, American Society for Microbiology, Washington, D.C., 1977.

31. Schachter, J.; Hill, E. C.,; King, E. B.; Coleman, V. R.; Jones, P.; Meyer, K. F. Chlamydial infections in women with cervical dysplasia. Am. J. Obstet. Gynecol., 123:753–757, 1975.

32. Paavonen, J.; Vesterinen, E.; Meyer, B; Saikku, P.; Suni, J.; Purola, E.; and Saksela, E. Genital Chlamydia trachomatis infections in patients with cervical atypia. Obstet. Gynecol., 54:289–291, 1979.

33. Hare, M. J.; Taylor-Robinson, D.; and Cooper, P. Evidence for an association between Chlamydia trachomatis and cervical intraepithelial neoplasia. Br. J. Obstet. Gynecol., 89:489–492, 1982.

34. Schachter, J.; Hill, E. C.; King, E. B.; Heibron, D. C.; Ray, R.; Margolis, A. J.; and Greenwood, S. A. Chlamydia trachomatis and cervical neoplasms. JAMA, 248:2134–2138, 1982.

35. Infectious Diseases, February 1983, pp. 1, 4.

36. Judson, F. N. Epidemiology and control of nongonococcal urethritis and genital chlamydial infections: a review. Sex. Trans. Dis., 8:117–126, 1980.

37. Bowie, W. Urethritis in men. In: Holmes, K. K., and Mardh, P. A., eds., International Perspectives on Neglected Sexually Transmitted Diseases. Washington, D.C.: Hemisphere, 1983.

38. Paavonen, J. Chlamydia trachomatis-induced urethritis in female partners of men with nongonococcal urethritis. Sex. Trans. Dis., 6:60–71, 1979.

39. Paavonen, J.; Saikku, P.; Vesterinen, E.; Meyer, B.; Vartiainen, E.; and Saksela, E. Genital chlamydial infections in patients attending a gynaecological outpatient clinic. Br. J. Vener. Dis., 54:257–261, 1978.

40. Paavonen, J.; Kousa, M.; Saikku, P.; Vesterinen, E.; Jansson, E.; and Lassus, A. Examination of men with nongonococcal urethritis and their sexual partners for Chlamydia trachomatis and Ureaplasma urealyticum. Sex. Trans. Dis., 5:93–96, 1978.

41. Johannisson, G.; Lowhagen, G. B.; and Lycke, E. Genital Chlamydia trachomatis infection in women. Obstet. Gynecol., 56:671–675, 1980.

42. Stamm, W. E.; Wagner, K. F.; Amsel, R.; Alexander, E. R.; Turck, M.; Counts, G. W; and Holmes, K. K. Causes of the acute urethral syndrome in women. N. Eng. J. Med., 303:409–415, 1980.

43. Panja, S. K. Urethral syndrome in women attending a clinic for sexually transmitted diseases. Br. J. Vener. Dis., 59:179–181, 1983.

44. Mardh, P. A.; Ripa, K. T.; Svensson, L.; and Westrom, L. Chlamydia trachomatis infection in patients with acute salpingitis. N. Eng. J. Med., 296:1377–1379, 1977.

45. Treharne, J. D.; Ripa, K. T.; Mardh, P. A.; Svensson, L.; Westrom, L.; and

Darougar, S. Antibodies to *Chlamydia trachomatis* in acute salpingitis. Br. J. Vener. Dis., 55:26–29, 1979.

46. Paavonen, J.; Saikku, P.; Vesterinen, E.; and Aho, K. *Chlamydia trachomatis* in acute salpingitis. Br. J. Vener. Dis., 55:203–206, 1979.

47. Paavonen, J. *Chlamydia trachomatis* in acute salpingitis. Am. J. Obstet. Gynecol., 138:957–959, 1980.

48. Ripa, K. T.; Svensson, L.; Treharne, J. D.; Westrom, L.; and Mardh, P.A. *Chlamydia trachomatis* infection in patients with laparascopically verified acute salpingitis: results of isolation and antibody determination. Am. J. Obstet. Gynecol., 138:960–964, 1980.

49. Svensson, L.; Westrom, L.; and Mardh, P. A. Acute salpingitis with *Chlamydia trachomatis* isolated from the Fallopian tubes: clinical, cultural, and serologic findings. Sex. Trans. Dis., 8:51–55, 1981.

50. Moller, B. R.; Mardh, P. A.; Ahrons, S.; and Nussler, E. Infection with *Chlamydia trachomatis*, *Mycoplasma hominis* and *Neisseria gonorrhoeae* in patients with acute pelvic inflammatory disease. Sex. Tans. Dis., 8:198–202, 1981.

51. Gjonnaess, H.; Dalaker, K.; Anestad, G.; Mardh, P. A.; Kvile, G.; and Bergan, T. Pelvic inflammatory disease: etiologic studies with emphasis on chlamydial infection. Obstet. Gynecol., 59:550–555, 1982.

52. Mardh, P. A.; Westrom, L.; Ripa, K. T.; and Moller, B. R. Pelvic inflammatory disease: clinical, etiologic, and pathophysiologic studies. In: Holmes, K. K., and Mardh, P. H., eds., International Perspectives on Neglected Sexually Transmitted Diseases. Washington, D.C.: Hemisphere, 1983.

53. Henry-Suchet, J.; Catalan, F.; Loffredo, V.; Serafty, D.; Siboulet, A.; Perol, Y.; Sanson, M. J.; Debache, C.; Pigeau, F.; Coppin, R.; deBrun, J.; Poynard, T. Microbiology of specimens obtained by laparoscopy from controls and from patients with pelvic inflammatory disease or infertility with tubal obstruction: *Chlamydia trachomatis* and *Ureaplasma urealyticum*. Am. J. Obstet. Gynecol, 138:1022–1025, 1980.

54. Litt, I. F. and Cohen, M. I. Perihepatitis associated with salpingitis in adolescents. JAMA, 240:1253–1254, 1978.

55. Semchyshyn, S. Fitz-Hugh and Curtis syndrome. J. Reprod. Med., 22:45–48, 1979.

56. Muller-Schoop, J. W.; Wang, S. P.; Munziger, J.; Schlapfer, H. U.; Knoblaugh, M.; and Amman, R. W. *Chlamydia trachomatis* as a possible cause of peritonitis and perihepatitis in young women. Br. Med. J., 1:1022–1024, 1979.

57. Paavonen, J., and Valtonen, V. V. *Chlamydia trachomatis* as a possible cause of peritonitis and perihepatitis in a young woman. Br. J. Vener. Dis., 56:341–343, 1980.

58. Wolner-Hansen, P.; Westrom, L; and Mardh, P. A. Perihepatitis and chlamydial salpingitis. *The Lancet*, 1:901–904, 1980.

59. Wang, S.; Eschenbach, D. A.; Holmes, K. K.; Wager, G.; and Grayston, J. T. *Chlamydia trachomatis* infection in Fitz-Hugh Curtis syndrome. Am. J. Obstet. Gynecol., 138:1034–1038, 1980.

60. Dalaker, K; Gjonnaess, H.; Kvile, G; Urnes, A.; Arnestad, G.; and Bergan, T. *Chlamydia trachomatis* as a cause of acute perihepatitis associated with pelvic inflammatory disease. Br. J. Vener. Dis., 57:41–43, 1981.

61. Clair, J. and Kurtz, J. B. *Chlamydia trachomatis* and upper abdominal pain. *The Lancet*, 1:1044–1045, 1983.

62. Mardh, P. A.; Helin, I.; Bobeck, S.; Laurin, J.; and Nilsson, T. Colonization of pregnant and puerperal women and neonates with *Chlamydia trachomatis*. Br. J. Vener. Dis., 56:96–100, 1980.

63. Wager, G. P.; Martin, D. H.; Koutsky, L.; Eschenbach, D. A.; Daling, J. R.; Chiang, W. T.; Alexander, E.R.; and Holmes, K. K. Puerperal infectious morbidity: relationship to route of delivery and to antepartum *Chlamydiatrachomatis* infection. Am. J. Obstet. Gynecol, 138:1028–1033, 1980.

64. Qvigstad, E.; Jerve, F.; and Skaug, K. *Chlamydia trachomatis* at first trimester of pregnancy: a microbiologic and serologic study. Br. J. Vener. Dis., 58:179–183, 1982.

65. Moller, B. K.; Ahrons, S.; Laurin, J.; and Mardh, P. A.; Pelvic infection after elective abortion associated with *Chlamydia trachomatis*. Obstet. Gynecol., 59:210–213, 1982.

66. Westergaard, L.; Philipsen, T.; and Scheiber, J. Significance of cervical *Chlamydia trachomatis* infection in postabortal pelvic inflammatory disease. Obstet. Gynecol., 60:322–325, 1982.

67. Martin, D. H.; Koutsky, L.; Eschenbach, D. A.; Daling, J. R.; Alexander, E. R.; Benedetti, J. K.; and Holmes, K. K. Prematurity and perinatal mortality in pregnancies complicated by maternal *Chlamydia trachomatis* infections. JAMA, 247:1585–1588, 1982.

68. Harrison, H. R.; Alexander, E. R.; Weinstein, L.; Lewis, M.; Nash, M.; and Sim, A. Cervical *Chlamydia trachomatis* and mycoplasmal infections in pregnancy. JAMA, 250:1721–1727, 1983.

69. Sexually Transmitted Diseases Treatment Guidelines 1982. MMWR supplement, 31:33S–60S, 1982.

70. Waugh, M. A., and Nayyar, K. C.; Triple tetracycline (Deteclo) in the treatment of chlamydial infection of the female genital tract. Br. J. Vener. Dis., 53:96–97, 1977.

71. Paavonen, J.; Kousa, M.; Saikku, P.; Vartiainen, E.; Kanerva, L.; and Lassus, A. Treatment of nongonococcal urethritis with trimethoprim-sulfadiazine and with placebo. Br. J. Vener. Dis., 56:101–104, 1980.

72. Lassus, A.; Paavonen, J.; Kousa, M.; and Saikku, P. Erythromycin and lymecycline treatment in *Chlamydia*-positive and *Chlamydia*-negative non-gonococcal urethritis: a partner controlled study. Acta Derm. Vener. 59:278–281, 1979.

73. Bowie, W. R.; Manzon, L. M.; Borrie-Hume, C. J.; Fawcett, A.; and Jones, H. D. Efficacy of treatment regimens for lower urogenital *Chlamydia trachomatis* infection in women. Am. J. Obstet. Gynecol., 142:125–129, 1982.

74. Robson, H. G.; Pramod, P. S.; Lalonde, R. G.; Hayes, L.; and Senikas, V. M. Comparison of Rosarimicin and Erythromycin stearate for treatment of cervical infection with *Chlamydia trachomatis*. Sex. Trans. Dis., 10:130–133, 1983.

75. Gjonnaess, H. Doxycycline in pelvic inflammatory disease. In: Sexually Transmitted Disease, Symposium Proceedings. New York: Science and Medicine, 1979.

76. Sweet, R. L.; Schachter, J.; and Robbie, M. O. Failure of B-lactam antibiotics to eradicate *Chlamydia trachomatis* in the endometrium despite apparent cure of acute salpingitis. JAMA, 250:2641–2645, 1983.

77. Black, F. T. *Ureaplasma urealyticum* and *Mycoplasma hominis*. In: Holmes, K. K., and Mardh, P. A., eds., International Perspectives on Neglected Sexually Transmitted Diseases. Washington, D.C.: Hemisphere, 1983.

78. McCormack, W. M.; Braun, P.; Lee, Y.-H.; Klein, J. O.; and Kass, E. H. The genital mycoplasmas, N. Eng. J. Med., 288:78–89, 1973.
79. Taylor-Robinson, D., and McCormack, W. M. The genital mycoplasmas. N. Eng. J. Med., 302:1003–1010, 1063–1067, 1980.
80. McCormack, W. M.; Moller, B. R.; and Mardh, P. A. Symposia: *Mycoplasma hominis*, a human pathogen. Sex. Trans. Dis., 10:160–165, 1983.
81. Klein, I. O.; Buckland, D.; and Finland, M. Colonization of newborn infants by mycoplasmas. N. Eng. J. Med., 280:1025–1030, 1969.
82. Foy, H. M.; Kenny, G. E.; Levinson, E. M.; and Grayston, J. T. Acquisition of mycoplasmata and T-strains during infancy. J. Inf. Dis., 121:579–587, 1970.
83. McCormack, W. M.; Almeida, P.C.; Bailey, P. E.; Grady, E. M.; and Lee, Y.-H. Sexual activity and vaginal colonization with genital mycoplasmas. JAMA, 221:1375–1377, 1972.
84. Hammerschlag, M. R.; Alpert, S.; and Rosner, I. Microbiology of the vagina in children: normal and potentially pathogenic organisms. Pediatrics, 62:57–62, 1978.
85. Mardh, P. A. An overview of infectious agents of salpingitis, their biology, and recent advances in methods of detection. Am. J. Obstet. Gynecol., 138:933–951, 1980.
86. Osborne, N. G.; Grubin, L.; and Pratson, L. Vaginitis in sexually active women: relationship to nine sexually transmitted organisms. Am. J. Obstet. Gynecol., 142:962–967, 1982.
87. Mardh, P. A., and Westrom L. Tubal and cervical cultures in acute salpingitis with special reference to *Mycoplasma hominis* and T-strain mycoplasmas. Brit. J. Vener. Dis., 46:179–186, 1970.
88. Mardh, P. A., and Westrom, L. Antibodies to *Mycoplasma hominis* in patients with genital infections and in healthy controls. Br. J. Vener. Dis., 46:390–397, 1970.
89. Mardh, P. A. Increased serum levels of IgM in acute salpingitis related to the occurrence of *Mycoplasma hominis*. Acta Pathol. Microbiol. Scand., 78:726–732, 1970.
90. Eschenbach, D. A.; Buchanan, T. M.; Pollock, H. M.; Forsyth, P. S.; Alexander, E. R., Lin, Y.-S.; Wang, S. P.; Wentworth, B. B.; McCormack, W. M.; and Holmes, K. K. Polymicrobial etiology of acute pelvic inflammatory disease. N. Eng. J. Med., 293:166–171, 1975.
91. Mardh, P. A.; Lind, I.; Svensson, L.; Westrom, L.; and Moller, B. R. Antibodies to *Chlamydia trachomatis*, *Mycoplasma hominis*, and *Neisseria gonorrhoeae* in patients with acute salpingitis. Br. J. Vener. Dis., 57:125–129, 1981.
92. Moller, B. R.; Freundt, E. A.; Black, F. T.; and Fredericksen, P. Experimental infection of the genital tract of female grivet monkeys by *Mycoplasmahominis*. Infect. Immun., 20:248–257, 1978.
93. Mardh, P. A.; Westrom, L.; von Mecklenburg, C.; and Hammar, E. Studies on ciliated epithelium of the human genital tract, I: Swelling of the cilia of Fallopian tube epithelium in organ cultures infected with *Mycoplasma hominis*. Br. J. Vener. Dis., 52:52–57, 1976.
94. Stray-Pedersen, B. Female genital colonization with *Ureaplasma urealyticum* and reproductive failure. In Sexually Transmitted Disease, Symposium Proceedings. New York: Science and Medicine, 1979.
95. Quinn, P. A.; Shewchuk, A. B.; Shuber, J.; Lie, K. I.; Ryan, E.; Sheu, M.; and

Chipman, M. L. Serologic evidence of *Ureasplasma urealyticum* infection in women with spontaneous pregnancy loss. Am. J. Obstet. Gynecol., 145:245–250, 1983.

96. Kundsin, R. B. Mycoplasma in genitourinary tract infection and reproductive failure. In: Sturgis, S. H., and Taymor, M., eds., Progress in Gynecology, Vol. V. New York: Grune and Stratton, 1970.

97. Friberg, J. Mycoplasma and infertility. In Sexually Transmitted Disease, Symposium Proceedings. New York: Science and Medicine, 1979.

98. Friberg, J., and Gnarpe, H. Mycoplasma and human reproductive failure, III: Pregnancies in "infertile" couples treated with doxycycline for T-mycoplasmas. Am. J. Obstet. Gynecol., 116:23–26, 1973.

99. DeLouvois, J.; Blades, M.; Harrison, R. F.; Hurley, R.; and Stanley, V. C. Frequency of mycoplasma in fertile and infertile couples. *The Lancet*, i:1073–1075, 1974.

100. Stray-Pedersen, B.; Eng, J.; and Reikvam, T. M. Uterine T-mycoplasma colonization in reproductive failure. Am. J. Obstet. Gynecol., 130:307–311, 1978.

101. Stray-Pedersen, B.; Bruu, A. L.; and Molne, K. Infertility and uterine colonization with *Ureaplasma urealyticum*. Acta Obstet. Gynecol. Scand., 61:21–24, 1982.

102. Toth, A.; Lessner, M. L.; Brooks, C.; and Labriola, D. Subsequent pregnancies among 161 couples treated for T-mycoplasma genital tract infection. N. Eng. J. Med., 308:505–507, 1983.

103. Dunkleberg, W. E. *Gardenerella (Haemophilus) vaginalis*. In: Holmes, K. K., and Mardh, P.A., eds., International Perspectives on Neglected Sexually Transmitted Diseases. Washington, D.C.: Hemisphere, 1983.

104. Vontver, L. A., and Eschenbach, D. A. The Role of *Gardnerella vaginalis* in nonspecific vaginitis. Clin. Obstet. Gynecol., 24:439–460, 1981.

105. Gardner, H. L., and Dukes, C. D. *Haemophilus vaginalis* vaginitis. Am. J. Obstet. Gynecol., 69:962–976, 1955.

106. McCormack, W. M.; Hayes, C.H.; Rosner, B.; Evrard, J. R.; Crocket, V. A.; Alpert S.; and Zinner, S. H. Vaginal colonization with *Corynebacterium vaginale (Haemophilus vaginalis)*. J. Inf. Dis., 136:740–745, 1977.

107. Pheifer, T. A.; Forsyth, P. S.; Durfee, M. A.; Pollock, H.M.; and Holmes, K. K. Nonspecific vaginitis: role of *Haemophilus vaginalis* and treatment with metronidazole. N. Eng. J. Med., 198:1429–1434, 1978.

108. Spiegel, C. A.; Amsel, R.; Eschenbach, D.; Schoenknecht, F.; and Holmes, K. K. Anaerobic bacteria in nonspecific vaginitis. N. Eng. J. Med., 303:601–607, 1980.

109. Amsel, R.; Totten, P. A.; Spiegel, C. A.; Chen, K. C. S.; Eschenbach, D.; and Holmes, K. K. Nonspecific vaginitis: diagnostic criteria and microbial and epidemiologic associations. Am. J. Med., 74:14–22, 1983.

110. Robbie, M. O., and Sweet, R. L. Metronidazole use in obstetrics and gynecology: a review. Am. J. Obstet. Gynecol., 145:865–881, 1983.

Menstrual Cycle Symptoms from a Developmental Perspective

INTRODUCTION

Symptoms in Normal Women

Women are caught in a double bind when it comes to menstrual cycle symptoms. If they admit to having menstrual cramps or the mood changes that sometimes accompany the premenstrual phase of the cycle, accusations of female impairment quickly follow. On the other hand, if women deny or play down menstrual pain, breast tenderness, symptoms of water retention, and so on, researchers give menstruation short shrift and physicians minimize the importance of menstrual discomfort.

The truth is that premenstrual symptoms are widespread. Common symptoms are weight gain, headache, skin disorders, cramps, backache, fatigue, painful breasts, irritability, mood swings, anxiety, and depression. Studies differ as to the incidence of many of these symptoms, but several studies of U.S. and European nonclinical populations report a symptom incidence of more than 25 percent (1–5). Thus the data suggest that a significant proportion of women are affected by menstrual symptoms. However, it is important to note that only a small proportion (2 to 8 percent) suffer disabling symptoms.

The symptoms seem to divide fairly readily into two groups. Those more characteristic of the menstrual phase of the cycle are cramps, backache, tension, and fatigue. In the premenstruum, irritability, depression, anxiety, water retention, and breast tenderness are more likely. Categorizing symptoms as menstrual or premenstrual is particularly useful in studying developmental changes because the prevalence and intensity of each group appears to be age-related.

Anecdotal and research data suggest that young women more often experience dysmenorrhea and mood disturbance during menstruation, with less premenstrual discomfort, whereas older women are more likely to complain of premenstrual distress (6–9, 3). Premenstrual complaints have been reported to rise in the mid-20s and peak in the mid-30s (10–14).

While few studies specifically address the relationship between age and menstrual cycle symptoms, many have relevant data. This chapter will present the results of a review of the literature that focused on developmental changes. However, it is important to keep in mind that the studies reviewed are not all of comparable quality.

Research Problems

In trying to find the causes and effects of menstrual-cycle-related symptoms, researchers are confronted with a number of methodological problems. For example, who are the subjects? Are they normal women, gynecological patients, psychiatric patients, schoolgirls, prisoners, or some other select group? In reviewing the literature one finds that all these groups have been studied. However, in view of their obvious differences in age, socioeconomic status, and physical and mental health, the comparability of much of the data obtained from these different groups is questionable.

Similarly, what methods have been used to collect the data? The retrospective questionnaire has probably been used most often in menstrual research. Women are asked to report their recollections of symptoms at different times during the cycle. The problem here is how well do the women remember? Are the recollections reliable? Do the women tend to average-out their experiences with menstrual symptoms, or do they report their worst cycles? When studies in which daily self-reports or mood scales taken at specific points in the cycle are compared with retrospective questionnaires, they often do not agree (15, 7, 16, 18). This disparity between daily measures and retrospective reports may be due to any number of things, among them flaws in the instruments used (the instruments may not be sensitive enough to pick up subtle changes that the women perceive in themselves), symptom variability from month to month, or stereotypic attitudes about menstruation causing women to report what is expected. Parlee (19) found that both men and women respond similarly when asked to describe the menstrual symptoms women experience, suggesting that questionnaires may tap stereotypic beliefs about symptoms rather than actual experience.

There is also the problem of experimenter bias. Experimenters share the same negative attitudes about menstruation that pervade the rest of the culture. Most studies of the menstrual cycle have focused on the negative consequences of menstruation, for example, the relationship between violent crime or suicide and cycle phase (6, 20–22). Many researchers have looked for menstrual debilitation, and most assume that whatever fluctuations are found are hormonally based, despite the lack of experimental evidence to support such a supposition (23, 24, 18). The complex interplay of physiological, personality, and experiential variables is often ignored, and there is an attempt to gain understanding of a complex phenomenon by reducing it to something that seems more easy to study.

Koeske (25) points out that we seem to assume that women's negative behavior must be explained by biology. Female behavior that differs from that traditionally associated with femininity, such as yielding or being cheerful or affectionate, is treated as unhealthy and undesirable (26, 27). And feminists are not immune to these mistakes. In a recent paper, Koeske (28) observes that even feminist researchers have to struggle to find a rational balance that acknowledges the importance of physiological influences on women's bodies as well as the psychosocial factors that interact with them.

All these caveats notwithstanding, menstrual cycle research has improved in the last ten years. Today more studies are being done in which there is a simultaneous determination of hormone levels and psychological variables. Phases of the cycle and related symptom constellations are more consistently defined, and there is a greater awareness of the psychosocial and subcultural factors that influence the menstrual experience, such as religion, attitudes about sexuality, general health, and even secondary gain.

What we do not have are studies that will tell us the incidence and demographic patterns of menstrual disorders. Nor do we have longitudinal studies directed toward answering questions about menstrual-cycle and menstrual-symptom variability over the course of a woman's life. Although there are a few studies of special populations, such as psychiatric patients (29–31, 33), more are needed. And these should include a greater number of studies of subgroups of normal women. For example, do women of different ages, sexual orientations, or religious backgrounds experience menstruation differently? There is some evidence that they do (8, 34). More qualitative data—case studies, in-depth interviews, and naturalistic observations—are needed too.

CULTURAL INFLUENCES

Attitudes

It is difficult to ignore the pervasive negative mental set that exists regarding menstruation in our culture. We have only to look at some of the most popular terms used to allude to it: "the curse," "falling off the roof," "on the rag." Language influences our perception of ourselves and the world around us. In a study of menstruation euphemisms, Ernster (35) found that females reported a much wider variety of terms for menstruation than did males, with the greatest number falling into the category of negative references ("being unwell" and "I've got the misery"). An interesting age-related finding was that females tended to learn menstrual expressions at menarche whereas males learned them later, in high school, college, or the service. Girls, then, learn the menstrual euphemisms before they have had much experience with menstruation, and Ernster suggests that the power of suggestion and social expectations may influence both girls' early attitudes about menstruation and their experience of menstrual distress.

Even preadolescents have negative beliefs about menstruation. In a survey of seventh- and eighth-grade boys and girls, Brooks-Gunn and Ruble (36) found that both sexes had similar and mostly negative perceptions. Most thought that menstruation was accompanied by physical discomfort, increased emotionality, and a disruption of activities. Further, there was an age effect, with younger girls reporting fewer symptoms than the older girls (fifth and sixth grade vs. seventh and eighth grade). Other studies of adolescents also found that menstruation is generally perceived negatively and that postmenarcheal girls have been found to show a greater dislike for menstruation than premenarcheal girls (37).

In 1981 Tampax Incorporated commissioned a large-scale study of attitudes toward menstruation. That research, based on a survey of 1,034 Americans ranging in age from 14 to over 65 who were interviewed by telephone, found that most Americans are still reticent about discussing menstruation openly and that most believe that women experience a significant amount of stress during menstruation. About half believe that menstruation is painful, and 87 percent thought that women are particularly emotional when menstruating. A substantial minority believed that women cannot function as well at work when menstruating. And those who were most likely to perceive menstruation as restrictive were subjects in the youngest and oldest age-groups (14–17 and over 55 years of age).

Education as well as age may be an important variable. Brooks, Ruble, and Clarke (38) found that college women held some positive attitudes toward menstruation. Most of the college women saw it as a way of keeping in touch with their bodies and felt that menstruation reflected a reoccurring affirmation of womanhood. Further, more than half found it predictable, indicating some feeling of control. Although these women also found menstruation to be bothersome, they did not perceive it to be particularly debilitating.

In an attempt to look at age differences in attitudes toward menstruation, Golub and Donnolo (unpublished manuscript) compared a group of mothers and their college-student daughters. The mean ages of the two groups were 46 and 20 years, respectively. Daughters were found to have significantly more positive attitudes than did their mothers, and no significant correlation was found between mothers' and daughters' attitudes toward menstruation. Further, subjects who used tampons or had more liberal sexual attitudes or described themselves as feminists also had significantly more positive attitudes. Educational background may explain some of these mother-daughter differences. Only 47 percent of the mothers had completed one or more years of college, and those with some college education did have more positive attitudes. Also, only 35 percent of the mothers, as opposed to 53 percent of the daughters, considered themselves feminists. Very likely, recent changes in societal attitudes toward women and the current more egalitarian perspective also affects the younger women's more positive attitudes about themselves as women as well as their attitudes about menstruation.

In another study, by Golub, Daly, Ingrando, and Murphy (unpublished manuscript), attitudes of college women, college men, professional nurses, and gay women toward menstruation were studied. The college students ranged in age from 18 to 23, the nurses' age-range was 23–50, and the age-range for the gay women was 17–47. Significant differences were found between the women and the men, with all the female groups demonstrating significantly more positive attitudes. This finding is in keeping with other studies that have found sex differences (39). However, no age differences were found. Gay women had the most positive attitudes toward menstruation, significantly more positive than those of either the male or female college students or the nurses. The gay women were also the most profeminist group.

Attitudes and Symptoms

The relationship between attitudes toward menstruation and symptoms of menstrual distress is a controversial subject. Most of the studies have been only correlational in nature, but that has not stopped some investigators from speculating that women who have negative attitudes are more likely to have symptoms. Few of the studies suggest the possibility that experiencing pain or other symptoms might influence a woman's attitude, a hypothesis that generally appeals to women who have symptoms.

Levitt and Lubin (40), in a study of menstrual complaints and menstrual attitudes, found a correlation of .32 between menstrual complaints and unwholesome attitudes. They concluded that attitude and personality are factors in the etiology of menstrual symptomatology.

Other researchers have also suggested a link between psychological problems and menstrual symptoms (41–44). Some of these studies have been criticized by a number of different authors on methodological grounds (45, 19, 46). And the evidence supporting a relationship between personality and symptoms contradicts studies by Coppen and Kessel (47) and Hirt, Kurtz, and Ross (48), among others, finding no correlation. Nevertheless, in an article discussing the *DSM*-III, painful menstruation is cited as an example of a disorder that might be placed in the category "Psychological Factors Affecting Physical Condition" (49), a conclusion that seems out of keeping with current knowledge. Recent work, particularly looking at dysmenorrhea, failed to find a causal link between attitudes and symptoms (50, 51). Similarly, Goudsmit (52) reviews a number of studies and concludes that there is little evidence that premenstrual symptoms are influenced by attitudes.

Whereas the studies cited above presented data that were not age-related, some researchers have suggested that menarcheal experiences, particularly a lack of preparation for menarche, lead to negative attitudes and the subsequent development of perimenstrual symptoms (53, 54, 44). However, in at least three recent studies no significant relationship was found between adequacy of preparation or early experiences with menstruation and the subsequent experience of menstrual symptoms (55–57). Golub and Catalano (55) found no relationship between attitudes and symptoms or between preparation for menstruation and symptoms. Woods, Dery, and Most (57) did find attitudes to be moderately associated with symptoms, but these authors suggest that the attitudes are probably influenced by the symptoms rather than the other way around.

DYSMENORRHEA

Definition and Incidence

Primary dysmenorrhea is defined as painful menstruation without evidence of anatomic abnormality or other precipitating cause (58). The reported incidence of primary dysmenorrhea ranges from 3 to 70 percent of menstruating women. The wide range reflects the variation in definition and in diagnostic criteria found in the literature (59, 58). A commonly given figure is about 50 percent, with 5 to 10 percent experiencing pain severe enough to be incapacitating for an hour to three days of each month (60). Dysmenorrhea is the most common menstrual disorder, and it is often cited as the greatest single cause of lost school or working days among young women (61). However, studies supporting this observation are contradictory and inconclusive (58).

Typically, menstrual cramps are described as sharp pains in the lower mid-abdomen which may radiate to the lower back or upper thigh. Alternatively, some women complain of congestive dysmenorrhea, in which the pain is described as a steady dull ache, sometimes radiating down the legs and to the suprapubic area (60). Pelvic pain may be accompanied by headache, nausea, and vomiting (61).

Age-Related Changes

Generally the incidence of dysmenorrhea is low around menarche and becomes more severe sometime in the next two years. Dysmenorrhea is usually not observed until after six months of cyclic menstruation, probably because of the frequent occurrence of anovulatory cycles during the first year (63). It is generally agreed that primary dysmenorrhea is related to ovulation (64), but some women report the onset of pain before the end of the first year of menstruation, and some note that the pain started with the earliest menstrual periods. For example, Golub and Catalano (55) found that 30 percent of the women they studied reported pain at menarche.

Dysmenorrhea thus begins in the early teens and becomes most severe in the late teens and early 20s. Bickers (65) noted that the incidence of menstrual cramps in girls under the age of 15 is less than 5 percent but that from the age of 15 to 22 the incidence rises progressively, going from 5 to 30 percent. Other studies also indicate an increasing incidence of dysmenorrhea during the teen years, ranging from 28 to 49 percent (66). Gray (67) found that dysmenorrhea generally appears at age 15 or 16, becomes more severe at 17 or 18, and continues to age 25. Widholm and Kantero (63) found that after the first gynecological

Table 12.1
Menstrual Distress Questionnaire Pain Scale Scores

REFERENCE	MENSTRUAL		PREMENSTRUAL		INTERMENSTRUAL	
	M.	S.D	M.	S.D.	M.	S.D.
Golub & Harrington (1981) Ages: 15–16	17.84	6.52	13.93	7.01	11.95	6.76
Gruba & Rohrbaugh (1975) Ages: 17–23	14.85	5.93	11.70	5.04	–	–
Moos (1968) Ages: mean 25.2	12.59	4.99	10.13	4.25	7.71	2.71
Golub (1983) Ages: 30–45	12.56	4.84	11.56	4.35	8.09	2.86
Maddocks (1983) PMS subjects Ages: 20–45 Mean age: 35	12.67	5.67	16.94	5.31	10.17	3.73

year the incidence of dysmenorrhea tripled, going from 7.2 percent to 25.6 percent in five years. Overall, although about 47 percent of the more than 5,000 girls studied by Widholm and Kantero had completely painless menstruation, 38 percent had pain occasionally and 13 percent experienced it regularly. Moos (3) also found that the younger women in his sample, those under 21, complained of significantly more menstrual pain than did the women over 31 years of age.

After the high incidence of dysmenorrhea seen during the teen years, dysmenorrhea seems to decrease gradually with increasing age. Kessel and Coppen (2) found a significant negative correlation between menstrual pain and age in their sample of 500 women between the ages of 18 and 45. And in a recent study, Woods, Most, and Dery (5) found that the severe dysmenorrhea was reported by 20 to 25 percent of the 18-to-25-year-old women in the sample, but by only 7 percent of the 31-to-35-year-old age-group. Other studies similarly found a decline in dysmenorrhea after age 25 or 30 (1, 68–70, 4).

Age differences in the magnitude of pain experienced are also of interest. Table 12.1 shows Menstrual Distress Questionnaire Pain Scale scores obtained from subjects of different ages in different studies. Younger subjects do experience more menstrual pain.

There have been a few studies that found no significant correlations between age and dysmenorrhea. However, this research was generally done using samples with a limited age-range or groups comprised primarily of young women. For example, Cox, McMahon, and Pennebaker (71) found age to be unrelated to dysmenorrhea, but their subjects ranged in age from "less than 18 years" to "greater than 25 years" with a mean age of 19. Similarly, Gough (42) found no significant correlation between age and pain, but he did not specify the range of his subjects' ages (the mean age was 25.8). Thus most of the research literature to date seems to confirm a relationship between age and dysmenorrhea.

One question remains: How do we separate the effects of age and parity? For the most part, as women get older they are also more likely to bear children. Anecdotally, women will often say that their periods got better after they had a child. And in the past, physicians used to tell women that the pain would disappear when they had a baby. Old wives' tale? Probably not. Svennerud (72), in a study of 890 women, found the frequency of dysmenorrhea to be similar in married and unmarried women in the 20-to-24-year age-group. However, the frequency of dysmenorrhea decreased with age more rapidly in the married women. Although these data were not examined for the effect of parity, it can be assumed that the married women were more likely to have had children. Similarly, over 30 percent of a group of women between the ages of 30 and 45 reported that childbirth had altered their menstrual cramps (55). And in a study of perimenstrual symptoms in which the effect of parity was specifically addressed, Woods, Most, and Dery (5) found that women who had been pregnant were significantly less likely to experience menstrual cramps than were the nulliparas (12.5 percent vs. 21 percent). Thus it seems reasonable to conclude that both age and parity affect the incidence of dysmenorrhea. Dingfelder (59) suggested that the gains in connective tissue and uterine vascularity which occur during pregnancy are related to the subsequent relief of pain.

Etiology and Treatment

Earliest theories about the etiology of dysmenorrhea were anatomical. Cervical obstruction was thought to inhibit the flow of menstrual blood, and the resulting retention of menstrual fluid was thought to cause dysmenorrhea (73). Yet Jollie (74) notes that women who had cervical stenosis secondary to cauterization, cone biopsy, or other gynecological problems did not necessarily experience dysmenorrhea. Similarly fraught with flaws were theories addressing primary dysmenorrhea primarily as a psychosomatic disorder. Current recognition of prostaglandin as the major cause of primary dysmenorrhea has put to rest the idea that menstrual pain is "all in the head."

In 1965, British researcher V. R. Pickles found that prostaglandin was produced by the menstruating uterus and could stimulate contractions of the myometrium. The majority of women with primary dysmenorrhea do have increased contractions of the uterus. Prostaglandins cause these uterine contractions, which result in a reduction in the blood supply to the myometrium, ischemia, and pain that has sometimes been referred to as "uterine angina" (75).

According to Chan (76), it was in 1971 that aspirin and related nonsteroidal anti-inflammatory drugs were found to inhibit prostaglandin synthesis. A new group of prostaglandin synthetase inhibitors was then developed. Flufenamic acid, a prostaglandin synthetase inhibitor, was used for the first time in the treatment of dysmenorrhea in 1972 (77), and since that time a number of other nonsteroidal, anti-inflammatory drugs have been used. These include ibuprofen (Motrin), indomethacin (Indocin), mefenamic acid (Ponstel), and naproxen (Naprosyn). All have been effective in alleviating symptoms of dysmenorrhea. Motrin, Ponstel, and Naprosyn are most commonly prescribed for dysmenorrhea and are relatively free of side effects (78). Contraindications include aspirin-induced asthma, other allergies to aspirin (such as nasal polyps, angioedema, and bronchospastic reactivity to aspirin), ulcers, chronic inflammation of the upper or lower gastrointestinal tract, and renal disease (79).

Oral contraceptives have also been used in the treatment of dysmenorrhea. Since primary dysmenorrhea characteristically occurs in ovulatory cycles, suppression of ovulation leads to a reduction of dysmenorrhea (80). Although there is some evidence that dysmenorrhea may be present in anovulatory cycles as well as (60), Chan (76) suggests that oral contraceptives are effective in treating dysmenorrhea because they inhibit ovulation and also produce hypoplasia of the endometrium, thus reducing the capacity of the endometrium to produce prostaglandin during menstruation. Whether a woman with dysmenorrhea should be treated with oral contraceptives or the prostaglandin synthetase inhibitors depends on several things, among them her need for contraception. The risks and side effects of oral contraceptives may exceed those of the prostaglandin inhibitors, particularly in older women. Therefore, if pain relief is the primary objective, long-term endocrine therapy would seem to be inappropriate. This is especially true in view of the relative safety of the prostaglandin synethetase inhibitors and the need to take them for only one or two days a month.

PREMENSTRUAL SYMPTOMS

Incidence

There is no clear definition of what has come to be known as the premenstrual syndrome (PMS). The number and variety of symptoms included vary widely from one study to another, from one woman to another, and within the same woman from one cycle to another. At best, PMS can be loosely characterized as a group of psychological and somatic symptoms that are limited to the week preceding menstruation and are relieved by the onset of menses. Physical complaints include headache, backache, painful breasts, and symptoms of water retention. Psychological complaints include depression, anxiety, irritability, lethargy, and aggressiveness.

Since there is no accepted general definition of premenstrual syndrome, efforts to compare published data in order to determine the incidence or prevalence of premenstrual problems are apt to be unrewarding. Hence we see cited incidence rates of up to 95 percent among normal women (47, 81–85, 3, 5). In a recent summary of a group of U.S. and European studies of the prevalence of premenstrual symptoms among adult women, the incidence of symptoms ranges from a low of 4 percent for fatigue to a high of 70 percent for irritability (5). These authors also found that their estimates for many symptoms closely resembled those from other studies. However, when they restricted their attention to severe symptoms, as opposed to mild or moderate ones, their prevalence estimates were considerably lower.

Changes Over Time

What is the relationship between age and premenstrual symptoms? In reviewing the literature, one finds that it was Lloyd (12) in 1963 who first noted a realtionship between age and premenstrual symptoms. He referred to these symptoms of irritability and depression as the "mid-thirties syndrome," pointing out that the modal age seems to lie around the thirty-fifth year. There have been many studies since, but few have included a direct look at the relationship between age and symptoms in normal women. Nevertheless, there is some support for the belief that moderate-to-severe premenstrual symptoms are more likely to occur in the 30s and 40s (10, 6, 7, 9, 3, 13, 14), and among patients with premenstrual complaints, the average age reported is in the 30s (10, 86, 32, 9).

It is particularly difficult to assess the relationship between premenstrual symptoms and age because so few studies include women over the age of 30. Most studies are of college or nursing students, who are usually women under 25. And the other populations that have been studied vary greatly, including normal women, PMS patients, prisoners, and psychiatric patients.

However, the incidence of premenstrual symptoms does seem to increase after adolescence. Widholm and Kantero (63) found that edematous symptoms tripled in five years, going from 4.8 percent at age 11.9 to 15.1 percent at age 17. These authors also found a higher incidence of premenstrual symptoms in mothers as compared with their daughters (76 percent for the mothers, compared with 67.5 percent for the daughters).

Moos (3), in a study of 700 women, compared subjects under 21 with those over 31 and found that the older women were significantly more like to complain of symptoms in the premenstrual phase of the cycle. In doing correlations between age and symptoms, Moos noted that the correlation coefficients were low, perhaps indicating that age is not important in explaining menstrual cycle symptoms.

However, the women in this sample were generally young, with a mean age of 25.2 years.

Kramp (9) found an incidence of premenstrual symptoms of 50 percent in his sample of women ranging in age from 15 to 45. There was a peak in the incidence of premenstrual symptoms of about 23 percent among women between the ages of 30 and 39, and another peak between the ages of 20 and 24 of about 20 percent. Kramp also noted an incidence of 30 percent among a group of psychiatric patients between the ages of 35 and 39. He concludes that premenstrual syndrome is most common in the 30-to-40-year age group.

In a study of 145 normal women and psychiatric patients between the ages of 15 and 45, Rees (13) found an incidence of moderate premenstrual tension of about 25 percent among the women who were between 15 and 24 years of age, rising to 31 percent in the 25-to-34-year-old age-group. Severe premenstrual tension was considerably more likely to be found after the age of 24, with an incidence of 30 percent. Rees also found a higher incidence of premenstrual tension among the psychiatric patients. He observed that nearly 80 percent of patients with premenstrual tension started before age 35, and in some, symptoms became worse after childbirth. In another study (14) of a group of patients suffering from severe premenstrual tension, Rees again found an increased incidence with increasing age. In this group the incidence was: 15–24 years, 8 percent; 25–34 years, 56 percent; 35–44 years, 36 percent.

Focusing on the effects of oral contraceptives in a sample of normal women aged 18 to 46, Andersch and Hahn (11) found that nonusers of oral contraceptives over the age of 25 had a significantly higher incidence of premenstrual symptoms. The incidence of irritability among nonusers of oral contraceptives over 25 was 80 percent, while about 40 percent experienced anxiety and sadness. In contrast, among the 18-year-old women the incidence of sadness and anxiety was only 20 percent, half as much.

Dalton (6), who has been studying patients with premenstrual syndrome for many years, reported on the increase in incidence with increasing age both among the childless and in parous women. Again the incidence reaches a peak of about 30 percent among women between the ages of 35 and 44.

A few studies permit comparison between the menstrual and premenstrual scores of subjects of different ages on the Negative Affect Scale of the Menstrual Distress Questionnaire (see Table 12.2). It is notable that the younger women experience more negative affect during the menstrual phase of the cycle, whereas the older women have more negative affect during the premenstrual phase. The youngest group (15-to-16-year-old high school students) have menstrual phase negative affect scores that were higher than those reported by Moos (3), and their premenstrual scores were lower (17.66 vs. 15.79, and 14.66 vs. 16.96).

In order to explore further the relationship between age and premenstrual mood changes, Golub and Harrington (8) gave the Menstrual Distress Questionnaire (MDQ), the Depression Adjective Check List (DACL), and the State Trait Anxiety Inventory to a group of high school students with a mean age of

Table 12.2
Menstrual Distress Questionnaire Negative Affect Scores

REFERENCE	MENSTRUAL		PREMENSTRUAL		INTERMENSTRUAL	
	M	S.D.	M	S.D.	M	S.D.
Golub & Harrington (1981) Ages: 15–16	17.66	7.58	14.66	7.57	13.64	7.11
Gruba & Rohrbaugh (1975) Ages: 17–23	22.15	9.02	20.08	9.86	–	–
Moos (1968) Mean age: 25.2	15.79	7.18	16.96	8.05	10.93	4.60
Golub (1983) Ages: 30–45	14.77	6.39	19.71	8.28	10.87	3.84
Maddocks (1983) PMS subjects Ages: 20–45 Mean age: 35	18.33	8.76	25.41	8.82	14.73	6.85

15–16. Significant differences in negative affect related to cycle phase were found on the MDQ. However, although these young women complained of more negative affect during the menstrual phase of the cycle, no significant mood changes were found on the DACL or the Anxiety (A)-State in this group in either the premenstrual or menstrual phases of the cycle. This stands in contrast to the significant differences found between intermenstrual and premenstrual depression and anxiety scores in a group of normal women between the ages of 30 and 45. It is important to point out that although the premenstrual mood change in this sample of older women was statistically significant, on the average the level of anxiety these women experienced was mild, comparable to that of college freshmen at an orientation session and less than that experienced by hospital patients or students during an examination. Similarly, depression scores were comparable to those of a group of pregnant women during the first trimester of pregnancy and far lower than those found in depressed patients (see Table 12.3).

Women who seek treatment for premenstrual syndrome appear to be quite different from the normal subjects discussed above. Goudsmit (52) focused on 20 outpatients attending a PMS research clinic at St. Thomas' Hospital in London. These women ranged in age between 24 and 45, with an average age of 34.4. Mean premenstrual DACL scores for these women were about 17.5, and premenstrual state anxiety scores averaged about 55 (see Table 12.3).

Table 12.3
Magnitude of Premenstrual Depression and Anxiety: Depression Scores (DACL) and Anxiety Scores (A-State)

REFERENCE	DACL	A-STATE
Golub & Harrington (1981)		
High school students		
Ages: 15–16		
Premenstrual	8.93	41.41
Intermenstrual	8.82	41.79
Golub (1976)		
Adult women		
Ages: 30–45		
Premenstrual	9.30	38.10
Intermenstrual	6.84	33.64
Lubin (1967)		
Normal adult		
women	7.80	
Depressed		
psychiatric	16.03	
patients		
Spielberger		
Gorsuch, & Lushene		
(1970)		
Unstressed college		
students		35.12
Students during		
an exam		43.69
Goudsmit (1983)		
PMS patients		
Ages: 24–45,		
mean 34.4	17.50[*]	55.00
Controls		
Ages: 21–44		
mean 26.7	4.50	27

*Mean scores taken from a graph.

There are also differences between normal women and those with psychiatric morbidity. Abplanalp, Haskett, and Rose (10) observed that psychotic episodes that appear to be cyclic and associated with the premenstrual phase of the cycle may be more prevalent in younger age-groups. They cite several studies indicating age of onset to be before age 23 and suggest that premenstrual psychosis in adolescents and young women represents a disorder that is different from that commonly referred to as premenstrual syndrome. One must therefore be cautious in generalizing from data on psychiatric patients to normal women (87).

Etiology and Treatment

Although the available data do suggest an increase in both the incidence and magnitude of premenstrual negative affect with increasing age among normal women, why this occurs is not known. It might be related to hormonal or neurohormonal changes, to target organ changes, or perhaps to a heightened sensitivity to paramenstrual body and mood changes among older women. (Are women in this age-group more tuned in to their bodies?) It might also be related to greater stress in the lives of women in their mid-30s. All are viable hypotheses and represent only a few of the theories as to the etiology of premenstrual symptoms. Reid and Yen (88) review the most salient of these, namely, progesterone deficiency, vitamin deficiency, hypoglycemia, hormone allergy, psychosomatic causes, fluid retention, neuroendocrine causes, catecholamines, and neurointermediate lobe peptide dysfunction. To date, no one hypothesis has adequately explained premenstrual symptoms or PMS, and Herz (89) suggests that many of the present difficulties in dealing with premenstrual syndrome arise from atttempts to find a single physiological or psychological etiology.

In view of the lack of a consistent definition of PMS or any satisfactory explanation of the cause(s), it is not surprising that a wide variety of different treatments have been proposed over the years. Abplanalp (90) notes that PMS has been treated with oral contraceptives, estrogen alone, natural progesterone, synthetic progestogens, minor tranquilizers, nutritional supplements (pyridoxine), minerals (magnesium and calcium), lithium, diuretics, bromocriptine, exercise, and psychotherapy. Because few studies of treatment efficacy have involved double-blind evaluations of the various treatment agents, it is not known which are truly effective. For example, uncontrolled studies and reports from some clinics suggest that progesterone is helpful, but in a double-blind controlled study of the efficacy of progesterone in the treatment of PMS, Sampson (91) found that whether patients received progesterone or a placebo, 60 percent were helped. The placebo was at least as effective as progesterone in this study. (For a more complete review of the treatment literature, see Abplanalp [90], Clare [29], and Reid and Yen [88].)

Although there is no universally agreed upon program for the treatment of PMS, several clinicians have proposed a generally accepted regimen for helping women with symptoms (92, 94, 89). This includes careful evaluation of both the somatic symptoms and the psychological status of the patient, since intra-psychic and environmental factors causing stress may play a role. An individualized treatment program that addresses both the specific symptoms and lifestyle changes that aim at alleviating intra- and interpersonal stress is recommended. Herz (89) advocates a biopsychosocial approach, beginning with daily records of basal temperature, weight, and symptoms over two to three cycles. Dietary change is advised: no caffeinated beverages; no sugar; frequent small meals comprised of high protein, high complex carbohydrates, and low fat foods; reduced sodium intake. In addition, some clinicians suggest vitamin and mineral supplements. For example, Herz (89) recommends 100 mg of magnesium two times a day and 100 mg of Vitamin B_6 twice a day during the second half of the cycle. Abraham (92) also advocates a therapeutic trial of B-complex vitamins.

Daily exercise is proposed as an effective way to alleviate tension and increase a woman's sense of control over her life. Other stress-reducing techniques, such as relaxation exercises, yoga, meditation, and music, are prescribed for symptoms of tension and anxiety. Psychotherapy can help a woman explore her attitudes and expectations regarding menstruation as well as the specific stress in her life, with an eye toward making changes that will enable her to manage more comfortably. In recognizing and accepting premenstrual mood swings, for example, a woman can learn to nurture herself when she needs it. Other symptom-specific treatments include diuretics for water retention. Budoff (93) specifically recommends Dyrenium because it fosters sodium and water loss without lowering potassium levels as the other antihypertensive diuretics do.

A great deal of research aimed at discovering the cause(s) of premenstrual syndrome is now going on. Until this research leads to more definitive treatment, acknowledging the validity of the patient's symptoms and providing specific suggestions such as those outlined above may be helpful in the treatment of premenstrual symptoms.

SUMMARY AND CONCLUSIONS

The emphasis in this chapter has been on the relationship between age and symptoms of menstrual distress. A review of the literature suggests that young women more often experience dysmenorrhea whereas older, parous women are more likely to complain of the amorphous set of symptoms that have been labeled "premenstrual syndrome." Prostaglandins have been identified as the cause of primary dysmenorrhea, and the prostaglandin inhibitors are often the treatment of choice. No such clear-cut alternative exists for premenstrual symptoms. Theories about etiology were briefly reviewed, and a generally accepted treatment regimen was presented. In order to further clarify the relationship between age and menstrual symptoms, studies of large numbers of normal women taking into account the physiological changes occurring over time as well as the different stresses experienced by women at different stages of their lives are needed. It is also important to emphasize that although a substantial proportion of women do experience pain or other symptoms of menstrual cycle distress during their lives, only a relatively small number of women (about 5 to 10 percent) suffer severe symptoms.

Cultural and attitudinal factors and their connection with menstrual symptoms also were explored. The link between attitudes and symptoms remains unclear, with some studies finding an association between them and others not finding one. However, contemporary researchers are acknowledging that attitudes may be influenced by symptoms rather than the other way around. The effects of age on attitudes appear to be less important than those of sex or education. Women have more positive attitudes toward menstruation than do men, and college-educated women were found to have the most positive relationship between attitudes toward feminism and attitudes toward menstruation, indicating that the way a woman feels about herself as a woman influences her beliefs about menstruation.

ACKNOWLEDGEMENTS

The assistance of Michelle Schwartz in reviewing the literature for this chapter is gratefully acknowledged. Thanks are also due to Dr. Richard C. Friedman and Dr. Leon M. Golub for their helpful comments on an earlier draft.

REFERENCES

1. Bergsjo, P.; Jenssen, H.; and Vellar, O. Dysmenorrhea in industrial workers. Acta Obstetrics Gynecology Scandinavia, 54:255–259, 1975.
2. Kessel, N., and Coppen, A. The prevalence of common menstrual symptoms. The Lancet, 2:61–65, 1963.
3. Moos, R. The development of a menstruation distress questionnaire. Psychosomatic Medicine, 30:853–867, 1968.
4. Sobczyk, R. Dysmenorrhea, the neglected syndrome. Journal of Reproductive Medicine, 25(4):198–210, 1980.
5. Woods, N. F.; Most, A.; and Dery, G. K. Prevalence of perimenstrual symptoms. American Journal of Public Health, 72(11):1257–1264, 1982.
6. Dalton, K. The Premenstrual Syndrome. Springfield, Ill. Charles C. Thomas, 1964.
7. Golub, S. The magnitude of premenstrual anxiety and depression. Psychosomatic Medicine, 38:4–12, 1976.
8. Golub, S., and Harrington, D. M. Premenstrual and menstrual mood changes in adolescent women. Journal of Personality and Social Psychology, 5:961–965, 1981.
9. Kramp, J. Studies on the premenstrual syndrome in relation to psychiatry. Acta Psychiatrica Scandinavica, 203:261–267, 1968.
10. Abplanalp, J. M.; Haskett, R.; and Rose, R. The premenstrual syndrome. Psychiatric Clinics of North America, 3:327–347, 1980.
11. Andersch, B., and Hahn, L. Premenstrual complaints, II: Influence of oral contraceptives. Acta Obstetrics Gynecology Scandinavia, 60:579–583, 1981.
12. Lloyd, T. S. The mid-thirties syndrome. Virginia Medical Monthly, 90:51, 1963.

13. Rees, L. Psychosomatic aspects of the premenstrual tension syndrome. British Medical Journal, 99:62–73, 1953.
14. Rees, L. The premenstrual tension syndrome and its treatment. British Medical Journal, 1:1014–1016, 1953.
15. Abplanalp, J. M. The menstrual cycle: costs and benefits. Paper presented at the meeting of the American Society of Psychosomatic Obstetrics and Gynecology. San Francisco, 1982.
16. McCance, R. A.; Luff, M. E.; and Widdowson, E. E. Physical and emotional periodicity in women. Journal of Hygiene, 37:571–611, 1937.
17. Moos, R.; Kopell, B.; Melges, R.; Yalom, I.; Lunde, D.; Clayton, R.; and Hamburg, D. Fluctuations in symptoms and moods during the menstrual cycle. Journal of Psychosomatic Research, 13:37–44, 1969.
18. Parlee, M. B. The premenstrual syndrome. Psychological Bulletin, 80:454–465, 1973.
19. Parlee, M. B. Stereotypic beliefs about menstruation: a methodological note on the Moos Menstrual Distress Questionnaire and some new data. Psychosomatic Medicine, 36:229–240, 1974.
20. Mandell, A. J., and Mandell, M. Suicide and the menstrual cycle. Journal of the American Medical Association, 200:792–793, 1967.
21. Morton, J. H.; Addison, H.; Addison, R. G.; Hunt, L.; and Sullivan, J. A clinical study of premenstrual tension. American Journal of Obstetrics and Gynecology, 65:1182, 1953.
22. Wetzel, R. D.; Reich, T.; and McClure, J. N. Phase of menstrual cycle and self-referrals to a suicide prevention center. British Journal of Psychiatry, 119:523–524, 1971.
23. Abplanalp, J. M.; Rose, R. M.; Donnelly, A. F.; and Livingston-Vaughan,L. Psychoendocrinology of the menstrual cycle, II: the relationship between enjoyment of activities, mood, and reproductive hormones. Psychosomatic Medicine, 41:605–615, 1979.
24. Lahmeyer, H. W.; Miller, M.; and DeLeon-Jones, F. Anxiety and mood fluctuation during the normal menstrual cycle. Psychosomatic Medicine, 44(2):183–194, 1982.
25. Koeske, R. D. Theoretical perspectives on menstrual cycle research: the relevance of attributional approaches for the perception and explanation of premenstrual emotionality. In: Dan, A. J.; Graham, E. A.; and Beecher, C. P., eds. The Menstrual Cycle, Vol. I. New York: Springer, 1980.
26. Bem, S. L. The measurement of psychological androgyny. Journal of Consulting and Clinical Psychology, 42:155–162, 1974.
27. Hyde, J. S., and Rosenberg, B. G. Half the human experience. Lexington, Mass.: D. C. Heath, 1980.
28. Koeske, R. D. Lifting the curse of menstruation: toward a feminist perspective on the menstrual cycle. Women and Health, 8(2/3):1–16, 1983.
29. Clare, A. W. Psychological aspects of women with the premenstrual syndrome. Current Medical Research and Opinion, 6:11–18, 1979.
30. Clare, A. W. The relationship between psychopathology and the menstrual cycle. Women and Health, 8(2/3):125–136, 1983.
31. Coppen, A. The prevalence of menstrual disorders in psychiatric patients. British Journal of Psychiatry, 111:155–167, 1965.
32. Kashiwagi, T.; McClure, J. N., Jr.; and Wetzel, R. D. Premenstrual affective syn-

drome and psychiatric disorder. Diseases of the Nervous System, 37:116–119, 1976.

33. Tourghele, J. R. Premenstrual tension in psychotic women. The Lancet, 77:163–170, 1957.

34. Paige, K. E. Women learn to sing the menstrual blues. Psychology Today, 4:41–46, 1973.

35. Ernster, V. L. American menstrual euphemisms. Sex Roles, 1(1):3–13, 1975.

36. Brooks-Gunn, J., and Ruble, D. N. Menarche: the interaction of physiological, cultural, and social factors. In: Dan, A. J.; Graham, E. M.; and Beecher, C., eds., The Menstrual Cycle, Vol. I. New York: Springer, 1980.

37. Clarke, A. E., and Ruble, D. N. Young adolescents' beliefs concerning menstruation. Child Development, 49:201–234, 1978.

38. Brooks, J.; Ruble, D. N.; and Clarke, A. College women's attitudes and expectations concerning menstrual-related changes. Psychosomatic Medicine, 39:288–298, 1977.

39. The Tampax Report. New York: Tampax Incorporated, 1981. (Available from Ruder, Finn & Rotman, 110 East 59th Street, New York, NY 10022.)

40. Levitt, E. E., and Lubin, B. Some personality factors associated with menstrual complaints and menstrual attitude. Journal of Psychosomatic Research, 11:267–270, 1967.

41. Berry, C., and McGuire, F. L. Menstrual distress and acceptance of sexual role. American Journal of Obstetrics and Gynecology, 114:83–87, 1972.

42. Gough, H. Personality factors related to reported severity of menstrual distress. Journal of Abnormal Psychology, 1:59–65, 1975.

43. Israel, S. L. Menstrual Disorders and Sterility. New York: Harper and Row, 1975.

44. Shainess, N. A re-evaluation of some aspects of femininity through a study of menstruation: a preliminary report. Comprehensive Psychiatry, 2:20–26, 1961.

45. Gannon, L. Evidence for a psychological etiology of menstrual disorders: a critical review. Psychological Report, 48:287–294, 1981.

46. Sommer, B. The effect of menstruation on cognitive and perceptual-motorbehavior: a review. Psychosomatic Medicine, 35:515–534, 1973.

47. Coppen, A., and Kessel, N. Menstruation and personality. British Journal of Psychiatry, 109:711–721, 1963.

48. Hirt, M.; Kurtz, R.; and Ross, W. D. The relationship between dysmenorrhea and selected personality variables. Psychosomatics, 8:350–353, 1967.

49. Spitzer, R. L.; Williams, J. B. W.; and Skodol, A. E. DMS–:III: the major achievements and an overview. American Journal of Psychiatry, 137:151–163, 1980.

50. Lawlor, C., and Davis, A. Primary dysmenorrhea. Journal of Adolescent Health Care, 1:208–212, 1981.

51. Stolzman, S. M. Menstrual attitudes, beliefs, and symptom experiences of adolescent females, their peers, and their mothers. Paper presented at the meeting of the Society for Menstrual Cycle Research, San Francisco, 1983.

52. Goudsmit, E. M. Psychological aspects of premenstrual symptoms. Journal of Psychosomatic Obstetrics and Gynecology, 2:20–26, 1983.

53. Brooks-Gunn, J., and Ruble, D. Dysmenorrhea in adolescence. In Golub, S., ed., Menarche. Lexington, Mass.: Lexington Books, 1983.

54. Garwood, S. G., and Allen, L. Self-concept and identified problem differences between pre- and postmenarcheal adolescents. Journal of Clinical Psychology, 35:528–537, 1979.

55. Golub, S., and Catalano, J. Recollections of menarche and women's subsequent experiences with menstruation. Women and Health, 8(1):49–61, 1983.

56. Slade, P., and Jenner, F. A. Performance tests in different phases of the menstrual cycle. Journal of Psychosomatic Research, 24:5–8, 1980.

57. Woods, N. F.; Dery, G. K.; and Most, A. Recollections of menarche, current menstrual attitudes, and perimenstrual symptoms. In: Golub, S., ed., Menarche. Lexington, Mass.: Lexington Books, 1983.

58. Morrison, J. C., and Nicolls, E. T. Epidemiologic, social, and economic aspects of dysmenorrhea. In: Dawood, M. Y., ed. Dysmenorrhea. Baltimore: Williams and Wilkins, 1981.

59. Dingfelder, J. R. Primary dysmenorrhea treatment with prostaglandin inhibitors: a review. American Journal of Obstetrics and Gynecology, 140(8):874–879, 1981.

60. Lamb, E. J. Clinical features of primary dysmenorrhea. In: Dawood, M. Y. ed., Dysmenorrhea. Baltimore: Williams and Wilkins, 1981.

61. Ylikorkala, O., and Dawood, M. Y. New concepts in dysmenorrhea. American Journal of Obstetrics and Gynecology, 130:833–847, 1978.

62. Chesney, M. A., and Tasto, D. L. The development of the menstrual symptom questionnaire. Behavior Research and Therapy, 13:237–244, 1975.

63. Widholm, O., and Kantero, R. L. Menstrual patterns of adolescent girls according to chronological and gynecological ages. Acta Obstetrics Gynecology Scandinavia, 50(14):19–29, 1971.

64. Friederich, M. A. Dysmenorrhea. Women and Health, 8(2/3):91–106, 1983.

65. Bickers, W. Dysmenorrhea and menstrual disability. Clinical Obstetrics and Gynecology, 3:233–240, 1960.

66. Frisk, M.; Widholm, O.; and Hortling, H. Dysmenorrhea—psyche and soma in teenagers. Acta Ostetrics Gynecology Scandinavia, 44:339, 1965.

67. Gray, L. Gynecology in adolescence. Pediatric Clinics of North America, 7:42–57, 1960.

68. Drillien, M. B. A study of normal and abnormal menstrual function in the auxiliary territorial service. Journal of Obstetrics and Gynecology, 53:228–241, 1946.

69. Gruba, G. H., and Rohrbaugh, M. MMPI correlates of menstrual distress. Psychosomatic Medicine, 37(3):265–273, 1975.

70. Schucket, M. A.; Daly, V.; Herrman, G.; and Hineman, S. Premenstrual symptoms and depression in a university population. Diseases of the Nervous System, 36:516–517, 1975.

71. Cox, D.; McMahon, E.; and Pennebaker, J. Virginia inventory of premenstrual and menstrual symptoms: standardization data. University of Virginia, 1983.

72. Svennerud, S. Dysmenorrhea and absenteeism, some gynaecologic and medico-social aspects. Acta Obstetrics Gynecology Scandinavia, 164:638–640, 1959.

73. Rosenwaks, Z., and Seegar-Jones, G. Menstrual pain: its origin and pathogenesis. Journal of Reproductive Medicine, 25:207–212, 1980.

74. Jollie, W. P. Anatomy of the female reproductive organs in reference to dysmenorrhea. In: Dawood, M. Y., ed., Dysmenorrhea. Baltimore: Williams and Wilkins, 1981.

75. Chan, W. Y.; Dawood, M. Y.; and Fuchs, F. Prostaglandins in primary dysmenorrhea. Comparison of prophylactic and nonprophylactic treatment with ibuprofen and use of oral contraceptives. American Journal of Medicine, 70:535–541, 1981.

270   Sexuality

76. Chan, W. Y. Prostaglandins in primary dysmenorrhea: basis for the new therapy. In: Golub, S., ed., Menarche. Lexington, Mass.: Lexington Books, 1983.
77. Schwartz, A.; Zor, U.; Lindner, H. R.; and Naor, S. Primary dysmenorrhea. Alleviation by an inhibitor of prostaglandin synthesis and action. Obstetrics and Gynecology, 44:709–712, 1974.
78. Murray, L. Dysmenorrhea. Sexual Medicine Today, 5(9):6–14, 1981.
79. Physicians' Desk Reference. Oradell, N.J.: Medical Economics, 1983.
80. Dawood, M. Y. Hormones, prostaglandins, and dysmenorrhea. In: Dawood, M. Y., ed., Dysmenorrhea. Baltimore: Williams and Wilkins, 1981.
81. Ferguson, J. H., and Vermillion, M. B. Premenstrual tensions: two surveys of its prevalence and a description of the syndrome. Obstetrics and Gynecology, 9:615–619, 1957.
82. Perr, I. N. Medical, psychiatric, and legal aspects of premenstrual tension. American Journal of Psychiatry, 115(3):211–219, 1958.
83. Paulson, M. J. Psychological concomitants of premenstrual tension. American Journal of Obstetrics and Gynecology, 81:733–738, 1956.
84. Pennington, W. M. Meprobamate in premenstrual tension. Journal of the American Medical Association, 164:638–640, 1957.
85. Sutherland, H., and Stewart, I. A critical analysis of the premenstrual syndrome. The Lancet, 1:1180–1183, 1965.
86. Anderson, A. N.; Larsen, J. F.; Streenstrup, O. R.; Svendstrup, B.; and Nielson, J. Effect of bromocriptine on the premenstrual syndrome: a double-blind clinical trial. British Journal of Obstetrics and Gynecology, 84:370–374, 1977.
87. Friedman, R. C.; Hurt, S. W.; Arnoff, M. S.; and Clarkin, J. Behavior and the menstrual cycle. Signs, 5(4):719–738, 1980.
88. Reid, R. L., and Yen, S. S. C. Premenstrual syndrome. American Journal of Obstetrics and Gynecology, 139:85–104, 1981.
89. Herz, E. K. Menstrual changes: medical evaluation and treatment. Paper presented at the meeting of the American Psychological Association, New York City, 1983.
90. Abplanalp, J. M. Premenstrual syndrome: a selective review. Women and Health, 8(2/3):107–123, 1983.
91. Sampson, G. Premenstrual syndrome: A double-blind controlled trial of progesterone and placebo. Brit. J. Psychiatry, 135:209–215, 1979.
92. Abraham, G. E. The nutritionist's approach. In: Debrovner, C., ed., Premenstrual Tension. New York: Human Sciences Press, 1982.
93. Budoff, P. S. No More Menstrual Cramps. New York: Penguin Books, 1980.
94. Harrison, M. Self-Help for Premenstrual Syndrome. Cambridge, Mass.: Matrix Press, 1982.
95. Golub, S. The Magnitude of premenstrual anxiety and depression. Psychosomatic Medicine 38:4-12, 1976.
96. Golub, S. Menstrual distress questionnaire scores. Unpublished raw data, 1983.
97. Maddocks, S. E. The investigation of symptom response patterns on a sample of women with severe premenstrual syndrome. Master's thesis, Queens University, Canada, 1983.
98. Lubin, B. Manual for the Depression Adjective Check List. San Diego, Calif.: Educational and Industrial Testing Service, 1967.
99. Spielberger, D. C.; Gorsuch, R. L.; and Luschene, R. E. STAI Manual. Palo Alto, Calif.: Consulting Psychologists Press, 1970.

The Role of Sleep Studies in the Differential Diagnosis of Impotence

The determination of whether erectile impotence in an adult male is organic, psychogenic, or mixed often presents a diagnostic dilemma for the clinician. This distinction has become increasingly important in recent years because significant advances have been made in the treatment of both inhibited sexual excitement (ISE; also referred to in the literature as psychogenic impotence) and organic impotence. These include psychological techniques pioneered by Masters and Johnson (1) and modified by Kaplan (2), improved methods for diagnosing and treating endocrinopathies that cause impotence (3), techniques for correcting vascular causes of impotence (4), and surgical techniques for the implantation of a penile prosthesis (5–7).

This chapter will outline a comprehensive clinical evaluation of impotence, describe the physiology of normal sleep relevant to the use of sleep studies for the differential diagnosis of impotence, describe and discuss the use of sleep studies for the differential diagnosis of impotence, and discuss problems associated with using sleep studies for this purpose.

CLINICAL EVALUATION OF IMPOTENCE

The clinical evaluation of all patients with erectile impotence except those with selective impairment of erections (see below) should include a complete sexual and medical history, a physical examination, and appropriate laboratory tests (3).

Sexual History

A comprehensive sexual history should be elicited. Special attention should be directed to the following details of the history which can help distinguish ISE from organic impotence:

Selective impairment of erections. The presence of sustained (arbitrarily defined as five minutes or more) full erections in some circumstances but not in others is *indicative* of ISE.* For example, if a patient can have intercourse with one partner but not another, or is able to attain full sustained erections when he masturbates but not when he attempts intercourse, his impotence is psychogenic. In such cases a physical exmination and laboratory tests are not required. If the patient gives a history of impaired erections in all circumstances, that is, in attempts at intercourse and masturbation, on awakening from sleep, and in erotically stimulating circumstances, this information is not helpful in distinguishing ISE from organic impotence.

Abrupt onset. An abrupt onset over one month or less is *suggestive* of ISE. The more abrupt the onset, the more suggestive the history is. An obvious exception is an abrupt onset following surgery such as a prostatectomy (10) or radical colon surgery for carcinoma. Impotence following such procedures can be due either to organic impotence or to ISE. A gradual onset over six months or more is *suggestive* of an organic cause such as impotence secondary to diabetes mellitus, but it can also occur with ISE.

Precipitating psychological cause. The presence of a precipitating psychological cause, for example, discovering that his partner is having an affair, is *suggestive* of ISE but is not diagnostic. The absence of such a finding is of little help diagnostically. In practice, the history will often reveal "psychological causes" that are less dramatic and more chronic than the above example and therefore more difficult to interpret diagnostically.

Previous transient episode(s) of impotence. Previous transient episodes of impotence *suggest* a psychogenic origin, provided the previous episode was psychogenic. Because past ISE does not protect against current organic impotence, this criterion must be used cautiously.

Maintenance of sexual desire. Loss of sexual desire has been associated with ISE, but there is so much overlap between psychogenically and organically impotent patients in the degree of maintenance of sexual desire that this criterion is of little or no practical value in the differential diagnosis of impotence.

It should be emphasized that the only finding in the sexual history that is *diagnostic* of ISE is the presence of selective impairment of erections. No findings in the history are diagnostic of organic impotence. The diagnosis of organic impotence can be made with a relatively high degree of probability based on the

---

*It is the author's view (9) that although for clinical and discussion purposes we speak of "ISE" and "organic impotence" such pure categories do not actually exist. Erection is the end result of a complex interaction of physiological and psychological processes, and a distrubance of erectile capacity invariably involves both. This view (at least as it applies to what is usually called ISE) is in agreement with what I understand Kaplan to mean when she stresses (2: p. 264) that in ISE "constitutionally determined organic vulnerabilities such as an especially reactive sexual system" may play a role. Any reference in this chapter to "ISE" or "organic impotence" should therefore be understood to mean "primarily ISE" or "primarily organic impotence."

convergence of data from the history and the multiple sources to be described below, but never with as much certainty as the diagnosis of ISE.

Medical History

The comprehensive medical history should focus on physical disorders and drugs that are known to be associated with impotence. The presence of an organic disease known to be sometimes associated with impotence, for example, diabetes mellitus, *supports* the possibility of organic impotence but is not diagnostic. Obviously diabetes mellitus does not protect a patient from ISE.

A partial list of physical disorders associated with impotence includes:

1. *Cardiorespiratory disorders*—coronary insufficiency, myocardial infarction, emphysema
2. *Endocrine disorders*—Acromegaly, Addison's disease, pituitary adenoma, diabetes mellitus, myxedema, thyrotoxicosis, estrogen ingestion, Klinefelter's syndrome, Cushing's syndrome
3. *Genitourinary disorders*—Prostatectomy, prostatitis, urethritis, hydrocele, Peyronie's disease
4. *Hematologic disorders*—Hodgkin's disease, leukemia, anemia
5. *Infections*—Genital tuberculosis, gonorrhea
6. *Neurologic disorders*—Amytrophic lateral sclerosis, spinal cord tumors or transection, multiple sclerosis, Parkinson's disease, peripheral neuropathies, tabes dorsalis, temporal lobe lesions
7. *Vascular disorders*—Hypertension, thrombotic obstruction of the aortic bifurcation, arthritis

A partial list of drugs that may be associated with impotence includes phenothiazines, tricyclic antidepressants, monamine oxidase inhibitors, most antihypertensive medications, alcohol, opiates, anticholinergics, and amphetamines.

Physical Examination

The patient should have a complete physical and neurological examination, including the following, which are not always routinely done:

1. Blood pressure check that includes evaluation for orthostatic hypotension
2. Evaluation of hair distribution
3. Evaluation of thyroid gland
4. Examination of skin for signs of above disorders, e.g., Cushing's syndrome
5. Breast examination
6. Examination of penis and testes
7. Pulses, including femoral, popliteal, posterior tibial, and dorsalis pedis

8. Neurologic examination including motor and sensory examination of lower extremities, deep tendon reflexes of the lower extremities, bulbocavernosus reflex, and anal wink

Laboratory Tests

Laboratory tests should include complete blood count, SMA-12, testosterone, luteinizing hormone, follicle-stimulating hormone, prolactin, thyroxine, plasma cortisol, three-hour glucose tolerance test, urinalysis, and if possible a penile blood pressure measurement.

If the cause of the impotence is unclear following the above described evaluation, optimally the patient should have sleep studies to further clarify the diagnosis. This would include *all* patients who are not diagnosed as having ISE based on selective impairment of erections. Any other finding or combination of findings in the comprehensive clincial evaluation, no matter how suggestive, is not diagnostic of either ISE or organic impotence. Under these circumstances it is best to obtain the additional information that sleep studies can provide before proceeding with treatment.

PHYSIOLOGY OF NORMAL SLEEP

Normal sleep in young adult humans consists of repeated sleep cycles of approximately 90–minute duration. The number of cycles per night varies from four to six, depending on the duration of sleep. Each cycle typically consists of five stages which are defined electroencephalographically and are passed through in a relatively orderly way during each cycle, except as noted below.

Stage 1 is characterized by a relatively low voltage and mixed frequency electroencephalogram (EEG) pattern and comprises about 5 percent of the total sleep time.

Stage 2 is characterized by sleep spindles and K complexes superimposed on a background of relatively low voltage and mixed-frequency EEG activity. It comprises approximately 50 percent of total sleep time.

Stages 3 and 4 are defined by high-voltage slow waves. If 20 to 49 percent of the record shows such slow waves it is called Stage 3, and if more than 50 percent of the record shows such slow waves it is called Stage 4. Stages 3 and 4 comprise approximately 20 percent of total sleep, occur mainly during the first few sleep cycles, and are often absent during the later sleep cycles.

Rapid eye movement (REM) or dreaming sleep has an EEG pattern similar to Stage 1 but is accompanied by episodic binocularly synchronous rapid eye movements (12) and a low amplitude electromyogram (EMG). REM sleep comprises 20 to 25 percent of total sleep. The first REM period is usually short or occasionally absent. Each successive REM period is typically longer. REM sleep is characterized by autonomic nervous system activation including increased heart and respiratory rates, by a higher incidence of gross body movements, and by a higher incidence of recall of vivid multisensory dream images than in other sleep stages. Most relevant to this chapter, REM sleep is also usually associated with penile erections in males (13).

The first published report of erections during sleep was in 1940, when Halverson noted erections in sleeping infants (14). In 1944, Ohlmeyer (15) first systematically measured nocturnal erections and reported a cycle of erections during sleep that occurred on the average of every 85 minutes and lasted an average of 25 minutes. Nine years later Aserinsky and Kleitman (16) first described REM sleep and two years later noted (12) that the length of nocturnal erections appeared to correspond to the length of REM periods during normal sleep. However, it was not until the mid-1960s that Fisher et al. (17) and Karacan et al. (18) independently documented that 80 to 95 percent of REM periods in men in their 20s and 30s were accompanied by full or partial erections. Karacan et al. (19–24) subsequently reported that all 125 normal males studied between 3 and 79 years old had nocturnal penile tumescence (NPT) during normal sleep, with the amount being a function of age.

Initially it was believed that NPT occurred only during REM sleep, but it was subsequently shown that REM-related NPT typically begins before and/or ends after the associated REM period, with 27 to 41 percent (depending on age) of the NPT actually occurring during non-REM (NREM) sleep immediately before or after the REM period. It was also shown that 5 to 15 percent of NPT episodes (varying with the age of the subject) occur totally unassociated with REM sleep (20). Further questions about the relationship between NPT and REM sleep were raised by recent preliminary findings which indicate that slightly more than half the actual tumescing, defined as increase in penile circumference, occurs during NREM sleep in patients with ISE (25).

SLEEP STUDIES FOR THE DIFFERENTIAL DIAGNOSIS OF IMPOTENCE

In 1970, Karacan (26) first reported using NPT measurements to distinguish ISE from organic impotence, providing for the first time an objective measure to help make this often difficult distinction. He *assumed* that relevant psychological factors would be inoperative during sleep in men with ISE and that NPT would therefore be present. In contrast, in organically impotent men the organic factors would continue to operate during sleep, and NPT would therefore be absent. Problems with these initial assumptions will be discussed in the following section. Using these assumptions, he divided a group of clinically indistiguishable impotent diabetics into two distinct groups based on the presence or absence of NPT. Subsequently Karacan et al. (27, 28) have indicated that NPT can be impaired to varying degrees but continue to report that NPT provides an objective basis for distinguishing organic impotence from ISE (19, 20, 27–32). Since 1970, NPT evaluations have become increasingly widely used to help in the diagnosis of difficult-to-diagnose impotent patients (10, 19, 20, 27–32).

The evaluation of impotent patients at the Sleep-Wake Disorders Center at New York Hospital/Westchester Division is conducted by an interdisciplinary-team consisting of a psychiatrist, a psychologist, a neurologist, a urologist, and polysomnographic technologists. Consultants in other subspecialties are available when indicated. As described above under "Clinical Evaluation of Impotence," a sexual and medical history is elicited from each patient during two interviews with a psychiatrist, a physical and neurological examination is performed by a neurologist, and laboratory tests including a penile blood pressure measurement are performed. Psychometric testing includes the Minnesota Multiphasic Personality Inventory (MMPI), the Derogatis Sexual Functioning Inventory, and the Beck Depression Inventory. When indicated, the patient's sexual partner is interviewed and additional consultations are obtained.

Technique of Polysomnogram-NPT Study

A polysomnogram (PSG), or sleep recording, is obtained for three consecutive nights in the sleep laboratory using standard measurements for NPT. These include (a) two EEG channels, (b) three electroculograph (EOG) channels, (c) one electromyogram (EMG) channel that measures mentalis (chin) muscle activity (which helps in determining REM sleep), (d) one electrocardiograph (EKG) channel, (e) two penile channels that measure changes in penile circumference with two mercury strain gauges, one placed at the base of the penis and one at the tip of the penis just behind the glans, (f) one EMG channel that measures contractions of the ischiocavernosus and bulbocavernosus muscles (muscles thought to be involved in erection) using surface electrodes placed between the base of the scrotum and the anus.

Penile circumference is measured at both the base and tip because certain pathologic conditions such as Peyronie's disease can cause marked differences between increases measured at the base and tip, which could be missed if only one was recorded.

The patient sleeps in a private sound-attenuated room and retires and arises at his regular times. A technologist is present throughout each night of recording, and all measurements are made continuously throughout the night. If the largest increase in penile circumference at the base or tip of the penis is 5 mm or more during the three nights of recording, the patient is awakened one to three times, and direct observations of the patient's erections are made. It is *crucial* that one of the patient's largest erections be directly observed. This is because there are large interindividual but only small intraindividual variations in the increases in circumference associated with erections sufficiently rigid for intercourse. The reported range for such erections is 10–48 mm at the tip of the penis and 15–45 mm at the base (23, 30, 35, 36). If the measured increases in penile circumference fall within these ranges, the only way to be sure that the particular patient has an erection adequate for vaginal penetration is to directly observe it.

The patient is informed prior to the study that he will be awakened one or more times during the three nights and asked to estimate the rigidity of his erection on a 0 to 10 scale. The ratings are made by his both looking at and feeling his penis. A rating of 8 or more defines an erection sufficiently rigid for vaginal penetration (a full or maximum erection). He is already familiar with this scale since it was used in eliciting his sexual history. He is also informed prior to the sleep recordings that the rigidity of his erection may be measured by briefly placing a rigidity gauge on the glans of his penis and pressing down (39). This measurement also provides the technologist an opportunity to feel the erection, which provides additional, often important, information.

The awakening is done during the second half of the second night or during the third night. The timing of the awakening is based on data obtained from earlier erections, including the previous largest change in circumference and the time it took to reach that change from the flaccid state. The technologist attempts to time the awakening so that there are circumference increases of 81 percent or more of the largest previous increases at both the base and tip (the amount of increase in normals usually associated with an erection sufficiently rigid for vaginal penetration [28]). If the first awakening shows an erection clearly sufficient for vaginal penetration, further awakenings are not performed. No attempt has ever been made in sleep laboratory studies to take into consideration the tightness or laxness of the partner's vagina in determining whether an erection is sufficiently rigid for vaginal penetration. A hypothetical ''average expectable vagina'' has always been assumed.

After the sleep recordings have been scored, the results of the entire evaluation are reviewed at a conference attended by all who participated in the evaluation, and a decision is reached about the diagnosis.

Indications for the NPT Evaluation

An NPT evaluation should be performed on:

1. All impotent patients in whom there remains a differential diagnostic problem after performing a complete medical and sexual history, physical examination, and relevant laboratory tests. In practice, this includes all patients who do not clearly have ISE, i.e. a history of full sustained erections in some circumstances but not in others. This is the case because, as indicated earlier, no matter how suggestive the history, physical exmaination, and laboratory tests may be of organic impotence, this diagnosis can never be certain and can only be based on the convergence of evidence from multiple sources. An NPT evaluation can provide important information to support or refute such a diagnosis and should be performed on all patients who are believed to be organically impotent. This is especially important if surgical implantation of a penile prosthesis is being considered as a possible treatment.

2. Patients with ISE who have a clear history of selective impairment of erections but who are unwilling to accept this diagnosis and enter psychological treatment without ''objective evidence.'' In such cases an NPT evaluation can *sometimes* be helpful in overcoming the patient's resistance to therapy.

NPT Criteria for Diagnosis of Impotence

There is currently disagreement about the criteria to be used in making a diagnosis based on NPT studies. Most workers in the field have relied, to some degree, on reported normal values for NPT. However, there is disagreement about which normal values should be used, that is, should frequency of full erections and/or duration of full erections be used and should data from all erections or only full erections be used. There is also disagreement about whether different criteria should be used for patients of different ages and whether the criteria for diagnosing ISE should be based entirely or only partially on normative data. Examples of NPT criteria that have been used to diagnose ISE include (a) one or more full NPT episodes (28), (b) one maximum (full) erection per night that is maintained for five or more minutes (36), and (c) "total minutes and number of full episodes within the normal range" (30).

These difficulties in arriving at NPT criteria for diagnosing ISE led Wasserman et al. (9) to question the usefulness of reported normal NPT values for the diagnosis of impotence, especially since Karacan et al. (18, 40), Fisher et al. (35, 41), Jovanovic (42), and Wasserman et al. (38) agree that pyschological factors can at least partially inhibit NPT (see the following section for a more complete discussion of this issue). Any disagreement concerns not whether but to what degree psychological factors inhibit nocturnal erections.

Wasserman et al. (58) asked, "What are we trying to demonstrate when we measure NPT that will justify diagnosing a patient psychologically impotent?" They concluded that the goal is "to demonstrate that the patient has sufficient physiological capacity to attain an erection sufficiently rigid for vaginal penetration and to maintain it for a period of time sufficiently long for satisfactory intercourse." The purpose is not to determine if the patient can equal values for frequency and/or duration of full and/or partial erections of age-matched potent normals. "Looked at in this way the question becomes what NPT findings demonstrate the physiological capacity to attain and maintain an erection adequate for satisfactory intercourse, rather than how normal NPT is defined."

Based on this reasoning the following criteria were suggested and are used at the Sleep-Wake Disorders Center of New York Hospital/Westchester Division:

ISE

The presence of one or more full erections during the entire three nights of NPT recording confirmed by direct observation to be adequate for vaginal penetration *and* maintained at this level for five or more consecutive minutes. The occurence of such an erection even once during the three nights of recording demonstrates that the physiological mechanisms for erection during sleep are sufficiently intact for the patient to obtain a full erection. The clinical usefulness of this finding is based on the assumption that the same physiological mechanisms for erection operate during both waking and sleeping. This assumption needs to be validated. The duration of five minutes originally suggested by Fisher et al.

(36) (though he requires one five-minute full erection *each* night to make the diagnosis of psychogenic impotence), while somewhat arbitrary, was chosen because it was our clinical impression that this period is sufficiently long for satisfactory intercourse for most men.

It should be noted that the diagnosis of ISE in this classification system is based solely on the NPT finding of one full erection sustained for five minutes. The diagnosis is ISE if this occurs, regardless of the history and/or presence of an organic disease known to be associated with impotence, for example, the presence of diabetes mellitus and/or the total absence of full erections during waking under all circumstances.

Organic Impotence

The patient has (a) no full erections during three nights of NPT recording, (b) independent evidence from his history, physical examination, or laboratory tests of an organic disease known to be associated with impotence, (c) no evidence of severe depression (depression has been reported to be associated with marked impairment of NPT patterns [43]), and (d) the absence of a history suggestive of a psychogenic cause, that is, full erections in some circumstances but not in others.

Unlike the diagnosis of ISE, the diagnosis of organic impotence cannot be made solely on the basis of NPT findings. It requires positive findings in the history, physical examination, or laboratory tests to support the diagnosis. Even with such supportive evidence, the diagnosis is never as certain as the diagnosis of ISE, which is made on the basis of positive NPT evidence that sustained erectile capacity is present.

Mixed

The patient has: (a) one or more full erections during the three nights' recording confirmed by direct observation to be adequate for vaginal penetration, but none is maintained in the maximum range for five or more consecutive minutes, (b) independent evidence of an organic disease known to be associated with impotence, and (c) a history strongly suggestive of a psychogenic component, for example, brief (less than five minutes) full erections in some circumstances but not in others.

Undetermined

The patient has (a) one or more erections with an increase of 10 mm or more at the tip or 15 mm more at the base (the smallest increase reported associated with full erections), but an adequate direct observation was not possible to determine whether these erections were sufficiently rigid for vaginal penetration (under these circumstances, additional studies are required to perform an adequate observation), or (b) no full erections during three nights of NPT recording and no evidence of organic disease known to be associated with impotence. The absence of full erections without the presence of an organic disease known to be associated with impotence is *not* sufficient to make the diagnosis of organic impotence.

PROBLEMS WITH THE USE OF NPT EVALUATIONS FOR THE DIFFERENTIAL DIAGNOSIS OF IMPOTENCE

The major problems with using NPT measurements for the differential diagnosis of impotence include the basic assumptions behind such evaluations, difficulties meeting the requirement for a direct observation of one of the patient's largest erections, and the use of portable NPT monitors rather than a sleep laboratory for NPT evaluations.

Basic Assumptions

As indicated previously, when Karacan (26) initially reported using NPT monitoring for the differential diagnosis of impotence he *assumed* that if the patient had ISE, NPT would be present, since the psychogenic factors would be inoperative during sleep, and that if the patient was organically impotent noctural erections would be absent, since the organic factors would continue to operate during sleep. He then recorded NPT in clinically indistinguishable diabetics. If NPT was present he diagnosed them as having ISE, and if NPT was absent he diagnosed them as organically impotent. On this basis he concluded that NPT measurements provided objective evidence to distinguish ISE from organic impotence. *His reasoning is circular.* Although clinical evidence strongly suggests that NPT monitoring is a useful aid in the differential diagnosis of impotence in most cases, the assumption that NPT measurements can distinguish patients with ISE from patients with organic impotence has never been validated in patients shown to have ISE or organic impotence independent of NPT measurements themselves. Such studies are therefore necessary to determine definitvely whether NPT is useful for all cases of impotence in which the diagnosis is unclear and, if not, to identify the exceptions.

It is of interest in this regard that 20 percent of the patients with impaired NPT studied by Karacan had no demonstrable organic disease known to cause impotence. He believes that these patients may have subtle physiological defects not detectable by available techniques (44). In contrast, Fisher et al. (33–36), Wasserman et al. (8, 38), and Marshall et al. (45) raised the possibility that at least some of these patients may have psychogenic impotence. Supporting this possibility are the following findings indicating that psychological factors can inhibit NPT:

1. Karacan et al. (8) found that NPT was impaired or absent in normal men in association with dreams that had a high anxiety content.
2. Fisher (41) found that erections were impaired in normal men in association with dreams that had a manifest content containing aggression, anxiety, or other negative affects.
3. Jovanovic (42) reported decreased total tumescence time, a decreased number of tumescence episodes, and a preponderance of weak and moderate episodes over stronger

episodes on the first night of recording in a sleep laboratory as compared with the second night. This "first night effect" is presumably due to the novelty of the recording situation and the anxiety associated with it.

4. Fisher et al. (33) found a marked discrepancy between impaired waking erections and the relatively intact NPT in men diagnosed to have ISE. However, careful review of their data indicates some decreases in the patients with ISE compared with normals in total nightly duration and length of NPT episodes, as well as an increased tendency for the tumescence episodes to be interrupted early.

5. Karacan et al. (27) found that 11 patients with ISE spent significantly more time in and had a larger number of partial erections than 11 aged-matched normal subjects. The men with ISE also had fewer full erections per night (2.00 ± 0.95 compared with 2.59 ± 1.1), but the difference was not statistically significant.

6. Kahn and Fisher (46) described two otherwise normal subjects between 71 and 96 years old who did not have full nocturnal erections when recorded in a sleep laboratory but who reported being able to have intercourse. One of these, a 76–year-old subject, was recorded for five nights without an erection but reported successful intercourse every one or two months.

7. Jovanovic (47) noted a reduction in the number of erections, a 45 percent decrease in total nightly duration of erections, and a complete absence of full erections in 53 men diagnosed on clinical grounds to have ISE. However, his criteria for making the diagnosis were not clear, and these results have not been replicated.

8. Fisher et al. (36) described three patients with significant impairment of NPT but no evidence of organic disease. They believed that they had ISE despite the NPT findings. They described what I believe is the single strongest piece of evidence to support the hypothesis that some patients with ISE have markedly impaired NPT when recorded in a sleep laboratory for the usual three nights. One of their patients was recorded for four nights with virtually no NPT. On the morning following the fourth night of recording, the patient was observed to attain a full erection by masturbating. One year later he was still able to get a full erection when he masturbated but not when he attempted intercourse.

9. Roose et al. (43) in a preliminary report described two men with severe depressions who had virtually no NPT while they were depressed but had normal NPT when they recovered. Though this study has methodological problems acknowledged by the authors, the findings suggest that severe depression can severely impair NPT. While some might view this as a type of physiological impotence, it certainly is not what is usually thought of when one speaks of organic impotence.

Because of these empirical findings suggesting that NPT can be severely impaired by psychological factors, and because of the circular reasoning initially employed in arguing that NPT can distinguish ISE patients from organically impotent patients, it is important that the basic assumptions behind NPT evaluations for impotence be tested in patients known to have ISE independent of NPT measurement themselves. One possible protocol might go as follows: Subjects would be selected who could be clearly diagnosed as having ISE on clinical grounds, that is, who can attain full sustained erections in some circumstances but not in others. In addition, they would have no history, physical abnormalities, or laboratory tests indicative of a physical disorder known to be associated with impotence. In other words, they would be the subgroup of impotent patients in whom NPT evaluations would not normally be indicated. In this study they would have NPT recorded prior to psychological treatment and then would be treated with both the patient and the therapist blind to the NPT results. Patients who fully recovered their potency would be diagnosed as having ISE for the purpose of the study, and those who did not fully recover would be eliminated from the study's statistical analysis. The NPT recordings of the patients shown by their recovery of potency with psychological treatment to have ISE would then be analyzed to determine if any of them demonstrated significantly impaired NPT. In a similar way the NPT patterns recorded prior to treatment in patients with reversible organic causes of impotence could be studied to see if any showed full nocturnal erections.

Until such studies are done to definitively determine the limits of NPT measurements in distinguishing ISE from organic impotence, it seems wisest to be cautious and not make the diagnosis of organic impotence solely on the basis of impaired NPT, but also to require for this diagnosis the presence of a documented organic illness known to be associated with impotence and the absence of a history of selective impairment of erections.

Requirement for Direct Observation of Erection

There are large interindividual differences in the increase in circumference associated with full erections at the tip of the penis (10–48 mm) (23, 30) as well as at the base (15–45 mm) (35, 36). Because of this, there is general agreement that if the increases in circumference fall within the above ranges, the only way, at present, to determine whether the erection is adequate for vaginal penetration is to observe the erection directly (36, 38, 40). However, an adequate direct observation is technically the most difficult step in the NPT evaluation. It is sometimes not possible to time the awakening so that the observed erection is sufficiently rigid for vaginal penetration and/or the increases in circumference at both the base and tip of the penis are 81 percent or more of the largest increases recorded during the three nights. This can occur if the erections are brief, if the patient has only one or two erections in the full range during the three nights' recording, or if the technologist is not well trained and/or alert. If an adequate awakening is not possible, an alternative to additional sleep studies employed at our center as well as by Fisher et al. (36) is to have the patient masturbate with a strain gauge in place at the base of his penis. An observation is then made, if possible, when the increase in circumference reaches 81 percent or more of the largest increase recorded during the three nights of sleep. The practical difficulty in obtaining an adequate observation may explain why in practice a direct observation has not always been used to determine whether an erection is full, despite the general acknowledgment of the importance of this step. For example, in one study in which most of the patients who had increases in circumference of 5 mm or more at the tip were awakened to observe one or more of their fullest erections, the amount of increase in circumference and not the information obtained from the direct observation was used to classify the erections as full or partial. In this study an increase of 16 mm or more at the tip (chosen on the basis of average findings in normals) was used to define a full erection (28). In other studies no direct observations of erections were reported (37, 48).

The crucial importance of a direct observation is illustrated by the following brief case report:

A 49–year-old married man had a three-year history of gradually progressive erectile difficulties. Two years before our evaluation he had consulted a urologist who could find no organic cause for the impotence and suggested sex therapy. In the month before his evaluation at our center he had not been able to achieve a single erection sufficient for vaginal penetration.

The results of three nights of PSG recording indicated that the largest increase in circumference at the base of the penis was 21 mm and at the tip 14 mm—both within the range associated with full erections in some normal men. However, on awakening the patient and observing an erection with an increase at the base of the penis of 17 mm (81 percent of the largest increase at the base) and an increase at the tip of the penis of 14 mm (100 percent of the largest increase at the tip), both the patient and the observer agreed that this erection was not adequate for vaginal penetration and rated it 5 to 6 on a scale of 10.

If an awakening had not been performed and the diagnosis was based entirely on circumference changes, this patient's condition might well have been diagnosed as ISE, and he might again have been referred for sex therapy. However, the awakening clearly showed that his erections were inadequate for vaginal penetration. He was subsequently shown to have an elevated prolactin level of 461 ng/mL (5–18 ng/mL). A skull roentgenogram, polytomograms of the sella turcica, and a computerized tomographic scan of the brain were all normal. The patient reported that he had a complete return of potency when treated for his hyperprolactinemia with bromocryptine mesylate 10 mg per day. Five months later, NPT was re-recorded and demonstrated rigid "stand-up" erections during sleep.

Portable Monitors for NPT Evaluations

The standard sleep laboratory evaluation of NPT is a complicated, expensive, time-consuming procedure that requires a great deal of technical expertise and costly equipment. It would be desirable if the procedure could be simplified and made less expensive without compromising the quality of the evaluation. Several portable monitoring devices that measure NPT continuously through the night have been marketed with these goals in mind. However, the monitors are often given to the patient to take home and use on himself for only one night without a direct observation of one of his largest erections and without any measurement of sleep stages. The diagnosis is made solely on the basis of penile circumference changes recorded by the monitor on a strip of paper similar to an EKG strip. A circumference change based on reported changes associated with full erections in average normals is usually chosen to define organic impotence and ISE in place of the findings of a direct observation of one of the patient's largest erections. Anyone who attains an increase in circumference equal to or greater than the designated circumference change is diagnosed as having ISE, and anyone who does not is diagnosed organically impotent.

Use of such monitors in this way is inadequate for diagnostic purposes for the following reasons. First, there is evidence that NPT is decreased (42) and that other sleep variables are altered the first night a patient is recorded in the sleep laboratory (49). The results of one night's recording are therefore suspect and cannot be presumed to accurately characterize the usual NPT pattern of a patient. Second, the monitors do not give information about whether the patient slept adequately or had a normal amount of REM sleep. This cannot be accurately determined either by asking the patient or directly observing him. It requires continuous polygraphic monitoring of EEG, EOG, and chin EMG. Third, and most important, unless the patient's erection is directly observed during a period of maximum tumescence, it is impossible to know whether an increase in circumference of 10 mm or more at the base is indicative of an erection adequate for intercourse for that particular individual.

There is no reason why portable NPT monitors cannot be used for three consecutive nights rather than one, or why a technologist cannot be present to awaken the patient and directly observe one of his largest erections. In fact, a minority of people who use portable monitors have employed them in this way. If the patient does have full sustained erections that are directly observed, portable NPT monitors provide a satisfactory and economical way to make the diagnosis of ISE. However, if the patient does not have full sustained erections and sleep is not polygraphically monitored, it is impossible to know whether the decreased or absent NPT is due to impaired NPT in a patient who slept well and therefore is suggestive of organic impotence, or is reflective of decreased REM sleep or the patient not sleeping at all and therefore indicative of an inadequate study.

In summary, portable monitors provide a satisfactory and economical technique for diagnosing ISE, provided a direct observation is performed, but they are *inadequate* for making the diagnosis of organic impotence. It is especially important to be correct about this latter diagnosis because it is often the basis (if there is not a treatable organic cause of the impotence) for recommending the surgical implantation of a penile prosthesis, which may result in irreversible damage to penile tissues (7). All such patients should have NPT evaluations in a sleep laboratory prior to recommending such surgery.

SUMMARY

A comprehensive clinical evaluation for impotence was described, focusing on findings helpful in differentiating ISE from organic impotence. Relevant findings in the sexual and medical history, physical examination, and laboratory tests were presented. The physiology of sleep relevant to the differential diagnosis of impotence was described, including the characteristics of the different sleep stages, the finding of nocturnal penile tumescence (NPT) in all normal males studied, and the relationship between NPT and REM sleep. The rationale for using NPT measurements to distinguish ISE from organic impotence was presented, the technique and indications for performing such a study were described, and the criteria for diagnosing impotence as ISE, organic, mixed, or undetermined were set forth. Finally it was emphasized that although clinical experience strongly suggests that NPT monitoring is a useful aid in the differential diagnosis of impotence in most cases, there are several significant problems with the technique. First, the basic assumptions behind these studies are based on circular reasoning and have never been definitively validated in patients shown to have ISE or organic impotence indepenent of NPT measurements themselves. One possible method for doing this was outlined. In addition, empirical findings suggesting that psychological factors can significantly impair NPT in some men were presented. Second, difficulties in performing the crucial step of awakening the patient and directly observing one of his largest erections were described, and it was emphasized that omitting this step and making the diagnosis solely on the basis of circumference changes can result in misdiagnosing an organically impotent patient as having ISE. This is illustrated with a brief case report. Third, problems associated with using portable NPT monitors to perform NPT evaluations, rather than doing them in a sleep laboratory, were discussed. The danger of misdiagnosing a patient with ISE who does not sleep adequately as organically impotent was stressed.

REFERENCES

1. Masters, W. H., and Johnson V. E. Human Sexual Inadequacy. Boston: Little, Brown, 1970. Pp. 137–213.
2. Kaplan, H. S. The New Sex Therapy. New York: Brunner/Mazel. Pp. 255–288.
3. Spark, R. F.; White, R.A.; and Connolly, M. S. Impotence is not always psychogenic. J. Amer. Med. Assoc., 243:750–755, 1980.
4. Michal, V.; Kramar, R.; and Bartak, V. Femoro-pudendal by-pass in the treatment of sexual impotence. J. Cardiovasc. Surg., 15:356–359, 1974.
5. Scott, F. B.; Bradley, W. E.; and Timm, C. W. Management of erectile impotence: use of implantable inflatable prosthesis. Urology, 2:80–82, 1973.
6. Small, M. P.; Carrion, H. M.; and Gordon, J. A. Small-carrion penile prosthesis. Urology, 5:479–486, 1975.
7. Scott, F. B.; Byrd, G. J.; Karacan, I.; Olsson, P.; Beutler, L. E.; and Attia, S. L.

Erectile impotence treated with an implantable, inflatable prosthesis. J. Amer. Med. Assoc., 241:2609–2612, 1979.

8. Wasserman, M. D. Morning erections and the clinical evaluation of impotence. Med. Aspects Hum. Sex., 16:95–99, 1982.

9. Wasserman, M. D.; Pollak, C. P.; Spielman, A. J.; and Weitzman, E. D. Theoretical and technical problems in the measurement of nocturnal penile tumescence for the differential diagnosis of impotence. Psychosom. Med., 42:575–585, 1980.

10. Wasserman, M. D.; Pollak, C. P.; Spielman, A. J.; and Weitzman, E. D. Impaired nocturnal erections and impotence following transurethral prostatectomy. Urology, 15:552–555, 1980.

11. Berger, R. J. The sleep and dream cycle. In Kales, A., ed., Sleep Physiology and Pathology. Philadelphia: J. B. Lippincott, 1969. Pp. 17–32.

12. Aserinsky, E., and Kleitman, N. Two types of ocular motility occuring in sleep. J. Appl. Physiol., 8:1–10, 1955.

13. Berger, R. J. Physiological characteristics of sleep. In Kales, A., ed., Sleep, Physiology and Pathology. Philadelphia: J. B. Lippincott, 1969. Pp. 66–79.

14. Halverson, H. M. Genital and sphincter behavior of the male infant. J. Genet. Psychol., 56:95–136, 1940.

15. Ohlmeyer, P.; Brilmayer, H.; and Hullstrung, H. Periodische vorgange im schlaf. Pflueggers Arch., 248:559–560, 1944.

16. Aserinsky, E., and Kleitman, N. Regularly occurring periods of eye motility and concomitant phenomena during sleep. Science, 118:273–274, 1953.

17. Fisher, C.; Gross, J.; and Zuch, J. Cycle of penile erection synchronous with dreaming (REM) sleep. Arch. Gen. Psychiatry, 12:29–45, 1965.

18. Karacan, I.; Goodenough, D. R.; Shapiro, A.; and Starker, S. Erection cycle during sleep in relation to dream anxiety. Arch. Gen. Psychiatry, 15:183–189, 1966.

19. Karacan, I.; Williams, R. L.; Thornby, J. I.; and Salis, P. J. Sleep related tumescence as a function of age. Amer. J. Psychiatry, 132:932–937, 1975.

20. Karacan, I.; Salis, P. J.; Thornby, J. I.; and Williams, R. L. The ontogeny of nocturnal penile tumescence. Waking and Sleeping, 1:27–44, 1976.

21. Karacan, I.; Hursch, C. J.; Williams, R. L.; and Thornby, J. I. Some characteristics of nocturnal penile tumescence in young adults. Arch. Gen. Psychiatry, 26:351–356, 1972.

22. Hursch, C. J.; Karacan, I.; and Williams, R. L. Some characteristics of nocturnal penile tumescence in early middle-aged males. Comp. Psychiatry, 13:539–548, 1972.

23. Karacan, I.; Hursch, C. J.; Williams, R. L.; and Littell, R. C. Some characteristics of nocturnal penile tumescence during puberty. Pediat. Res., 6: 529–537, 1972.

24. Karacan, I.; Hursch, C. J.; and Williams, R. L. Some characteristics of nocturnal penile tumescence in elderly males. J. Gerontol., 27:39–45, 1972.

25. Wasserman, M. D.; Pressman, M.R.; Pollack, C. P., Spielman, A. J.; DeRosairo, L.; and Weitzman, E. D. Nocturnal penile tumescence: is it really a REM phenomenon? Sleep Res., 11:44, 1982.

26. Karacan, I. Clinical value of nocturnal erection in the prognosis and diagnosis of impotence. Med. Aspects Hum. Sex., 4:27–34, 1970.

27. Karacan, I.; Scott, F. B.; Salis, P. J.; Attia, S. L.; Ware, N. C.; Attila, A.; and Williams, R. L. Nocturnal erections, differential diagnosis of impotence and diabetes. Biol. Psychiatry, 12:373–380, 1977.

28. Karacan, I.; Salis, P. J.; Ware, J. C., Dervent, B.; Williams, R. L.; Scott, F. B.; Attia, S. L.; and Beutler, L. E. Nocturnal penile tumescence and diagnosis in diabetic impotence. Amer. J. Psychiatry, 135:191–197, 1978.
29. Karacan, I. Advances in the psychophysiological evaluation of male erectile impotence. In: LoPiccolo, J., and LoPiccolo, L., eds., Handbook of Sex Therapy. New York: Plenum, 1978. Pp. 137–145.
30. Karacan, I.; Salis, P. J.; and Williams, R. L. The role of the sleep laboratory in diagnosis and treatment of impotence. In: Williams, R. L. and Karacan, I., eds., Sleep Disorders, Diagnosis and Treatment. New York: John Wiley and Sons, 1978. Pp. 353–382.
31. Karacan, I. Nocturnal penile tumescence as a biologic marker in assessing erectile dysfunction. Psychosomatics, 23:349–360, 1982.
32. Karacan, I. Evaluation of nocturnal penile tumescence and impotence. In: Guilleminault, C., ed., Sleeping and Waking Disorders: Indications and Techniques. Reading, Mass.: Addison-Wesley, 1982.
33. Fisher, C.; Schiavi, R.; Lear, H.; Edwards, A.; Davis, D. M.; and Witkin, B. A. The assessment of nocturnal REM erection in the differential diagnosis of sexual impotence. J. Sex. Marriage Ther., 1:277–289, 1975.
34. Fisher, C.; Schiavi, R.; and Edwards, A. Assessment of nocturnal REM erection in differential diagnosis of sexual impotence. Sleep Res., 5:42, 1976.
35. Fisher, C.; Schiavi, R.; Edwards, A.; Davis, D.; Reitman, M.; and Fine, J. Quantitative differences in nocturnal penile tumescence (NPT) between impotence of psychogenic and organic origin. Sleep Res., 6:49, 1977.
36. Fisher, C.; Schiavi, R. C.; Edwards, A.; Davis, D.; Reitman, M.; and Fine, J. Evaluation of nocturnal penile tumescence in the differential diagnosis of sexual impotence. Arch. Gen. Psychiatry, 36:431–437, 1979.
37. Hosking, D. J.; Bennett, T.; Hampton, J. R.; Evans, D. F.; Clark, A. J.; and Robertson, G. Diabetic impotence: studies of nocturnal erection during REM sleep. Br. Med. J., 2:1394–1396, 1979.
38. Wasserman, M. D.; Pollak, C. P.; Spielman, A. J.; and Weitzman, E. D. The differential diagnosis of impotence: measurement of nocturnal penile tumescence. J. Amer. Med. Assoc., 243:2038–2042, 1980.
39. Hahn, P. M., and Leder, R. Quantifications of penile "buckling" force. Sleep, 3:94–97, 1980.
40. Karacan, I., and Ilaria, R. L. Nocturnal penile tumescence (NPT): the phenomenon and its role in the diagnosis of impotence. Sexuality Disability, 1:260–271, 1978.
41. Fisher, C. Dreaming and sexuality. In: Loewenstein, R. M.; Newman, L. M.; Schur, M.; and Solnit, A. J., eds., Psychoanalysis—A General Psychology. New York: International Universities Press, 1966. Pp. 537–569.
42. Jovanovic, V. J. Der effekt der ersten untersuchungsnacht auf die erektionen im schlaf. Psychother. Psychosom., 17:295–308, 1969.
43. Roose, S. P.; Glassman, A. H.; Walsh, B. T.; and Cullen, K. Reversible loss of nocturnal penile tumescence during depression: a preliminary report. Neuropsychobiology, 8:284–288, 1982.
44. Impotence: psyche vs. soma. Med. World News, 17:28, June 28, 1976.
45. Marshall, P.; Surridge, D.; and Delva, N. The role of nocturnal penile tumescence in differentiating between organic and psychogenic impotence: the first stage of validation. Arch. Sex. Behav., 10:1–10, 1981.

46. Kahn, E., and Fisher, C. REM sleep and sexuality in the aged. J. Geriatr. Psychiat., 2:181–199, 1969.

47. Jovanovic, V. J. Sexuelle Reaktionen und schlafperiodik bei menschen. Ergebnisse experimentaller untersuchungen. Beitr. Sexualforsch., 51:1–292, 1972.

48. Madorsky, M. L.; Ashamalla, M. G.; Schussler, I.; Lyons, H. R.; and Miller, G. H. Postprostatectomy impotence. J. Urol., 115:401–403, 1976.

49. Agnew, J. W., Jr.; Webb, W. B.; and Williams, R. L. The first night effect: an EEG study of sleep. Psychophysiology, 2:263–266, 1966.

AHMED MOBARAK and
CHARLES A. SHAMOIAN

14

Aging and Sexuality

People are living longer and the number of the elderly is increasing steadily. The aged and society at large are becoming increasingly interested not only in the fact that there is a longer life span but also in the quality of later life. Society is now more aware of the physical, financial, and psychological needs of the elderly. However, an important facet of their life, sexuality, has been ignored. Sexuality offers many older persons the opportunity to express intimacy, passion, and affection while providing affirmative evidence that the body is still reliable and functional (1). To recognize and accept the sexual needs of an older person is to accept that person as a whole (3).

Only recently has the sexual behavior of the elderly been the subject of investigation and research. Unfortunately, the myths and misconceptions about sexuality and the aged have been a serious impediment to availability of older subjects for research and to our understanding of sexuality in old age. In the monumental work of Kinsey (3, 4) there were only 106 men who were 60 years old or older among the 14,084 men who participated in the study, and only 56 women were 60 years old or older among the 5,940 women studied. In Masters and Johnson's (5) pioneer work in human sexual response, among the population who actively participated in the laboratory studies there were 312 men, of whom only 20 were 60 or older, and of the 382 women only 11 were 60 or older.

Duke University's longitudinal studies (6, 7) were successful in attracting their older population probably because the sexual aspects of the studies were part of a more broadly based longitudinal study of how people adapt to growing old. Pfeiffer (2) pointed out the difficulties in recruiting subjects for such studies. First, subjects are reluctant to participate, and even if they do cooperate, the data that can be collected are generally of a limited nature. Aged individuals themselves may agree to participate in such studies, but relatives who learn of their participation sometimes become "concerned" and insist that the subjects withdraw from the study. Even referring physicians may express "concern" that such studies may prove upsetting to their patients, or they may contend that such matters are essentially private and should not be studied scientifically. Finally, investigators themselves need to overcome the initial hesitancy and embarrassment before they can comfortably inquire into the sexual lives of their subjects.

SOCIOCULTURAL ATTITUDES TOWARD SEXUALITY IN THE ELDERLY

In spite of society's more liberal attitudes toward sexuality in general, the traditional notion that sexual activity is primarily for procreative purposes and only secondarily for recreational purposes is still considered sacred by many. Many of the taboos concerning sexuality in adolsecence and adulthood have been largely laid aside, since the production of offspring is still a possibility and thus sexual activity is sanctioned. But in old age the fiction that sex is being carried on for procreational purposes can no longer be maintained and is therefore not easily accepted. This may be an extension of the incest taboo. Children of all ages experience a great deal of anxiety at the thought of their parents' engaging in sexual activity. Since the elderly constitute the parent generation, the seeming cultural prohibition against their becoming involved in active sexual expression may be accounted for on this basis (2). Another possible explanation is the fear among the young that their own sexual viability might be lost with age (8). To deal with this fear is to discount the importance of sex in old age. If sexual behavior is not important then, certainly neither is the loss of it. The young may also seek to eliminate the aged as competitors for sexual objects by fostering and generating the stereotype of the aged, asexual elderly (9).

These myths about the sexuality of the elderly lead to cultural stereotypes which are not substantiated by the scientific data that has accumulated in recent years. It is assumed that older people (a) do not have sexual desires, (b), could not make love even if they desired, (c) are too fragile physically, and (d) are physically unattractive and therefore sexually undesirable (10). The psychological response to these societal cues may be the greatest threat to continued sexual activity in later years.

In recent years, studies of the sexual behavior of the elderly have been gaining popularity. The monumental work of Kinsey et al. (3, 4) was the first to address the issue of sexual behavior in the elderly. Though Kinsey acknowledged the underrepresentation of the aged, his findings opened the door for a better understanding of the effects of aging on sexuality. Although the cross-sectional studies indicated that sexual activity persisted in late life, there was a general decline in all measures of sexual activity across the adult age-range. This pattern was true for both men and women, although women typically reported lower levels of activity than men at all ages.

Kinsey et al. (3, 4) also reported that at age 60 only one out of five men was no longer capable of sexual intercourse, but at the age of 80 this proportion had risen to three out of four men. This constitutes a steep decline in the proportion of men still sexually capable over a 20–year age-span. But Kinsey also concluded that the rate of decline in absolute frequency of all sexual outlets (which in his studies included sexual intercourse, masturbation, and nocturnal emissions) on the average did not decline any more rapidly in old age than at ages between 30 and 60.

Women showed the same pattern of decline with age and typically reported lower levels of activity than men at all ages. Women also indicated that their pattern of sexual activity was dependent mostly on the availability and preference of their male partners. Finke et al. (11) reported that 65 percent of men aged 70 years and younger in their samples indicated that they had engaged in sexual activity within one year. Freeman (12) reported that in a sample of men with an average age of 71 years, 55 percent indicated that they were sexually active. These studies support the findings of Kinsey et al. that a majority of older men remain sexually active in late life. Masters and Johnson's pioneering work (5, 13) in the studies of the physiology of sexual response indicated that though there is general slowing in the different phases of the sexual response cycle, the elderly are sexually active in their 70s, 80s, and even in their 90s, given reasonable good health.

Other cross-sectional studies (14, 15) similarly concluded that, though sexual activities tend to decline with age, some level of sexual activity persists in late life. George and Weiler (16) addressed the problems with cross-sectional design of previous studies: First, results may be skewed by the selected survival of a cohort of the study population having a nonrandom distribution of the variables studied (e.g., men with a higher sex drive might also live longer). Second, possibilities for examining the patterns of change over time are precluded. Third, there is the risk of making invalid comparisons between generations. Finally, in such studies there is no way for individual variation of patterns to emerge from the population.

Pfeiffer et al. (17) and Verwoerdt et al. (18) conducted longitudinal studies of sexual behavior with aging. They concluded that: (a) Sex continues to play an important role in the lives of many elderly persons and sexual interest and activity continue in late life. (b) Sexual activity declines gradually over time for both men and women, although over the ten years, studied the gradual decline pattern was not representative of all individuals; some showed a steady level of sexual interest, and even for a small group of men actual increases in sexual interest and activity occurred over the ten-year period of the study. (c) Sexual interest declined over time, though more slowly than sexual activity. (d) Men were more sexually active than women at any given age, though the gap narrows at advanced age. (e) Sexual activity among women is heavily dependent on the availability of a functionally capable, socially sanctioned male partner. In addition, cessation of sexual activity among both men and women is most commonly attributed to men. George and Weiler (16) in their longitudinal study corroborated the findings of other investigators. They found that women report significantly lower levels of sexual interest and activity than their male aged peers and that both men and women attribute the responsibility for cessation of sexual activity to the male partner. Unlike other longitudinal studies, their data suggested that levels of sexual activity tend to remain stable over middle and late life. George and Weiler also suggested the importance of distinguishing the effects of aging per se from those of cohort differences or other factors. The fact that there are apparent cohort differences in the frequency of sexual activity suggests that older persons of the future may not have the same patterns as older persons do today.

AGE-RELATED SEXUAL CHANGES: A CONTINUOUS PROCESS

There is no specific age at which someone suddenly becomes old. Different societies have different points of reference at which someone is considered elderly. In our society we have accepted the chronological age in a rigid manner as a measure of phases of life. As a result we have generalized judgments and stereotypes about aging. The effects of aging on sexuality involve a complex interaction of biological, sociocultural, and psychological factors. There are certain universal biological changes associated with aging, but responses of individuals to these changes differ tremendously. We now turn to a review of the physiology of the reproductive system and the normal physiological and anatomical changes that occur with aging.

Age-Related Changes in Sex Steroid Hormones in the Male

In recent years, many investigations have addressed the subject of testicular endocrine functions in aging and have shown consistent evidence for a decrease in circulating plasma testosterone. The data of Vermeulen et al. (19) show that although mean testosterone levels fall after age 50, there is a very wide scatter of individual testosterone values. In their study, 230 ng/dl is taken as the lower limit of normal, so that even after age 80 the majority of men still have total testosterone concentrations in the normal range.

Since the nonprotein-bound testosterone is now widely accepted as representing the biologically active fraction, a number of investigations of free and bound testosterone in subjects of different ages have been undertaken (20). An increase with age has been found in the fraction of testosterone bound to globulins, with a corresponding decrease in the free fractions. The fall in free testosterone begins earlier and is steeper than that of total testosterone (21), but there is a considerable scatter of values with some overlap between older and younger men. Vermeulen et al. (19) reported a decrease in the overall rate of metabolism and the secretion of testosterone with age, which they attributed to the lowering of the fraction of testosterone available to cells. A review (22) of the nature of changes with aging in sexual function and endocrinology confirmed the decrease of total plasma testosterone with a greater decrease in the free fraction. They aso reported that although all aspects of sexuality declined with aging, libido showed a lesser decline than potency.

Male Hormone Replacement Therapy

Hormonal replacement in aging men has generated controversy. Numerous reports (23–27) suggest impovement in the sexual functioning of elderly men by androgen administration, but many of these studies were without controls and therefore of questionable validity. Only recently, adequate controlled studies have documented improvement in sexual behavior with sex steroid replacement therapy in hypogonadal men (28, 29). Since hormonal therapy may be hazardous, with unknown risks of exacerbating benign prostatic hypertrophy and urinary retention, or induction of prostatic carcinoma, as well as a possible relationship between androgen secretion and arteriosclerosis, routine androgen treatment of aging men cannot be recommended at this time (20).

Changes in Male Sexual Physiology

Aging is a continuous process which begins with life itself, and the physiological changes of aging must be viewed on a continuum. Data from different studies (5, 13, 30) show that men reach the peak of their sexuality in their late teens or early 20s. With mild sexual stimulation the young man achieves an erection and reaches the highest level of excitement easily, and orgasm is experienced as intense and biphasic. The first phase of orgasm is felt when the internal genital organs contract; one to three seconds later the second phase follows, with ejaculation with strong ryhthmic contractions. The detumescence after orgasm is slow, and the refractory period is very brief. For a young man to have four to eight orgasms in a day is not unusual. Kinsey et al. (3) described the earliest age-related change in their male subjects as loss of capacity for multiple orgasms in a short period of time. Masters and Johnson (5) described other changes of aging in the pattern of the male sexual response. Erection occurs more slowly, and the older man needs more direct stimulation of the genitals. The erection is frequently maintained for an extended period of time without ejaculation. The full penile erection frequently is not obtained until just before ejaculation. In addition, increased ejaculatory control is associated with the aging process. Some elderly men experience what Masters and Johnson termed an "adverse refractory period," which means that after the elderly male obtains full erection and subsequently experiences a detumescence without ejaculation, for example, because of long foreplay, 12 to 24 hours might pass before he can have another erection. Testicular elevation, scrotal sac vasocongestion, and vascular engorgement of the testis are diminished. The emission phase of the ejaculatory experience is minimal or absent, and the ejaculatory force is diminished and its biphasic characteristic is almost absent. The subjective level of ejaculatory demand is reduced, and a man of 60 is often satisfied to ejaculate every second or third time coitus occurs. Detumescence after orgasm is rapid, and the refractory period is much lengthened. It is evident that the male orgasm is the most vulnerable to the effects of aging, while the erection response remains relatively unaffected (30).

Anatomical Changes in the Male

Despite generalized reduction in elastic tissues with aging, elasticity of the corpora cavernosa of the penis does not seem to be significantly affected. Older men can maintain the capacity for full erections into their very late years. However, atherosclerosis in the deep arteries of the penis may limit the vasocongestion necessary for full erection. The angle of the fully erect penis relative to the abdomen tends to be reduced, probably due to loss of elasticity of the suspensory and fusiform ligaments. The scrotal sac tends to be elongated, shows multiple folding, and sags away from the underlying testis. Though these changes are quite noticeable, they do not affect coitus. Aging changes in the testicular tissues may account for some of the reduction in the volume of the ejaculate as well as for the gradual decline in sex steroids. Atrophic changes in the perineal muscles can contribute to decreased rigidity of erection and force of ejaculation in the aged man. Benign prostatic hypertrophy is common in elderly men. While it might cause difficulties with the act of urination, it has no specific effect on sexual functioning.

Age-Related Sexual Behavior in Males

Men reach the peak of their sexuality in their late teens or early 20s, after which there is a gradual decline. Kaplan (30) reports that by their 40s men show a noticeable change in their sexual expression and behavior. The focus gradually shifts from the intense, genitally localized sensation of the younger years to the more sensuous, romantic, but diffuse and generalized experience characteristic of middle age and later life. More attention is paid to the sexual ambience and wish to be seductive and to be seduced. Orgasm gradually assumes less importance within the sexual experience. By the 50s the physiological changes in the sexual response cycle play a major role in the sexual behavior. There is a need for longer foreplay and for more direct stimulation to the genitals. Men of this age have better control over the ejaculatory urgency and are generally satisfied with fewer orgasms. They are usually satisfied with one or possibly two orgasms per week. Men who are secure in their sexual relationships and confident in their sexuality can usually adjust to their altered and somewhat diminished sexual response. They often feel that their gained sexual experience and better control over ejaculatory urgency make them better lovers. However, some men are threatened by their slowed sexual responses and worry about virility and performance. They may become depressed and irritable and withdraw from sexuality. Others, in their panic, try to recapture the sexual excitement of their younger years by leaving their older partners and becoming involved with younger women. Middle age is a period of sexual adjustment, and the fortunate are able to continue a healthy pattern of sexual activity and enjoyment for the rest of their lives.

Physiology of the Female Reproductive System

In the female, aging changes occur prior to menarche, between menarche and menopause, and finally between menopause and death. The effects of estrogen and progesterone on the anatomy and physiology of the female reproductive organs, on the secondary sexual characteristics, and on pregnancy, delivery, and lactation are all well understood. Androgen is thought to activate cerebral sex centers and to increase sexual desire in women as well as in men. Testosterone may be an effective aphrodesiac for women, especially when the androgen-estrogen ratio is on the low side. For many years the libidinal effects of androgen have been clearly understood for men, but recently they have been found to be equally influential on the sexual desires of women. Estrogen and progesterone may have no specific effect on sexual behavior, but there is some evidence that progesterone inhibits female sexuality, possibly indirectly, to the extent that it antagonizes the action of androgen (30).

In spite of considerable anatomical changes in the female reproductive system at the time of menopause, the sexual response cycle of the older female remains essentially the same as that of her younger years. She continues to be capable of multiple orgasmic response with almost no refractory period throughout her life. This may be because the female orgasm lacks the emission phase of ejaculation, which seems to be most vulnerable to the aging process. Masters and Johnson (5, 13, 31) have concluded that age-related changes in female sexual physiology are functionally minimal, but they did report certain changes that are related to the anatomical changes of aging. A slowing in the rate of production and a reduction in the volume of vaginal lubricating fluid occurs. In addition, there is usually some loss in the elasticity of the vaginal wall. This leads to a significant reduction in the woman's involuntary capacity for lengthening and increasing the transcervical diameter of the vaginal barrel in response to sexual stimulation. Thus more time is needed for precoital stimulation to allow for this slowed excitement phase. Also, many aging women report that their orgasmic experience is also somewhat slowed. The duration of an orgasm is shortened, and its intensity is somewhat reduced. However, the subjective levels of sensual pleasure derived from coitus usually continues unaltered. Infrequently, some elderly women experience the uterine contractions during orgasm as painful spasms. The resolution phase of the sexual response cycle is shortened considerably in postclimacteric women.

Anatomical Changes in the Female

The changes in the female reproductive system are related both to aging and to ovarian hormonal depletion. It is impossible to separate the respective effects of aging from the hypoestrogenic state because both occur concurrently. There may be some thinning of the pubic hair, and the mons veneris becomes less prominent due to the reduction in fatty tissue. The hood over the clitoris, formed by the anterior ends of the labia minora, recedes with age, and this shrinkage, in a kind of paradox, exposes the clitoris more readily to sexual stimulation during foreplay and during intercourse itself (32). Shrinkage of the vagina occurs, especially at the vault. There is thinning of the vagina and reduced elasticity of the walls. Vulvo-vaginal lubrication is reduced during sexual stimulation. Aging atrophy of the perineal muscles may add to the earlier effects of childbirth and lack of exercise. This may limit the muscular response during orgasm.

Because some of these changes are not directly degenerative in nature but rather induced by hormonal insufficiency, the rate of "aging" can be diminished or even considerably reversed by the administration of female sex hormones. Over the years, the role of hormonal replacement therapy has changed. An approach popular in the 1950s suggested that estrogens would maintain eternal youthfulness and therefore should be given to everyone. To the contrary, however, estrogens were found to be associated with side effects and complications. A second approach was that estrogens should never be given because their use was not natural. This was harsh, for estrogens may indeed be helpful for many women. The third approach, currently shared by many investigators (33, 34), is to evaluate the patient and determine a presenting symptom. If vaginal atrophy or severe uterine cramps are presenting a threat to sexual life, estrogens would be advised. Given the understanding of the beneficial effects and the risks of the treatment, however, the woman must share in the responsibility of the decision.

The importance of regular sexual activity in decreasing the effects of aging on the vagina has been emphasized by several investigators (35, 36). Leiblum (37) investigated the effect of sexual activity on vaginal atrophy in postmenopausal women. Fifty-two subjects (mean age 57 years) were divided in two groups: sexually active (intercourse frequency three to four times monthly) and sexually inactive (intercourse frequency less than ten times yearly). As predicted, less vaginal atrophy was apparent in the sexually active women, as opposed to the sexually inactive women. Further, women with less vaginal atrophy had significantly higher mean levels of androgens and gonadotropins, suggesting the importance of androgens in reducing atrophy and maintaining sexual interest.

Age-Related Sexual Behavior in Females

Studies (4, 14, 5, 13, 38, 39) have shown that sexual activity in women, as in men, persisted in late life. In addition, a general decline in all sexual activity with aging has been reported. However, these studies showed variation in the quality and the quantity of the sexual activity in females as compared with males. In young women during early marriage the frequency of intercourse is at its peak. This seems to be primarily motivated by the young husband's intense sexual desire. By their late 30s, women tend to reach their peak of sexual responsiveness. Masters and Johnson (5, 13) observed rapid and intense sexual responsiveness during this period. Kaplan (30) also observed that many but not all women in this age-group report that they experience more interest in sexuality than during their earlier years. This is speculated to be not primarily biologically determined but rather due to a combination of gradual loss of inhibition and a degree of sexual autonomy. In contrast to the reported better sexual responsiveness in the middle-aged female, Udry et al. (40), in a cross-national comparison, reported that recent data from the United States, Thailand, Belgium, and Japan confirm the finding that female age and not male age is the more important contributor to the decline in the frequency of marital intercourse in women 45 years old or younger. They postulate that the most probable explanation is the decline in the female (but not male) androgen levels during adult years.

The female sexual function during the menopausal years is extremely variable and depends on the woman's general psychic state, the security in her relationship with her husband, as well as the endogenous hormonal changes. Dennerstein and Burrows (33) report a decline in sexual activity and responsiveness in women during this period. There have been different and conflicting explanations for this. Kinsey (4) attributed these changes either to aging changes in the male or to the opportunity for women to use the excuse of menopause for discontinuing sexual relationships in which they were not particularly interested. Pfeiffer et al. (38, 39) showed a dramatic decline in the sexual interest of women between the ages of 45 and 55. A parallel decline in male sexual interest was not evident. Hallstrom (41) also confirmed this finding and was able to demonstrate that decreased sexual function was significantly associated with menopausal status rather than age. Conversely, Kaplan (30) reported that while some women experienced a decrease in sexual desire, many women actually feel an increase in erotic appetite during the menopausal years. She has also postulated from a purely physiological standpoint that sexual desire should theoretically increase at menopause, because the action of androgen, which is not materially affected by menopause, is now unopposed by estrogen. She observed that some women do behave in this manner, especially if they are not depressed and have an available suitable partner. Hallstrom (41) also observed that while women with decreased sexual interest were more likely to suffer from dyspareunia due to vaginal atrophy, no direct relationship was evident between impairment of sexual interest and urinary total estrogens.

Psychological factors play an important role in how women will adjust sexually to menopause. Most psychological theories focus on loss. Deutsch (42) referred to the loss of the reproductive capacity as "a partial death." The decline of sexual attractiveness, usefulness, and biological function were experienced by some women as loss with an ensuing depression. However, decline in sexual interest may occur secondarily to the depressed mood. Hallstrom (41) found declining sexual interest to be significantly associated with Hamilton Rating Scores of depression and also with personality traits of introversion. The importance of premorbid personality has been emphasized by Dennerstein and Burrows (33). Women who have effective capacity and positive secure relationships and who have enjoyed sex in their younger years are more likely to maintain sexuality throughout their menopause.

Sociologically, women's attitudes through the menopause are correlated with a social role performance. The loss of a role (e.g., "mothering") may be crucial in a woman who had few role alternatives unless this is balanced by important cultural gains after the menopause. Van Keep and Kellerhals (43) found fewer symptoms when children were still at home. Crowford and Hooper (44) found more menopausal symptoms present when a daughter had married than when a son had married. Conversely, two studies, by Schneider and Brotherton (45) and Krystal and Chiriboga (46), failed to confirm the importance of loss of parental role or "the empty nest syndrome." This might be a reflection of changes in women's role in present-day society. Van Keep and Kellerhals (43) reported that women in the higher social classes had fewer menopausal complaints. Hallstrom also noted that the higher social class was an important factor in maintaining sexual response after menopause, as were the presence of positive, intact marital relationships, higher educational level, and being employed.

After the 50s, the postmenopausal years also show great variations in female sexual responsiveness. Heterosexual women of this age-group depend on a dwindling supply of men, whose sexual needs have declined markedly. Since the women who are older now were socialized to sexual activity in a traditional way, the loss of their mate or of his interest in sex puts an extreme limitation on their own current activity. It seems that intact marriages or the presence of a socially acceptable partner are crucial factors in the continued sexual activity of the elderly woman. Verwoerdt et al. (18) noted that relatively small numbers of unmarried women (single, divorced, separated, or widowed) reported any degree of sexual activity in their senior years. However, separated and divorced women reported somewhat relatively higher sexual interest and activity than widowed women. This is in contrast to the reports that unmarried men in later life are not so restricted by the absence of full marital status and that they maintain the same sexual expression as married men. Palmore (6, 7) reported that the best predictors of continued sexual functioning in old age for men were past sexual experience, age, health, and social class. In contrast, the best predictor for women is marital status.

Many studies (16–18, 5, 13) confirm that spouses agree that the husband was responsible for any decline or cessation in sexual intercourse in the marriage. These studies have focused only on vaginal intercourse. Other forms of sexual expression, which definitely exist—like masturbation, oral sex, and homosexuality—have rarely been investigated. It may be that as other sexual practices gain more acceptance, investigators will broaden the scope of studied sexual practices.

SEXUAL ACTIVITY AMONG THE ELDERLY

As noted previously, studies have indicated that continued sexual activity of elderly women is heavily dependent on the availability of suitable men. This places older women in our culture at a greater disadvantage. Women live an average of seven years longer than men and marry men four years older. Of 12 million older women, more than 6 million live alone, and an additional 1.2 million are divorced or single. Older men have a tremendous advantage compared with women in finding companionship, sexual partners, or remarriage. Also, because they tend to marry younger women who outlive them, men are much less likely to be widowed.

Some 53 percent of older women are widowed, compared with only 15 percent of older men. Men 65 and older are much more likely to be married than women at this age: 78 percent of older men are married, as opposed to only 39 percent of older women (1). Even widowed older men tend to remarry younger women. When men 75 years old or older remarry, over half marry younger women, and one-fifth of these are below age 65.

In intact marriages, husbands are primarily responsible for the decline or cessation of sexual activity. Thus it is important to examine the factors in male sexual involution. Aside from physical and mental disabilities, Masters and Johnson (5, 13) indicate that other possible factors are (a) sexual boredom, which may be the greatest detriment to sexual interaction between men and women in any long-standing relationship, (b) overindulgence in food or drink, (c) preoccupation with outside activities, (d) physical or mental fatigue, and (e) fear of performance. There are also many symbolic associations between sexual activity and death, evidenced in the French word for orgasm, which is *petit mort*, or "little death." Fear of heart attacks or strokes during intercourse may lead to abstinence, which may or may not be medically justified.

To summarize, women report significantly lower levels of sexual interest and activity than their male aged peers, sexual activities for men and women continue into later life, women before the middle years of life report more activity than interest in marital intercourse, while afterward they report more interest than activity, and sexual activity among women is heavily dependent on the availability of a functioning capable socially sanctioned male partner. In addition, cessation of sexual activity among both men and women is most commonly attributed to the men. In the older population as a whole, sexual activity is less frequent than among younger persons, regardless of the particular factors that account for that difference.

The Effects of Physical Illness on Sexual Activity

Multiple ilnesses are common in old age, so there is relatively a greater likelihood of adverse effects on the sexuality of the males and the females. There is also a greater possibility of individuals requiring a multiple-drug regimen that may further interfere with their sexuality. Addressing all physical illnesses that interfere with the sexuality of the elderly is beyond the scope of this chapter, but some of the more common physical illnesses warrant specific mention, especially degenerative illnesses.

Arteriosclerosis in its cerebral form may lead to the loss of sexual desire, with impotence or sometimes disinhibition with hypersexuality and inappropriate sexual behavior. Its local effects on the deep arteries of the penis may limit the vasocongestion necessary for full erection. Strokes with or without prior history of hypertension may affect sexuality, depending on which part of the brain is involved (47, 48). A stroke can also create marital conflicts on a psychological and/or physical basis. Partner rejection because of altered physical appearance and the physical difficulties of intimacy may all require guidance and help. Couples can then be advised about different positions for intercourse or alternatives to intercourse. In myocardial infarction, a common fear for both patient and the spouse is that sexual activity might precipitate another attack or even death. Sexual activity to orgasm imposes a strain on the heart roughly equivalent to walking two city blocks at a measured pace. Although arrhythmias may occur during sexual activity, they are the exception not the rule, and postcardiac patients may maintain a satisfying sexual adjustment. Generally the physician should encourage the couple to resume sexual activity about three months after the initial heart attack. About one-third of the patients who resume sexuality at that time return to their former level of activity. The majority have a more-or-less permanent reduction in activity, while up to 10 percent abstain permanently (49, 50).

Patients with degenerative joint diseases in the form of osteoarthritis with pain and stiffness often need counseling about careful timing of analgesics in relationship to sexual activity. Suggestions about more comfortable positions for sexual play and intercourse can contribute to continuation of regular sexual intimacy (32).

Endocrine disorders can lead to sexual impairment in the young as well as in the elderly. Diabetes mellitus is the most common medical disorder causing erectile dysfunction (51). Between 30 and 60 percent of all diabetic men (750,000 to 1,700,000) develop erectile dysfunction (52). No correlation has been found between erectile dysfunction and the severity of the diabetic process, the duration of the illness, or the type or amount of the antidiabetic medication (53). However, erectile dysfunction increases in frequency in the older diabetic age-group, from a prevalence of 25 to 30 percent among diabetics in their 20s and 30s to 50 to 70 percent in diabetic men over 50 (53, 54). It is hypothesized that this difference in prevalence is related to the microvascular changes with the accelerated arteriosclerosis seen in the aging diabetics. Adult-onset diabetes can cause loss of potency that tends to precede loss of sexual desire. Adequate control of the diabetes and encouragement of continuing sexual intimacy might help restore potency or help the couple to find alternative forms of sexual expression.

Hypothyroidism, commonly seen in later life, decreases sexual desire and diminishes potency. This condition seems to be more common in females, for unknown reasons. Hormonal replacement for life can correct the sexual dysfunction. Patients over 70, however, who have been hypothyroid for 18 months or more may fail to show significant return of sexual functioning (32).

Mental Illness and Sexual Activity

The literature hardly addresses the effects of mental illness on the sexuality of the elderly. The possibility that late-onset psychopathology (i.e., depression, mania, paraphrenias) might affect the sexuality of the elderly in a different manner than the younger age-group has yet to be explored. In primary degenerative dementia there is a general decline in sexual interest and activity. Even if sexuality persists in severely demented patients, the spouses usually are very upset by their partner's misidentification of them and/or their inappropriate sexual behavior.

The Effects of Drugs on Sexual Activity

Pharmacological agents may affect any phase of the sexual response cycle. Some alter sexual desire, while others affect erection, orgasm, and ejaculation. Unfortunately, most of these agents inhibit rather than enhance sexuality. The effects of drugs on male sexuality are far better understood than their effects on female sexuality. This is partly because the male response is more visible and quantifiable.

Drugs that influence sexual interest by acting on the brain either as stimulants or as depressants may have similar sexual effects on both genders. Also, the peripheral effects of certain drugs on the sexual response cycle may be similar on both men and women. However, since there is no emission phase in the female orgasm, antiadrenergic drugs which impair emissions in the male may be expected to have no particular effect on orgasm in women (30, 55) . It is important to be aware of the potential side effects of various drugs when selecting alternative medication. Such knowledge could be helpful in enhancing compliance and reducing psychological distress.

The effects of drugs on sexuality have been extensively reported (13, 30, 54–59, 48, 51). Some of the drugs commonly used in the geriatric population that might affect sexuality are summarized below:

1. *Anti-Anxiety Drugs* (e.g., diazepam and clorazepate dipotassium). These decrease sexual desire and cause orgasmic difficulty by action on the limbic system and internuncial neurons of the spinal cord.

2. *Sedative-Hypnotic Drugs* (e.g., alcohol and barbiturates). These may decrease sexual desire and sexual response because of general depression of the central nervous system (CNS), causing interference with the reflex transmission pathways of sexual arousal. Effects are dose-related, with higher doses producing impaired response in all phases. Chronic alcohol abuse results in neurological and hepatic damage with resulting impaired sexual functioning in all phases.

3. *Antipsychotic Agents*

A. Phenothiazines (e.g., thiothixene, thioridazine, and chlorpromazine). Retrograde ejaculation may be caused by internal vesical sphincter paralysis, causing semen to empty into the bladder, often seen with thioridazine. Decrease in desire is reported only at very high doses, and impotence is rare.

B. Butyrophenones (e.g., haloperidol). The mechanism of action is unkown; may involve central or peripheral antiadrenergic and/or antidopaminergic activity. This may decrease desire and may cause impotence (rare), but apparently has no effect on orgasm.

4. *Antidepressants*

A. Tricyclic antidepressants (e.g., amitriptyline, imipramine). The anticholinergic side effects might rarely affect sexual desire or cause impotence.

B. Monoamine oxidase inhibitors (e.g., phenelzine sulphate and isocarboxazid). There have been some reports of impairment in orgasmic phase in some females.

C. Antimanic drugs (e.g., lithium carbonate). The hypersexuality of manic behavior may diminish. There are some reports of difficulties with different phases of the sexual response cycle in males with these drugs (60).

5. *Antihypertensive and Cardiac Drugs*. These drugs warrant special mention in detail because they are frequently prescribed.

A. Diuretics (e.g. thiazides, furosemide). These may cause erectile dysfunction and difficulties with ejaculation. This might be due to blunting of vascular reflexes via influence on smooth muscle reactivity or to hyperglycemic and hypocalcemic effects. The incident of dysfunction may reach more than 30 percent.

B. Centrally acting sympatholytic drugs (e.g., alpha-methyl-dopa). These inhibit all phases of the sexual response. This effect is dose-related and increases in incidence up to 50 percent of patients when the dose exceeds 2 grams per day. Effects are mediated by CNS catecholamine depletion and production of false neurotransmitters. Clonidine may also cause inhibition of all phases of the sexual response in 10 to 20 percent of patients. Effects may be mediated by alpha-adrenergic blocking activity (centrally and peripherally).

C. Alpha-adrenergic blockers (e.g., phenotolamine, phenoxybenzamine). These cause erectile dysfunction and ejaculation difficulties and may be due to alpha-adrenergic block-ade with inhibition of emission and ejaculations.

D. Beta-adrenergic blockers (e.g., propanolol). These might decrease libido and cause erectile dysfunction, but these sexual side effects, although possible, are less common. The incidence of decreased sexual desire is low (1 to 3 percent).

E. Ganglion blockers (e.g., mecomylamine, pentolinium). These lead to loss of entire sexual response due to paralysis of the peripheral autonomic nervous system. They are rarely used in the United States.

F. Sympathetic nerve terminal agents (e.g., guanethidine). In males, these cause either failure of ejaculation or retrograde ejaculation in as many as 60 percent of patients; impotence is reported in 30 percent. These drugs deplete norepinephrine stores and prevent its release.

G. Noradrenergic vasodilators (e.g., hydrolazine). These cause direct relaxation of the arteriolar smooth muscles and are relatively free of sexual side effects except at doses more than 200 mg per day, when 5 to 10 percent of men report decreased sexual desire occasionally accompanied by erectile dysfunction.

H. Digitalis. Might decrease sexual desire and cause erectile dysfunction. This might be due to estrogen-like effects (chemical similarity) with decreased serum testosterone.

In an isolated study, Hogan (59) studied 861 male patients receiving antihypertensive medication and found a positive history of sexual dysfunction in 9 percent of patients receiving hydrochlorothiazide (HCTZ) (60 mg per day), in 13 percent of patients receiving methyldopa (500 mg to 2 grams per day) plus HCTZ (50 mg per day), 15 percent of patients receiving clonidine (0.2 to 1 mg per day) plus HCTZ (50 mg per day), and in 23 percent of patients receiving propanolol (160 to 320 mg per day) plus hydrolazine (100 mg per day) plus HCTZ (50 mg per day). The incidence of sexual dysfunction was 4 percent in an age-matched control group of 177 normotensive males taking no medication. From this data and those of others Hogan reports the incidence of sexual dysfunction to range from 6 percent to 40 percent for propanolol, up to 26 percent for methyldopa, and 1 to 20 percent for clonidine. However, continued research is needed to clarify the magnitude of sexual side effects of frequently prescribed pharmacologic agents.

SEXUAL DYSFUNCTION IN THE ELDERLY

Sexual activity can still give pleasure to older persons, and sexual problems may trouble them. Masters and Johnson (13) showed more than a 50 percent success rate in treating sexual dysfunctions in older people even when the problem may have existed 25 years or longer. Counseling an older person or couple successfully on a sexual problem can be rewarding to both the practitioner and the patient.

Besides the different types of sexual dysfunctions that are encountered in both the young and the old, Masters and Johnson (31) described two sexual syndromes associated with aging. These clinical syndromes are encountered frequently enough to warrant special attention. They have been termed the Widow's and the Widower's Syndromes. These usually occur in men and women in their late 50s and beyond who have been abstinent from coitus for a year or longer because of their spouse's failing health. When the sexual opportunity presents itself to the man (who usually has no history of prior sexual dysfunction) after such a long period of abstinence, an erection cannot be achieved or maintained. The psychological trauma resulting from this totally unexpected failure often leads to partial or complete impotence.

For the women, the long abstinence from coitus encourages the postmenopausal genital changes, that is, the reduction in elasticity and atrophic changes in the vaginal wall. The vaginal barrel and the vaginal outlet constricts, and lubrication is severely reduced. Attempted coitus after the long abstinence becomes difficult and painful. If these widowers and widows have been fortunate enough to experience their sexual difficulties with cooperative and sexually knowledgeable partners, they may return to full capacity for coitus after several episodes of unhurried and undemanding sexual interaction. Failing to find the ideal partner, they may need professional help and guidance. Engaging in regular masturbatory activity does not appear to prevent or reverse the widower's or widow's syndrome. Thus, neither older men nor older women can afford long periods of coital abstinence if they are to continue as fully capable sexual partners.

ALTERNATIVE SEXUAL EXPRESSION

Masturbation

Researchers have reported difficutly in obtaining information about masturbation from older people. Christenson and Gagnon (61) found in interviews with 241 women over 50 that masturbation among married women occurred less frequently than coitus and showed some decrement with increasing age. Also, they found that almost twice as many postmarital women as married women reported masturbation. More than half of 15 formerly married women studied by Ludeman (62) reported masturbation. Kaplan (30, 55) reported that 25 percent of 70–year-old women still masturbated.

For men, about 25 percent of males over age 60 masturbated regularly (63). Although no recent studies are available on masturbation in older men, Nigola and Peruzza (64) provide one comparison study. In their interviews, they found that 32 women between ages 60 and 80 reported more frequent masturbation than 53 men of approximately the same age.

Bisexuality and Homosexuality

In contrast to exclusive homosexuality, which has not generally been seen as an acceptable sexual outlet, bisexuality is regarded as acceptable by a substantial minority of women, especially in the younger age-group. Wall and Kaltreider (65) interviewed 100 randomly selected female gynecology outpatients ranging in age from 19 to 75 with a mean age of 31. Almost one-third of the women envisioned bisexuality as a possibility they had seriously considered, and nearly all regarded bisexuality as an acceptable alternative for others. Some 63 percent of the women regarded themselves as purely heterosexuals, 23 percent reported incidental homosexual feelings, 11 percent noted considerable homosexual awareness but felt predominantly heterosexual, and 3 percent believed themselves to be bisexual.

For men in the gay community, physical attractiveness and youth are highly valued (66). This has led to the stereotyping of the old male homosexual as one who is disengaged from the homosexual world, lonely, rejected, and unhappy.

Furthermore, many previous studies regarding age and homosexuals have grouped subjects past the ages of 40–46 as old. There has been limited research in the older gay population, and only recently has the question of what happens to older gay men been addressed. Although limited, the available research does not support the stereotype of the older homosexual. Weinberg and Williams (68), who explored homosexual adaptation in the United States, Holland, and Denmark, report that older (over 46) homosexuals are higher on some measurements of psychological well-being than are younger homosexuals. Bennett and Thompson (69), in their study of 478 homosexual men in Australia with diverse backgrounds, corroborated other studies that found that the older homosexual's involvement in the gay community is as satisfying as that of his younger counterpart. They reported that some age difference exists between younger and older homosexuals if their involvement in a relationship is less than one year. The older homosexuals are more likely to be either in long-term relationships or in none at all, with only 10 percent in relationships of one year or under. Although the gay world values youth highly, many homosexual men do age in a positive and healthy manner.

THE INSTITUTIONALIZED ELDERLY

The institutionalized aged are clearly more controlled by their environment than are the noninstitutionalized aged. The lack of knowledge about the sexuality of older individuals of both sexes exerts deleterious and often irrational influence over their personal lives and freedoms (1). Homes for the aged, nursing homes, and mental institutions apparently subscribe to the notion that old age is essentially sexless. Ordinarily, no provisions for privacy exist in these institutions; men and women are often rigidly segregated and are not allowed to visit in one another's rooms. Despite environmental pressures to the contrary, sexual activity is for some residents a difficult issue (70).

Wason and Loeb (71), in a study on sexual behavior in nursing homes, reported that some residents of these nursing home were sexually active. White (72) also reports that institutionalization does not preclude sexual activity, though the absence of privacy and the availability of willing and desired partners present obvious substantial obstacles to sexual behavior. Studies about staff attitudes toward sexual behavior of the institutionalized elderly showed varied responses. Wason and Loeb (71) observed that "medical and behavioral people showed great reluctance to discuss the subject." In contrast, Szasz (73) reported in his study that a majority of the staff freely described the sexual behavior and their feelings about it. Three types of behavior by men were identified as sexual and "causing problems": sex talk (i.e., using foul language), sexual acts (i.e., touching, grabbing, exposing genitalia), and implied sexual behavior (i.e., openly reading pornographic magazines). Sexual behaviors identified as acceptable by the staff were limited to hugging and kissing on the cheek. In contrast, sexual incidents involving women residents were fewer and more sympathetically reported by the staff.

Institutions should provide a physical environment that ensures the privacy and dignity of the residents. For the staff, in-service sex education programs about the residents' sexual needs and the management of problematic sexual behavior should be conducted. Residents do not lose their valuation of sexuality simply because they are institutionalized.

OVERVIEW OF ISSUES IN AGING AND SEXUALITY

The field of sexuality and aging has been taboo, and until recently there have been no systematic studies in this area. Although the current literature provides interesting information, there is still a need for further investigation of the issues. Social limitations and prejudices against sexuality in the elderly must be addressed. There is a need to educate physicians and health professionals so that they will be able to accept the elderly as sexual people. Lief (74, 75) pointed out that physicians may have difficulty dealing with sexual matters because their training in this area has been generally inadequate. Normal changes in sexuality need to be understood by the elderly themselves, so that they do not mistake such changes as being signs of an end to sexuality. Families of the elderly and society at large need to learn to accept the elderly as whole persons with definite sexual needs and a right to express them fully. It is important that further research be done to distinguish the effects of the aging process on sexuality from other factors (e.g., sociocultural factors). We know now that in the sexuality of the elderly there are enormous individual differences that cannot be explained simply by aging. This may suggest that with changing sociocultural factors the older persons of the future may not present the same pattern of sexuality as today's elderly. Further understanding of the sexual aspects of the aging process will be beneficial to the aged of today as well as to ourselves as we age.

REFERENCES

 1. Butler, R. N. Psychosocial aspects of reproductive aging. In: Schneider, E. L., ed., Aging, Vol. IV, The Aging Reproductive System. New York: Raven Press, 1978.
 2. Pfeiffer, E. Sexual behavior. In Howells, J. ed., Modern Perspectives in the Psychiatry of Old Age. New York: Brunner/Mazel, 1975.
 3. Kinsey, A. C.; Pomeroy, W. B.; and Martin, C. R. Sexual Behavior in the Human Male. Philadelphia: W. B. Saunders, 1948.
 4. Kinsey, A. C.; Pomeroy, W. B.; Martin, C. R.; and Gebhard, P. H. Sexual Behavior in the Human Female. Philadelphia: W. B. Saunders, 1953.
 5. Masters, W. H., and Johnson, V. E. Human Sexual Response. Boston: Little, Brown, 1966.
 6. Palmore, E. Normal Aging: Reports from the Duke Longitudinal Studies, 1966–1969. Durham, N.C., Duke University Press, 1970.

7. Palmore, E. Normal Aging, II: Reports from the Duke Longitudinal Studies, 1970–1978. Durham, N.C., Duke University Press, 1974.

8. Lobenz, N. Sex After Sixty-Five. Public Affairs Pamphlet No. 519. New York: Public Affairs Committee, 1975.

9. Busse, E. W., and Pfeiffer, E., eds., Behavior and Adaptation in Late Life. Boston: Little, Brown, 1969.

10. Butler, R. N., and Lewis, M. I., eds., Aging and Mental Health, 3rd edition. St. Louis: C. V. Mosby, 1982.

11. Finkle, A. L.; Moyers, T. G.; Tohenkin, M. I., et al. Sexual potency in aging males. JAMA, 207:113–115, 1969.

12. Freeman, J. T. Sexual capacities in the aging male. Geriatrics, 16:37–43, 1961.

13. Masters, W. H., and Johnson, V. E. Human Sexual Inadequacy. Boston: Little, Brown, 1970.

14. Newman, G., and Nichols, C. P. Sexual activities and attitudes in older persons. JAMA, 173:117–119, 1960.

15. Martin, C. E. Sexual activity in the aging male. In: Money, J., and Mousefh, M., eds., Handbook of Sexology. Amsterdam: ASP Biol. Med. Press, 1977.

16. George, L. K., and Weiler, S. J. Sexuality in middle and late life: the effects of age, cohort, and gender. Arch. Gen. Psychiat., 38:919–923, 1981.

17. Pfeiffer, E.; Verwoerdt, A.; and Wang, H. S. The natural history of sexual behavior in a biologically advantaged group of aged individuals. Journal of Gerontology, 24:193–198, 1969.

18. Verwoerdt, A.; Pfeiffer, E.; and Wang, H. S. Sexual behavior in senescence. Geriatrics, 24:137–154, 1969.

19. Vermeulen, A.; Rubens, R.; and Verdonick, L. Testosterone secretion and metabolism in male senescence. J. Clin. Endocrinol. Metab., 24:730–735, 1972.

20. Harman, S. M. Clinical aspects of aging of the male reproductive system. In: Schneider, E. L., ed., Aging, Vol. IV, The Aging Reproductive System. New York: Raven Press, 1978.

21. Baker, H. W. G.; Burger, H. G.; GeKretser, D. M.; and Hudson, B. Endocrinology of aging, pituitary testicular axis. In: Proceedings of the Fifth International Congress of Endocrinology. Amsterdam: Excerpta Medica, 1976.

22. Davidson, J. M.; Gray, G. D.; and Smith, E. R. The sexual psychoendocrinology of aging. In: Meites, J., ed., Neuroendocrinology of Aging. New York: Plenum Press, 1982.

23. Carmichael, H. T., and Noonan W. T. The effects of testosterone propionate in impotence. Am. J. Psychiat., 79:917–943, 1941.

24. Reiter, T. Testosterone implantation: a clinical study of 240 implantations in aging males. J. Am. Geriat. Soc., 11:540–550, 1963.

25. Wesson, M. B. The value of testosterone to men past middle age. J. Am. Geriat. Soc., 12:1149–1153, 1964.

26. Forti, G.; Pozzagli, M.; Calabresi, E., et al. Radio-immuno-assay of plasma testosterone. Clin. Endocrinol., 3:5–17, 1974.

27. Greenblatt, R. B.; Oettinger, M.; and Bohler, C. S. S. Estrogen, androgen levels in aging men and women: therapeutic considerations. J. Am. Geriat. Soc., 24:173–178, 1976.

28. Skakkebaek, N. E.; Bancroft, L.; Davidson, D. W., and Warner, P. Androgen

replacement with oral testosterone undecanoate in hypogonadal men: a double-blind controlled study. Clinical Endocrinology, 14:49–61, 1980.

29. Luisi, M., and Franchi, F. Double-blind group comparative study of testosterone undecanoate and mesterolone in hypogonadal male patients. Journal of Endocrinological Investigation, 3:305–308, 1980.

30. Kaplan, H. S. Disorders of Sexual Dsire. New York: Brunner/Mazel, 1976.

31. Masters, W. H., and Johnson V. E. Sex and the aging process. J. Am. Geriatr. Soc., 29:385–390, 1981.

32. Felstein, I. Sexual function in the elderly. Clinics in Obstetrics and Gynecology, Vol. VII, no. 2, 1980.

33. Dennerstein, L., and Burrows, G. Hormone replacement therapy and sexuality in women. Clinics in Endocrinology and Metabolism, Vol. XI, no. 3, 1982.

34. Schiff, I., and Wilson, E. Clinical aspects of aging of the female reproductive system. In: Schneider, E. L., ed., Aging, Vol. IV, The Aging Reproductive System. New York: Raven Press, 1978.

35. Easley, E. B. Sex problems after the menopause. Clin. Obstet. Gynecol., 21:269–277, 1978.

36. Natelovitz, M. Gynecologic problems of menopausal women, III: Changes in extragenital tissues and sexuality. Geriatrics, 33:51–53, 1978.

37. Leiblum, S.; Bachmann, B.; Kemmann, E.; Calburn, D.; and Swartzman, L. Vaginal atrophy in the postmenopausal woman, the importance of sexual activity and hormones. JAMA, 249:2195–2198, 1983.

38. Pfeiffer, E., and Davis, G. C. Determinants of sexual behavior in middle and old age. J. Am. Geriatr. Soc., 20:151–155, 1972.

39. Pfeiffer, E.; Verwoerdt, A.; and Davis, G. C. Sexual behavior in middle life. Am. J. Psych., 128:82–87, 1972.

40. Udry, J. R.; Deven, F. R.; and Coleman, S. J. A cross-national comparison of the relative influence of male and female age on the frequency of marital intercourse. J. Biosoc. Sci., 14:1–6, 1982.

41. Hallstrom, T. Sexuality in the climacteric. In: Clinics in Obstetrics and Gynecology, Vol. IV, no. 3, 1977.

42. Deutsch, H. The Psychology of Women, Vol. II, Motherhood. New York: Grune and Stratton, 1945.

43. Van Keep, P. A., and Kellerhals, J. M. The impact of sociocultural factors on symptom formation. Psychotherapy and Psychosomatics, 23:251–263, 1974.

44. Crowford, M. P., and Hooper, D. Menopause, aging, and family. Social Science and Medicine, 7:469–482, 1975.

45. Schneider, M., and Brotherton, P. Physiological, psychological, and situational stresses in depression during climacteric. Maturitas, 1:153–158, 1979.

46. Krystal, S., and Chiriboga, D. A. The empty nest process in middle-life men and women. Maturitas, 1:215–222, 1979.

47. Smith, A. D. Causes and classification of impotence. Urol. Clin. North Am., 8:79–89, 1981.

48. Smith, P. The sexual recovery of the stroke patient. Sex. Med. Today, 5:6–11, 1981.

49. Tuttle, W. B.; Cook, W. L., Jr.; and Fitch, E. Sexual behavior in post-myocardial infarct patients. Am. J. Cardiol., 13:140, 1964.

50. Glover, B. Sex in the aging. Post Grad. Med., 57:165–169, 1975.

51. Vliet, L. W., and Meyers, J. K. Erectile dysfunction: progress in evaluation and treatment. Johns Hopkins Medical Journal, 151:246–258, 1982.
52. Cooper, A. J. Diagnosis and management of "endocrine impotence." Br. Med. J., 2:34–36, 1972.
53. Martin, L. M. Impotence in diabetics: an overview. Psychosomatics, 22:318–329, 1981.
54. Kolodny, R. C.; Masters, W. H.; and Johnson, V. E. Textbook of Sexual Medicine. Boston: Little, Brown, 1979.
55. Kaplan, H. S. Disorders of Sexual Desire. New York: Brunner/Mazel, 1979.
56. Papadopoulous, C. Cardiovascular drugs and sexuality: a cardiologist's review. Arch. Intern. Med., 140:1341–1345, 1980.
57. Cole, N. J. Drugs that influence sexual expression. Consultant, 20:280–286, 1980.
58. Munjack, D. J., and Oziel, L. J. Sexual Medicine and Counseling in Office Practice: A Comprehensive Treatment Guide. Boston: Little, Brown, 1980.
59. Hogan, M. J.; Wallin, J. D.; and Baer, R. M. Antihypertensive therapy in male sexual dysfunction. Psychosomatics, 21:234–237, 1980.
60. Blay, S. L.; Ferraz, M. P. I.; and Calil, H. M. Lithium-induced male sexual impairment: two case reports. J. Clin. Psych., 43:497–498, 1982.
61. Christenson, C. V., and Gagnon, J. H. Sexual behavior in a group of older women. Journal of Gerontology, 20:351–356, 1965.
62. Ludeman, K. The sexuality of the older person: review of literature. The Gerontologists, 21 (2):203–208, 1981.
63. Rubin, I. Sexual Life After Sixty. New York: Basic Books, 1965.
64. Nigola, P., and Peruzza, M. Sex in the aged. J. Amer. Geriat. Soc., 22:481–484, 1974.
65. Wall, S., and Kaltreider, N. Changing social-sexual patterns in gynecological practice. JAMA, 237:565–568, 1977.
66. Harry, J., and DeVall, W. B. The Social Organization of Gay Males. New York: Praeger Publishers, 1978.
67. Bell, A. P., and Weinberg, M. S. Homosexualities. New York: Simon and Schuster, 1978.
68. Weinberg, M. S., and Williams, C. J. Male Homosexuals: Their Problems and Adaptation. New York: Oxford University Press, 1974.
69. Bennett, K. C., and Thompson, N. L. Social and psychological functioning of the aging male homosexual. Brit. J. Psychiat., 137:361–370, 1980.
70. Comfort, A. Sexuality in old age. J. Am. Geriat. Soc., 22:422–440, 1974.
71. Wason, M., and Loeb, M. B. Sexuality in nursing homes. J. Am. Geriatr. Soc., 27:73–79, 1979.
72. White, C. B. Sexual interest, attitudes, knowledge, and sexual history in relation to sexual behavior in the institutionalized aged. Archives of Sexual Behavior, 11(1):11–21. 1982.
73. Szasz, G. Sexual incidents in an extended-care unit for aged men. J. Am. Geriatr. Soc., 31(7):407–411, 1983.
74. Lief, H. I. Sex education of medical students and doctors. Pacif. Med. Surg., 73:52–58, 1965.
75. Lief, H. I. Sex and the medical educator. J. Am. Med. Wom. Ass., 23:195–196, 1968.

PART FOUR

ATTITUDES, VALUES, AND ETHICS

Changes in American Sexual Attitudes During the Past Century

What follows is an historical overview of changes that have occurred over the past one hundred years in the sexual attitudes and ideals held especially by college students. Its aim is to show how variform factors—including the work of Havelock Ellis, Sigmund Freud, Alfred Kinsey, and William Masters and Virginia Johnson—have influenced views on nonmarital heterosexual relations, contraception and abortion, masturbation, and on the sex roles and sexuality of women.

THE "SPERMATIC ECONOMY," 1880–1900

The concept of a "spermatic economy" (1) held that in the male "the spermatic receptors are composed of the most precious properties of which the blood is comprised. Thus it is that the vital resources of the individual are severely taxed when any undue strain on them takes place" (2: p.30). "Spending" was a word frequently used to describe any type of seminal discharge, and the way a man managed his sexual discharge was often regarded as "continuous with the way in which he handled money, specifically debt and expenditure" (3: p.179). It was commonly believed that heterosexual relations should not occur oftener than once a month and that excessive sex could cause some women to become invalids (4) and some men to suffer genital dysfunction, dyspepsia, loss of strength, and cardiac palpitations.

Medical authorities propounded the view that women who were educated and from the middle and upper classes lacked sexual passions. For example, in 1883 an American doctor told his medical class, "I do not believe one bride in a hundred, of delicate, educated, sensitive women, accepts matrimony from any desire for sexual gratification; when she thinks of it at all, it is with shrinking, or even with horror, rather than with desire" (5: p.62). While some college-educated women came to enjoy marital sexuality (6), others believed that sexual passion was "associated almost exclusively with the male, with prostitutes and women of the lower class (7: p.31). In 1886 one woman wrote that it was the urgent task of wives to civilize their husbands by curbing their "animal" instincts (8).

The view that educated women were sexually abstinent led to the view that contraceptive information and devices were "obscene materials." This then led to the passage of anticontraception and antiabortion legislation in the late nineteenth century. The Comstock Law of 1873, which persisted through the 1920s, made it a felony to "sell . . . or in any manner exhibit . . . any obscene book, pamphlet, paper . . . or any drug or medicine, any article whatever, for the prevention of conception, or for causing unlawful abortion" (8: p.22). This legislation was supported by physicians and women reformers, who held that the only way to limit family size was through sexual continence (8).

With only a few exceptions, nineteenth-century American physicians taught that masturbation, in both men and women, could cause many physical illnesses and was a major cause of insanity. As evidence for the latter contention, physicians observed that "large numbers of patients in mental hospitals masturbated. From this they concluded that it was such practices that originally had caused them to become ill" (9: p.60). It was then held that there was a "characteristic form of 'masturbatory insanity,' " five times as common in males as in females, which began between 13 and 20 years of age and in the majority of cases resulted in "a rapid decline into agitated dementia" (10: pp.7–8). Toward the end of the nineteenth century, however, the belief that masturbation could cause insanity waned and was replaced by the belief that masturbation was a "common cause" of neurotic disorders (10: p.9).

Treatment of masturbation consisted of a potpourri of remedies from scientific medicine and medical folklore: a variety of drugs and foods, hydropathy and mineral baths, different kinds of mechanical restraints, and different kinds of restraining clothes. For a time there was a society of professionals—publishing a *Journal of Orificial Surgery*—which held that "the solution for masturbation as well as any number of other problems was circumcision, clitoridectomy, and forcible dilation of the anus (9: p.69). Castration, ovariotomy, and section of the pudendal nerves were also sometimes advocated and performed (10).

Male and female homosexuality were regarded as immoral and sometimes criminal, and merited expulsion from school, college, or job. Most physicians viewed homosexuality as an illness caused by excessive masturbation and/or as an inherited weakness in the nervous system (9).

THE "REPEAL OF RETICENCE," 1900–1919

In the first two decades of the twentieth century, youthful Americans began to experience a weakening of some sexual interdictions. These interdictions had been upheld by the family, church, and local community, with each usually reinforcing the other. When large numbers of young people migrated to the cities, either for jobs or for higher education, they confronted new individuals and institutions that had a morality which seemed distant, casual, and transient. Freedom from supervision by elders, and private romantic contacts, were facilitated first by the telephone and then by the automobile. "The real value of the telephone," observed one social historian, "was to a man determined to carry out a 'whirlwind courtship.' With its aid he could multiply flatteries, underline cajolements, be the first to say good morning or the last to say good night" (11: p.220). For young couples the automobile was at first "an incredible engine of escape" from supervision by elders (12) and then a place where physical intimacies could begin to be initiated. To some couples, at first, petting in a car seemed like a "desperate adventure" (13: p.460).

As a traditional morality began to weaken, there was an upsurge of a new purity movement led by educators, psychologists, and physicians. This new movement was more pragmatic and "scientific" in approach than previous movements. It campaigned for public dissemination of accurate information about prostitution and venereal disease (methods for diagnosing and then treating syphilis had recently been discovered) (7). Elsie Parsons, who had taught sociology at Barnard College in New York City, called for an "open discussion of sex morals" and an end to what she described as "the taboo of direct reference" to matters of sex (14: p.392).

At this time the ideas of Havelock Ellis and Sigmund Freud began to exert an influence, especially among college students and teachers. Both Ellis and Freud were physicians who viewed sexual activity as "neither a threat to moral character nor a drain on vital energies . . . [but] on the contrary [an] entirely worthwhile, though often precarious, human activity, whose proper management was essential to individual and social well being" (15: p.2). Both criticized prevailing interdictions on sexuality and published case histories of men and women in which inhibited sexuality was posited as a cause of various illnesses. Both were reticent about advocating premarital intercourse. Freud's psychoanalytic method, which encouraged patients to free-associate and recollect repressed experiences—making no distiction between men and women patients—and which encouraged psychoanalysts to attentively listen and to explore sexual experiences, dealt an especially heavy blow to prevailing reticence about sex. The early American psychoanalysts became therapists who "unearthed the sexual demon with a leveling zeal that also characterized muckraking" and who saw themselves as "fighters against irrational oppressive conventions" (7: p.463).

It began to be publicly stated that women had sexual desires, but it was thought that these desires had to be evoked by men. In 1914 two male authors stated: "Men's sexual appetites are on the average far keener and more insistent than those of a normal woman. Women's desire for sexual gratification often needs clamant awakening" (16: p.67). The extent to which a male-dominated culture inhibited women's sexuality was ignored, even by Ellis and Freud.

During these first two decades of the century, women began to spend less time doing housework (because of new mechanical appliances) and more time away from home. Increasing numbers of women were gainfully employed. The number of college-educated women climbed dramatically. In 1900, some 85,000 women were enrolled in colleges; by 1920 the number reached 250,000 and the number of females college graduates began to approximate the number of men graduates. The "ideology of educated motherhood" developed the ideal of a woman who, because of her college education, would create "more ideal surroundings" for her children and who could become "the companion and friend for all time" of her boys. College-educated women were also expected to take part in politics and political reforms, and this later activity led to women's obtaining the right to vote in 1920. For women, college education did not lead to postgraduate professional training, as it did for men. In 1920 about 53,000 men were enrolled in professional programs (e.g., law, medicine), but there were only 4,000 women (8).

In his *Sexual Inversion* (1897), the first volume in his epochal *Studies in the Psychology of Sex*, Havelock Ellis had argued that homosexuality was neither a disease nor a crime but simply a congenitally acquired sexual orientation. Ellis was the first English writer to support this view (17). In the first part of the twentieth century, however, most states passed laws that defined homosexuality, along with the perversions, as "crimes against nature." Many of these state laws also prohibited fellatio and cunnilingus among heterosexual couples (18).

Although no longer regularly regarded as a cause of insanity, masturbation was thought to lead to impairment of character, especially in males. Winfield S. Scott, Professor of Psychology at Northwestern University and author of pamphlets distributed by the Young Men's Christian Association (YMCA), claimed that masturbation was "debilitating and unmanning" and "would lead to loss of virility" (7: p.250). Ellis, although holding that masturbation was universal and not the cause of serious psychological illness, believed that it could cause "slight nervous disorders" and that extensive masturbation in adolescence could leave the masturbator incapable of associating sexuality with affection (15). Freud thought that masturbation was the cause of the psychiatric illness neurasthenia (19). In 1916 the leading American psychoanalyst, A. A. Brill, stated that "although masturbation was nearly universal and would do no physical harm, it could stifle the development of an aggressive, extroverted personality." He argued for a "cautious, gentle" correction of masturbation in children (20: p.214).

In 1915, James Exner, a physician who was Secretary of the Student Department of the International Committee of the YMCA, made the first attempt to secure statistical data on the sexual behavior of American college students. Exner prepared a questionnaire and obtained replies from 948 college students, 562 from the West and 386 from New York City. In the western group, 61.5 percent admitted to having masturbated—it was described in the questionnaire as "having practiced self-abuse"—and 36 percent said they had had sexual intercourse with women. In the New York City students, replies showed that

"34.7 percent confess to having practiced self-abuse," and 13.2 percent said they had had sex with women (21: p.16).

THE "REVOLUTION IN SEXUAL MORALS," 1920–1939

In the years after World War I there developed what one historian has described as a "revolution in sexual morals" (22). During the prohibition era there was greatly enhanced social drinking between the sexes (23). The development of the closed automobile (in 1919 some 90 percent of American cars had been roofless) and the proliferation of automobiles made sexual contacts more private and more available. Wrote one historian, "The motor-car (like the hansom cab) became an intimate and exciting little box, and it is a basic if little-advertised human law that men and women cannot be tucked into cozy little boxes without getting ideas into their heads" (11: p.220). There was an upsurge in the belief that "one's sex life is a private matter in which neither law nor public opinion has any right to interfere" (24), disapproval of religious sex sanctions, and some approval of the scientific ideas of Freud, Ellis, and Dutch gynecologist Theodore van de Velde.

In his book *Ideal Marriage* published in an American edition in 1930, van de Velde gave an account of heterosexual lovemaking which has been summarized as follows. "He . . . prescribed in detail the specific bodily technique—the kisses, the caresses, the thrusts—by means of which his patients and his readers could translate their emotional commitments into physiological responses and orgasms—mutual, simultaneous orgasms" (25: p.84). Van de Velde stressed the mutual joys of simultaneously giving and receiving while making love, and the "myriad subtle interweavings of sensation and emotion" which bind two lovers together (25: p.85). *Ideal Marriage* was widely read by college students. Some used it as a guide to lovemaking, others regarded its prescriptions as ideals on which they were still too inhibited to act.

Colleges developed and popularized a new ideal of woman as wife-companion. A female college graduate need not necessarily become a mother, but she must appeal—and reappeal—to her husband by being sensuous and loving, beautiful, and intellectually interesting. Young women learned these attributes not only from their college teachers but in a new kind of organization—the sorority house. "The sorority's primary aim," wrote one feminist historian, "was to train its members to become ideal wife-companions. . . . The sororities taught good appearance—how to apply cosmetics, how to bob hair . . . the talents of being good hostesses. . . . They also defined the standards of sexual permissiveness—how far to go to interest a man (petting) without going too far (premarital intercourse). . . . Most important of all, the sororities organized dances and socials so that a member could meet the right kind of man; she could then make the marriage that would be so central to her life" (8: p.82).

There was greatly increased discussion about different contraceptive methods

(24)—although the Comstock laws were still operative—and an increase in the use of condoms by men of all social classes (12). Among educated women, use of the vaginal diaphragm increased, while douching and withdrawal, the previous methods of contraception, decreased (26). Middle-class college women who wanted to marry could frequently find doctors who would advise them on contraception. Such doctors would sometimes, if indicated, perform an (illegal) abortion. Poor women remained, on the whole, ignorant of contraception and unaffected by these changes (8).

In 1938, Dorothy Bromley and Florence Britten, two women with journalistic backgrounds, published *Youth and Sex: A Study of 1,300 College Students*, which consisted of replies to questionnaires filled out by 1,364 male and female students in 46 colleges and universities of all types scattered from coast to coast. This was the largest survey of college sexuality to date (12). The most striking finding was that "half of the men and one quarter of the women juniors and seniors in American colleges today have had pre-marital sex intercourse" (12: p.11). This finding agreed with those of other studies of college students (27). It suggested that premarital sexuality among college females was markedly increasing. Whether premarital sex among college males had also increased was unclear; college men may have consorted less with prostitutes and correspondingly more with other women. "A very modern note," reported Bromley and Britten, "was the tolerance expressed by men for the girl who had sex experience. Three-quarters of the men were willing to marry non-virgin girls, and this number included men who had not yet indulged in sex relations themselves" (12: p.11).

Youth and Sex gave some statistics on masturbation and homsexuality. Out of 122 college females who admitted to experiencing sexual desire, 11 "confessed to finding an outlet" in masturbation. Of the 285 college males who had no sexual experience, 14 said they had masterturbated. Of the 243 males who had had intercourse, 38 said they had masturbated (12). These figures, especially among the male, are much lower than the figures in other studies (28). Some of the college males may have been reluctant to talk about their masturbation to women questioners. *Youth and Sex* reported that 4 percent of female students (13 out of 375) and 8 percent of males (46 out of 470) "admitted having indulged in the practice of homosexuality at some time in their lives" (12). These low figures may also have been caused by a reluctance of many students to reveal their homosexuality because of prevailing prejudice (12).

Despite the increase of heterosexual interactions between college students, half the states in the union had laws making this interaction a crime, and nearly all states considered it a crime if the girl was under 18 (29). Practically all colleges had enforced rigid dormitory separation of male and female students, and most colleges had prohibitions against any campus expression of sex. An event that typified campus sexual attitudes occurred in the spring of 1927 at Indiana University. At this time two students published an article in the university magazine, *Vagabond*, using the term "phallic worship" and other "unacceptable phrases." Charges against the article were presented by the dean of men to an assembly of all male members of the Indiana University faculty, and the two student authors were penalized (30).

One Indiana University faculty member who deplored sexual prudery and who argued that the *Vagabond* authors "had a natural impulse to try their elders by exhibiting their animal spirits" was Alfred Kinsey, Professor of Zoology (30). At this time and during most of the 1930s, Kinsey was establishing himself as an authority on gall wasps. He studied several million of these wasps, learning how to classify large numbers of objects and developing skills in interviewing the diverse individuals who lived and worked on the land where the wasps were found. In July 1938, Kinsey was asked to give lectures on the biological aspects of sex and marriage for junior and senior students at Indiana University. He soon found that although much had been written about sex only a small number of individuals had been studied. As the marriage course progressed, students would come to Kinsey for advice on sexual matters, and he would question them about their sex history. From these contacts he developed a special interviewing technique that enabled him to rapidly elicit a sexual history from an individual (29).

One evening in 1938 he gave a talk on sex to the students at one of the university's fraternities. Afterward the students pressed him with questions that revealed their deep concerns about certain specific areas of sex: "Is masturbation harmful?" "Is homosexuality abnormal?" "What effect does petting have on subsequent marital adjustment?" Kinsey then turned to his audience and proclaimed: "Neither I nor anyone else knows the answers to many of these questions because of our lack of knowledge, but if you, and many like you, will be willing to contribute your own sexual histories, I will be able eventually to discover enough about human sexual behavior to answer at least some of these questions." The response was enthusiastic (31).

By the end of a year, Kinsey had obtained 300 sex histories, mainly from students. He began to discern that there was a deep difference between the histories of college students and those who had not attended college, so in 1939 he began taking histories from persons in surrounding Indiana towns and from inmates in Indiana jails, most of whom were not college students or college graduates. He was launched on the most extensive study of human sexual behavior that had ever been undertaken (29).

THE WORK OF ALFRED KINSEY AND ITS AFTERMATH, 1940–1965

From 1940 until his death in 1956, Kinsey elicited, through personal interviews, the sexual histories of 17,500 men and women throughout the United States. He was aided by three other interviewers, by assistants, and by financial grants. To administer his work he founded and headed Indiana University's Institute for Sex Research, now familiarly known as the Sex Institute. He published the results of his interviews in two books: *Sexual Behavior in the Human Male* (1948) and *Sexual Behavior in the Human Female* (1953).

Some of his findings were as follows. Almost all men (92–97 percent) masturbated. Masturbation was "the great source of premarital sexual outlet for the upper educational levels. For that group masturbation provides nearly 80 percent of orgasms during the earlier adolescent years, as against little more than half the outlet (52 percent) for the lower educational level" (27: p.552). Some 62 percent of all women masturbated, and women who were college graduates masturbated more frequently than those who had not gone beyond grade school (although the social differences were not as great as among men) (28). Kinsey claimed that masturbation caused no harm and that it sometimes aided the development of healthy interpersonal sexual fantasies and helped some individuals adjust to marriage (28).

Premarital heterosexual petting provided orgasms for many more college-level males than for males who never go beyond grade school. "Petting," Kinsey wrote, "is pre-eminently an occupation of the high school and college levels" (28: p.552). College males had much less premarital heterosexual intercourse (about 67 percent) than high school males (84 percent) and grade school males (98 percent) and had intercourse much less frequently than the less-educated groups. College males showed a greater willingness to indulge in oral erotic contacts (kissing and mouth to genitals and breasts) and to try different positions in intercourse than other groups (27).

About two-fifths of women up to age 25 had experienced orgasm through petting. At age 20–25, some 26 percent of the noncollege females had had premarital intercourse, as against 15–20 percent of the college and graduate school females. By age 25, however, the college-educated women were ahead of the noncollege women by a small margin, because the latter tended to marry earlier and thus be removed from any further possibility of premarital experience. Educational differences were less pronounced among women than among men. Kinsey observed that among married women there was (with some qualification) "a marked positive correlation betweeen experience in orgasm obtained from premarital coitus, and the capacity to reach orgasm after marriage" (25: p.148).

It was shown that over one-third of all males had experienced at least one homosexual contact. College males experienced the least homosexual contacts, high school males the most, and grade school males were intermediate between these two groups (27). Some 28 percent of all women had had homosexual contacts; these occurred most often among college women and those who had gone on to graduate work, and much less among grade school and high school girls (28).

The deepest and most enduring impact of Kinsey's work was that it allowed sex to be regarded essentially as a commonplace experience. Kinsey has been called "this century's foremost sexual demystifier" (15: p.14). His work stimulated further scientific investigations of sexuality and helped create varying degrees of tolerance for different sexual practices. A 1960 study, based on interviews with 200 male college students, confirmed Kinsey's findings on the prevalence of masturbation and heterosexual petting and found that students were generally accepting of these practices. The majority of students engaged in "relatively little premarital intercourse"—reserving this for girls they expected to marry—and regarded it as "more acceptable for the male than female (double standard)." Although some students condoned homosexuality, most regarded it with "shame, dread and guilt" (32).

Between 1959 and 1965 a series of Supreme Court decisions nullified many obscenity laws and made it possible to market pornographic materials—books, magazines, movies, shows, and music—which publicized sexual nudity and sexual interactions (33).

At this time the social position of women underwent several changes. An increasing number of married women, and mothers, were becoming part of the work force, so that during the 1950s and 1960s for the first time in American history more women than men took jobs (34).

During the fifteen years after World War II the 1920s ideal of a woman as wife-companion appealed to women in all social classes (8), but then this ideal in many cases turned out to be frustrating and embittering. In her 1963 book, *The Feminine Mystique*, Betty Friedan explored the lives of college graduates who had become suburban housewives and found that, occupied with an endless routine of household chores, they had lost their self-respect. As one woman expressed it, "The problem is always being the children's mommy, the minister's wife, and never being myself." Friedan wrote that the only way for women to find themselves was through creative work, and she urged women—speaking mainly to college students and college graduates—to develop careers as men did. In 1966 the National Organization of Women (NOW) was founded to help women attain opportunities for jobs that were equal to those of men.

Another change that deeply enhanced women's new sense of equality and independence was the development of new contraceptives. In 1960 the first intrauterine device, the Lippes Loop, was marketed in the United States. Other improved devices followed. In 1961, the Searle drug company began to market Enovid, a pill that if taken at regular intervals by a woman effectively prevented pregnancy (26). Although changes in anticontraceptive laws were slow in coming, by 1965 many college students were viewing contraceptive information as a right that was due them and were using contraceptives when indicated (35). By 1974 at least 10 million American women would be taking "the pill" (26). The discovery of the pill has been compared to the discovery of fire and with a half-dozen or so major innovations of human history. With the pill it became possible, for the first time in history, for large numbers of sexually active men and women to free themselves from the fear of pregnancy and to enjoy sex for its own sake (36).

The above changes occurred at a time when increasing numbers of students were participating in radical political organizations and in civil rights demonstrations that challenged existing laws. The coexistence of changing sexual behavior and political activism encouraged students to challenge prohibitions against sex in college dormitories and to demand "with increasing militancy their right to privacy and self-determination in matters pertaining to their own sexual activity (35: p.44). Some colleges tried relaxing existing dormitory regulations and curfews (37). Most college authorities, along with the parents of students, became increasingly fearful, confused, and uncertain about how to confront ever-pressing student demands. A 1965 report, *Sex and the College Student*, stated that there was a "wide gap between rules and regulations . . . designed to inhibit sexuality on campus and the insistent reality of student behavior" (35: p.11).

THE REVOLUTION IN SEX INFORMATION AND ATTITUDES, 1966–1983

The revolution in sex information and attitudes occurred simultaneously in the areas of scientific research on sex and moral attitudes toward sex. The most important, and most publicized, scientific research on sex was done by the team of William Masters, an obstetrician and gynecologist, and Virginia Johnson, working at the Reproductive Biology Research Foundation at Washington University in St. Louis. In 1966 they published their first book, *Human Sexual Response*, and in 1970 their second book, *Human Sexual Inadequacy*.

Human Sexual Response gave an account of the normal sexual cycle in 694 men and women who, for study purposes, were either masturbating or copulating. It showed that the male and female sexual cycle consists of four stages: arousal, plateau, orgasm, and resolution. It concluded: "The parallels in reaction to effective sexual stimulation emphasize the physiologic similarities in male and female responses rather than the differences. . . . Men and women are homogeneous in their physiological responses to sexual stimuli" (38: p.285). There were, however, differences between the sexes. Because of a refractory period, the male could achieve only one orgasm at a time, and the pattern of his sex cycle was essentially the same. The woman could maintain an orgasm for a relatively long time, and because she did not have a refractory period she could sometimes follow one orgasm with another, or several other patterns of orgasm (38). Thus Masters and Johnson viewed female sexuality as more powerful, complex, and variable than male sexuality. This disputed the views of Ellis and Kinsey, who had regarded female sexuality as essentially passive and less intense than that of the male (15). Masters and Johnson also argued that Freud's distinction of two kinds of female orgasm—vaginal and clitoral—was erroneous because it ignored the fact that all orgasms (regardless of where the stimulation began) involved contractions of the congested walls of the vagina and what was called the "vaginal platform" (15).

Human Sexual Inadequacy reported on the results of treating 790 men and women (mostly married couples) who suffered from such sexual dysfunction as impotence, premature ejaculation, and retarded ejaculation in the male, and orgasmic dysfunction, vaginismus, and dyspareunia in the female. The standard treatment came to be known as dual sex therapy: daily meetings, for two weeks, between the couple with the problem and a male and female sex therapist. Here the couple were instructed in different sexual techniques and in techniques in psychotherapy for recognizing and dealing with attitudes toward sexuality. Masters and Johnson claimed that by their methods of therapy about eight out of ten cases of sexual dysfunction were successfully treated (39). Although these success claims have been disputed (40), the publication of this book created an ambience of therapeutic optimism about treating sexual dysfunctions and led to the development of different methods of sexual counseling (41).

Masters and Johnson went beyond all previous sexual researchers in extolling the virtues of masturbation. They stated that masturbation produced a more intense orgasm than coitus and that sexually normal couples should observe how each other masturbates and then use this masturbatory technique during intercourse. During sex therapy couples were usually taught how to masturbate each other. *Sexual Inadequacy* reported the cases of 11 women who could attain orgasm during coitus but were unable to be orgasmic through masturbation (either by self or by partner). These women were diagnosed as suffering from the sexual dysfunction of ''masturbatory orgasmic inadequacy,'' and 10 of them were taught how to achieve orgasm through masturbation (39). Thus, whereas less than a century previously masturbation had been regarded as something to be shunned and a cause of illness, now it was regarded as something worth cultivating and as a source of sexual health and happiness.

Masters and Johnson had a feminist orientation. In discussing the treatment of female sex dysfunction they contended that sex therapists must always consider two points. First they must consider the impact of society, and most of human history, on women's feelings about their sexuality: ''Sociocultural influence more than not places woman in a position in which she must adapt, sublimate, inhibit, or even distort her natural capacity to function sexually in order to fulfill her genetically assigned role. *Herein lies a major source of women's sexual dysfunction*'' (39: p.240; italics in original). Then they observed that a woman's ''physiological capacity for sexual response infinitely surpasses that of man,'' and they inferred that a woman's ''significantly greater susceptibility to negatively based psychosocial influences may imply the existence of a natural state of psycho-sexual-social balance between the sexes that has been culturally established to neutralize women's biophysical superiority'' (39: p.219).

In planning treatment for a couple, Masters and Johnson instructed the woman to assume at least an equal share of the responsibility for carrying out the therapeutic regimen. In the course of treatment, the couple was usually urged to experiment with the female-superior position, which allowed the woman freedom of movement and a measure of control not available in the traditional male-superior (missionary) position (39). The views of Masters and Johnson deeply influenced concepts of female sexuality.

During the early 1970s, as the student radicalism of the 1960s subsided, it became clear that two dramatic and lasting changes in college sexuality had occurred. First there was the institution, in many colleges, of "co-residential living"or co-residency, whereby men and women shared the same dormitories, often living on the same corridors and sometimes sharing bathrooms (42). The second change concerned premarital intercourse. Between the mid-1940s and the mid-1960s, however, "almost every new campus survey showed distinctly higher rates of premarital coitus than had been typical for the past two decades or so" (43). The 1974 survey by Morton Hunt showed that by age 17 half the males who eventually went to college had had premarital sexual experience, more than double the figure in Kinsey's comparable sample, and that among women in their late teens and mid-20s, including college women, the percentage had roughly doubled since Kinsey's time. There was also, no doubt, an increase in sex on the college campus. From a study of his data, Hunt concluded that the students who had premarital intercourse were not just being promiscuous but that they usually felt "strong affection" and a "deep emotional commitment to each other" and that it was "the force of this conviction, translated into action, that has made parents and deans change their rules, rather than the reverse" (44: p. 148).

Previous studies on premarital sexual standards had found that, among students and nonstudents, both men and women tended to believe in the traditional "double standard": to accept coitus before marriage for men but to believe that it was wrong for women. In a 1979 study of premarital sexual attitudes of 1,376 unmarried men and women—985 students at the University of Wisconsin at Madison and 656 nonstudents living in Madison—it was found that this double standard had disappeared. The study reported:

The ideologies of our respondents for males and females were essentially the same: their standards did not differ as a function of gender. . . . In general, our interviewees reported a personal standard which accepts premarital intercourse, though they varied in whether they believed persons who engaged in it should be in love, feel mutual affection, or both desire it. The dominant ideology among our respondents, irrespective of gender or educational status, was . . . permissiveness with affection; a substantial minority believed intercourse to be acceptable "if both want it," . . . [what has been termed] "permissiveness without affection." (45: p.227)

There were no major differences in attitudes between students and nonstudents.

Another change in student sexuality was that male and female students masturbated with less guilt than previously and that the social differences in male masturbation—noted by Kinsey in 1948 as being high among the college educated and low among the less educated—had largely disappeared.

During the 1970s the student radical political parties and demonstrations of the 1960s were largely replaced by organizations that advocated and debated the needs of special groups of students. Thus on many campuses there were organizations of male and female homsexuals which met regularly for political meetings and social events in specially designated rooms. Homosexual student sexual relations ranged from loving couples who lived together, and who went to campus classes and events together (lesbian couples were especially monogamous), to individuals who met for one casual sex encounter and then never met again. Serious scientific studies of homosexuals showed that there was an enormous range of behavioral and social variations among homosexuals (just as there was among heterosexuals) (46) and also that there were no differences in the biological sexual responses of homosexuals and heterosexuals (47). The cause, or causes, of homosexuality, although much debated, remained undetermined. In 1974, however, the American Psychiatric Association rejected the "homosexuality as illness" concept (49). Student attitudes toward homosexuals became more tolerant, and most students favored legislation that would guarantee civil rights for homosexuals (48).

College women's organizations were politically divided into two groups: a reform movement using traditional democratic mehtods to win legal and economic rights for women, exemplified by NOW, and more radical women's liberation groups, which advocated reevaluation of male and female sex roles, new sexual standards, and an end to the patriarchal family (50). Despite differences, most women espoused a new view of "woman as a person," a person who was active, energetic, and had powerful sexual feelings and capacities—as shown by the work of Masters and Johnson—and who was fully competent in the area of work and a career (8). During the 1970s, the number of women in graduate studies proliferated (34), and women achieved more in every area of human endeavor—religion, education, sports, the arts, politics, the law—than they had achieved in all recorded history (51).

For women the most significant event of the 1970s was probably the Supreme Court decision of January 1973 which declared unconstitutional all state laws that prohibited or restricted abortion during the first trimester of pregnancy. One historian wrote that the right of abortion defined women as individuals within the family and made their bodies "truly their own, at the disposal of neither their unborn offspring nor of their husbands" and that, because women could now have abortions even if their husbands did not agree, women were now the "final authority over the size of the family" (34: p. 418). Following the Supreme Court decision, many colleges provided services for instructing pregnant students on how to have an abortion.

In 1966 the Supreme Court permitted contraceptive practices. In 1970 Congress rewrote the Comstock Law of 1873, taking contraceptive information and appliances off the obscene list. In 1972 the Supreme Court ruled that the unmarried have the same right to contraceptives as the married. Following these changes, many colleges began to provide contraceptive services. However, it seems to be a fact of college student sexuality that women students—who know about contraceptives—still become pregnant unintentionally. This often occurs because of unconscious motivations and conflict (35).

Although the new sexual openness and permissiveness has had a positive effect on some students, it has also had several different negative effects on varying numbers of other students. Campus permissiveness has pressured many students to have sex before they were emotionally ready for it. Some women, in the course of having sex with men, expressed their newly discovered sense of rage over women's exploitation (discovered and discussed in feminist groups) by an "aggressive manner and overassertiveness." Their manner has enhanced the man's castration anxiety and fear of the vagina and has resulted in his becoming impotent—what has been dubbed "the new impotence" (52). Women complain that men are inept, or at best ignorant, about how to stimulate them to orgasm and that their best orgasms are achieved by self-stimulation or by stimulation from other women (53).

Recently, increasing numbers of students are attempting to live with their sexual tensions by learning new facts about sex. There are several sources of information. In 1972 Herant Katchadourian and Donald Lunde published *Fundamentals of Human Sexuality*, which stressed information and not advice and which had grown out of an innovative course that the authors had taught to undergraduates at Stanford University. A decade later, many colleges were offering comprehensive courses in sex, and *Fundamentals of Human Sexuality* had gone through three editions and become the first successful textbook about sex which in scope, reliability, and level of sophistication compares favorably with the better textbooks in the biological and social sciences.

Students and young adults have also learned about sex through attending and participating in—either singly or with a partner—different sex discussion groups (groups that aim at psychotherapy, sex therapy, consciousness-raising, or exchange of information), which are usually conducted by psychologists or psychiatrists who have researched sex problems. Here they have discussed variegated sex experiences and thoughts and learned, for instance, that (contrary to the assertion of Masters and Johnson) men can experience three patterns of orgasm (54) and that for some women there is a difference between a clitoral orgasm and a vaginal orgasm (55). New kinds of women's orgasms, showing uterine contractions without accompanying vaginal contractions and showing orgasmic expulsion of fluid, have been described (56). New kinds of women's sexual dysfunctions continue to be reported, and one sex therapist has observed: "The unhappy truth of the conjugal world is that women have many more sexual disorders than scientists have so far described. Naming and defining has hardly begun" (57: p.140).

Couples have learned old truths about sexual interactions between two individuals: (a) that a relationship goes through stages where obstacles are overcome and illusions are shed, and that "as the work of each stage is completed or realized, a new developmental task emerges with its own illusions to be overcome" (58: p.3); (b) that mutually satisfying sex and emotional intimacy are sometimes different modalities and that, "while satisfying sex . . . can add depth to an already intimate raltionship," "close and intimate relationships can survive and sometimes thrive without good sex, or even without any sex at all"; and (c) that "the devastating aspect of a sexual problem is not the specific problem itself but the distance created between the two partners when sex doesn't proceed according to expectations'' (59: p.282).

For many young adults an especially important and beneficial insight has been that—in order to have a satisfying sexual relationship in today's atmosphere of sexual permissiveness and pressure for sexual experimentation and innovation—it is necessary that they remain true to their own values. While they may be able to change their values over a period of time, ''discomfort and conflict rather than intimacy and satisfaction can result if behaviors are tried which are too divergent from personal values and attitudes'' (59: p. 282).

NOTES

1. Barker-Benfield, B. The spermatic economy. Feminist Studies, 1:45–74, 1972.
2. Duffy, E. B. The Relation of the Sexes. New York: Wood and Holbrook, 1876.
3. Barker-Benfield, G. J. The Horrors of the Half-Known Life: Male Attitudes Toward Women and Sexuality in Nineteenth-Century America. New York: Harper Colophon Books, 1977.
4. Trall, R. T. Sexual Physiology and Hygiene; or, The Mysteries of Man. New York: M. L. Holbrook, 1885.
5. Napheys, G. The Physical Life of Women. Philadelphia: David McKay, 1890.
6. Degler, C. N. What ought to be and what was: women's sexuality in the nineteenth century. American Historical Review, 79:1468, 1974.
7. Hale, G. N. Freud and the Americans: The Beginnings of Psychoanalysis in the United States, 1876–1917. New York: Oxford University Press, 1971.
8. Rothman, S. M. Woman's Proper Place: A History of Changing Ideals and Practices, 1870 to the Present. New York: Harper Colophon Books, 1978.
9. Bullough, V. L., and Bullough, B. Sin, Sickness, and Sanity: A History of Sexual Attitudes. New York: Garland, 1977.
10. Hare, E. H. Masturbatory insanity: the history of an idea. Journal of Mental Science, 108, 1962.
11. Turner, E. S. A History of Courting. London: Michael Joseph, 1954.
12. Bromley, D. D., and Britten, F. H. Youth and Sex: A Study of 1,300 College Students. New York: Harper and Brothers, 1938.
13. Fitzgerald, F. S. Echoes of the jazz age. Scribner's, 90:460, 1931.
14. Parsons, E. C. Sex morality and the taboo of direct reference. The Independent, 113, 1914.
15. Robinson, P. The Modernization of Sex. New York: Harper and Row, 1976.
16. Geddes, P., and Thompson, A. J. Sex. New York: Henry Holt and Co., 1914.
17. Grosskurth, P. Havelock Ellis: A Biography. New York: Alfred A. Knopf, 1980.
18. Bullough, V.L. Sexual Variance in Society and History. Chicago: University of Chicago Press, 1980.
19. Jones, E. The Life and Work of Sigmund Freud: The Formative Years and the Great Discoveries, 1856–1900. New York: Basic Books, 1953.
20. Brill, A. A. Masturbation, its causes and sequelae. American Journal of Urology and Sexology, 12:214, 1916.
21. Exner, M. J. Problems and Principles of Sex Education: A Study of 948 College

Men. New York: International Committee of Young Men's Christian Associations, 1915.

22. Morrison, S. E. The Oxford History of the American People. New York: Oxford University Press, 1965.

23. Allen, F. L. Only Yestrday: An Informal History of the Nineteen-Twenties. New York: Harper and Row, 1964.

24. President's Research Committee on Social Trends. Report: Recent Social Trends in the United States, Vol. I. New York: McGraw-Hill, 1933.

25. Brecher, E. M. The Sex Researchers. Boston: Little, Brown, 1969.

26. Reed, J. From Private Vice to Public Virtue: The Birth Control Movement and American Society Since 1830. New York: Basic Books, 1978.

27. Kinsey, A. C.; Pomeroy, W. B.; and Martin, C. E. Sexual Behavior in the Human Male. Philadelphia, W. B. Saunders, 1948.

28. Kinsey, A. C.; Pomeroy, W. B.; Martin, C. E.; and Gebhard, P.H. Sexual Behavior in the Human Female. Philadelphia: W. B. Saunders, 1953.

29. Pomeroy, W. B. Dr. Kinsey and the Institute for Sex Research. New York: New American Library, 1972.

30. Christenson, C. V. Kinsey: A Biography. Bloomington: Indiana University Press, 1971.

31. Pomeroy, W. B. The Institute for Sex Research: The Encyclopaedia of Sexual Behavior, edited by A. Ellis and A. Abarbanel, Vol. II. New York: Hawthorne Books, 1961.

32. Kronhausen, P., and Kronhausen, E. Sex Histories of American College Men. New York: Ballantine Books, 1960.

33. Nobile, P., ed. The New Eroticism: Theories, Vogues, and Canons. New York: Random House, 1970.

34. Degler, C. N. At Odds: Women and the Family in America from the Revolution to the Present. New York: Oxford University Press, 1980.

35. Group for the Advancement of Psychiatry. Sex and the College Student. Report No. 60. New York: Group for the Advancement of Psychiatry, 1965.

36. Montagu, A. Sex, Man, and Society. New York: G. B. Putnam's Sons, 1969.

37. Randal, J. Relaxed Campus Rules Reflect Liberalized Attitudes on Sex. New York Times, April 25, 1966.

38. Masters, W. H., and Johnson, V. E. Human Sexual Response. Boston: Little, Brown, 1966.

39. Masters, W. H., and Johnson, V. E. Human Sexual Inadequacy. Boston: Little, Brown, 1970.

40. Zilbergeld, B., and Evans, M. The inadequacy of Masters and Johnson. Psychology Today, August 1980.

41. Kaplan, H. S. The New Sex Therapy. New York: Brunner/Mazel, 1974.

42. Reid, E. A. Effects of coresidential living on the attitudes, self-image, and role expectations of college women. American Journal of Psychiatry, 131:554, 1974.

43. Smigel, E. O., and Seiden, R. The decline and fall of the double standard. Annals of the American Academy of Political and Social Science, 376:15, 1968.

44. Hunt, M. Sexual Behavior in the 1970s. Chicago: Playboy Press, 1974.

45. DeLamater, J., and MacCorquodale, P. Premarital Sexuality: Attitudes, Relationships, Behavior. Madison: University of Wisconsin Press, 1979.

46. Bell, A.P., and Weinberg, M. S. Homosexualities: A Study of Diversity Among Men and Women. New York: Simon and Schuster, 1978.
47. Masters, W. H., and Johnson, V. E. Homosexuality in Perspective. Boston: Little, Brown, 1979.
48. Katchadourian, H. A., and Lunde, D. T. Fundamentals of Human Sexuality, 3rd edition. New York: Holt, Rinehart, and Winston, 1980.
49. Bayer, R. Homosexuality and American Psychiatry: The Politics of Diagnosis. New York: Basic Books, 1981.
50. Lerner, G. The feminist: a second look. Columbia Forum, 13:24–30, 1972.
51. The decade of women. New York Times Sunday Book Review, March 30, 1980.
52. Ginsberg, G. L.; Frosch, W. A.; and Shapiro, T. The new impotence. Archives of General Psychiatry, 26:219, 1972.
53. The Hite Report: A Nationwide Study on Female Sexuality. New York: Macmillan, 1976.
54. Zilbergeld, B. Male Sexuality: A Guide to Sexual Fulfillment. Boston: Little, Brown, 1978.
55. Kline-Graber, G., and Graber, B. Woman's Orgasm: A Guide to Sexual Satisfaction. Indianapolis: Bobbs-Merrill, 1975.
56. Perry, J. D., and Whipple, D. The varieties of female orgasm and female ejaculation. Siecus Reports, May–July 1981.
57. Offit, A. K. The Sexual Self. Philadelphia: J. B. Lippincott, 1977.
58. Cambell, S. The Couple's Journey: Intimacy as a Path to Wholeness. San Luis Obispo, Calif.: Impact Publishers, 1981.
59. Barbach, L. For Each Other: Sharing Intimacy. New York: Anchor Press/Doubleday, 1982.

On Sexual Morality

MORAL PHILOSOPHY AND SEX

Since Freud, the disciplines of psychology, sociology, anthropology, and medicine have done much to illuminate the empirical side of human sexuality. Psychology has given us insight into the motivations that affect us when we are engaged in sexual activity and the origins of sexual preference; sociology has examined the causal connections that exist between human sexuality and our political and economic forms of life; anthropology has accumulated a body of materials on the customs of primitive peoples and shown how the individual's sex life is shaped by the social environment in which he or she is born and reared; and medicine has explored the physiological basis of human sexual response and sexual inadequacy. The contributions of philosophy, by contrast, have been relatively slow in coming. For several decades of this century, due in no small measure to the influence of a school of Anglo-American philosophy called logical positivism, moral philosophy in the English-speaking world was preoccupied with the distinction between fact and value and the analysis of moral language and therefore had little to say about substantive problems of contemporary life. There were undoubtedly also reasons for this neglect that were mainly of historical or sociological interest. But fashions in and conceptions of the role of philosophy do change, and philosophy has recently begun to align itself once again with the tradition of practical moral thinking that goes back to Plato. In the past ten years, a new field called ''applied ethics'' has sprung up as philosophers have turned their techniques, skills, and knowledge to the study and resolution of practical moral problems and public policy options. The response to this development from the nonphilosophical community has been mixed. Philosophers, like all latecomers, have on occasion been greeted with suspicion or hostility, and for their part, philosophers have been known to counter with exaggerated claims about the importance of their contributions. The result is a lamentable but hopefully temporary political obfuscation of the real contributions philosophy can make to the burgeoning discussion of a topic such as human sexuality. (The term "sex" or "sexual" refers to at least four separate, though related, sets of physical/psychological data: [a] biological sex, defined by six anatomical and physiological characteristics—chromosomes, gonads, internal and external genitalia, hormones, and secondary sexual characteristics; [b] gender, composed of gender identity ["I am male"/"I am female"], gender-role identity ["I am masculine"/"I am feminine"], and gender-role behavior; [c] sexual behavior, overt and fantasied, expressed by type of activity as well as by choice of object, or alternately by pleasurable genital activity or any sensual experience having an erotic meaning for the individual; and [d] reproduction. In this chapter, I am principally interested in [c], although some of the issues I raise inevitably spill over into the other areas as well. I am indebted to Rosemarie Tong for these points.)

What are the contributions philosophy can make? Most philosophers characterize the main job of moral philosophy as that of providing nonarbitrary moral principles that are mutually consistent, in keeping with the facts of the world, and adequate for resolving moral difficulties. (There is profound disagreement among moral philosophers about the foundations of ethics. This coexists, however, with substantial consensus about the factors that should be taken into account in real life. Utilitarian moral philosophers, for example, are not alone in holding that the positive and negative utility of predicted outcomes of action is an important factor to consider in resolving ethical controversies.) But the attempt to state and evaluate principles by which difficult problems may be solved does not exhaust the functions of moral philosophy, and other kinds of issues arise in the course of ethical deliberation as well. It is with some of these that I begin.

Moral philosophy provides general criteria that a judgment must satisfy in order to count as a *moral* judgment at all. A "moral judgment," as the expression is used in philosophy rather than in, say, anthropology or sociology, does not merely refer to any opinion that some individual or group happens to hold regarding the propriety of human conduct, qualities, or goals, however arbitrary or prejudiced this opinion might be. On the contrary, the point of calling something a moral judgment is precisely to distinguish it from beliefs of this sort. If the issue is whether someone's belief in the wrongness of homosexuality or lesbianism or promiscuity is a moral belief in this narrow sense, then at the very least we need to know whether there is some feature or aspect of these practices in virtue of which he regards them as wrong or whether his judgment is groundless. But even if we have reasons for the stand we take, they may be inadequate in several ways. We may base our views about homosexuality, lesbianism, or promiscuity on a personal emotional reaction and say something like "They are wrong beause they make me sick." To be sure, the strength of feeling people display about a matter is one criterion of their having strong or serious moral views about it, and it is desirable for persons to have strong moral views about certain matters. However, moral judgments are supposed to justify the emotional reactions, not the other way around, and our positive or negative emotional response to an act or practice never by itself makes our approval or condemnation of it a moral approval or condemnation. Where the emotional reaction is based on ill-founded factual beliefs—the notorious example of masturbation's causing illness, and the like, comes to mind—we have yet a further reason for denying moral status to the judgment based on that reaction. Again, a view is not a moral one because it is the view of one's parents, teachers, or even society at large. I must have my own reasons, not in the sense that they are original with me but in the sense that I have used my critical faculties to determine that they are worthy of ethical commitment.

This is perhaps an appropriate place to say a word about the relationship between a moral position and a religious one. The need to do so is evident, for it is scarcely possible for most people in our society to think about sex in nonreligious terms, so strongly have Western conventional attitudes in this area been influenced by Christian teaching. The sexual norms of the Christian tradition constitute the dominant conception of sexual relations in the West and usually serve as the point of departure for discussions of sexual morality. Moreover, this tradition has had a powerful effect on our conception of morality. In the post-Christian world, sex is not merely *a* but *the* moral issue; that is, acting morally is commonly regarded as a matter of behaving in accordance with the sexual customs of the Christian tradition. Outside the specialized discussions of philosophical ethics, the language of morality is largely used to comment on some aspect of a person's sexual activity, while the rest of that person's character is ignored.

Religious moralists may base their norms and value judgments about sexual conduct on beliefs about the function or purpose of human organs or faculties and institutions such as marriage and the family, but in their view these functional assertions have moral import because of religious or theological connections. For the religious moralist, sexual morality depends on religion or theology in the sense that ethical principles can be justified by appeal to theological premises and to these alone. To the question why one ought to do what God commands, religious moralists can respond in a number of ways. They may say that "ought" just means "what God commands" or that if one believes that God is a perfectly moral being it would be irrational of a person not to do what God commands. But neither of these responses seems satisfactory. A definition alone never solves the problem of justification, for the definition itself needs to be justified, and justifying it is tantamount to justifying the principle that the definition supplanted. Further, if we ought to do what God commands because God is perfectly moral, and if God is perfectly moral because he only approves of what is good (which goodness is not derivative from or identical with God's approval), then there is a preexisting standard of goodness that God's judgment accords with rather than creates. In this case, the fundamental truth about ethics is not theological. A genuinely theologically based ethics, on the other hand, would be faced with the problem of explaining why God could not or would not make such things as murder or rape right by commanding them.

Moral philosophy identifies and distinguishes among those aspects of a problem that must be considered if a decision about living is to be made in a morally responsible and intelligent manner; in other words, like any discipline, it defines its own subject matter. It also places certain definite constraints on the kind of belief that can count as moral and confines its attention to those moral judgments for which one is prepared to offer reasons of a certain kind. This philosophical concern with rational justification in ethics is more than a quest for objective moral truth. It is also an attempt to make sense of, and to render coherent, ordinary persons' deepest convictions about how they ought to conduct their lives. Here a necessary preliminary step is the philosophical explanation of our moral convictions, by which I mean the articulation of those general principles presupposed by them—supposing that these convictions are genuinely moral ones—and in the light of which our positions can be accounted for. Often these principles take the form of unstated assumptions or assumptions that we do not have in mind when we speak, and philosophical investigation may force us to become aware of and to reassess the principles to which we have tacitly committed ourselves. For example, conventional attitudes toward family and marriage might be shown to rest largely on the principle that procreation of children is the only moral function of sexual intercourse, and this would allow discussion to proceed beyond the level of cultural contingency. We may also discover that the principles presupposed by a range of cases provoking moral judgment are inconsistent with one another. Consider an example involving abortion, a problem discussed elsewhere in this volume. Suppose I endorse an unrestricted right to abortion and when pressed to provide a justification argue that self-consciousness is a necessary condition of personhood, that only persons have rights, that killing nonpersons violates none of their rights, and that killing is morally wrong only when it violates the victim's rights. At the same time, I do not endorse a right to infanticide. What reasons can I offer for this distinction? If I argue that infants are persons, I abandon my earlier contention that self-consciousness is a necessary condition of personhood. If I maintain that infants have rights because they have the capacity to experience pleasure and pain, I deny the proposition that only beings possessing self-consciousness have rights. If I contend that killing infants is wrong because it leads to a certain coarsening or brutalizing of the persons engaging in it, I repudiate the principle that killing is morally permissible so long as it does not violate the victim's rights. Once these inconsistencies are brought to light, a number of options are available. I can change my position on infanticide; I can change my views on abortion; I can continue to distinguish between the morality of at least some abortions and the morality of infanticide but base my acceptance of abortion on different grounds—by arguing, for example, that though killing may be wrong for reasons having nothing to do with the rights of the victims, no other type of reason for condemning killing is available in this particular case, or that though the fetus is a person with rights it may pose a threat of imminent danger to the mother which justifies abortion. The alternative I decide to pursue may depend on the relative strengths of my pretheoretical convictions regarding the morality of abortion and infanticide. Unwilling to countenance infanticide but less sure about abortion, I may be moved to alter my position on the moral status of the fetus. Strong convictions, of course, render us vulnerable to rationalization, and undoubtedly there is a great deal of rationalization surrounding the topic of human sexuality in particular. But it is one thing to condone rationalization and quite another to maintain that when a hypothesized general principle conflicts with some strongly held prephilosophical belief, we ought to reconsider just how strongly warranted the principle actually is. Indeed, one test of a principle's adequacy is that it is able to support our intuitively compelling moral judgments by explaining the underlying assumptions they reflect.

Once the suppressed premises of our moral beliefs have been brought to light by philosophical investigation, the process of critical evaluation can begin. Consider, for example, the tacit assumption, frequently encountered in arguments about sexual morality, that public attitudes toward extreme deviations from sexual norms are in no way responsible for the bad social consequences of these activities or for the moral vices and objectionable character traits of those who engage in them. This assumption enables us to take the unworthwhile features of certain types of sexual conduct as justification for these attitudes, whereas in fact they may largely result from these attitudes, and in this way we never get to the question of whether these should have been adopted in the first place. No independent justification of the attitudes seems to have been provided. The case of homosexuality can illustrate this point. Homosexual relationships, it is argued, typically fall short of the ideal form of interpersonal relationship in that they lack stability, mutual trust, and loving concern for the other person. Yet an atmosphere of social intolerance is hardly conducive to stable relationships of personal love and trust, and until homosexuals are accorded the opportunity to form love relationships according to their desires and to receive whatever institutional recognition is necessary to perfect such relationships, we are not in fact judging homosexual relationships on the same footing as heterosexual ones. (I do not wish to deny that some homosexuals regard promiscuity as integral to the gay life-style or to address the question of what value, if any, promiscuous relations have. It should be pointed out, however, that it is one thing to condemn promiscuity and quite another to condemn homosexuality for being a promiscuous way of life.)

Detection of logical fallacies and clarity about what we are doing when we make moral judgments will not by themselves enable us to decide difficult moral problems. Argument on the substantive issues raised by these problems, and rational adjudication among different, competing moralities, are still needed. At the same time, the preliminary logical and conceptual work helps us avoid deciding these problems in a muddled way.

WHAT IS SEXUAL MORALITY?

Some contemporary philosophers have argued that there is no such thing as a specifically *sexual* morality. Whatever is moral or immoral in the sexual realm, they contend, is so not because of the sexual nature of the activity but because this activity conforms or fails to conform with general moral rules and principles that are applicable to a wide range of human activities. Thus, child molestation, rape, and adultery, though they are sexual acts and are wrong, are wrong not *because* they are sexual but because they violate general moral norms forbidding manipulation of innocent persons without regard for their interests, condemning the use of violence against innocent persons, and prohibiting deception and betrayal of trust. Morality is a system of norms governing relations among individuals and groups of people, and sexual behavior falls within the domain of morality because one way human beings relate to one another is sexually. On this view, "sexual experiences," like experiences in business, politics, or medicine, and for the very same reason, "render us liable to specific moral situations"(1). Though the particular precepts of a sexual morality specify acts in terms of their sexual characteristics alone, these precepts must be understood as instantiating general rules that are independent of practical context.

Underlying this approach to the nature of sexual morality is an assumption about what I shall call the *unity* of morality, namely, that there is only one kind of ethics, an ethics of universal principles, and that while talk about an ethics of sex, of business, of politics, and so on, can be justified on the ground that it makes possible the most efficient examination of ethical issues, it cannot be justified on the ground that there are formally different types of ethics. Why moral philosophers make this assumption is difficult to say. With respect to sexual morality, the assumption of unity might sometimes be a reaction against conventional and largely unreflective attitudes toward human sexuality or against the habit of virtually equating immorality with sexual impropriety. On a deeper theoretical level, the unity assumption might reflect an unwillingness to accept the possibility of conflicts in ethics that cannot be resolved by the application of a single method of decision. Different types of ethics, if such were allowed, might correspond to incommensurable types of value and might invoke fundamentally disparate considerations that support two or more incompatible courses of action. Again, the postulation of a special ethics of sexual morality might be regarded as symptomatic of a relatively backward stage in the evolution of the moral consciousness of the human race. Such is Agnes Heller's view:

Is the existence of a separate "sex morality" a lasting value? Our answer is a definite "no." It is no because the existence of all partial or restricted moralities (and this applies not only to sex morality, but similarly to "business morals" or "political morals") is an expression of moral alienation. . . . If . . . we examine the problem from the point of view of the development of the properties of the species . . . it becomes clear that in the relation between the sexes the same factors—and only those factors—impair universal values which are detrimental to all other aspects of morality.(2: p. 540)

That the only morally relevant factors in the assessment of human sexuality are those that involve "universal values" is, Heller believes, the position of the genuinely civilized moral consciousness. Whatever the explanation, there is no question that the notion of unity has a powerful hold on our thinking about ethical problems.

However, this thesis about the status of a sexual morality seems difficult to reconcile with the fact that sexual morality is not only concerned with the effects that our sexual behavior has on others. The so-called sexual perversions, for example—bestiality, coprophilia, necrophilia, and, more controversial, homosexuality—are regarded as immoral not because or only because they inflict harm on others but because they are degrading to the persons themselves engaging in them. (Religious moralists like Saint Augustine go further and proclaim that sexual activity as such is personally degrading.) Many of the precepts of our sexual morality—indeed, the precepts of any plausible sexual ethic—stem from beliefs about the self-regarding rather than just other-regarding consequences of sexual experiences and acts. It seems to follow, therefore, that sexual morality must in part be a morality of "prudence" or "self-interest" according to which what is good is good for us and what is good for us is what enables us to live well and/or to be good persons. (By "good" person I do not mean someone who follows or makes an effort to follow moral rules, but someone who, external circumstances permitting, lives in a good, valuable, or desirable way.) But this thesis, namely, that sexual morality is not merely compatible with self-interest but that sexual morality necessarily involves the identification of types of behavior and traits of character that help the individual live a good life and make him a good person, interprets self-interest very differently from the traditional conception of the relation between morality and self-interest. This conception is enunciated in the following quote: "Morality . . . is social or it is nothing; and this not merely in the sense that our obligations are in fact directed toward others, but also in the sense that they are sanctioned by an impersonal authority which transcends our personal inclinations or preferences"(3: p.297). An important function of morality is to issue injunctions that constrain the pursuit of self-interest and that apply equally to all relevantly similar persons in relevantly similar circumstances regardless of their "personal inclinations or preferences." Clearly a great deal more must be said about personal preferences before we can accept this as a characterization of the function of *sexual* morality.

Defenders of the view that all special "moralities" are derivable from a single set of universal and impartial moral prescriptions might take the following line. They might argue that though sexual morality is certainly concerned about the self-regarding aspect of sexual conduct, this is not sufficient to establish that prudence or self-interest in any reasonable sense of the term plays a leading role in such morality. Sexual morality undeniably has a strong personal component, but it is not the person in all his or her concrete particularity or with his or her idiosyncratic inclinations and preferences that sexual morality or any morality is interested in. It is rather the humanness in or of persons, that is, a general feature or set of features of the person that all persons possess to the same degree. (The personal component of sexual morality, even in a nonparticularistic sense, is sometimes insufficiently appreciated. See the next section for a discussion of how proponents of the new sexual permissiveness may be guilty of this.) Thus, expressions like "You owe it to yourself to do x" or "You wrong yourself when you do y" are to be interpreted not as bits of prudential advice but as admonitions to display in your conduct a respectful attitude toward your own humanness, just as expressions like "You owe it to another to do x" or "You wrong another when you do y" are to be understood as injunctions to display in your conduct a respectful attitude toward the humanness of others. In short, the supposedly prudential side of sexual morality is either not prudential at all but of a piece with the morality of interpersonal conduct, or else it is not part of sexual *morality*.

This analysis may depersonalize sexual morality, but this is deemed necessary in order to keep morality from collapsing into egoism, that is, into the view that all people should always look out for themselves first. Yet on further reflection, the distinction between the moral and the impartial, on the one hand, and the immoral and the partial, on the other, does not seem to do justice to the complexity of our moral lives. We value friendship, for example, not only because it promotes the general welfare of society but also because it enhances the lives of the friends and is a vital ingredient of the good life. Morality, in one of its roles, reflects on practices from the point of view of individual agents as they perform self-regarding actions in the context of friendships and other personal relationships. This function of morality cannot be fulfilled in abstraction from personal preferences and inclinations, for obviously these are not and cannot be transcended in personal relationships. I am not friends with just anyone, but only with those whom I have selected out as being somehow special to me. In dealing with my friend, moreover, I both expect myself to and am expected to make allowances for and adjust my actions to my friend's particular tastes and personality, plans and moods, and the form of our relationship on the whole is determined in large measure by the configuration of our desires over time. In addition, though friends do not only do things for one another in order to advance their own interests, a friendship will endure only if each individual involved considers the relationship to be on balance good because it is good for him or her. To discuss friendship, which is a personal relationship, in isolation from personal preferences is to treat friendship as just another relationship between any two or more arbitrarily chosen individuals, and to discuss the morality of friendship in isolation from self-interest is to trivialize morality by detaching it from the most intimate concerns of everyday life.

The extent to which self-interest must be taken into account by morality varies, because there are certain situations in which morality requires us to disregard our personal preferences and others in which morality leaves us free and even encourages us to act according to our personal inclinations. An example of the former is the institutional setting. In such a setting, persons relate to one another as members of a group, and being a member of this group means, among other things, being subject to a public system of rules which defines social positions with their rights and duties. Persons who relate to one another institutionally do not, as such, pursue interests unconnected to their social positions or functions, and the one who is in charge of the group is morally required to distribute the benefits and burdens of group membership in an impartial and impersonal manner. From that person's point of view, no individual in the group is, and no individual may be treated as, special and noninterchangeable with any other individual occupying the same social position or performing the same institutional function. Friendship, by contrast, is not an institutional but a personal relationship, without antecedently defined roles, and sexual relations too can be viewed as personal relationships having a sexual dimension.

To view sexual relations in this way is to deny that sexual attraction is entirely a matter of natural instinct. Such phrases as "the unreasoning fury of sexual passion," suggesting as they do that other persons only function as vehicles for the satisfaction of some diffuse sexual desire of ours, are misleading, because choices, preferences, and individual likings are a significant part of our sexual lives as well as of our friendships and love relationships. Moreover, good sex, like friendship or love, is enriching both to self and to other and is valued for this reason. This notion of personal enrichment through sex, so essential to our assessment of human sexuality, cannot be captured by a morality that demands interchangeability of the subjects and interchangeability of the objects of moral practices (4). (In a critique of Lawrence Kohlberg's theory of moral development, Carol Gilligan [4] argues that females employ moral categories having to do with affective, affiliative, and relational variables much more than men do. If Gilligan is correct, then one explanation for the failure of moral philosophy to take seriously a plurality of "moralities" may be that moral philosophy has been dominated by men. Further, Gilligan's work suggests another interpretation of the expression "sexual morality," namely, male/female differences as regards conceptual categories employed in moral thinking.)

If sexual morality cannot be considered apart from a prudential morality, and if the approach of impersonal morality is also valid in certain contexts, perhaps we should say that there are at least two systems in ethics and that the diverse considerations that motivate us in our moral lives cannot all be subsumed under a single moral system. If conflicts arise between the deliverances of personal and impersonal morality, and these moralities are distinct and both ultimate, then a solution that uses a common standard of evaluation will not be available. Sex can be and often is symbolic of as well as conducive to commitment to another particular person, and this particularistic commitment which sex expresses and cements may collide with the universalistic requirements of social morality. In these cases, we have to choose between being faithful to our partners and being completely impartial, that is, refusing to be influenced by particular interests. Either way, we are being true to ourselves, only in one case to ourselves as unique individuals, in the other to ourselves as embodiments of some general characteristic of persons as such.

Those who embrace the unity assumption will find this suggestion hard to accept, but moral progress may consist both in the neat resolution of practical problems where possible *and* in the recognition that our moral lives are influenced by factors and responsive to values so disparate that a final resolution is sometimes in principle unattainable. (To concede this is to accept the inevitability of tragedy in moral life.) If so, then it will be necessary to broaden our conception of what a moral theory of, say, human sexuality does. One of its jobs will surely be to provide universal and impersonal principles for application to the domain of sexual conduct, principles that may need further clarification and refinement. Another will be to indicate the limitations of this enterprise and to locate human sexuality within the moral life by describing the type of value and basis of decision-making peculiar to it. (For a discussion of what might be called "the unitarian fallacy in ethics," see the work of Thomas Nagel [5].)

CONSENT AND PERMISSIVENESS: SEXUAL MORALITY TODAY

The contemporary sexual revolution asserts three interconnected freedoms: the freedom to break traditional codes of sexual conduct, the freedom to diverge from majority sexual patterns into deviant behavior, and the positive freedom to lead a fully expressive sexual life in the pursuit of fulfillment and happiness. Out of this setting of freedom and opportunity to experiment, a new standard for the control of sexual behavior is emerging. As one commentator put it:

In contrast with the old mode of externally imposed control, the new one is a mode of *internal* control. It works on a basis of what the individual *feels* is right as a result of his own experience, rather than on a basis of what he has been *told* is right—rules drawn from the handed-down experience of someone else, in a different place and at a different time. (6: p.136)

Insofar as this new mode simply amounts to a repudiation of the view that in sexual matters individuals ought to do what others tell them to do just because they have been told to do it, and an affirmation of individuals' rights to take responsibility for their own sexual conduct, the change in standards is no doubt salutary. It is a good thing for persons to fulfill their potential as moral agents, and this requires that they acknowledge responsibility for their actions and achieve autonomy wherever and whenever they can, in sexual matters as in other matters. They may listen to the advice of others regarding proper sexual conduct, but as moral agents they must make this advice their own by determining for themselves whether it is good advice. On the other hand, the so-called new sexual morality is to be decried if it does not merely call for independence of judgment in moral decision-making but calls also for a new normative principle of the right to govern our sexual lives. According to this principle, what feels right *is* right, and since what feels right is a result of one's own experience, and the experiences of individuals vary enormously, what is right or good for one individual will not necessarily be right or good for another, even if the situations involved are similar. The principle "in sex if it feels right do it" entails that sexual morality is a relativistic morality.

While the rejection of conventional sexual morality does not logically entail the position of relativism, the two are frequently connected both by advocates and by critics of the new sexual values. Critics often condemn contemporary developments because they regard them as antithetical to moral standards of any kind, and in overemphasizing the extent of disagreement among individuals concerning what is right and wrong, advocates often seem to be embracing this moral nihilism. Advocates and critics often share another assumption as well, namely, that a relativistic sexual morality not only is compatible with but actually lends support to a morality of toleration and noninterference with respect to deviant sexual conduct. If "right" can only coherently be understood as meaning "right for a given individual," it seems to follow that it is wrong for one individual to condemn, interfere with, and so on, the sexual values and practices of another—a conclusion that some liberals feel reinforces a subjective conception of the nature of sexual morality and some conservative critics regard as a *reductio ad absurdum* of this conception.

Whatever one may think of the relativist analysis of right—whether one regards it as the only inference to draw from the wide disagreement about moral issues or (correctly, I believe) as a thoroughly untenable position to hold in moral philosophy—it is not difficult to show that a doctrine of toleration or permissiveness cannot consistently be derived from it. If all standards of value or ideals are relative, then so too is the ideal of tolerance. One person may feel that it is right to be tolerant, another may espouse the most ruthless intolerance, but consistent relativists could hardly criticize the latter for being mistaken, for this would be tantamount to judging his values in terms of those of the former. In short, a morality of toleration employs a nonrelative sense of "right" that is not allowed for by the normative principle of relativism. The consistent relativist could no more agree with the advocate of intolerance than disagree, but by having no principled basis on which to condemn intolerance, relativism also undermines the effectiveness of moral criticism as an instrument for social reform, and in so doing gives de facto support to repressive laws and public policy regarding sexual conduct.

Freudian psychology, or its popularized version, has helped spread the belief that sexual matters belong in the realm of science, not morals, and relativism, representing as it does the destruction of morality, fits together with this view. But alongside the strong current of relativism in the writings of proponents of a new sexual morality is another, in fact incompatible, position. Instead of a relativistic destruction of ethics, we now find a nonrelative and allegedly nonarbitrary moral norm for sexual conduct, that is, that nothing is really wrong as long as nobody else "gets hurt." To the obvious objection that it is often difficult, if not impossible, to know what in the long run will hurt others and what will not, the reply may be that harm is not to be determined "in the long run" at all. It is to be determined rather by discovering whether the parties involved in a sexual interaction have consented to it, for nobody gets hurt or is harmed by actions to which he or she has consented. For example, the fact that teenage girls who consent to sexual intercourse may become pregnant and may suffer in many ways as a result is no counterexample to this principle, for if they are old enough to consent, they are not harmed in the sense employed by the principle, that is, they are not injured or treated unjustly. Sexual acts between consenting adults are not immoral in this view, no matter how harmful to them the consequences might be, for to one who freely consents no wrong is done. To use the words of the Roman law, *Volenti non fit inuria*.

The consent referred to in the *volenti* maxim has three requirements: power, capacity, and voluntariness. The qualification "harmful to them" is relevant to the power to consent, for while rational adults may have the right to consent to actions that harm them, they have no right to consent to actions that harm others. Unless specifically authorized to do so, no person can waive another's right to be free of intrusions that result in harm to that other. In other words, the power to consent is lacking when the rights involved are not solely those of the persons whose consent is in question. With respect to capacity, the persons involved in a sexual interaction must not only be inherently competent to consent, that is, have the general ability to know or understand the nature, character, and effects of their actions, but must also be in a rational frame of mind at the time they perform this particular action. Voluntariness, of which competence is a precondition, suggests more specifically that people are in a situation where they can exercise their choice freely, that is, without fraud, deceit, duress, or coercion.

In order to decide whether the *volenti* maxim should be taken as the basic principle of sexual morality, we must say more about the conditions or circumstances that full consent precludes. Coercion that involves the deliberate effort on the part of someone to pressure another into a particular decision clearly renders consent involuntary and thus vitiates and invalidates it. Coercion in this sense is present in any particular sexual interaction that involves the imposition of one will on another. In the specific case where sexual intercourse is performed against the will of the victim, the act of coercion is rape. Force, beyond what is involved in the very act of intercourse itself, is not necessary for rape, but as a violation of respect for persons it is seriously immoral whether it exploits another's weaknesses, dependencies, or fears. (The frequent occurrence of rape and its less-than-frequent successful prosecution are symptomatic of the secondary legal and social status of women in our culture. Another indication of this is the widespread assumption that married women have granted general consent to intercourse with their husbands. This allows little room for the notion that husbands can rape their wives.)

But there seem to be other factors that can vitiate an apparently free consent as well, and if the *volenti* maxim is interpreted to rule out only the kind of coercion that flows from the deliberate efforts of individuals, then there is a kind of moral objection to sexual relations that cannot be grounded in the *volenti* maxim. I have in mind here what might be called 'institutional coercion,'' that is, the coercion that flows from the structure of economic and social relations between men and women in general. The relation between man and woman is at present characterized by great disparities of social, economic, and political power, and the pervasive powerlessness of women often subverts sexual relations into relations of dominance and submission, regardless of the wishes and choices of the particular persons involved. If the *volenti* maxim is to occupy a central place in a sexual ethic, then it seems both individual and institutional constraints on freedom of choice must be allowed to be coercive.

There is an objection to this attempt to salvage consent as the cornerstone of a sexual morality. It might be argued that those who accept this defense of the *volenti* maxim are being led by their intense opposition to male dominance to distort the meaning of the word "coercion," and that even if we go along with this usage the links between social practices and freedom in making choices are too indirect and obscure to support the claim that institutional constraints can invalidate consent by rendering it involuntary. (It should be noted, however, that choices regarding sexual behavior are made against the background of existing social norms and conventions and that these can still be criticized for making a fully expressive and satisfying sexual life extremely difficult for many to achieve. Consider the plight of many young women on our campuses who find themselves caught in the bind of sexual liberation. If they consent to sexual relations, they are branded "easy"; if they refuse, they are branded "prudes.") Questions of institutional coercion aside, it seems plainly false to say that a person cannot freely consent to an arrangement that is violative of his or her own rights or that one cannot voluntarily engage in activities (sexual and otherwise) that show insufficient concern for one's moral status as a person. If, as I believe, the tendency to enter into such arrangements and to engage in such activities is usually indicative of a *moral* defect—the moral defect of self-contempt—and therefore not merely foolish or distasteful but morally wrong, consent cannot be the whole story about the rights and wrongs of sexual conduct. A full theory of sexual morality must recognize the existence of distinct and independent kinds of wrong, the wrong of coercion as well as the wrong of certain attitudes toward the self, and must formulate principles that reflect the complexity of our moral lives.

The new sexual permissiveness is closely connected to shifts in normative conceptions of sex roles, and the traditional prohibitions, with their double standard, are being eroded. This aspect of modern sexual morality cannot but be welcomed by anyone who believes that the unequal and inferior social status of women is unjust and needs to be eliminated. But in conceptualizing the theoretical underpinnings of the new permissiveness, we should be careful not to embrace either ethical relativism or the misconception that there can be nothing wrong with sexual activity to which those involved have given their consent.

TWO PROBLEM CASES

AIDS and Promiscuous Sex

The sexual revolution of the 1960s and 1970s had a particularly liberating effect on many homosexual men. A significant segment of the homosexual population came to openly reject the heterosexual model of lifelong monogamous unions and embraced the alternative life-style of frequent noncommittal sex with a variety of partners. For these men, promiscuity was inseparable from being gay. In the last few years, however, the spread of a new lethal disease known as AIDS (acquired immune deficiency syndrome) among promiscuous male homosexuals has touched off deep fear in the gay community about the medical consequences of indiscriminate sexual contact and has forced it to reassess this life-style from a prudential (not moral) point of view. Many homosexuals also worry—not without good cause—about society's reaction to their problem, fearing an erosion of their civil rights under the guise of preventing a spread of the so-called epidemic.

The medical establishment was slow to respond to the illness until AIDS-related diseases were discovered among a number of hemophiliacs. It is now believed that AIDS can be spread to the general population through blood donations and that a single donor with AIDS might contaminate an entire batch of blood products that can be used by as many as 100 hemophiliacs. To counteract this danger, a variety of measures have been suggested, ranging from a call for a moratorium on blood donations by homosexuals to screening of potential donors for homosexuality. The latter has aroused the most antagonism from the gay community.

Proposals to ban blood donations by homosexuals at high risk of contracting AIDS have confronted at least the following two objections: the right to offer the gift of blood is being denied homosexuals in this group who are unaffected by AIDS, and the potential donor's right to privacy is violated by invasive screening procedures. With regard to the first, doing good for others, for example, by donating blood, is certainly praiseworthy and virtuous, perhaps even morally required. We might also agree that the duty to be beneficent is a *right* of ours because it is vitally important not only to the community in general but also to the agent himself that this duty be discharged, and further that the opportunity to promote the good of others should be guaranteed us. It does not follow, however, that any particular way of doing good for others can be demanded as a right. Moreover, because there is an uncertain risk of transmitting a life-threatening disease to many others in the community, the case for not allowing homosexuals in the high-risk group to give the gift of blood is a strong one.

Another difficulty in the proposal to ban blood donations by certain homosexual men arises in connection with the interviews, which at one time, before the development of a test to detect the presence of the antibody to the AIDS virus, might have been used to screen potential donors. Questions about sexual pratices and orientation or about numbers of sexual partners infringe on the potential donor's right to privacy, on his right to determine for himself when, how, and to what extent information about his private life is communicated to others. Yet the right to privacy is not absolute; it can be infringed without being violated. As Justices Warren and Brandeis (7) observe, under certain circumstances "the dignity and convenience of the individual must yield to the demands of the public welfare or of private justice." The case under consideration involves such demands because of the health interests at stake.

Even if the right to privacy of potential blood donors would not have been unjustifiably infringed by questioning about sexual life-styles, the effectiveness of this procedure is open to question. Since there is no test for homosexuality, identification of promiscuous gay men requires their cooperation and honesty. Yet where discrimination against homosexuals and fear of homosexuality are widespread, as in our society, any policy aimed at preventing homosexuals from being able to do what most heterosexuals can do is bound to be viewed by many subject to the exclusion as a further instance of social prejudice and to be resisted by them. Before the development of the antibody test, the best protection for those in need of blood was not a ban on blood donations by homosexuals but a demonstration of society's goodwill and sincere concern for the interests of homosexuals themselves. With the test in use, the possibility that its results will be used for purposes other than blood screening or research is a new source of legitimate concern for homosexuals.

Parental Involvement in Teenage Abortion

The sexual revolution is nowhere more apparent than in the lives of young people, and one of its most troublesome problems is the dramatic increase in recent years of sexual activity among minors. Young people are reaching physical and sexual maturity at earlier and earlier ages, but lacking the ability and willingness to carry out the responsibilities of adult life, they may be unprepared for parenthood. At a time when a young person may be in need of parental protection and guidance herself, she may be forced to choose between obtaining an abortion and giving birth to a child that she herself cannot properly care for and whose needs will not be met. To choose the latter would seem to be morally irresponsible; to choose the former is to make a decision that may have profoundly traumatic consequences for her. As for the minor's parents, they have an obligation to prevent her as far as possible from acting in morally irresponsible ways and to protect her from psychological and other harm, and they may interpret this obligation in various ways: as giving them the right to prohibit all sexual activity by their minor child, as giving them the right to educate their child in sexual matters, as giving them the right to veto their minor child's decision to have an abortion, or at least as giving them the right to be informed of their minor child's decision to have an abortion before it takes place. As for the state, having assigned primary responsibility for a child's care to its parents, it must seek to preserve the integrity of family life and must not subvert parental authority. How this is to be done with respect to teenage sexuality is a concern of the 1981 U.S. Supreme Court decision in the case of *H.L. v. Matheson* (101 S.Ct. 1164, 1981).

In this case, the court upheld the constitutionality of a Utah statute requiring a doctor to inform a teenage girl's parents before performing an abortion on her or face criminal penalties, at least when the girl is an "immature, dependent minor." Parental notification in such instances, the Court argued, serves state interests important enough to outweigh a teenager's right to privacy and to unobstructed access to abortion, interests it identified as "family integrity" and "protecting adolescents" from the "medical, emotional, and psychological consequences of an abortion." The notification requirement serves these interests, the Court explained, by preserving parental authority in the home and by ensuring that teenage girls receive their parents' guidance in making a decision whose consequences are "potentially traumatic and permanent." Both parents' rights and the best interests of the minor child justify notifying parents.

In discussing the issues raised by this case, we should distinguish between moral and legal aspects. Do immature, dependent minors have a moral right to get an abortion in the absence of parental knowledge? Should immature, dependent minors have a legal right to do so? A reasonable moral principle is that a child should have the right to decide about her own treatment or care, provided that in exercising this right she does not endanger her physical, emotional, or psychological development or well-being. If, as the Court maintained, abortions performed on immature patients do endanger their welfare, then it seems irresponsible not only to grant them the right to get an abortion without prior notification of their parents but also to let them get abortions regardless of whether their parents have consented to them.

The merits of a law conferring on parents a right to notification must be evaluated differently. In arguing that such a law promotes family integrity, the Court assumed that most parents would respond to their daughter's predicament with compassion and understanding, not rejection. Only if this is true would the notification requirement actually strengthen families rather than just erect a barrier to pregnancy termination. However, this assumption is not supported by available data, nor is it likely that empirical evidence can support it. In a society like ours, where parents tend to deny their own sexuality to their children and consider the control of sexual impulses in their children to be one of their primary functions as parents, it is unlikely that most of them will be comfortable enough with a daughter's sexuality to respond to her pregnancy with love and understanding. The Court *is* legitimately concerned about the further erosion of parental authority in our society, but sentimental ideals of the supportive family cannot be the foundation for sound law. Further, laws requiring parental consent to or notification of a minor's abortion may reduce somewhat the high rate of abortions among minors and may cause some to postpone sexual activity, but the central problem of teenage sexuality is how to help adolescents prevent pregnancy and handle their sexuality in a responsible way. Such legislative approaches are of limited usefulness in accomplishing these goals (8).

REFERENCES

1. Ruddick, S. Better sex. In: Baker, R., and Elliston, F., eds., Philosophy and Sex. Buffalo, N.Y.: Prometheus Books, 1975.
2. Heller, A. On the future of relations between the sexes. International Social Science Journal, 21(4):540, 1969.
3. Kekes, J. Morality and impartiality. American Philosophical Quart., 18(4):297, 1981.
4. Gilligan, C. In a different voice: women's conception of self and of morality. Harvard Educational Review, 47:481–517, 1977.
5. Nagel, T. The fragmentation of value. In: Mortal Questions. Cambridge, Eng.: Cambridge University Press, 1979.
6. Nixon, R. E. Sex or guilt. In: Grunwald, H. A., ed., Sex in America. New York: Bantam Books, 1964.
7. Warren, C., and Brandeis, L. The right to privacy. Harvard Law Review, 4(5):214, 1890.
8. Dryfoos, J. The epidemiology of adolescent pregnancy: incidence, outcomes, and interventions. In: Stuart, I. R., and Wells, C. F., eds., Pregnancy in Adolescence. New York: Van Nostrand Reinhold, 1982.

SUGGESTIONS FOR FURTHER READING

Atkinson, R. Sexual Morality. New York: Harcourt, Brace and World, 1966.
Baker, R., and Elliston, F., eds. Philosophy and Sex. Buffalo, N.Y.: Prometheus Books, 1975.
English, J., ed. Sex Equality. Englewood Cliffs, N.J.: Prentice-Hall, 1977.
Soble, A. Philosophy of Sex. Totowa, N.J.: Littlefield, Adams and Co., 1980.
Verene, D. P., ed. Sexual Love and Western Morality. New York: Harper and Row, 1972.
Vetterling-Braggin, M.; Elliston, F.; and English, J., eds. Feminism and Philosophy. Totowa, N.J.: Littlefield, Adams and Co., 1977.
Wilson, J. Logic and Sexual Morality. Baltimore: Penguin, 1967.

Bibliographical Essay

The term sexuality subsumes a broad spectrum of sexual behaviors, and the literature on the various aspects of sexuality is so voluminous as to preclude a comprehensive coverage in a brief bibliographic essay—this despite the fact that sex as a subject of scientific study is a relatively recent phenomenon. Although individuals have expatiated endlessly on sex and its "meanings" and through the ages have considered it to be the essence of individual identity, it did not become a matter for systematic investigation until just before the turn of the century. A few rudimentary studies of the clinical medical aspects of sex were in evidence from the mid-nineteenth century, but it was Freud's concentrated and exhaustive delving into mechanisms that legitimized its study. His "Three Essays on the Theory of Sexuality" and "My Views on the Part Played by Sexuality in the Etiology of the Neuroses" were published in 1905. Since Freud's time there has been an explosion of investigative approaches to describe, formulate, predict and explicate the origins and influences of the biological, psychological and sociological determinants of sexuality throughout the various phases of human development.

From the "number collecting" investigative techniques of the earliest sexologists, highly complex and sophisticated research methodologies have evolved over the past few decades among researchers in the variety of disciplines that are concerned with illuminating the many facets of sexual behavior.

This volume has focused its attention primarily on some pertinent and timely clinical investigations in the fields of psychiatry, psychology and medicine (including philosophy and history to round out the perspective) that expand our understanding of sexual behavior in the life cycle. Because its subject matter covers only a limited segment of literature in the field of sexuality, we have chosen to highlight readings in the field that provide an overview of sexuality. We have not seen fit to supply listings of references for the specific subject matter of each chapter since we believe that the individual authors have sufficient expertise to have already culled the most important reference material pertaining to their areas of inquiry. (These references can be found at the end of each chapter.) In our selection of books for further reference we have selected current as well as some less recent works. The latter have been chosen either because they can be considered classics in the field or are particularly germaine to some of the specific subject matter elaborated in this volume.

Before enumerating these references, it should be noted that in the area of sexual behavior four investigators stand out as having the most profound influence in the field in that their particular research techniques and findings constituted monumental breakthroughs in previously unexplored sexual territory. Freud, Kinsey and Masters and Johnson (with Freud the acknowledged giant) are almost too obvious to mention. Each of these investigators' emergence on the scene was highly controversial although time has worn away the sensationalism their writings initially created. All are now recognized as seminal influences that spawned an incalculable number of further investigations. References to Freud's approaches to sex are to be found throughout these writings. Two specific references alluded to earlier in this essay have been singled out in that they are the forerunners of the many subsequent formulations on sexuality; both are to be found in *Collected Papers*, Vol. 1, E. Jones, ed., London: Hogarth Press, 1950. For Kinsey's major writings see A. Kinsey, et al., *Sexual Behavior in the Human Male*, Philadelphia: W. B. Saunders, 1948; and *Sexual Behavior in the Human Female*, Philadelphia, W. B. Saunders, 1953. For W. H. Masters and V. E. Johnson, see *Human Sexual Response*, Boston, Little-Brown, 1966.

The historical significance and the impetus given to further study of various aspects of sexual behavior by the above can hardly be exaggerated. Concurrent with, in between, and subsequent to these major works is a body of literature too vast to be enumerated in its entirety. For readers wishing up-to-date information the following references, published in the 1980s, are noteworthy, as are several volumes from the 1970s that remain current and present original material or important reviews of work in the specific subjects addressed.

E. R. Mahoney, *Human Sexuality*, McGraw-Hill, 1984; D. C. McCarthy, ed., *Handbook on Critical Sexual Issues*, Doubleday, 1984; C. Landes, *Sex in Development*, Arden Library, 1984; Stewart Meckle, et al., *Sex in Adolescence*, College Hill, 1984; *Human Sexuality* (a series of addresses, essays and lectures) Sage Publications, 1984. J. H. Block, *Sex Role Identity and Ego Development*, Jossey-Bass, 1984; M. Lewin, *In the Shadow of the Past: Psychology Portrays the Sexes*, Columbia University Press, 1984; A. K. Offit, *The Sexual Self*, Congdon and Weed, 1983; M. C. Hermantz, *Human Sexuality*, Harper and Row, 1983; S. A. Rathus, *Human Sexuality*, Holt Rinehart and Winston, 1983; I. Gross, J. Downing, and A. D. D'Heurle, Sex role attitudes and cultural change, *Priority Issues in Mental Health*, Vol. 3, Reidel, 1983; G. R. Freedman, *Sexual Medicine*, Edinburgh: Churchhill Livingston, 1983; C. Nadelson and D. B. Marcotti, *Treatment Interventions in Human Sexuality*, Plenum Press, 1983; C. S. Chilman, *Adolescent Sexuality in a Changing American Society: Social and Psychological Perspectives for the Human Services Professions*, 2nd ed., Wiley, 1983. G. W. Albee, S. Gordon and H. Lutenberg, eds., *Promoting Sexual Responsibility and Preventing Sexual Problems* (from Sex Disorders Congress), Published by the Vermont Conference on Primary Prevention of Psychopathology, University Press of New England, 1983; H. Kaplan, *The Evaluation of Sexual Disorders: Psychological and Medical Aspects*, Brunner/Mazel, 1983; R. B. Weg, *Sexuality in the Later Years*, Academic Press, 1983; H. S. Stream, *The Sexual Dimension: A Guide for the Helping Professional*, The Free Press, Collier MacMillan Publishers, 1983; G. Hrentwicz, and G. Schmidt, eds., *The Treatment of Sexual Disorders*, Basic Books, 1983; R. W. Russo, et al., *Advanced Textbook of Sexual Development and Disorders in Childhood and Adolescence*, Medical Examination, 1983; T. L. Altherr, ed., *Procreation a Pleasure?: Sexual Attitudes in American History*, Kroeger, 1983. S. Seemans, *Sexuality*, Lippincott, 1982; J. S. Weinberg, *Sexuality*, Saunders, 1982; M. Vellerling-Braggan, ed., *Femininity, Masculinity and Androgeny*, Rowan and

Littlefield, 1982; N. Reeves, *Womankind: Beyond the Stereotypes*, 2nd ed., Aldine, 1982; L. H. Croft, *Sexuality in Later Life: A Handbook for Physicians*, John Wright P. S. G., 1982; I. Al-Issa, *Gender and Psychopathology*, Academic Press, 1982; L. Greenspoon, ed., *Psychiatry*, The American Psychiatric Association Annual Review, American Psychiatric Press, 1982; David E. Scharff, *The Sexual Relationship: An Object Relations View of Sex and the Family*, Routledge and Kegan, 1982; M. Kirkpatrick, *Woman's Sexual Experience*, Plenum Press, 1982; Alfred C. Kinsey Institute for Sex Research, *Sex Studies Index*, G. K. Hall, 1982; E. D. Machlin and R. H. Ruben, eds., *Contemporary Families and Alternative Life Styles: Handbook on Research and Theory*, Sage, 1982; J. Edelwich, *Sexual Dilemmas for the Helping Professional*, Brunner/Mazel, 1982; R. C. Friedman, ed., *Behavior and the Menstrual Cycle*, Marcel Dekker, 1982; L. L. Constantine, and F. M. Martinson, eds., *Children and Sex: New Findings, New Perspectives*, Little Brown, 1981; S. B. Ortner, and H. Whitehead, *Sex Roles*, Cambridge University Press, 1981; M. Guttentag, S. Sulasen, and D. Belle, *The Mental Health of Women*, Academic Press, 1980; B. B. Walman, ed., *Handbook of Human Sexuality*, Prentice Hall, 1980; J. Money, *Love and Love Sickness: The Science of Sex, Gender Difference and Pair Bonding*, Johns Hopkins University Press, 1980; J. K. Meyer, ed., *Symposium on Sexuality* (Psychiatric Clinics of North America, Vol. 3, No. 1), Saunders, 1980.

Less recent but still current are the following references from the 1970s: R. C. Kolodny, *Textbook of Sexual Medicine*, 1st ed., Little Brown, 1979; D. Symonds, *The Evaluation of Human Sexuality*, Oxford University Press, 1979; T. B. Karasu, and C. W. Socarides, eds., *On Sexuality: Psychoanalytic Observations*, International University Press, 1979. H. A. Katchadurian, ed., *Human Sexuality: A Comparative and Developmental Study*, University of California Press, 1979; T. E. McGill, et al., *Sex and Behavior: Status and Prospectus*, Plenum, 1978; J. Money and H. Masoph, eds., *Handbook of Sexology*, Exerpta Medica, Elsevier, 1977; W. H. Masters, et al., *Ethical Issues in Sex Therapy and Research*, Little Mead, 1977; F. A. Beach, ed., *Human Sexuality in Four Perspectives*, Johns Hopkins University Press, 1977; M. S. Weinberg, ed., *Sex Research: Studies from the Kinsey Institute*, Oxford University Press, 1976; B. J. Sadock, H. I. Kaplan, and A. Freedman, eds., *The Sexual Experience*, Williams and Wilkins, 1976; E. A. Rubenstein, et al., eds., *New Dimensions in Sex Research* (Perspectives in Sexuality Series), Plenum Publishers, 1976; E. Maccaby, and J. C. Maccaby, *The Psychology of Sex Differences*, Stanford University Press, 1975; H. S. Asten, *Sex Roles: A Research Bibliography*, National Institute of Mental Health, U.S. Government Printing Office, 1975; W. I. Gadpaille, *The Cycles of Sex*, Scribners, 1975; E. A. Rubinstein, R. Green, and E. Brecher, *New Directions in Sex Research*, Plenum Press, 1975; J. M. Tanner, *Control of the Onset of Puberty*, John Wiley, 1974; R. C. Friedman, R. M. Richart, and Vandewiele, eds., *Sex Differences in Behavior*, John Wiley, 1974; J. L. McCary, *Human Sexuality: Psychological Factors*, 2nd. ed., Van Nostrand, 1973; R. Sorensen, *Adolescent Sexuality in Contemporary America*, William Collins, 1973; J. Money and A. Ehrhardt, *Man and Woman, Boy and Girl*, Johns Hopkins University Press, 1972.

Index

AIDS (Acquired Immune Deficiency Syndrome), 189–211, 221; risk factors, 190, 192(table); transmittal, 190, 203; retrovirus, 190, 200, 201–202; cases reported, by state, 191(fig.); cases in U.S, by quarter of diagnosis, 192(fig.); distribution of, by risk factors, 192(table); immunologic abnormalities in, 194(table); distribution of, by disease category and sexual orientation, 198(table); genetic factors, 198; and environmental factors, 198, 200, 202; and prior immune deficit, 200–201; anti-LAV antibody in patients, 204(table); carriers of, 205–206; sequence of immune disruption, 206–207; and number of sex partners, 207, 208(table); treatment of patients, 209; complications of, 210(table); prevention of, 210, 211; morality issues concerning, 344–5

Abortion, 7, 21–25; legalization of, 23–25, 325; among unmarried adolescents, 55–58; laws against, 314; and questions of sexual morality, 334; morality issues concerning parental involvement in teenage, 345–7. *See also* Miscarriage

Acquired Immune Deficiency Syndrome. *See* AIDS

Adolescent females: and motivations for pregnancy, 5; and rape, 33, 39; premarital conception, 45–46, 53–54; childbirth in, 45–46; sexual activity in, 46–48; contraceptive usage among, 48–50; reasons given for not using contraceptives, 50–53; impact of conception on, 54–55; abortion among, 55–58; childbirth outside marriage among, 59–60; health consequences òf childbirth among, 60; and adoption, 60–61; educational consequences of childbirth in, 61–62; social, vocational, economic consequences of childbirth in, 62–63; psychological effects of premarital childbirth, 63–64; development of sexual identity in, 74–76, 83–85; sexual problems in, 76–82; sexual behavior and sex roles, 92–96; moral questions concerning parental involvement in abortion for, 345–7

Adolescent males: and pregnancy, 5–6; sexual activity in, 46–48, 80; contraceptive usage among, 48–50; reasons given for not using contraceptives, 50–53; development of sexual identity and autonomy, 74–76; sexual behavior and sex roles, 92–96

Adoption, 60–61

Golub, Sharon, on menstrual cycle, 251–
70
Group for the Advancement of Psychiatry
Guilt: pregnancy, childbirth and, 5, 11;
and voluntary abortion, 24, 57; and
rape, 35; and adoption, 61; of incest
victim, 166

HLA. *See* Histocompatibility antigens
HTLV-I (T cell leukemia virus), and
AIDS, 202–203
HTLV-III antibody, 205–206
HTLV-III/LAV virus antibody, 203,
204(table), 205
Haitians, and AIDS, 190
Hamilton Rating Scores for depression,
298
Heller, Agnes, on sexual morality, 336–7
Hemophiliacs, and AIDS, 190
Hepatitis A and B virus, 190, 195
Hermaphrodites, 101. *See also*
Pseudohermahrodites
Herpes Simplex virus, 221
Heterosexuality as social norm, 141–2,
147–8
Histocompatibility antigens (HLA), 195;
Class I and II, 196, 206
Home vs. hospital childbirth, 12–13
Homosexuality, female, 160, 161, 172–3,
174, 255, 304, 325
*Homosexualitat, Heterosexualitat, und
Perversion*, 152
Homosexuality, male, 314, 325, 335; and
boyhood femininity, 101, 108–9, 120;
and psychoanalysis, 141–57; vs. latent
homosexuality, 146–47, 154; and borderline psychopathology, 160–61, 171–
2; and Don Juanism, 180; and AIDS,
190, 191(fig.), 192(fig.); number of
partners and AIDS, 207, 208(table);
sexual practices and AIDS, 208–9; and
elderly, 304–305; Havelock Ellis on,
316; rejected as illness, 325
Hormones, 107; and psychological variables, 252–3; replacement therapy, 293,
296. *See also* Androgens; Estrogen;
Progesterone; Prostaglandin;
Testosterone

Hostility toward men: in mothers of ex-
tremely feminine boys, 115; in incest
victims, 166–7
Human Sexual Inadequacy, 322–3
Human Sexual Response, 322
Hypersexuality, in borderline patients,
164–5
Hyperthyroidism, 301
Hyposexuality, 78

ISE. *See* Inhibited sexual excitement
Ideal Marriage, 317
Illness, and sexual activity, 300–301
Immune system: dysfunction, 189; abnormalities in AIDS, 193, 194(table); cell-
mediated immunity, 193; communication among cells, 195–7. *See also*
AIDS
Imperato-McGinley, Julianne, on impact
of androgens on male gender identity,
125–38
Impotence: clinical evaluation of, 271–4;
sleep study for diagnosis of, 275–80;
problems with NPT evaluation in diagnosis of, 280–84; and sexual permissiveness, 326
Imprinting: theory of, and gender-identity, 109; sex-steroid, 125
Incest: and promiscuity, 162; and hypersexuality, 164–5; impact on psychosexual development, 165–8; and
dysmorphophobia, 169–70; and jealousy, 173–4
Indiana University, 318, 319
Infants, and AIDS, 200
Infertility, 228, 237–8
Influenza, 195
Information about sex, 315; and female
sexuality, 82–83; revolution in, 1966–
83, 322–7
Inhibited sexual excitement (ISE), 271,
284, 285; distinguishing, from organic
impotence, 271–3, 278–9. *See also*
Impotence
Institute for Sex Research, 319
Institute Pasteur, Paris, 203
Institutionalization of the elderly, and
sexuality, 305–306

About the Editors

ZIRA DEFRIES, M.D., is Clinical Assistant Professor of Psychiatry, College of Physicians and Surgeons, Columbia University, and Director of Mental Health Services at Barnard College. She has contributed articles to the *American Journal of Psychiatry*, *The Journal of the American Academy of Psychoanalysis*, *The American Journal of Orthopsychiatry*, *The Bulletin of the New York Academy of Medicine*, *The Journal of Communication Disorders*, and *Medical Aspects of Human Sexuality and Adolescence*, among others.

RICHARD C. FRIEDMAN, M.D., is Clinical Associate Professor of Psychiatry at the Cornell University Medical College and Collaborating Psychoanalyst at Columbia University Center for Psychoanalytical Studies. He has edited *Sex Differences in Behavior* and *Behavior and the Menstrual Cycle* and has contributed many articles to other texts. Some of the many journals in which his publications appear include *The New England Journal of Medicine*, *The American Journal of Psychiatry*, *The Journal of Nervous and Mental Diseases*, and *The Journal of the American Academy of Psychoanalysis*.

RUTH CORN is Lecturer of Social Work in Psychiatry at Cornell University Medical College. She is the Assistant Director of Social Work Services for Staff Development and the Coordinator of Social Work Services for the Acute Treatment Services Division at the Westchester Division of the New York Hospital/Cornell Medical Center. She has contributed to *Behavior and the Menstrual Cycle*, *The American Journal of Psychotherapy*, and the *American Journal of Psychiatry*, among many others.